AFRICAN HISTORICAL DICTIONARIES
Edited by Jon Woronoff

1. *Cameroon,* by Victor T. LeVine and Roger P. Nye. 1974. *Out of print. See No. 48.*
2. *The Congo,* 2nd ed., by Virginia Thompson and Richard Adloff. 1984. *Out of print. See No. 69.*
3. *Swaziland,* by John J. Grotpeter. 1975.
4. *The Gambia,* 2nd ed., by Harry A. Gailey. 1987.
5. *Botswana,* by Richard P. Stevens. 1975. *Out of print. See No. 70.*
6. *Somalia,* by Margaret F. Castagno. 1975.
7. *Benin (Dahomey),* 2nd ed., by Samuel Decalo. 1987. *Out of print. See No. 61.*
8. *Burundi,* by Warren Weinstein. 1976.
9. *Togo,* 3rd ed., by Samuel Decalo. 1996.
10. *Lesotho,* by Gordon Haliburton. 1977.
11. *Mali,* 3rd ed., by Pascal James Imperato. 1996.
12. *Sierra Leone,* by Cyril Patrick Foray. 1977.
13. *Chad,* 2nd ed., by Samuel Decalo. 1987.
14. *Upper Volta,* by Daniel Miles McFarland. 1978.
15. *Tanzania,* by Laura S. Kurtz. 1978. *Out of print.*
16. *Guinea,* 3rd ed., by Thomas O'Toole with Ibrahima Bah-Lalya. 1995.
17. *Sudan,* by John Voll. 1978. *Out of print. See No. 53.*
18. *Rhodesia/Zimbabwe,* by R. Kent Rasmussen. 1979. *Out of print. See No. 46.*
19. *Zambia,* by John J. Grotpeter. 1979.
20. *Niger,* 3rd ed., by Samuel Decalo. 1996.
21. *Equatorial Guinea,* 2nd ed., by Max Liniger-Goumaz. 1988.
22. *Guinea-Bissau,* 3rd ed., by Richard Lobban and Peter Mendy. 1996.
23. *Senegal,* by Lucie G. Colvin. 1981. *Out of print. See No. 65.*
24. *Morocco,* by William Spencer. 1980. *Out of print. See No. 71.*
25. *Malawi,* by Cynthia A. Crosby. 1980. *Out of print. See No. 54.*
26. *Angola,* by Phyllis Martin. 1980. *Out of print. See No. 52.*
27. *The Central African Republic,* by Pierre Kalck. 1980. *Out of print. See No. 51.*

59. *Comoro Islands,* by Martin Ottenehimer and Harriet Ottenehimer. 1994.
60. *Rwanda,* by Learthen Dorsey. 1994.
61. *Benin,* 3rd ed., by Samuel Decalo. 1995.
62. *Republic of Cape Verde,* 3rd ed., by Richard Lobban and Marlene Lopes. 1995.
63. *Ghana,* 2nd ed., by David Owusu-Ansah and Daniel Miles McFarland. 1995.
64. *Uganda,* by M. Louise Pirouet. 1995.
65. *Senegal,* 2nd ed., by Andrew F. Clark and Lucie Colvin Phillips. 1994.
66. *Algeria,* 2nd ed., by Phillip Chiviges Naylor and Alf Andrew Heggoy. 1994.
67. *Egypt,* 2nd ed., by Arthur Goldschmidt, Jr. 1994.
68. *Mauritania,* 2nd ed., by Anthony G. Pazzanita. 1996.
69. *Congo,* 3rd ed., by Samuel Decalo, Virginia Thompson, and Richard Adloff. 1996.
70. *Botswana,* 3rd ed., by Jeff Ramsay, Barry Morton, and Fred Morton. 1996.
71. *Morocco,* 2nd ed., by Thomas K. Park. 1996.
72. *Tanzania,* 2nd ed., by Thomas P. Ofcansky and Rodger Yeager. 1997.

Historical Dictionary of Tanzania

Second Edition

Thomas P. Ofcansky
Rodger Yeager

African Historical Dictionaries, No. 72

The Scarecrow Press, Inc.
Lanham, Md., & London
1997

SCARECROW PRESS, INC.

Published in the United States of America
by Scarecrow Press, Inc.
4720 Boston Way
Lanham, Maryland 20706

4 Pleydell Gardens, Folkestone
Kent CT20 2DN, England

British Library Cataloguing-in-Publication Information Available

Library of Congress Cataloging-in-Publication Data

Ofcansky, Thomas P., 1947–
    Historical dictionary of Tanzania / Thomas P. Ofcansky, Rodger
Yeager.—2nd ed.
        p.   cm.—(African historical dictionaries ; no. 72)
    1st. ed. entered under: Kurtz, Laura S.
    Includes bibliographical references.
    ISBN 0-8108-3244-5
    1. Tanzania—History—Dictionaries.   I. Yeager, Rodger.
II. Title.   III. Series.
DT444.O33 1997
967.8'003—DC20   96-35043
                                                         CIP

ISBN 0-8108-3244-5 (cloth : alk.paper)

⊗ ™ The paper used in this publication meets the minimum requirements of
American National Standard for Information Sciences—Permanence of Paper
for Printed Library Materials, ANSI Z39.48-1984.
Manufactured in the United States of America.

*For Tanzania
yesterday, today, and tomorrow*

Contents

Editor's Foreword

When Tanganyika became independent in 1961, there seemed to be more cause for hope and enthusiasm than in most other parts of Africa. The people were united behind a widely backed party, they supported a charismatic leader who—unlike some of his peers—refrained from expressing extreme political views, and the economy was relatively promising in a vast country less densely populated than most. Indeed, in the first decade or so of independence substantial progress was made in education, health, and other sectors, if considerably less so in the national economy. During this period the young state also grew into the United Republic of Tanzania by merging with Zanzibar, offering a rare concrete demonstration of African unity. On the other hand, Tanzania's professed ideology of African socialism did not work, and attempts at control by the ruling party eventually became repressive. The leadership finally conceded that economic and political reforms were necessary, and some positive change has occurred over the past ten years. Today's mood is much less euphoric than it was in the heyday of early independence, but Tanzania may now be embarking on a more realistic and popularly acceptable course of economic and political development.

Tanzania has always attracted attention abroad, and not only because of the extraordinary leadership of President Julius K. Nyerere. The country is too large and strategically too well located to be ignored either in its earlier history or today. Hence, foreigners and citizens alike maintain a keen interest in knowing more about Tanzanian history, both since independence and also much further back in time. The political scene, usually more stable than elsewhere in Africa, is yet highly dynamic, as are the evolving social, economic, and cultural orders. Nor can historically significant people be overlooked, whether they be present-day leaders or those from the past. These public figures and other key subjects are covered in this dictionary's individual entries, while broader historical trends are recorded in the volume's chronology. Additional reading is suggested in a truly impressive bibliography.

This new edition of the *Historical Dictionary of Tanzania* was written by Thomas P. Ofcansky and Rodger Yeager. Dr. Ofcansky is currently senior analyst for East Africa in the U.S. Defense Intelligence Agency.

He has studied and written on East Africa, including Tanzania, and visits the region periodically. His most recent major study is *Uganda: The Tarnished Pearl of Africa*. Dr. Yeager is professor of political science and adjunct professor of African history at West Virginia University. He has published extensively on public policy problems and prospects in eastern and southern Africa, including *Tanzania: An African Experiment*. In the present volume, Ofcansky and Yeager have covered the ground admirably and provide a comprehensive and accessible historical reference to a very important African country.

Jon Woronoff
Series Editor

Acronyms

AIC	African Inland Church (formerly AIM)
AIDS	Acquired Immune Deficiency Syndrome
AIM	African Inland Mission
AMNUT	All-Muslim National Union of Tanganyika
ASP	Afro-Shirazi Party
ASU	Afro-Shirazi Union
ASYL	Afro-Shirazi Youth League
BCU	Bukoba Cooperative Union
CC	Central Committee
CCM	Chama Cha Mapinduzi (Revolutionary Party)
CCT	Christian Council of Tanganyika (later Tanzania)
CGA	Clove Growers' Association
CMS	Church Missionary Society
CO	Colonial Office
COMESA	Common Market of Eastern and Southern African States
COSATA	Cooperative Supply Association of Tanzania
CUF	Civic United Front
CUT	Cooperative Union of Tanzania
DOAG	Deutsch-Ostafrikanische Gesellschaft (German East Africa Company)
EAA	East African Airways
EAC	East African Community
EACM	East African Common Market
EACSO	East African Common Services Organization
EAHC	East African High Commission
ELCT	Evangelical Lutheran Church in Tanzania
ERP	Economic Recovery Programme
ESAP	Economic and Social Action Programme
FO	Foreign Office
FPTU	Federation of Progressive Trade Unions
GDP	Gross Domestic Product
GEA	German East Africa
GNP	Gross National Product
HIV	Human Immunodeficiency Virus

IA	Indian Association
IBEAC	Imperial British East Africa Company
IBRD	International Bank for Reconstruction and Development (World Bank)
IDA	International Development Association
IMF	International Monetary Fund
INA	Indian National Association
JUWATA	Union of Tanzania Workers
KAR	King's African Rifles
KBO	Kagera Basin Organization
KNCU	Kilimanjaro Native Cooperative Union
KNPA	Kilimanjaro Native Planters' Association
LEGCO	Legislative Council
MP	Member of Parliament
NACP	National AIDS Control Programme
NCCR	National Convention for Construction and Reform
NEC	National Executive Committee
NESP	National Economic Survival Programme
NGO	Nongovernmental organization
NPSS	National Party of the Subjects of the Sultan of Zanzibar
NUTA	National Union of Tanganyika Workers
OAU	Organization of African Unity
ODA	Official Development Assistance
OTTU	Organization of Tanzanian Trade Unions
PAFMECA	Pan-African Freedom Movement of East and Central Africa
PLA	People's Liberation Army
PRC	People's Republic of China
PTA	Preferential Trade Area for Eastern and Southern African States
RDA	Ruvuma Development Association
SADC	Southern African Development Community
SADCC	Southern African Development Coordination Conference
SAP	Structural Adjustment Programme
SGC	Society for German Colonization
TAA	Tanganyika African Association
TAGSA	Tanganyika African Government Servants' Association
TANU	Tanganyika African National Union
TAPA	Tanganyika African Parents' Association
TAZARA	Tanzania-Zambia Railway Authority
TEC	Tanganyika (later Tanzania) Episcopal Conference
TFL	Tanganyika Federation of Labour
TPDF	Tanzania People's Defence Force
TT	Tanganyika Territory

TTC	Tanzania Tourist Corporation
TYL	TANU Youth League
UDP	United Democratic Party
UEA	University of East Africa
UK	United Kingdom
UMCA	Universities' Mission to Central Africa
UN	United Nations
UNFPA	United Nations Fund for Population Activities
US	United States
UTP	United Tanganyika Party
UWT	United Women of Tanganyika (later Tanzania)
VDC	Village Development Committee
VFCU	Victoria Federation of Cooperative Unions
ZNP	Zanzibar National Party
ZPPP	Zanzibar and Pemba People's Party
ZRC	Zanzibar Revolutionary Council

Chronology

1000 B.C.	Original Khoi-San hunters and gatherers are disturbed by pastoral Cushitic migrations from Ethiopia.
Pre-A.D. to 2 C. A.D.	Early traders visit the coast from Egypt, India, Assyria, Phoenicia, Arabia, Persia, Greece, and Rome.
0–1000 A.D.	In-migration of West African Bantu-speaking agriculturalists begins. Arab and Persian merchants create settlements in coastal and offshore island locations.
ca. 1270	Sultan Hassan bin Sulaiman I establishes rule on Kilwa, probably builds the island's Great Mosque, and begins minting coins.
by 1290	Arab and Shirazi Muslims dominate the western Indian Ocean, spreading Islam along the coast.
1000–1300	Bantu settlements predominate in western Tanganyika, with a mixture of Bantu, Cushitic, and Nilotic peoples occurring in the central and northern areas.
1300–1500	An Afro-Arab "Swahili" coastal culture arises and flourishes.
1328	The Arabian geographer Ibn Battuta visits Kilwa, now ruled by Sultan Hassan bin Sulaiman II.
26 July 1500	Pedro Alvares Cabral, in command of six Portuguese ships, arrives at Kilwa.
14 July 1502	In command of 10 ships, Portuguese explorer Vasco da Gama pays a second visit to Kilwa and, on behalf of Portugal, imposes liability to tribute.
24 July 1505	Francisco de Almeida, in command of eight Portuguese ships, storms Kilwa and subsequently begins construction of a fort.
11 April 1593	The Portuguese dedicate Fort Jesus, built in present-day Kenya to protect the East African coast from a Turkish attack.
1652	Muscat (Omani) Arabs attack Zanzibar and Pemba.
1669	Omanis attack along the coast as far south as the Ruvuma River, the present-day border between Tanzania and Mozambique.
1698	Omanis capture Fort Jesus and occupy the mainland.
1700–1800	Cattle raids and wars become commonplace among the western interlacustrine African kingdoms.
1700–1850	Pastoral Maasai peoples expand into northern Tanganyika

xvii

	and dominate large areas of the eastern Rift Valley, highlands, and plains.
1753	An attempt by the localized Mazrui clan to conquer Omani-ruled Zanzibar is defeated, and the island remains loyal to the imam of Oman.
14 September 1776	The sultan of Kilwa, Hassan bin Ibrahim, signs a treaty with France agreeing to supply 1,000 slaves a year for French possessions in the Indian Ocean.
1780	The imam of Oman seizes Kilwa and places a local governor in charge to tax the slave traders.
1784	Saif bin Ahmad al Busaidi fails to create an independent Sultanate of Kilwa and Zanzibar, and the Omani imam reestablishes control over the coast.
1811–1820s	The Zanzibar slave market is established, and Arab and Swahili merchants and slave traders penetrate the coastal hinterland and interior.
21 September 1822	The Moresby Treaty outlaws the sale of slaves to Christian merchants, but not to Muslims.
1824	Seyyid Said ibn Saif establishes Zanzibar town.
21 September 1833	The US signs Treaty of Amity and Commerce with the sultan of Zanzibar, which allows American merchants to trade freely in Zanzibar.
17 March 1837	A US consulate opens in Zanzibar.
1840	Sultan Said of Oman transfers his capital from Muscat to Zanzibar.
17 November 1844	The sultan of Zanzibar signs a Treaty of Commerce and Consular Jurisdiction with France. The treaty is ratified on 4 February 1846.
1845	An Arab settlement is established at Ujiji on Lake Tanganyika.
2 October 1845	The Hamerton Treaty restricts slaving to Sultan Said's East African possessions by outlawing the slave trade north of Mogadishu.
11 May 1848	Johannes Rebmann, a European missionary, first sights Mount Kilimanjaro.
3 December 1849	Missionary Johann Ludwig Krapf first sights Mount Kenya.
1852	An Arab trading center is established at Tabora in central Tanganyika.
13 February 1858	Richard Burton and John Hanning Speke sight Lake Tanganyika.
3 August 1858	John Hanning Speke sights Lake Nyanza (later named Lake Victoria).
1859	A treaty of commerce is negotiated and signed between the sultan of Zanzibar and the Hanseatic German Republics.
10 March 1862	Great Britain and France sign a treaty recognizing Zanzibar's independence.
1863–1864	The Holy Ghost Fathers create a settlement for freed slaves in Zanzibar.

31 August 1864	Bishop William G. Tozer and Dr. Edward Steere, the first representatives of the Universities Mission to Central Africa (UMCA), arrive in Zanzibar.
1868	The Holy Ghost Fathers begin missionary work at Bagamoyo on the mainland coast opposite Zanzibar.
6 July 1871	A Select Committee of the House of Commons is appointed to inquire into the slave trade along the East African coast.
10 November 1871	Henry Morton Stanley "finds" David Livingstone in Ujiji.
5 June 1873	The sultan of Zanzibar signs a treaty that prohibits the export of slaves from the sultan's East African mainland possessions to Zanzibar.
15 January 1876	The sultan of Zanzibar abolishes slavery in Kisimayu and the Banadir.
18 April 1876	The sultan of Zanzibar outlaws slave caravans in the mainland interior.
April 1878	A White Fathers mission arrives in Bagamoyo and prepares to move inland to Lakes Tanganyika and Victoria.
25 December 1879	Eastern Telegraph Company completes a telegraphic cable from Aden to Zanzibar. Two days later, telegraphic communication is established between Zanzibar and Europe.
1 September 1883	The British Political Agency and consulate general's office in Zanzibar are transferred from the Indian administration to the British government to further the suppression of the East African slave trade.
4 November 1884	Dr. Carl Peters arrives in Zanzibar and subsequently signs 12 treaties with local mainland chiefs, ceding to Germany territorial rights over a 2,500 square mile (6,500 square kilometer) area in Usagara, Uzigua, Ukami, and Nguru.
27 February 1885	Emperor Wilhelm signs a *schutzbrief* that recognizes the territorial annexations made by Carl Peters.
1 May 1885	Sir Lloyd W. Mathews, with a 180-man force, travels from Zanzibar to the interior and claims a protectorate for Zanzibar at Mount Kilimanjaro.
19 August 1885	The coastal settlement of Dar es Salaam is ceded to the Germans.
1 November 1886	An Anglo-German Agreement is signed, which divides influence over the sultan of Zanzibar's territories between Great Britain and Germany.
8 November 1886	The sultan of Zanzibar signs the General Act of the Brussels Conference concerning the abolition of slavery and the slave trade.
18 April 1888	The British East African Association, founded by Sir William Mackinnon in 1887, becomes the Imperial British East Africa Company (IBEAC).
28 April 1888	Carl Peters's German East Africa Company (Deutsch-Ostafrikanische Gesellschaft, DOAG) concludes an agreement with the Sultan of Zanzibar for a 50-year lease of the coastline from the Umba to the Ruvuma Rivers.

3 September 1888	The IBEAC receives a royal charter.
4 September 1888	The Abushiri revolt against the DOAG begins near Pangani.
8 September 1888	The Abushiri revolt against the DOAG spreads to Bagamoyo.
22 November 1888	Germany proclaims a protectorate over Witu.
30 January 1889	The German Reichstag empowers Chancellor Otto von Bismarck to spend up to two million marks to suppress the slave trade and to protect German interests in East Africa.
7 February 1889	The German *Schütztruppe* is established.
8 May 1889	German military forces end the Abushiri revolt by attacking the rebel camp at Bagamoyo.
13 September 1889	Great Britain and sultan of Zanzibar sign an agreement whereby all indentured persons entering the sultan's domains after 1 November 1889 will be freed. In exchange, the British lift their blockade of Zanzibar.
22 October 1889	The DOAG proclaims a protectorate over the mainland.
1 April 1890	The German government takes partial control of German East Africa (GEA) from the DOAG.
18 June 1890	Great Britain proclaims a protectorate over Witu, challenging the German claim.
1 July 1890	An Anglo-German Agreement formally defines spheres of influence between the two countries in East Africa.
1 August 1890	The sultan of Zanzibar signs an Anti-Slavery Decree, which prohibits sales and exchanges of slaves, closes slave markets, and permits slaves to purchase their freedom.
5 August 1890	An Anglo-French Convention defines spheres of influence between the two countries in the Indian Ocean. Accordingly, Britain recognizes French claims to Madagascar while France withdraws its opposition to the British protectorate over Zanzibar.
28 October 1890	The sultan of Zanzibar cedes the lease of the Tanganyika mainland to Germany.
4 November 1890	Great Britain proclaims a protectorate over Zanzibar and Pemba.
20 November 1890	The German government and the DOAG sign a contract whereby Berlin guarantees a loan of 10,556,000 marks for the development of the coast and for an indemnity to the sultan of Zanzibar.
1 January 1891	The German government assumes full control over GEA from the DOAG and declares a protectorate over its sphere of influence.
7 April 1897	The sultan of Zanzibar signs a decree ending the legal status of slavery.
1 February 1892	Zanzibar becomes a free port. *The Gazette for Zanzibar and East Africa* becomes the first weekly newspaper to be published in East Africa.
30 May 1893	Chief Engineer Bernhardt arrives at Tanga and begins construction of the Central Railway.

December 1894	The IBEAC is bought out by the British government.
1894–1898	Uprisings are mounted against the Germans by the Gogo, Hehe, Yao, and Haya peoples.
1 April 1896	The Tanga-Muheza section of the Central Railway commences operations.
6 April 1897	Slavery is abolished in the Zanzibar Protectorate.
1897–1903	The development of GEA proceeds; Ocean Road Hospital is opened in Dar es Salaam; the Amani Agricultural Research Institute is founded near Tanga; the Tanga Railway is completed to Korogwe; and plantation farming of sisal, coffee, and rubber is initiated.
7 April 1899	The German government, the DOAG, and the *Usambara Linie* railway company sign an agreement whereby Berlin acquires the railway and its assets for 1,300,000 marks.
6 April 1905	The German government founds the German Colonial Railway Construction and Administration Company to operate the Tanga Railway.
31 July 1905	Soon to engulf the entire southeastern mainland, the Maji-Maji Rebellion breaks out in the Matumbi Hills and in Madaba. Not ending until 1907 with great loss of African life, the rebellion results in the appointment of GEA's first civilian governor, Baron Albrecht von Rechenberg.
9 June 1909	The sultan of Zanzibar issues a decree abolishing all slavery and arranging compensation payments for slave owners.
7 February 1912	The Tanga Railway's extension to Moshi officially opens.
1905–1914	Central Railway construction links Dar es Salaam with Tabora and Kigoma.
1 July 1913	The British Colonial Office assumes responsibility for Zanzibari affairs from the Foreign Office.
4 November 1914	Germans defeat British forces at Tanga at the outset of World War I in East Africa.
4 September 1916	British forces occupy Dar es Salaam.
25 November 1918	General Paul von Lettow-Vorbeck surrenders to British forces at Abercorn, Northern Rhodesia.
31 January 1919	Sir Horace Byatt becomes civil administrator of the territory occupied by British troops.
1 April 1919	British civil administration assumes responsibility for all mainland railways.
7 May 1919	The Supreme Council at the Versailles peace talks allocates all of GEA to the UK under mandate. Belgium, which still occupies Ruanda-Urundi, protests the decision.
31 May 1919	To prevent a rift between the two nations, the UK cedes the Ruanda-Urundi portion of GEA to Belgium.
28 June 1919	Germany renounces all claims to GEA.
10 January 1920	GEA is renamed Tanganyika Territory (TT).
22 March 1921	Belgium cedes Kigoma District to TT.
23 July 1921	The Indian rupee ceases to be legal tender in TT.
1 January 1922	The Metallic Currency Ordinance establishes the East African shilling as legal tender in TT.

16 June 1922	Colonial authorities enact the Involuntary Servitude (Abolition) Ordinance, which outlaws slavery throughout TT.
22 July 1922	The League of Nations confirms a British mandate over TT in the name of the League.
26 January 1923	Colonial authorities enact the Land Ordinance, which authorizes the governor to grant private titles to land.
1 April 1923	British authorities impose African hut and poll taxes, following the introduction of the first Native Authority Ordinance in 1921.
1 June 1923	The Railways Administration assumes responsibility for marine service on Lake Tanganyika.
5 August 1924	Great Britain and Belgium sign a protocol demarcating the TT/Ruanda-Urundi boundary.
7 December 1926	TT's recently formed European Legislative Council (LEGCO) holds its first session.
15 August 1928	The Tabora-Mwanza branch line of the Central Railway is opened to traffic.
13 December 1929	The Moshi-Arusha portion of the Tanga Railway is opened to traffic.
1 January 1930	The *Tanganyika Standard* begins publication.
1930s	Worldwide economic depression leads the Colonial Office to exert great pressure on colonial officials to generate more surplus wealth. Accordingly, the government of TT conducts plant-more-crops campaigns intended to expand African export production and to increase local revenues by bringing subsistence farmers into the cash economy.
3 September 1939	The British authorities detain all German nationals and place their assets under a custodian.
1 January 1940	A territorial income tax is introduced.
1945–1946	The first African members are permitted to sit on the LEGCO.
13 December 1946	The newly formed United Nations confirms British trusteeship over TT.
5 February 1947	The British government announces a 10-year development plan for Zanzibar to improve the island's educational, medical, and agricultural services.
7 October 1947	The Msagali-to-Kongwa segment of the Tanganyika Railway's Central Line opens for traffic.
19 December 1947	The East African High Commission (EAHC) and Central Legislative Assembly are established to conduct all regional affairs and to enact all legislation of an interterritorial nature for Kenya, Uganda, and TT.
1 March 1948	The British Overseas Food Corporation assumes responsibility for the ill-fated East African Groundnut Scheme in southeastern TT.
1 May 1948	Tanganyika Railways and the Kenya and Uganda Railways form one transport system, known as the East African Railways and Harbours.

1951–1953	A Committee on Constitutional Development recommends equal racial representation among the unofficial LEGCO members. A Local Government Ordinance is passed providing for elected local councils. Julius K. Nyerere returns from study in the UK and becomes president of the Tanganyika African Association (TAA).
7 July 1954	Julius Nyerere and some of his colleagues transform the TAA into the Tanganyika African National Union (TANU).
2 October 1955	The British government announces its intention to grant Zanzibar internal self-government within the Commonwealth.
5 February 1957	Leaders of the Zanzabari African Association and Shirazi Association form the Afro-Shirazi Party (ASP).
17 July 1959	Louis and Mary Leakey discover *Zinjanthropus* at Olduvai Gorge.
1 May 1961	Following several unsuccessful attempts at multiracial government, including TANU's electoral defeat of the multiracial United Tanganyika Party (UTP), Julius Nyerere becomes Tanganyika's first prime minister in a government granted internal self-rule. Similar attempts at multiracialism in Zanzibar have led to bloody African-Arab clashes.
29 July 1961	President Nyerere opens Kivukoni College in Dar es Salaam.
9 December 1961	TT gains full independence from Great Britain. Also, the East African Common Services Organization (EACSO) replaces the EAHC.
14 December 1961	Tanganyika is admitted to the UN.
1 January 1962	An Education Ordinance eliminates the division of schools along racial lines.
5 June 1962	The National Assembly, created in 1961 from the LEGCO, passes the National Development Corporation Act, which seeks to facilitate the industrial and economic development of Tanganyika. EACSO has already been formed from the colonial EAHC to facilitate the same purposes on a regional basis.
9 December 1962	Tanganyika becomes a republic, following Julius Nyerere's resignation as prime minister. Nyerere is elected as the republic's first president. Regional commissioners have been appointed to replace colonial provincial commissioners, and a concerted effort is made to fill civil service positions with Tanganyika citizens.
14 January 1963	TANU's National Executive Committee (NEC) decides to make Tanganyika a one-party state, following the passage of a Preventive Detention Act in 1962.
5 June 1963	Tanganyika, Uganda, and Kenya sign a declaration proposing the creation of an East African Federation. However, disagreements among the three countries prevent the establishment of this union.

24 June 1963	Zanzibar becomes an internally self-governing state.
29 June 1963	The University College in Dar es Salaam, created in 1961, becomes a constituent campus of the University of East Africa.
10 December 1963	After a constitutional conference in London, Zanzibar gains internal self-government and independence from Great Britain under a government controlled by the sultan.
16 December 1963	Zanzibar is admitted to the UN.
12 January 1964	John Okello, supported by the Afro-Shirazi Youth League (ASYL) and dismissed African policemen, overthrows the Zanzibar government.
18 January 1964	The People's Republic of Zanzibar is established.
20 January 1964	The First Battalion of the Tanganyika Rifles mutiny in Dar es Salaam for higher pay and the dismissal of their expatriate British officers. The government requests British troops to help quell the rebellion.
30 January 1964	President Abeid Amani Karume announces that Zanzibar will become a one-party state under the ASP.
21 February 1964	Swahili replaces English as the official language of Zanzibar.
26 April 1964	The Republic of Tanganyika and the People's Republic of Zanzibar unite to form the United Republic of Tanzania and Zanzibar.
29 October 1964	Following public consultations, the country is renamed the United Republic of Tanzania.
19–23 December 1964	Julius Nyerere visits Zanzibar for the first time since the formation of the union with the mainland.
3 September 1965	Julius Nyerere is reelected president for a second five-year term after Tanzania is constitutionally transformed into a one-party state. The parliamentary election ousts a significant number of incumbents in the National Assembly, setting a precedent to be repeated in future parliamentary elections.
15 December 1965	Tanzania breaks diplomatic relations with the UK over the Rhodesian Unilateral Declaration of Independence (UDI).
1964–1966	Tanzania experiences foreign policy difficulties with West Germany over an East German presence in Zanzibar, and with the US over an alleged plot to overthrow the Tanzanian government.
14 June 1966	The Bank of Tanzania commences operations and introduces a national currency to replace the East African shilling.
5 February 1967	TANU adopts Julius Nyerere's Arusha Declaration, which commits Tanzania to a policy of *ujamaa na kujitegemea* (socialism and self-reliance).
5 September 1967	The People's Republic of China (PRC) agrees to provide Tanzania and Zambia with an interest-free loan for the construction of the Tanzania-Zambia Railway.

6 June 1967	Tanzania, Kenya, and Uganda sign the Treaty for East Africa Co-operation which establishes the East African Community (EAC).
13 September 1967	Julius Nyerere issues an agricultural policy statement outlining his plans to create "a nation of *Ujamaa* villages." Later, in 1968, all middle-level and senior party and government officials are required to adhere to the Arusha Declaration's Leadership Code, which prevents them from having more than one source of income.
13 April 1968	Tanzania recognizes the independence of Biafra.
1 July 1970	The Tanzanian government nationalizes the University College of Dar es Salaam, which henceforth is known as the University of Dar es Salaam.
30 October 1970	Julius Nyerere is reelected president for a third term.
January 1971	TANU publishes and begins to implement its *Mwongozo* leadership guidelines, which assert absolute party supremacy over the government, the working population, and the national economy.
16 March 1971	Zanzibari President Abeid Karume announces that all non-citizen Asians must leave Zanzibar within a year. He justifies this action by claiming that Asians are attempting to control the islands' economy.
7 April 1972	Zanzibari President Abeid Karume is assassinated. Aboud Jumbe becomes president of Zanzibar and vice president of the union.
26 April 1972	The private *Standard* newspaper merges with TANU's *Nationalist* to form the government-owned *Daily News*.
6 November 1973	President Julius Nyerere announces a "villagization" policy whereby most rural Tanzanians must live in farming collectives by the end of 1976.
November 1974	TANU's Musoma Resolution calls for universal primary education by 1977.
23 October 1975	The Tanzania-Zambia Railway, linking Kapiri Mposhi in Zambia to Dar es Salaam, officially opens. Subsequently, the line is placed under the jurisdiction of Tanzania-Zambia Railway Authority (TAZARA).
26 October 1975	Julius Nyerere is reelected president for a fourth term.
14 July 1976	The Tanzania-Zambia Railway officially opens.
5 February 1977	TANU and ASP amalgamate to form the Chama Cha Mapinduzi (CCM).
11 March 1977	The government establishes Air Tanzania Corporation, following the demise of East African Airways (EAA). Flight operations begin in June 1977.
26 April 1977	Tanzania's first permanent constitution is proclaimed, recognizing the CCM as the country's sole political party.
1 July 1977	The EAC collapses as a result of financial and other disagreements among Tanzania, Uganda, and Kenya.
22 September 1978	Ugandan planes bomb Mwanza, killing two and wounding twenty others.

30 October 1978	Ugandan troops occupy about 90 square miles (234 square kilometers) of northwestern Tanzanian territory near Kagera.
4 March 1979	Tanzania invades Uganda.
10 March 1980	Having overthrown Idi Amin's government, Tanzania announces the withdrawal of one-half of its 20,000 troops from Uganda.
1979–1980	Tanzania becomes a founding member of the Southern African Development Coordination Conference (SADCC), an association of southern African states intended to promote joint development programs and to counter South Africa's economic and political domination of the region. In 1992 SADCC is converted into the Southern African Development Community (SADC), an even more ambitious common-market and services organization.
15 June 1981	Six members of South Africa's Pan Africanist Congress (PAC) are sentenced to 15 years in prison for the 1979 murder of PAC official David Sibeko in Dar es Salaam. Like other southern African liberation parties, PAC maintains a liaison office in Dar es Salaam, headquarters city to the African Liberation Committee of the Organization of African Unity (OAU).
26 November 1981	Tanzania deploys 400 troops to the Seychelles after a group of South African mercenaries invades the islands and attempts to overthrow the government.
21 December 1981	The Preferential Trade Area for Eastern and Southern African States (PTA) is established.
18 March 1983	Prime Minister Edward Sokoine initiates a nationwide campaign against economic "sabotage."
29 January 1984	Aboud Jumbe resigns as president of Zanzibar amid growing controversy over constitutional changes to reduce Zanzibari overrepresentation in the union government. Ali Hassan Mwinyi succeeds Jumbe.
19 April 1984	Ali Hassan Mwinyi is elected as Zanzibar's president.
26 September 1984	Julius Nyerere dedicates the Morogoro campus of the University of Dar es Salaam as the Sokoine University of Agriculture, named after recently deceased Prime Minister Edward Sokoine.
1985	National economic performance reaches an historic low because of flooding, droughts, and adverse international terms of trade, and also because of several policy factors including villagization, an overvalued currency, low agricultural producer prices, inefficient government corporations, and an industrial strategy oriented toward import substitution.
12 January 1985	Zanzibar adopts a new constitution that limits the presidency to two five-year terms.
15 October 1985	Idris Abdul Wakil is elected Zanzibari president.
1 November 1985	Ali Hassan Mwinyi is elected to succeed Julius Nyerere,

who has announced his retirement as president of Tanzania to enable policy reforms in the socialist economy increasingly demanded by foreign donors.

5 November 1985   Julius Nyerere steps down as president of Tanzania, but remains CCM chairman. Ali Hassan Mwinyi takes the presidential oath of office.

1985–1988   Bilateral and multilateral donor and lending agencies curtail assistance to Tanzania until policy reforms are introduced to reduce the country's US$3 billion debt by denationalizing the socialist economy. In June 1986 President Mwinyi introduces the Economic Recovery Programme (ERP) to effect currency devaluations, remove import restrictions, increase producer prices for food and export crops, and reform state corporations. The following month, the IMF responds with an $800 million allocation in standby credits, and in 1987 with a $90 million structural adjustment loan. Donors meet in Paris and agree to another $130 million in new loans and grants. By November 1988 Tanzania has received more than $100 million in IBRD loans and a second IMF standby credit facility to help finance economic privatization.

23 January 1988   Zanzibari President Idris Abdul Wakil dismisses his 18-member cabinet and takes control of the islands' military forces after claiming that he had uncovered a coup plot.

21 September 1988   The mainland government establishes two commissions to investigate corruption, theft, and misappropriation of public funds among leaders and civil servants in Zanzibar and Pemba.

29 December 1988   Tanzania deploys soldiers to Zanzibar and Pemba after rumors surface of a coup plot against the Zanzibari government.

1 August 1990   As part of an effort to encourage foreign-exchange earnings from tourism, Tanzania rescinds a 17-year ban on big game hunting and permits limited shooting between August and November. Prohibitions remain in place against hunting elephant, lion, and rhinoceros.

17 August 1990   To help pave the way for political reform, including an end to one-party rule, Julius Nyerere resigns as CCM chairman and turns over the post to President Ali Hassan Mwinyi.

21 October 1990   Salim Amour is elected as Zanzibar's president.

28 October 1990   Ali Hassan Mwinyi is reelected to a second term as president.

23 February 1991   President Mwinyi names members of a presidential commission that is charged with canvassing public opinion on the idea of introducing a multiparty system of government in Tanzania.

2 June 1991   Tanzania signs the Nuclear Non-Proliferation Treaty.

30 September 1991   The National AIDS Control Programme reports that about

	100,000 Tanzanians have AIDS and another 700,000 have the AIDS virus, HIV.
10 November 1991	The Bank of Tanzania announces that foreign banks can begin operations in Tanzania by 1993.
20 November 1991	Tanzanian authorities release Zanzibar's ex–Chief Minister Seif Sharif Hamad after 30 months in custody. Hamad had been jailed on charges of sedition.
20 January 1992	The CCM National Executive Committee (NEC) endorses a presidential commission's proposal that opposition parties be allowed to register.
19 February 1992	A CCM Special Congress endorses the principle of a multiparty system of government.
5 March 1992	Tanzania lifts its ban on elephant hunting.
31 March 1992	In the wake of Nelson Mandela's release from prison and the legalization of the African National Congress (ANC), Tanzania lifts its restrictions on personal travel to South Africa and ends its scientific and cultural boycott of that country. The bans on direct air links, sports, and tourism are likewise lifted, although Dar es Salaam continues to maintain economic and trade sanctions against Pretoria.
7 May 1992	The National Assembly endorses the Eighth Constitutional Reform Draft Bill, which legalizes opposition parties.
12 May 1992	The National Assembly legalizes private newspapers.
14 May 1992	Zanzibar's House of Representatives endorses a bill amending the islands' constitution to legalize opposition parties.
17 June 1992	The Tanzanian government permits opposition parties to petition for legal status.
5 September 1992	Former Foreign Minister Oscar Kambona returns to Tanzania after 25 years of political exile.
1991–1993	Despite economic reforms, Tanzania's perennial dependency on foreign aid has persisted. The country now ranks second only to Ethiopia as sub-Saharan Africa's largest recipient of official development assistance. Although averaging more than US$1 billion, annual aid transfers still leave a substantial balance-of-payments deficit and a long-term debt that has swelled from less than $2 billion in 1980 to more than $6 billion.
5 November 1993	Tanzania and 14 other nations sign a treaty that transforms the PTA into the Common Market of Eastern and Southern African States (COMESA).
11 November 1993	Tanzania lifts trade and economic sanctions against South Africa and announces that it will open a South African liaison office.
28 November 1993	The Tanzanian government bans tree harvesting on Mount Kilimanjaro to save Africa's highest peak from environmental degradation.
30 November 1993	Tanzania, Kenya, and Uganda sign a Treaty for Enhanced East African Co-operation. This treaty lays the groundwork

for regional cooperation in several areas, including trade, industry, agriculture, energy, transport, communication, law, and security.

8 February 1994   Tanzania's first private television station, the Coastal Television Network, commences operations.

12 May 1994   Tanzania and South Africa establish formal diplomatic relations.

30 June 1994   Tanzania, Uganda, and Kenya sign a treaty establishing the Lake Victoria Fisheries Organization, which supposedly will strengthen cooperation in the region.

24 October 1994   Tanzania announces that more than one million people are believed to have been infected with HIV and that approximately 840,000 Tanzanians will have acquired AIDS by the year 2000.

13 December 1994   The Tanzanian government announces that it needs at least US$12.3 million to provide care for the 548,000 Rwandan and Burundian refugees who are living in 10 camps in the Kagera region.

30 December 1994   Dar es Salaam announces that the South African hotel chain, Protea, will take over the management of four state-owned hotels in Tanzania. The takeover is part of Tanzania's open-door policy to attract private investors and to boost tourism.

9 January 1995   The National Museum of Tanzania reveals that researchers from Tanzania, the United States, Canada, Great Britain, and India have discovered fossils believed to be more than one million years older than those from Olduvai Gorge and Laetoli. These fossils, of mammals, reptiles, birds, and fish, were found in Manonga River valley in Shinyanga Region, about 180 miles (300 kilometers) south of Lake Victoria. The fossils, which date back five to six million years, are the oldest mammal remains ever found in Tanzania.

23 February 1995   Frustrated by the growing number of Rwandan and Burundian refugees in Tanzania, a group of parliamentarians calls for the Tanzanian government to annex Rwanda and Burundi.

24 February 1995   Tanzania and Israel restore diplomatic relations. Dar es Salaam had severed diplomatic ties with Tel Aviv in 1973 in reaction to the Arab-Israeli conflict.

27 February 1995   The Consultative Group meets in Paris and promises to provide Tanzania with US$1 billion in new foreign aid commitments for 1995/96.

31 March 1995   Tanzania closes its border with Burundi to prevent at least 50,000 Rwandan Hutus from seeking refuge in western Tanzania. The Rwandan Hutus had been living in Burundi since the mid-1994 genocide in Rwanda, which claimed up to 500,000 lives.

9 April 1995   Tanzania's first private university opens in Iringa. The first

	intake of students will be 600; eventually, the university will have about 2,000 students.
12 April 1995	Tanzania, Rwanda, and the United Nations High Commissioner for Refugees sign an agreement for the voluntary repatriation of the estimated 650,000 Rwandan refugees camped in Tanzania.
28–29 April 1995	Between 200,000 and 250,000 Rwandan refugees flee into Tanzania. These refugees are Hutu Rwandans who fear that the insurgent Rwanda Patriotic Front might exact revenge for the massacre of hundreds of thousands of Tutsi Rwandans. The refugees establish a camp, the largest in the world, at Benaco in Ngara District.
11 May 1995	A Rwandan newspaper, *The Express*, reports that the Rwandan government is recruiting Tanzanians into its army.
3 July 1995	Former President Nyerere denies allegations that he played a role in choosing CCM candidates to run in the October 1995 presidential elections.
14 July 1995	Three new political parties—the United People's Congress, the National Alliance for Mass Advancement, and the Popular Democratic Movement of Tanzania—submit their applications for registration.
19 July 1995	Denmark, Finland, the Netherlands, Norway, Sweden, and the European Union agree to provide Tanzania with US$15 millon to help finance the October 1995 national elections. These funds will be used to support the National Electoral Commission, the Zanzibar Electoral Commission, voter education, election observers, and media coverage of the elections.
22 July 1995	The CCM's NEC rejects at least 14 presidential aspirants and officially endorses former Foreign Minister Benjamin Mkapa as its potential presidential candidate.
6 August 1995	The Civic United Front (CUF), National Convention for Construction and Reform (NCCR), and the Party for Democracy and Development (PDD) form a coalition and agree to support Augustine Mrema as their sole presidential candidate. Within weeks the agreement collapses as CUF and PDD leaders accuse the NCCR of "imposing its will" on the coalition.
22 August 1995	Fifty-seven members of Tanzania's parliament call for a referendum to establish a separate government for the mainland to parallel the largely autonomous Zanzibari government.
30 August 1995	The CCM's National Electoral Commission endorses three presidential candidates; Benjamin Mkapa of the CCM, John Cheyo of the United Democratic Party (UDP), and Ibrahim Lipumba of the CUF.
18 September 1995	The CCM's National Electoral Commission invites foreign observers to monitor Tanzania's first multiparty elections,

scheduled for October 1995. Observers from 10 countries (Belgium, Canada, Denmark, Finland, France, Japan, the Netherlands, Norway, Sweden, and the United States) and five international organizations (the Association of Western Parliamentarians, the Commonwealth of Nations, the European Union, the OAU, and the UN) accept the invitation.

22 October 1995 National elections are held in Zanzibar, accompanied by widespread allegations of voting irregularities.

26 October 1995 The Zanzibar Electoral Commission announces that incumbent CCM candidate Salim Amour has won the Zanzibari presidency with 165,271 votes (50.2 percent), with 163,706 votes (49.8 percent) cast for the CUF candidate, Seif Sharif Hamad. The CCM also won 26 National Assembly seats as compared with the CUF's 24 seats.

29 October 1995 National elections are held on the mainland, accompanied by widespread allegations of voting irregularities.

13 November 1995 Tanzania's High Court dismisses a petition by 10 opposition parties to have the October 1995 elections nullified on the grounds that they were not free and fair.

23 November 1995 Benjamin Mkapa is sworn in as Tanzania's third president following an election in which he won 62 percent of the popular vote. His CCM party also won 186 parliamentary seats, as opposed to 46 for the three main opposition parties, the NCCR, CUF, and UDP. Mkapa's main presidential opponent, the NCCR's Augustine Mrema, won 28 percent of the popular votes. A few hours after his inauguration, President Mkapa authorizes the banning of the Swahili-language weekly *Rafiki* for publishing information likely to cause unrest in the country.

4 December 1995 Tanzania announces that at the end of October 1995 the country's external debt was US$6.8 billion.

16 December 1995 Tanzania and Uganda pledge to revive economic cooperation between the two former partner states in the EAC. Efforts to revive the EAC have most recently failed because of poor relations between Kenya and Uganda, each accusing the other of supporting rebels intent on overthrowing their respective governments. However, President Benjamin Mkapa now expresses optimism about the prospects of reinstituting the EAC because of a new spirit of cooperation that has arisen among Kenya, Tanzania, and Uganda.

17 December 1995 President Mkapa announces that the Tanzanian-Burundian border will remain closed until peace and stability are reestablished in Burundi.

21 December 1995 Tanzania and Kenya announce that train and ship service between the two countries will resume on 20 January 1997.

Maps

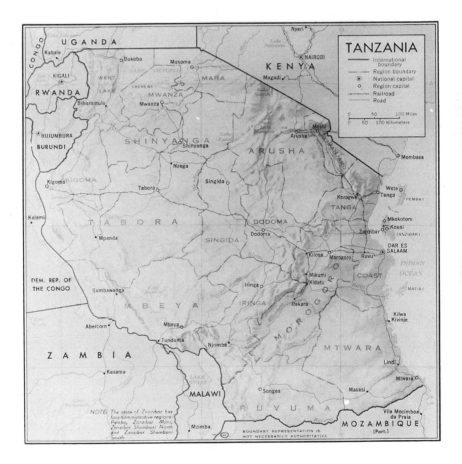

Zanzibar and Pemba

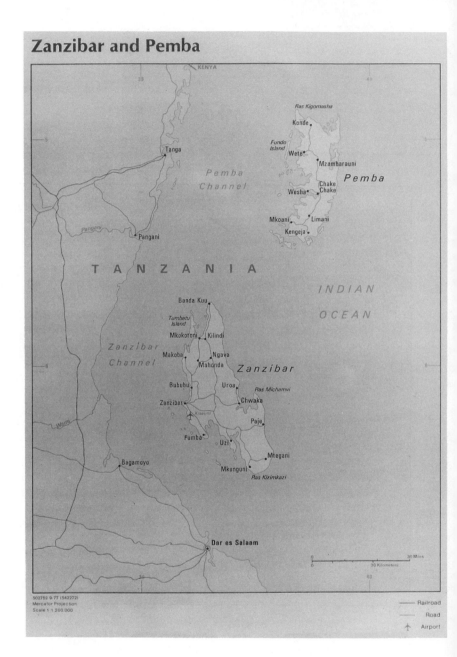

KENYA

Ras Kigomasha

Konde

Tanga

Fundo
Island   Wete

Mzambarauni

*Pemba
Channel*   *Pemba*

Wesha   Chake
         Chake

Mkoani   Limani

Pangani   Kengeja

T A N Z A N I A

I N D I A N

O C E A N

Banda Kuu

Tumbatu
Island

Mkokotoni   Kilindi

*Zanzibar
Channel*   Makoba   Ngava

Mahonda   *Zanzibar*

Bububu   Uroa   Ras Michamvi

Zanzibar   Chwaka

Paje

Fumba   Uzi

Mtegani

Bagamoyo   Mkunguni

Ras Kizimkazi

Dar es Salaam

30 Miles
30 Kilometers
60

502753 9-77 (542272)
Mercator Projection
Scale 1:1,200,000

——— Railroad
——— Road
↑ Airport

Introduction

Tanzania has evolved as one of East Africa's most significant and historically rich countries. Until recently, the work of archaeologists such as Louis and Mary Leakey enabled the country to claim that it was in fact the cradle of mankind. Newer discoveries in Kenya and Ethiopia have challenged this view. Nevertheless, Tanzania remains an important link to the human past. Indeed, *Homo habilis*, which was discovered at Olduvai Gorge near the Serengeti Plains, continues to be regarded as the most direct early ancestor of *Homo sapiens*.

Human history in Tanzania began about 10,000 years ago, when Khoi-San-speaking hunters and gatherers lived in the area south of Olduvai Gorge. In the first millennium B.C., Cushitic-speaking cattle herders from southern Ethiopia traveled via the Great Rift Valley to the same region. Beginning early in the first millennium A.D., a much larger influx occurred of Bantu-speaking, iron-working cultivators from the West African areas of what is now southern Nigeria and Cameroon. Since each of these groups relied on a different economic base, there was little competition or conflict among them. Between the tenth and eighteenth centuries, however, a succession of Central Sudanic, Nilotic, and Paranilotic migrations from the north and northwest upset this relatively peaceful balance. These grain-producing and herding peoples moved into western and northern Tanzania, where they clashed and mixed with the Bantu speakers who had already settled in these regions. At the same time, small numbers of Bantu-speaking cultivators settled in the lowlands adjacent to the Indian Ocean.

The early nineteenth century witnessed the beginnings of the modern colonial scramble for Zanzibar and mainland Tanganyika. In 1822 Great Britain and the sultan of Zanzibar signed the Moresby Treaty, which reflected British desires to end the East African slave trade. In 1833, 1844, and 1858, respectively, the sultan of Zanzibar concluded free-trade agreements with the United States, France, and Germany. From these initial contacts, by 1890 the British had completed the process of formal colonization in this part of East Africa by declaring a protectorate over Zanzibar.

During the middle to late nineteenth century, European explorers,

1

missionaries, traders, and imperialists used Zanzibar as a base of operations from which to penetrate the mainland. Their activities further stimulated British and German interest in the status of the mainland and nearby islands. As a result, Britain and Germany competed with one another to establish dominance in the region. In 1884 Carl Peters, a German imperialist who had founded the Society for German Colonization, arrived in East Africa and signed a series of treaties with local rulers that gave his society political and commercial rights over what eventually became German East Africa (GEA). The following year, the society received a German government charter to administer the mainland. Eventually Peters transferred the charter to a new organization he had formed called the German East Africa Company (Deutsch-Ostafrikanische Gesellschafort DOAG).

Britain, active elsewhere in East Africa, accepted German superiority in the area by agreeing to the establishment of a German protectorate north of the Ruvuma River and south of what is now the border between Tanzania and Kenya. An 1886 Anglo-German agreement allowed the sultan to retain control over Zanzibar, Pemba, Mafia, and Lamu Islands, together with a coastal strip extending 3.5 miles (6 kilometers) inland. Two years later, the sultan granted Germany a 50-year lease over the coastal strip, which provided the Germans with full political and economic jurisdiction over the mainland. Another Anglo-German agreement, concluded in 1890, determined GEA's western boundary, authorized the establishment of a British protectorate over Zanzibar and Pemba, and gave Germany permanent ownership of the coastal strip. The following year, Berlin assumed direct responsibility for GEA, largely because the German East Africa Company had become almost bankrupt following its often-brutal mismanagement of the mainland.

Scholars continue to debate the significance of the German colonial period. Apart from creating a European-dominated plantation economy, the German military administration introduced Western medicine, law, and education to GEA. Additionally, the Germans built railway and road networks throughout the northern and central parts of the colony. On the other hand, these accomplishments benefited few Africans and failed to extinguish widespread popular discontent over policies such as those involving European land alienation and labor impressment. The implementation of a hut tax further exacerbated anti-German feelings among the indigenous population.

African resistance to colonial rule culminated in the 1905–1907 Maji-Maji Rebellion, which spread from the coast to an area that today includes most of Morogoro and Ruvuma Regions. The Germans responded to this revolt by unleashing a reign of terror that claimed the lives of between 75,000 and 120,000 Africans. In the wake of German victory, famine and disease resulted in many more deaths. The widespread destruction and suffering associated with the Maji-Maji uprising caused a public outcry in Germany. In response, the German government installed GEA's first civilian governor, Baron Albrecht von Rechenberg, who introduced numerous reforms to improve the treatment of Africans, to encourage indigenous agricultural development, and to expand African educational opportunities. German settlers, who faced reductions in available African land and labor, vigorously opposed Rechenberg's policies and eventually forced him to resign. The debate over whether GEA should be ruled by German settlers or by expatriate colonial officials on behalf of the indigenous population persisted throughout the last years of German colonial rule.

Meanwhile, the British had consolidated their hold over Zanzibar and had persuaded the sultan to abolish slavery. In 1913 London transferred responsibility for the Zanzibar Protectorate from the Foreign Office to the Colonial Office and replaced the islands' consul general with a Resident who functioned largely as a colonial governor. Under this arrangement, however, the British continued to regard Zanzibar as a semiautonomous Arab enclave rather than as part of colonial East Africa. The sultan remained titular head of state, and his subjects received preference for government jobs. Arabs also controlled the economy, which was based primarily on the clove industry.

During World War I, British and Allied forces occupied GEA despite the brilliant guerrilla tactics of Major General Paul von Lettow-Vorbeck. This remarkable German general, who commanded an army that included thousands of African *askaris* (soldiers), was never actually defeated on the battlefield; Lettow-Vorbeck and his men surrendered only after peace had been concluded in Europe.

The postwar settlement changed the political status of the mainland but did little to alter conditions in Zanzibar. The League of Nations mandated the western African kingdoms of Ruanda and Urundi to Belgian administration and the rest of the mainland to Great Britain. The British portion was soon renamed Tanganyika. Under the terms of the League mandate, Brussels and London vaguely promised to rule these territories in the interests of "peace, order and good government" and to facilitate "the material well-being and the social progress of the inhabitants." The British continued to treat Zanzibar as an Arab state, which served to perpetuate centuries-old racial, religious, and political divisions between the islands and the mainland.

Several significant developments characterized the interwar period. On the mainland, Sir Donald Cameron, British governor from 1925 to 1931, introduced a form of local government that he had helped to develop during his earlier service in Nigeria. This system, known as indirect rule, sought to encourage the establishment of indigenous political institutions and leaders, both helping to prepare the territory for eventual independence under continuing British influence. The colonial authorities hoped to achieve these goals by creating native authorities to make local laws and to administer local courts and treasuries. Staffing all native authorities with traditional leaders proved to be an impossible undertaking, since formal governing systems had never existed in many societies. In others, organized political authority had been disrupted or destroyed by several factors, including local warfare, the Arab slave trade, German pacification campaigns, and large-scale migrations partly induced by outbreaks of human and livestock diseases.

To overcome the paucity of traditional leaders, the British appointed local notables, hoping that they would acquire traditional legitimacy. Unfortunately, nearly all of these new rulers were as foreign to local communities as were the British colonial officials. To make matters worse, many of the new rulers were corrupt or were inclined toward suppressing their subjects. Those who sought to implement government policies often succeeded in widening the gulf between rulers and ruled. Conversely, native authorities who resisted official policy were usually dismissed from their jobs.

The economic situation on the mainland remained as stratified as it had been during the German colonial period. Europeans and Asians controlled the productive and retail trade sectors, while a minority of Africans worked in small-scale commercial agriculture. British colonial authorities encouraged the production of coffee and cotton rather than food crops in order to expand indigenous export production and to increase tax revenues. As a means of promoting export crops, the government sanctioned the establishment of African cooperative societies. Some of these officially supervised organizations formed the basis of what later became interest groups and political parties expressing regime-challenging demands and agitating for independence.

Unlike the mainland, Zanzibar experienced little change during the interwar years. The British continued to recognize the protectorate as an Arab state and to dominate the senior levels of the civil service, while Arabs occupied midlevel positions and Asians worked in the lower ranks. Arabs also remained in control of the plantation economy and Indians held sway over Zanzibar's commercial sector. All political activity reflected the islands' ethnic divisions. And yet, despite the anticolonial attitudes of groups like the Indian Association and the Zanzibari African Association, there was no serious challenge to British colonial rule until the post-World War II era.

After 1945 a fundamental change took place in the nature of the relationship between Britain and Tanganyika. The British looked to the mainland for an increased supply of agricultural products needed to help repair their war-damaged economy. Even more important was Tanganyika's change in legal status from a League of Nations mandate to a

United Nations trust territory. This new arrangement required the British government to submit regular reports concerning the territory's progress toward self-government and eventual independence.

To achieve these goals, the British colonial authorities devised a number of programs. In 1946 the government introduced a 10-year development plan to expand African involvement in the cash economy. Plans were also mounted to increase the production of food oils and other agricultural commodities. In 1955 the British published another development plan that promised greater support for African commercial agriculture. Despite these initiatives, development expenditures remained concentrated on export crops rather than on the subsistence sector. Small-scale African farmers thus continued to suffer economic hardship, which became increasingly worse as population pressures and environmental problems such as soil erosion and depletion affected much of rural Tanganyika.

In the political arena, the colonial government sought to counter growing African nationalism by creating partly elected local councils that were intended to introduce reforms in the native authority system. This strategy failed to quell a rising tide of anticolonial nationalism among the country's African population. The emergence of the Tanganyika African National Union (TANU) in July 1954 fundamentally altered the nature of African political activity. Previously, expressions of anticolonial sentiment had been limited to the local level. Under the leadership of Julius Nyerere, TANU now moved the debate on Tanganyika's political future into the national and even international arenas.

As TANU grew in popularity and influence, Britain recognized the inevitability of self-government. Sir Edward Twining, governor of Tanganyika from 1949 to 1958, provided a "multiracial" alternative to TANU by encouraging the European and Asian communities to form the United Tanganyika Party (UTP). He also required racial parity on all local councils, despite the fact that few or no Europeans and Asians actually lived in many districts. According to his critics, Twining also launched an intimidation campaign against TANU, which culminated in the conviction of Julius Nyerere for libel after he had criticized two British district commissioners.

Once Sir Richard Turnbull became governor of Tanganyika in 1958, relations between the colonial authorities and TANU improved. Apart from announcing that racial parity was no longer required on local councils, he supported the UTP's dissolution. More important, Turnbull accelerated progress toward internal self-rule, which was proclaimed on 15 May 1961. Under this agreement, the colonial government retained control over Tanganyikan foreign relations and the armed forces until 9 December 1961, when the country gained its full independence.

During the post-1945 period in Zanzibar, the British found themselves in the middle of a three-way struggle for power among the African, Arab, and Shirazi communities. In 1954 the Arab Association, a group that had traditionally supported British policies, sought to persuade the colonial government to grant internal self-government by organizing an 18-month boycott of the Zanzibari Legislative Council (LEGCO). Over the next few years a Zanzibar Nationalist Party (ZNP) and Afro-Shirazi Union (ASU) also became politically active. The British hoped that this development would result in effective electoral competition. To their disappointment, a 1957 LEGCO election proved inconclusive as none of the parties succeeded in scoring a decisive victory.

Following the election, new political factions emerged. In 1959 Shirazis who lived on Pemba formed their own Zanzibar and Pemba People's Party (ZPPP) while Zanzibar's Shirazis joined the Afro-Shirazi Party (ASP), which had recently replaced the now-defunct ASU. The colonial government responded to this deepening political confusion by scheduling another LEGCO election for January 1961, which also failed to produce a winning party or party coalition. The increasingly frustrated British called for yet another LEGCO election for June 1961. A ZNP-ZPPP coalition obtained a three-seat majority but failed to establish a stable, functioning government. The British responded by promising to grant internal self-government by June 1963 and scheduled a final pre-independence election for July. In this poll the ZNP-ZPPP alliance won a majority of LEGCO seats, formed a government, reaffirmed its support of the sultanate, and announced that it intended to ban post-independence political opposition.

On 10 December 1963 Zanzibar received its independence. Within a month, a crisis emerged when a Ugandan immigrant named John Okello led a violent revolution against the ruling ZNP-ZPPP coalition. His action resulted in the overthrow of the government and the sultanate and the rise to power of Abeid Karume and his ASP. The Zanzibari Revolution had caused the deaths of more than 5,000 Arabs. This event and the chaos that followed precipitated the unification of the mainland with Zanzibar in April 1964 and led to the birth of the United Republic of Tanzania.

The new nation confronted numerous problems, the most immediate of which concerned Dar es Salaam's lack of control over Zanzibar. Indeed, the Zanzibari government retained control over its own foreign policy and continued to command the islands' armed forces, to supervise the immigration and emigration services, and to manage Zanzibar's foreign-exchange reserves. Even more alarming from the mainland's point of view, local leaders increasingly challenged TANU and its policies.

The TANU elite reacted to the latter issue by authorizing the legalization of a one-party state. Julius Nyerere also took several steps to suppress the opposition, including the amalgamation of private trade unions and cooperative societies into the TANU-affiliated National Union of Tanganyika Workers (NUTA). He likewise abolished the colonial native authorities and replaced them with district councils, which were elected but not autonomous. Nyerere fused TANU and local government structures by empowering the party to approve all candidates for district council seats.

Over the next few years, the country steadily moved away from the egalitarian and democratic principles enunciated by TANU during the struggle for independence. In 1967 Nyerere unveiled the Arusha Declaration, which committed Tanzania to a policy of *ujamaa na kujitegemea*, socialism and self-reliance. Shortly thereafter the Tanzanian government distributed several policy booklets throughout the country extolling the principles of socialist village development under the *Ujamaa* concept. In 1972 the Tanzanian government eliminated district councils altogether and authorized regional governments, operating under party scrutiny, to assume their functions. Between 1973 and 1977, moreover, fully 85 percent of the rural population was, sometimes forcibly, relocated into some 7,300 developmentally ill-conceived villages.

The Zanzibar problem was not resolved until 1977, when Dar es Salaam combined TANU and the ASP into a new governing party, the Chama Cha Mapinduzi (CCM). The CCM, dominated by mainland Africans, now assumed effective responsibility for governing Zanzibar's Arab population. All former TANU and ASP members were automatically enrolled in the CCM, but new recruits had to complete an indoctrination course on party policies and goals prior to applying for membership.

While party elections were under way, the National Assembly approved a permanent constitution to replace an interim 1965 constitution. This document asserted the CCM's supremacy over the entire country. In a concession to political reality, the new constitution also recognized Zanzibar's unique status by authorizing a separate Zanzibari cabinet and ministerial system. The number of elected National Assembly seats was also increased to provide Zanzibar with 10 constituency positions.

Over the coming years, it became increasingly evident that Nyerere's political, economic, and social policies had failed to unite the mainland with Zanzibar, to stimulate economic growth and diversification, and to improve the lives of average Tanzanians. In particular, Tanzania had become one of the most impoverished countries in the world. Persistent conflict with Zanzibar, corruption and incompetence in the CCM, a rapidly growing population, the large-scale emergence of the Acquired Immune Deficiency Syndrome (AIDS) and other emerging and newly reemerging diseases, and escalating demands for genuine democracy further isolated Nyerere. This troubled atmosphere undoubtedly contributed to his announcement in 1985 that he would not campaign again for the presidency. Later, in 1990, he resigned from the CCM chairmanship itself.

Nyerere's successor, Ali Hassan Mwinyi, also proved incapable of resolving the country's many problems, including the hegemonic tendencies and corruption of the CCM. Mwinyi gradually moved away from Nyerere's brand of socialism and slowly introduced economic reforms. After serving two terms as president, he announced his retirement, and in a multiparty election in October 1995 he was succeeded by CCM's Benjamin Mkapa.

It remains to be seen whether the 1995 elections will mark a turning point in Tanzania's history. Opinion about the country's future is divided. Optimists maintain that Tanzania is finally moving toward the establishment of a sound economy and a genuinely democratic society. Pessimists believe that Tanzania will remain economically and politically moribund as long as the CCM continues to dominate the country. No matter which vision proves to be true, it is certain that Tanzania will continue to be one of Africa's historically most dynamic, interesting, and important countries.

The Dictionary

— A —

ABDALLAH IBN HEMEDI EL AJJEMY (1840–1912). Distinguished Swahili historian and administrator who was born in Zanzibar (q.v.) to an Arab father and a Machinga mother. Abdallah served Kimweri za Nyumbai (q.v.) and joined the German colonial service. In 1905, after serving as *akida* (q.v.) of Sega and Muheza, he was appointed *liwali* (q.v.) of Tanga (q.v.). This made Abdallah one of the highest ranking non-European government officers in GEA. He served in this role until 1910. Abdallah died in 1912 at Tanga.

ABDULLAH IBN KHALIFA, SEYYID (1910–1963). Tenth Busaidi (q.v.) ruler of Zanzibar (1960–1963). Abdullah was 50 years of age when he succeeded his father, Seyyid Khalifa ibn Harub (q.v.). During his brief tenure, Seyyid Khalifa failed to prevent bitter communal politics from degenerating into intense racial hatred between Zanzibar's Arab and African communities. Although he reportedly was a Zanzibar National Party (ZNP) (q.v.) supporter, Seyyid Khalifa's ineffectiveness was probably due largely to the fact that he was a sick man when he acceded to the throne. His health continued to deteriorate until his death in July 1963.

ABDULLAH IBN NASIBU (?–1882). The Arab leader most disliked by Chief Mirambo (q.v.). He was one of the foremost Arab trader-warriors of the interior, earning the nickname *Kissessa* (Valiant) from his many victories. He also acquired a large and devoted following at Unyanyembe, near Tabora (q.v.), from his generosity in distributing the spoils of these exploits. At one point, disagreement arose between the Unyanyembe community and the *liwali* (q.v.) of Sultan Barghash (q.v.). With the support of Chief Isike of Unyanyembe, Abdullah replaced the sultan's *liwali*. The deposed *liwali* fled to Mirambo's protection at Urambo, and for years thereafter mutual animosity and mistrust continued between the former and latter *liwalis* and their supporters, and also between Abdullah and the sultan.

In 1881, the sultan recalled Abdullah to Zanzibar (q.v.). Abdullah supposedly had heavy debts with Zanzibar's Asian merchants, and had joined a faction seeking the overthrow of Sultan Barghash. In 1882 Abdullah died unexpectedly as he was preparing to return to Unyanyembe. Some reports claimed that Barghash had ordered him poisoned.

ABEDI, SHEIKH AMRI KALUTA (1924–1964). Born in Ujiji (q.v.) and educated at Tabora Secondary School (1937–1941). Between 1942 and 1953 Abedi trained as a postal worker and as an Islamic missionary. He also studied at Rabwah College in Pakistan (1954–1956). In 1959 Abedi was elected to TT's transitional parliament and served as mayor of Dar es Salaam (q.v.) in 1960 and 1961. In 1962 he became commissioner for Western Region and in 1963 minister of justice. A member of the Tanganyika Agricultural Corporation (TAC), Abedi became minister of community development and national culture shortly before his death in 1964.

ABUSHIRI REVOLT (1888–1889). Popular uprising by Tanzania's coastal peoples, who sought to resist the imposition of German colonial rule. In mid-1888, Abushiri, or Bushiri ibn Salim al-Harthi (q.v.), a slave-owning sugar planter from the Pangani River estuary, began the revolt after the Germans tried to collect custom duties from coastal traders. During the next year, Abushiri, who enjoyed support among the peoples who lived between Pangani and Dar es Salaam (q.v.), fought a running battle with German forces led by Hermann von Wissmann (q.v.). Mounting casualties and growing suspicion about Abushiri's political motives caused many rebels to stop fighting and to return home. In 1889 Abushiri tried to flee northward to join forces with the Zigua leader Bwana Heri ibn Juma (q.v.). However, German troops captured him, and on 15 December 1889 Abushiri was hanged at Pangani.

ADULT EDUCATION. In the late 1940s TT's Social Welfare Department began conducting adult education classes in the towns and cities and by 1952 extended these services to the rural areas. In both venues, voluntary agencies assumed responsibility for most teaching. The *Development Plan for Tanganyika, 1961/62–1963/64* (q.v.) allocated £230,000 for community development schemes to reduce illiteracy in a mass education campaign. In addition, extramural classes were taught at Dar es Salaam's Institute of Adult Education after it opened in 1963. The institute also conducted research into adult education and the training of adult education teachers and administrators. Classes were likewise conducted in other large urban centers, including Tanga, Morogoro, Iringa, and Moshi (qq.v.). Informal adult literacy education continued under the auspices of the post-independence Community Development Division and private voluntary agencies. Approximately 300,000 adults were enrolled in literacy classes in 1962 and more than 600,000 by 1969.

In the Education Act of 1969 (q.v.), the Ministry of National Education assumed responsibility for adult education. In that same year, a Commission of Inquiry into the University of Dar es Salaam (q.v.) recommended the further expansion of adult education services in the rural areas. Accordingly, the Tanzanian government hoped to increase "functional literacy" by underwriting radio programs, correspondence courses, and adult literacy classes.

President Nyerere declared 1970 Adult Education Year, and a Directorate of Adult Education was established in the Education Ministry in 1973. By late 1974 the literacy rate had risen to 50 percent of Tanzania's adult population, and 3.4 million people were enrolled in a variety of subjects, including arithmetic, Swahili (q.v.), history, political education, farming methods, health, and domestic science. By 1975 this number had grown to more than five million. In 1975 an examination was administered to adults in order to determine their degree of literacy. Nearly two million men and women demonstrated functional literacy in Swahili. By June 1976 an estimated 61 percent of all adults could read and write. Ten years later, the figure had increased to 90.4 percent, at which level it has remained since.

ADVISORY COMMITTEE ON AFRICAN EDUCATION. In 1926 the Colonial Office established this committee, which consisted of three government officials, two Africans, two representatives of trade and commerce, and no fewer than eight missionaries. One African member was a missionary appointee and the other a government civil servant. There was no Muslim representation. The committee held regular meetings until 1934, when it was replaced by a Central Advisory Committee, which had twice the official and half the missionary membership of the original committee. The pre-independence Education Ordinance of 1961 (q.v.), in turn, replaced the Central Advisory Committee with a multiracial Advisory Council of Education (q.v.).

ADVISORY COUNCIL OF EDUCATION. In 1961 this council replaced the Central Advisory Committee on education. The council consisted of 12 official and unofficial members and was chaired by the Ministry of Education's chief education officer. Meeting at least once each year, its decisions could not be overridden by the minister of education without special permission from the president, the cabinet, and the National Assembly (q.v.).

AFRICAN ASSOCIATION. In 1934 mainlanders formed this organization and requested official recognition as an affiliate of the Tanganyika African Association (q.v.). The organization sought to protect mainland laborers and squatters resident in Zanzibar. In February 1957 the African Association joined with the Shirazi Association (q.v.) to form the Afro-Shirazi Union (ASU). However, the associations kept their separate identities.

AFRICAN EDUCATION, GERMAN EAST AFRICA. Under German colonial rule, Africans attended mission and government schools. By 1913 10 missionary societies operated 1,119 schools for 87,207 students while, by 1914, the colonial government maintained 99 schools for 6,100 pupils. Mission and government school systems included elementary feeder schools, which offered a three-year course of morning instruction by African instructors in reading, writing, mathematics, gymnastics, and singing. In central schools, African and German teachers provided students a four-year curriculum with training in the Swahili (q.v.) and German languages, writing, geography, drawing, natural science, and mathematics. High or main schools, the most noted of which was the Tanga School (q.v.), offered a five- to six-year curriculum that included courses similar to those in central schools. Mission societies also operated bush schools, which enabled students to become minimally literate. Additionally, missions such as the Sisters of the Holy Ghost Mission and the White Sisters established a network of schools for women and girls. The outbreak of World War I (q.v.) caused government schools to close; however, some missionary schools remained open but operated with limited resources and staff. Also, see AFRICAN EDUCATION, TANGANYIKA TERRITORY.

AFRICAN EDUCATION, TANGANYIKA TERRITORY. In 1920 the British colonial authorities established the Department of Education, which sought to reestablish and expand an educational infrastructure that had been all but destroyed during World War I (q.v.). In 1926/27, the colonial government implemented a grant-in-aid code whereby missionary schools for the first time received public funds on the basis of the number of European instructors, the salaries of African teachers, maintenance costs, and the schools' relative efficiency. The African Education Ordinance of 1928 placed TT's educational system under government control. Financial shortages slowed the reconstruction process, but by 1930 there were 54 European and 238 African teachers and 48 industrial instructors. In addition, the government operated 95 schools with an average monthly attendance of 5,500, and the various missionary societies maintained 2,903 schools with an average monthly attendance of approximately 90,000. Between 1940 and 1961 there was a dramatic increase in the number of Africans who received formal education. By independence, there were 506,260 African students enrolled in TT's educational system.

Government and missionary village schools provided elementary education up to Standard II. Native Administration schools, managed by local African communities, served the sons of sub-chiefs and headmen. Central schools offered a four-year English course or a four-year industrial course. The British also maintained a government school for African teacher training at Mpwapwa, and various mission societies operated similar schools throughout TT. African girls could attend government schools at Tabora (q.v.) and at Malangali; however, female education was primarily the responsibility of mission societies. Also, see AFRICAN EDUCATION, GERMAN EAST AFRICA; and PHELPS-STOKES COMMISSION.

AFRICAN INLAND MISSION/CHURCH (AIM/AIC). In 1909 this missionary group, led by Rev. E. Sywulka, entered GEA from Kenya. Its members settled in Nassa, north of Mwanza (q.v.), and shared this area of influence with the Church Missionary Society (q.v.). In 1957 the AIM became the AIC, although the name of the church was not officially changed until 1965. By the mid-1970s, as a result of expansion in Sukumaland, the Mwanza-based church claimed one bishop, 70 pastors and 500 evangelists, about 70,000 adherents, two Bible schools, a print shop, bookstores, a hospital at Kolandoto, and 10 dispensaries.

AFRICAN NATIONAL CONGRESS. In February 1958 Zuberi M. Mtemvu, a former TANU (q.v.) secretary in Eastern Province, formed the Tanganyika African Congress. In a party manifesto, Mtemvu rejected TANU's moderate political philosophy and instead advocated an "Africa for Africans only" policy. After the authorities refused the organization's application for registration in May 1958, Mtemvu renamed it the African National Congress and was allowed to register. Despite the name change, Mtemvu's bid to lead a radical African nationalist party failed, largely because his narrow views alienated many Africans. Although it suffered decisive defeats in the 1958 and 1960 elections, the African National Congress managed to keep itself in existence by maintaining nine regional party branches. After visiting the PRC and several other communist nations in 1961, presumably for advice and funds, Mtemvu opened provincial headquarters and branches in five new areas. However, despite the party's expansion, Mtemvu received only 21,276 votes in the 1962 presidential election. His defeat paved the way for the dissolution of the African National Congress, and on 22 January 1963, Mtemvu rejoined TANU.

AFRICANIZATION. The process of indigenizing leadership positions, in most cases involving Africans taking over from non-Africans. In 1951 only one African occupied a top civil service position. Of the 4,000 top- and middle-level government positions gazetted in 1959, Africans occupied only five. Also in that year, there were only 13 African physicians, no African judges or magistrates, and no African assistant principal secretaries or permanent secretaries. By 1961 Africans held 14 percent of government jobs and 15 percent of senior civil service positions. District commissioner positions were Africanized very quickly, from one African in the 58 districts in 1959, to five in early 1961, to 53 by independence. By January 1963 40 percent of all civil servants were Tanganyika citizens. Even this rate of growth was too slow for many Africans and contributed to the 1964 army mutiny (q.v.) of the Tanganyika Rifles (q.v.). In the civilian sector, as late as 1964 only 17 of 685 secondary school teachers were Africans. In 1967, however, the authorities replaced all expatriate heads of boys' secondary schools and teacher training colleges with Africans. By this time, moreover, 78 percent of all commercial and manufacturing licenses were held by African businessmen. At least 70 percent of the civil service was also Africanized, and over 1,000 students were enrolled in preprofessional courses of study at the Dar es Salaam (q.v.) campus of the University of East Africa (q.v.). The name of the process was also changed to "localization," to acknowledge the hiring of citizens from any ethnic/racial group. In 1974 67 percent of senior public positions were filled by Tanzanians, and by 1980 the proportion had risen to an estimated 90 to 95 percent. By the 1990s virtually all public and private employment rosters were localized.

AFRO-SHIRAZI PARTY (ASP). On 5 February 1957 the leaders of the African Association (q.v.) and the Shirazi Association of Zanzibar created the Afro-Shirazi Union (ASU) to unite Zanzibar's African and Shirazi (Arab) communities. After the July 1957 elections the ASU renamed itself the ASP. This organization's leadership opposed the political and social dominance of the islands' Arab oligarchy and intended to transform Zanzibar into an African-ruled nation. After the 1964 revolution the ASP absorbed the Umma (Masses) Party (q.v.) and took power in Zanzibar. Abeid Karume (q.v.) became party leader and president of Zanzibar (1964–1972). In 1977 the ASP merged with TANU (q.v.) to form the CCM (q.v.).

AGE SET. Groupings of similar age within a lineage or clan whose members share certain identities, privileges, and responsibilities. In particular, Central Sudanic, Nilotic, and Paranilotic pastoralists adhere to this system, in which men and, to a certain extent, women belong to several graded age sets. These associations exist separately from residential neighborhoods and kin groups. Males become members of a specifically named set after passing through an initiation ceremony, usually involving circumcision, at puberty. They are thus bound together and remain peers for the rest of their lives. If one is a designated spokesman, he becomes first among equals. Every three to four years a new set is opened, signaling the advancement of older sets to more senior age grades. There are typically five grades of age sets; junior warrior, senior warrior, junior elder, senior elder, and retired elder. Each grade has its own duties. Once they reach senior warriorhood, members usually marry and settle down to raise families. All warriors remain active in herd management and protection. Junior elders participate in community affairs and fulfill important political and juridical functions. Elevation from warriorhood to elderhood is a significant event and is marked by elaborate ceremonies. At the same time, senior elders must be willing to retire. Senior warriors enjoy high esteem and are sometimes reluctant to become elders.

AGRICULTURE. About 10 percent of Tanzania's land area is under cultivation, and another 10 percent consists of fallow and pasture lands. Approximately 27 percent of the country's grasslands and woodlands is suitable for cultivation, and about one-third of Tanzania has sufficient water to support rain-fed cultivation. More than 65 percent of the population lives in the rural areas and consists primarily of subsistence farmers and pastoralists. In 1966 the value of marketed cash crops exceeded the total value of crops consumed on the farm for the first time. Since then, cash crop and food crop production has fluctuated considerably under the influences of world market factors, variable weather conditions, and government policies affecting agriculture. Today, the agricultural sector accounts for 60 percent of GDP and more than 80 percent of exports. Also, see BANANAS; CASHEW; CASSAVA; CLOVES; COCONUTS; COFFEE; COTTON; MAIZE; PYRETHRUM; SISAL; TEA; TOBACCO; and WHEAT.

AIDS. Although the first suspected AIDS case in Tanzania was diagnosed in the Kagera region in 1983, medical researchers believe that the spread of the Human Immunodeficiency Virus (HIV) probably began in the late 1970s or early 1980s. After the discovery of AIDS, the number of reported cases rose rapidly. After the government confirmed the presence of the AIDS epidemic in 1985, it established a national AIDS task force, which eventually became the National AIDS Technical Advisory Committee. In April 1988 officials created the National AIDS Control Programme (NACP), which is administered by the Ministry of Health. Since then the NACP has monitored the disease, supervised research, implemented a prevention program, and created an improved health care system for AIDS patients. Despite these efforts, the epidemic has continued to worsen. By the end of 1991 there were about 800,000 HIV-positive Tanzanians and 21,175 reported AIDS cases, with an annual AIDS-related death rate of up to 30,000. By 2010, an estimated 5 to 17 percent of the population will be HIV positive.

AIR TANZANIA CORPORATION. This airline was formed on 11 March 1977 after the collapse of East African Airways, which had been jointly operated by Tanzania, Kenya, and Uganda. On several occasions, the airline has suspended international flights because of financial and technical problems. In the early 1990s the airline flew to 18 towns in Tanzania and to various international destinations, including Djibouti, Bujumbura, Dubai, Entebbe, Gaborone, Harare, Kigali, Lilongwe, Lusaka, Muscat, and Johannesburg. Equipment problems prevented regular service to Europe. The airline's fleet included two Boeing 737s, two F-27–600s, and three de Havilland DHC-6 Twin Otters. Air Tanzania services international airports at Dar es Salaam and Kilimanjaro. In 1990 Zanzibar Airways commenced independent operations to cater to the tourist trade. Oman assisted in this effort with a project to extend the Zanzibar airport's runway in order to accommodate long-distance aircraft. In the following year, Air Tanzania Corporation, Zambia Airways, and Uganda Airlines agreed to form a new regional airline, African Joint Air Services. This enterprise never became operational, however, largely because of inadequate financing. In early 1995 Tanzania, Uganda, and South Africa announced the establishment of Alliance Airways, which will concentrate on developing intercontinental routes, leaving Air Tanzania and Uganda Airlines to operate domestic and regional service. Also, see AVIATION.

AKIDA. Originally a mainland administrative appointee of the sultan of Zanzibar. During colonial times, an *akida*, who usually was an Arab or a member of a minority African tribe, supervised a group of villages within each district and managed *jumbes* (q.v.), who administered individual villages.

ALI IBN AL-HASSAN IBN ALI. The first sultan of Kilwa (q.v.). Arab historians date his reign from 957 to 996 A.D., although most others claim it occurred two centuries later, according to the Western calendar. Ali most likely arrived at Kilwa around 1200 and established a new Shirazi (q.v.) dynasty at this trading post. Gaining the nickname *Nguo Nyingi* (Many Clothes), he built a strong fortress and raided other coastal towns. Sultan Ali placed his son Muhammed in charge of Mafia Island (q.v.) to the north of Kilwa.

ALI IBN HAMOUD, SEYYID (1884–1918). Eighth Busaidi (q.v.) ruler of Zanzibar (1902–1911). Although he spent three years at Harrow public school in England, Seyyid Ali was one of the most ill-prepared and impotent sultans ever to govern Zanzibar (q.v.). Because he was not yet of age when he acceded to the throne, the British appointed a regent, A. S. Rogers, to govern on behalf of the young sultan. The regency existed until June 1905, when Seyyid Ali attained his majority. As sultan, he did little more than to sanction British policy initiatives. These changes included the adoption of a new constitution, a reorganization of the Zanzibar civil service and the judicial system, the Europeanization of central administration and the expansion of social services. In 1911 the Foreign Office persuaded Seyyid Ali to abdicate, largely because of his ineffectiveness and lavish lifestyle. He died in Paris.

ALI IBN SAID, SEYYID (1855–1893). Fifth Busaidi (q.v.) ruler of Zanzibar (1890–1893) and last of Said ibn Seyyid's (q.v.) sons to occupy the throne. He was little more than a puppet torn between his British masters, who wanted to implement numerous reforms, and his Arab advisers, who resisted any change. During his tenure, several significant changes occurred in the political and economic life of Zanzibar (q.v.). On 1 August 1890 Seyyid Ali signed an Anti-Slavery Decree prohibiting the exchange, sale, or purchase of slaves and closing the houses of slave brokers. A British protectorate over Zanzibar was established on 4 November 1890, with Ali's agreement that future Zanzibari relations with foreign powers would be conducted exclusively through British government channels. He also acceded to the plans of Gerald Portal (later Sir), who arrived in Zanzibar on 6 August 1891 as British agent and consul general, to reorganize the island's administration and establish a free port in Zanzibar. Seyyid Ali died on 5 March 1893, after frequent periods of illness.

ALL-MUSLIM NATIONAL UNION OF TANGANYIKA (AMNUT). The AMNUT was formed in 1957 and acted as a Muslim pressure group, criticizing TANU (q.v.) for not supporting separate Islamic education. In general, AMNUT resisted social change, including the emancipation of women and secular education. In September 1959 AMNUT suggested that TT should not become independent until Muslim residents were afforded greater opportunities in the new country. Under attack by TANU and the majority of Muslim political leaders, the organization died before TT's independence in December 1961.

AMANI INSTITUTE. In 1902 the German colonial government established the Amani Biological and Agricultural Institute to address problems of plant diseases, insect pests, soil and plant chemistry, and other problems confronting farmers in GEA. With a budget equaling £10,000 per year, Amani scientists focused on research into improved cotton production. Quinine was also made here and at the Mpwapwa research station as well. During World War I (q.v.) the institute, which was some 50 miles (80 kilometers) from Tanga (q.v.), prepared many varieties of foodstuffs, spices, medicines, soaps, oils, and liquors.

After World War I the British Department of Agriculture maintained Amani. In 1927, however, the colonial authorities reconstituted Amani as a link in a chain of imperial research stations. The new facility, known as the East African Agricultural Research Station at Amani, conducted long-range scientific investigations into the difficulties facing the coffee and sisal (qq.v.) industries in East Africa and into pathological problems associated with plants and soils. In 1952 the colonial authorities closed the station, moved its staff and equipment to Nairobi, Kenya, and established a new organization known as the East African Agricultural and Forestry Research Organization. Amani subsequently became headquarters of the East Africa Malarial Research Unit and its constituent Tanganyika Malarial Service. In 1959 the colonial authorities moved the latter organization from Amani to Morogoro (q.v.).

AMOUR, SALIMIN (b. 1948). On 21 October 1990 Amour, who had served as the minister of home affairs (1983–1985), was elected the fifth president of Zanzibar and Pemba. His major goals included restoring the Zanzibaris' confidence in the CCM (q.v.), reviving the islands' moribund economy, and coming to terms with those who wanted a referendum to decide the future of the union with mainland Tanzania. Having also to contend with growing demands for democratic reforms, Amour made little progress toward achieving any of these goals. In the eyes of many Zanzibaris, the CCM is corrupt, inefficient, and incapable of resolving the country's many problems. By 1995 popular demand had grown for a referendum on the future of the union, despite Amour's often heavy-handed efforts to suppress such dissent. Although some economic improvements and reforms had occurred, most Zanzibaris remained desperately poor and blamed the government for their plight. In the eyes of his critics, Amour's greatest failing has been his harsh reaction to pro-democracy advocates. The Zanzibari authorities have harassed, beaten, or jailed opponents, including members of the Civic United Front (CUF), Tanzania's main opposition party. On several occasions Julius Nyerere (q.v.) blamed Zanzibar's difficulties and the controversy over the future of the union on Amour's poor performance.

ANGLICAN CHURCH IN TANZANIA. The Anglican Church began in Tanzania under two different groups, the Church Missionary Society and the Universities' Mission to Central Africa (UMCA) (qq.v.). In 1958 the bishops of both sects in TT and Kenya met and discussed the possibility of unification. In 1960, the Anglican Church of East Africa was founded under the direct authority of the British archbishop of Canterbury. Four dioceses were established in Tanganyika and one in Kenya. In 1970 the Tanzanian and Kenyan branches separated, with eight dioceses formed in Tanzania. One year later, the Southwestern Diocese was created and joined the Church of the Province of Tanzania. In the mid-1980s this church included 16 dioceses and claimed approximately 647,000 members.

ANGLO-GERMAN AGREEMENT (1886). Under this accord, Great Britain and Germany recognized the sultan of Zanzibar's control over the islands of Zanzibar (q.v.), Pemba (q.v.), Lamu, and Mafia (q.v.); all coastal islands; and a continuous line of coast from the Miningani River at the head of Tunghi Bay in the south, to Kipini in the north. The agreement also established Germany's sphere of influence from the Ruvuma to the Umba Rivers, and the British sphere from the Umba to the Tana Rivers. Also, see DELIMITATION COMMISSION.

ANGLO-GERMAN AGREEMENT (1890). Under this agreement's terms, Germany recognized a British protectorate over Zanzibar and abandoned the protectorate of Witu and all territorial claims north of Tana River. Great Britain gained effective control of Uganda, since Germany acknowledged the extension of the boundary dividing the British and German spheres of influence to Lake Victoria and thence to the Congo Free State. The British ceded Heligoland to Germany and persuaded Seyyid Khalifa ibn Said (q.v.) of Zanzibar to cede to Germany the land leased by the German East Africa Company (q.v.) in return for an indemnity. The 1890 agreement is also known as the Heligoland Treaty.

ANTI-SLAVERY DECREE (1890). Signed by Zanzibari Sultan Ali ibn Said (q.v.) on 1 August 1890, this British decree prohibited all sales and exchanges of slaves, closed down slave markets, ordered that the slaves of a childless master be freed upon the master's death, forbade the wives of Indians to hold slaves, threatened punishment of masters for ill-treatment of their slaves, and permitted slaves to purchase property. Also, see MORESBY TREATY.

ARAB ASSOCIATION. Established in Zanzibar (q.v.) in the 1920s to secure compensatory payments for former slave owners and later to represent the interests of the Arab land-owning community. In 1948 the Arab Association rejected a proposal for popular elections to replace governmental nomination as the method of selecting Arab and Asian unofficial LEGCO (q.v.) members. In 1954 the association split because of the British Resident's proposal for multiethnic representation within its ranks. The colonial authorities arrested most of the organization's leadership, prompting an 18-month Arab boycott of all government organizations. In January 1965 Zanzibari authorities deported Abdalla Suleiman el Harthy, who had been president of the Arab Association for 40 years.

ARABS. Tanzanian Arabs are a heterogeneous group, originating in the Arabian Gulf and Persian Shiraz regions of the Middle East. In the nineteenth century Arabs led caravans into the Tanganyikan interior in search of ivory, slaves, and other trade items. Coastal and inland Arab trading posts were situated in or near African population centers, many of whose inhabitants became Islamized. At the time of the Tanganyika-Zanzibar union, about 26,000 Arabs lived on the mainland and approximately 50,000 in Zanzibar and Pemba (qq.v.). The majority worked in wholesale and retail trade, fishing, and peasant farming. Arabs have been more reluctant than other Tanzanians to adopt secular education, many preferring Islamic schooling. This group's main contributions to Tanzanian culture include an Arabic basis for the Swahili language, the Islamic religion, and an Omani-Swahili civilization, with its unique varieties of architecture and graphic art, poetry, cuisine, and social manners and customs. Zanzibari Africans felt oppressed when Arabs were in political control, and vice versa. Tensions still exist between the two groups, compounding religious and territorial animosities between Muslim Zanzibar and the mainly non-Muslim population of mainland Tanzania.

ARMED FORCES. See ARMY MUTINY; POLICE; TANGANYIKA RIFLES; TANZANIA PEOPLE'S DEFENCE FORCE; UGANDAN-TANZANIAN WAR; WORLD WAR I; and WORLD WAR II.

ARMY MUTINY. On 20 January 1964 the First Battalion Tanganyika Rifles mutinied at Dar es Salaam (q.v.) to protest low pay, poor working conditions, and the fact that British officers still commanded the army. The following day, the Second Battalion Tanganyika Rifles also mutinied at Tabora (q.v.). Julius Nyerere (q.v.) reacted to the army mutiny by requesting British intervention. Consequently, on 25 January 1964 600 British marines landed at Dar es Salaam and quickly restored order. In the aftermath of the mutiny, Nyerere lessened the country's dependence on the British by reorganizing the armed forces with recruits drawn largely from TANU Youth League (TYL) (q.v.) and by placing African officers in command. He also organized a TYL-staffed army reserve, known as the United Republic Volunteer Corps, under the directorship of John A. Nzunda, who also was TANU's deputy secretary-general. This action ensured that the military remained politically loyal and subservient to TANU's (q.v.) goals and policies.

ARUSHA. Arusha is a town located in Arusha Region exactly halfway between Cape Town and Cairo on the Great Northern Road. Arusha is a rapidly growing agricultural and business center at the head of the railway line from Tanga (q.v.). It is also an important tourist center because of its proximity to the Serengeti, Arusha, and Tarangire National Parks (qq.v.) and to the Ngorongoro Crater and Olduvai Gorge (qq.v.). Its selection in 1967 as the headquarters city for the East African Community (q.v.) also enhanced its significance. Arusha lies at an altitude of 4,600 feet (1,380 meters) above sea level, and its mild climate is conducive to the production of both food and export crops. The city's population grew from about 10,000 in 1959 to more than 100,000 in 1977 and to 134,708 in 1988. If it reflects Tanzania's 11 percent average annual rate of urbanization, Arusha's population may have exceeded 350,000 by the early 1990s.

ARUSHA DECLARATION (1967). This major policy statement, drafted by President Julius Nyerere (q.v.), was approved by the TANU (q.v.) National Executive Committee at a 26–29 January 1967 meeting in Arusha. In effect, the declaration rejected the "improvement approach" to socioeconomic development of the late colonial and immediate postcolonial periods and extended the "transformation approach" of the early 1960s into a full-scale program of *ujamaa na kujitegemea* (socialism and self-reliance). It declared Tanzania to be a "nation of peasants and workers . . . involved in a war against poverty and oppression in our country." To win this struggle, the declaration called for the people of Tanzania to unite and work together for their own social and economic welfare. Its main aims were to establish democratically elected public control over the major means of production and exchange; to ensure economic self-reliance by rejecting an overreliance on foreign gifts, loans, and investment as well as on money itself as the major means of economic modernization; to emphasize self-help agriculture over capital-intensive industry as the principal engine of development; and to remove all distinctions based on class, wealth, and social status.

To help implement the latter goal, the declaration committed the ruling party, TANU, and the Tanzanian government to the following leadership code:

1. Every TANU and Government leader must be either a peasant or a worker, and should in no way be associated with the practices of capitalism or feudalism.
2. No TANU or Government leader should hold shares in any company.
3. No TANU or Government leader should hold directorships in any privately owned enterprise.
4. No TANU or Government leader should receive two or more salaries.
5. No TANU or Government leader should own houses which he rents to others.

The leadership category included middle-level and higher civil servants, elected government representatives, senior party officials, and executives of government corporations. The code also applied to the spouses of leaders.

In its implementation, the Arusha Declaration advanced social welfare and equality but failed to produce policies that lessened foreign-aid dependency while fostering economic growth. Although not officially abandoned, the declaration was increasingly ignored in the economic policy reforms and structural adjustments of the late 1980s and the 1990s, many of which were demanded by foreign donors and lenders, aimed at promoting economic growth through private enterprise and reduced governmental control over the national economy. Also, see DEVELOPMENT PLANS.

ARUSHA NATIONAL PARK. Gazetted in 1960, this park covers an area of 58 square miles (137 square kilometers) and is located about 21 miles (37 kilometers) north of Arusha town. It is noted for the Ngurdoto Crater, Mount Meru, and the Momela Lakes. Although it lacks large wildlife herds, Arusha National Park contains an array of fauna, including elephant, hippopotamus, red and forest duiker, dik-dik, reedbuck, buffalo, giraffe, warthog, and bushbuck.

ASIAN ASSOCIATION. In 1950 20 of TT's Asian leaders formed the Asian Association to foster the goal of a "non-racial, secular state."

In 1956 the association refused to support the United Tanganyika Party (UTP) (q.v.), which also sought to advance the cause of multiracialism. In the association's view, the UTP program would entrench racial differences because it advocated the continuation of a LEGCO (q.v.) based on racial parity. The Asian Association helped to form TANU (q.v.) and cooperated with African nationalists. After independence, most Asians realized that they had no place in a society that was multiracial in name but nearly monoracial in fact. As a result, the Asian Association terminated its activities and many wealthier Asians left Tanzania.

ASIANS. Tanzanians of Indian and Pakistani descent. Asians have never formed a cohesive community because of their differences in language, religion, and places of origin. The greater proportion of Asians who originally emigrated to East Africa were Shias, rather than orthodox Sunnis who now predominate, and were divided into three sects (Ismailis, Ithnasheris, and Bohras). Throughout the colonial period, TT's Asian population grew steadily. From a small community of 8,698 in 1912, the number of Asian residents expanded to 10,209 in 1921, 25,144 in 1931, 75,536 in 1957, and 92,000 in 1962. By independence, approximately 50 percent of the Asian population was employed in wholesale and retail trade, with others working in manufacturing, public services, forestry, agriculture, and fishing.

Historically, Asians played a key role in the opening and development of Tanganyika and Zanzibar (qq.v.). In addition to providing menial labor, they financed much of the slave trade, introduced imported consumer goods, and acted as middlemen and lenders for African agricultural producers and European businessmen. Asian associations contributed to community welfare by erecting schools and health clinics and by providing other social services.

After independence, the position of the Asian community became more precarious. From late 1961 through 1963, more than half of locally born Asians sought to avoid the possibility of discrimination by registering as citizens. To facilitate this process, the Aga Khan, leader of the Ismaili sect, urged his followers to take out citizenship. Privately, however, he encouraged Asians to consider leaving Tanzania because of widespread economic and political discrimination. Other factors also contributed to a growing exodus. Thousands of Asians left Zanzibar (q.v.) after the 1964 Zanzibar Revolution (q.v.), and a substantial number departed the mainland after the nationalization of Asian property and business enterprises began in 1970. Today the remaining Asian population resides in all parts of Tanzania but primarily in larger towns and cities and in Zanzibar.

The status of the Asian community remains uncertain, since many

Africans continue to regard Asians as interlopers. In April 1993 Tanzanian authorities were forced to quell an Asian Islamic riot that began because three butcher shops in Dar es Salaam were selling pork. According to several sheikhs, the incident demonstrated the government's repressive and discriminatory policies toward Asians.

The Asian issue also became a topic of concern during the 1995 presidential election. Rev. Christopher Mtikila, leader of the opposition Democratic Party, accused Asians of maintaining dual citizenship and of looting the country to smuggle wealth to India, Europe, North America, and the Middle East. Augustine Mrema (q.v.), leader of the opposition National Convention for Construction and Reform (NCCR), took a more moderate position by acknowledging that the Tanzanian government had ignored the needs of Asians and by promising to enhance educational opportunities for their children. Many Muslim leaders rejected Mrema's overture, however, because he had accused those who participated in the April 1993 riots of being "hooligans" (at the time, Mrema was minister for home affairs). Such confrontations reflect a racial gulf between Tanzania's African and Asian communities that is unlikely to be resolved in the near future.

ASKARI. The Swahili name applied to African professional soldiers. During the German colonial period *askaris* were recruited among former slaves and staffed German military outposts throughout the interior. The Germans organized *askari* units in sizes up to company level. During World War I (q.v.), the Germans deployed *askaris* with great effectiveness against British and Allied forces.

AUGUSTANA LUTHERAN MISSION. The Lutheran Church assumed responsibility for the work of the Leipzig Mission in the Iramba area after its German missionaries were forced to depart during World War I (q.v.). The Augustana Lutheran Mission assumed control of the earlier mission and later became known as the Central Synod of the Lutherans. The larger church eventually ordained local pastors and gained independence from the Augustana Mission. In 1963 the church extended itself to the Barabaig people and in 1967 to the Kindiga and Sukuma.

AVIATION. Civil aviation began in TT on 28 February 1920, when a Vimy commercial airplane landed at Tabora (q.v.). In 1929 P.E.L. Gethin, the father of civil aviation in TT, became director of civil aviation. In January 1932 Imperial Airways initiated a weekly flying-boat service to Cape Town via Moshi, Dodoma, and Mbeya (qq.v.). South African Airways and Southern Rhodesian Air Services also operated transcontinental flights via several points in TT.

World War II (q.v.) interrupted civil aviation, but by late 1945 British Overseas Airways Corporation had established two weekly flights between England and South Africa via Dar es Salaam (q.v.) and Lindi. Several other international carriers, including South African Airways, Air France, Scandinavian Air Services, and Sabena, operated services through TT.

On 1 January 1946 the colonial authorities established a Directorate of Civil Aviation for TT, Kenya, and Uganda. This organization created East African Airways (EAA). In 1956 EAA initiated regular flights to Britain and India. By 1960, the airline had begun jet services to India and elsewhere in Asia. Twenty-two Tanzanian airports were in use in the 1970s, and in 1975 EAA culminated nine straight profitable years by recording net earnings of TShs.41.1 million (US$5,871,428). Despite its profitability, EAA disintegrated when Kenya formed its own national airline, Kenya Airways, on 22 January 1977; Tanzania followed suit on 11 March 1977 by establishing Air Tanzania Corporation (q.v.). Air Zanzibar, founded in 1990, operates scheduled services between Zanzibar (q.v.) and destinations in mainland Tanzania, Kenya, and Uganda. By the mid-1990s, Tanzania had three international airports (Dar es Salaam, Kilimanjaro, and Zanzibar) and 50 smaller domestic airports and air strips. Also, see AIR TANZANIA CORPORATION.

AZANIA. The name given to East Africa's coast by Greek writers early in the first millennium A.D.

AZANIANS. An early civilization in mainland Tanzania, which dates from about 700 A.D. or earlier. Azanians were skilled in using dry stone for building, and some settlements consisted of as my as one hundred stone houses clustered together. One archaeological discovery of Azanian ruins is a city located in hill country along the Kenya-Tanzania border. Another characteristic of the Azanian civilization was its elaborate terracing of cultivated land. Azanians also dug irrigation canals, raised cattle, mined iron and other minerals, and worked these materials both for their own needs and for export. Trading appears to have been limited to a small-scale enterprise. The civilization ended in the fourteenth or fifteenth century at the hands of pastoral nomads who were militarily superior to the Azanians.

— B —

BABU, AHMAD ABDULRAHMAN MUHAMMAD (1924–1996). A Zanzibari political activist born of mixed Arab-Comorian descent.

After primary and secondary schooling in Zanzibar (q.v.), Babu en-rolled at Makerere University (q.v.) and later at London University, specializing in English literature, philosophy, social psychology, and journalism. In 1957 he entered Zanzibari politics, following six years of work with the Clove Growers' Association (q.v.) and another six years at a savings bank in West London. In particular, Babu became a leader of the Zanzibar National Party (ZNP) (q.v.) and won succes-sive electoral victories by linking Arab, Asian, and African ethnic groups through appeals to Islamic religious unity.

A two-year jail sentence for sedition (1962–1963) interrupted Babu's political activities. After his release he waged a two-year struggle to turn the conservative, pro-sultanate ZNP away from strict Koranic principles and toward socialism. Before the July 1963 elec-tions Babu resigned from the ZNP and founded the Marxist-oriented Umma (Masses) Party (q.v.). One week before the January 1964 revo-lution in Zanzibar, the authorities banned the Umma Party while Babu was on the mainland. After the revolution, he was appointed minister of defence and external affairs in the new Zanzibari govern-ment and his Umma Party merged with the Afro-Shirazi Party (ASP) (q.v.) of Abeid Karume (q.v.).

Following the union of Tanganyika and Zanzibar in April 1964, Babu held various portfolios including minister of state, minister for commerce and cooperatives, minister for health, minister for com-merce and industries, and minister of economic affairs and planning. On 7 April 1972 he was detained after the assassination of Zanzibari President and Union First Vice President Karume. Babu had opposed the union in the first place, and was accused of leading a group of largely Arab dissidents who had allegedly plotted to murder Karume and to introduce Marxist-Leninist socialism to Zanzibar. In 1973/74, Babu was tried and imprisoned on the mainland. His sentence was subsequently commuted and he left Tanzania to settle in Great Brit-ain, where he eventually secured a faculty position at the University of London. In recent years, while working as a freelance journalist, Babu became a strong advocate for multiparty democracy in Tan-zania.

On 4 August 1995 Babu returned to Tanzania and was selected as Augustine Lyatonga Mrema's (q.v.) vice presidential running mate in that year's parliamentary and presidential elections. The National Electoral Commission contested his right to stand, because of his al-leged involvement in the 1972 assassination of Abeid Karume. Babu filed a petition in the High Court challenging the Electoral Commis-sion ruling, but on 4 September 1995, before a decision could be handed down, he announced that he was removing himself from the vice presidential race and withdrawing his appeal to the High Court. Babu then withdrew from politics and died in 1996.

BAGAMOYO. A small coastal village located 47 miles (75 kilometers) north of Dar es Salaam (q.v.). Prior to the colonial era Bagamoyo was a hub of the slave trade (q.v.), serving as the mainland terminus of the slave caravan route extending from Lake Tanganyika through Tabora to Zanzibar (qq.v.) and beyond. By the mid-nineteenth century, approximately 50,000 slaves were shipped each year from Bagamoyo to Zanzibar. The name "Bagamoyo" ("Here I lay down my heart") probably refers to the town's role in the slave trade.

In 1888 Bagamoyo became GEA's first capital. On 1 April 1891, shortly after the German government had assumed control over GEA from the German East Africa Company (q.v.), the capital was moved to Dar es Salaam. Since the turn of the century, Bagamoyo's importance has declined. At present, it is a quiet, almost entirely Islamic community, depending for its livelihood on fishing and coconut production.

BANANAS. Probably introduced into East Africa from southeastern Asia before 500 A.D., bananas are grown for eating raw and cooked, as a major cash crop, and for brewing beer. Banana stalks provide fodder for cattle and thatching material for houses. Bananas flourish in the wetter northwestern and southwestern areas of Tanzania. They are the staple food of the Chagga and Haya (qq.v.) peoples.

BANK OF TANZANIA. Tanzania's central bank, which issues and controls the country's currency. It was created on 14 June 1966 and had as its first task the introduction of a new Tanzanian shilling to replace the East African shilling previously in use. The bank also afforded monetary authorities greater flexibility and independence in determining the total supply of money and credit, thus reducing one factor in the country's dependence on foreign economic forces. Another bank function was to regulate Tanzania's gold and foreign-exchange reserves. Since 1967 the Bank of Tanzania has provided financial advice to the National Bank of Commerce, which assumed the duties of private commercial banks nationalized in that year. On 11 November 1991 the Bank of Tanzania announced that in 1993 foreign banks would again be permitted to conduct business in Tanzania.

BANTU. A linguistic term referring to the ethnic progenitors of most modern Tanzanians. Probably originating in what is now southern Nigeria and Cameroon, these culturally diverse peoples were linked by a common root language and began migrating into eastern Africa early in the first millennium A.D. Here they interacted and partially assimilated with earlier and later migrants from southern Ethiopia, the central Sudan, and Arabia, helping to create Tanzania's contemporary mosaic of more than 120 cultural and linguistic minorities. Today, approximately 95 percent of all Tanzanians are Bantu speaking.

BAPTIST CHURCH. In 1956 the American Southern Baptist Convention sent its first missionaries to TT. They started work in Dar es Salaam (q.v.), established the Baptist Mission of Tanganyika (later Tanzania), and opened a hospital in Mbeya (q.v.). In 1958 Baptist missionaries opened Rungwe Mission Station, which engaged in agricultural education. Other stations opened during the 1960s in Kigoma, Tanga, Arusha, Mwanza, Moshi (qq.v.), Chunya, and Mbozi to service a membership that totaled about 12,000 in the mid-1970s. The mission operated one hospital and three dispensaries, a seminary in Arusha, a social center in Dar es Salaam, and four Bible schools.

BARGHASH IBN SAID, SEYYID (1837–1888). Third Busaidi (q.v.) ruler of Zanzibar (1870–1888). Seyyid Barghash devoted his energies to resisting encroachments on his domain from Oman and to expanding Zanzibar's commercial activity on the East African mainland. He also fostered considerable socioeconomic and political development in Zanzibar (q.v.). Among other innovations, he ordered the construction of a conduit to supply pure drinking water to Zanzibar town. Additionally, Barghash developed steamship, trade, and cable connections with the outside world. By assigning Muslim judges to the interior, Barghash helped to extend Arab influence over the indigenous peoples of Zanzibar and Pemba (qq.v.).

After an 1872 hurricane destroyed much of his naval fleet and many of Zanzibar's clove and coconut trees, Seyyid Barghash's military and economic influence waned. As a result, he had to rely more and more on the British for support. On 5 June 1873 the British persuaded Barghash to sign a treaty outlawing seaborne traffic in slaves; however, he failed to enforce the pact and continued to justify the lucrative slave trade (q.v.) by citing the teachings of the Koran. In subsequent years the British assumed greater control over Zanzibar's foreign relations and coerced Barghash into accepting a series of agreements that eventually ended most slave trading in East Africa.

In 1875 Barghash traveled to England and met with Queen Victoria and Prime Minister Benjamin Disraeli. In 1877 he failed to persuade Great Britain to accept a 70-year lease over all commercial activities in territories controlled by Zanzibar. During the same year, Barghash organized an army, which British officers trained and commanded. This force pacified the mainland interior and protected Zanzibari trade routes.

After declaring a protectorate over the mainland in 1885, Germany seized control of 60,000 square miles (156,000 square kilometers).

Barghash protested these actions, and on 7 August 1885 five German warships dropped anchor off Zanzibar town. Barghash submitted to this display of German power "in consequence of the demand which comes to us from His Majesty the Emperor of Germany as an Ultimatum and as indispensable to the commencement of friendly negotiations." He also reluctantly conceded his territorial claims to the East African interior. Afterwards, Seyyid Barghash confined his activities to Zanzibar, and watched helplessly as Britain and Germany divided the mainland between themselves.

In 1886, without Zanzibari participation, Germany and Britain signed a Delimitation Treaty, which reduced the Sultan's domain to Zanzibar, Pemba, Mafia (qq.v.), and Lamu Islands and to a mainland coastal strip averaging 10 miles (16 kilometers) in width and 600 miles (960 kilometers) in length. Between 1890 and 1895, even these territories came under European control, when the Germans and British established colonies on the mainland and when Britain declared a protectorate over Zanzibar. By that time, in 1888, Barghash had died of tuberculosis and elephantiasis.

BARONGO, EDWARD BARUGIRA (b. 1928). Born at Bukoba (q.v.) and educated through district primary school, Barongo joined the East Africa Army Medical Corps in 1946 and served until 1950. He then served in the Tanganyika Police from 1951 to 1954 and later worked as a coffee (q.v.) instructor for the Bukoba Native Co-operative Union. In 1955 Barongo entered politics as a Tanganyika African Association (TAA) (q.v.) member. The following year, he helped to transform the Bukoba TAA branch into a TANU (q.v.) branch, serving as its first district secretary. In 1957 he became the party's West Lake provincial secretary, and in 1958 he was elected provincial chairman. Barongo also served as a Buhaya District Council member from 1958 to 1961.

In 1960 Barongo entered national politics as a National Assembly (q.v.) member, and in 1961 he was appointed TANU deputy general secretary. He subsequently held several posts in the independent government, including regional commissioner for Northern and Ruvuma regions, parliamentary secretary in the Ministry of Agriculture, member of parliament for Busubi, executive chairman of the Tanganyika Tobacco Board, and, until 1975, executive chairman of the National Milling Corporation. Barongo left the latter position amid controversy over the corporation's inefficiency, and before his retirement he returned to the Ministry of Agriculture as junior minister.

BATTERSHILL, SIR WILLIAM DENIS (1896–1959). Battershill served as TT's governor from 1945 to 1949. During his tenure the colonial government supported the creation of the East African High Commission (EAHC) (q.v.) and its Central Legislative Assembly (q.v.). Battershill also participated in decisions to admit the first African members to the LEGCO (q.v.), to superimpose representative local government on the Native Authorities, to introduce a 10-year development plan (q.v.) and an accompanying education plan intended to facilitate TT's post-World War II (q.v.) reconstruction and development, and to launch the ill-fated Groundnut Scheme (q.v.).

BENEDICTINE MISSION OF ST. OTTILIEN CONGREGATION. The first German Roman Catholic missionaries to reach GEA. In November 1887 they began work at Pugu, about 12 miles (19 kilometers) west of Dar es Salaam (q.v.). In January 1889 Arab rebels headed by Bushiri (q.v.) raided Pugu Station and killed two brothers and one sister. The Benedictines carried on their proselytizing, however, and founded a mission house and sisters' convent at Dar es Salaam in 1890 and a mission at Kurasini in 1894.

In 1894 the Benedictines pushed into the Southern Highlands (q.v.) and established the Madibira Station. The following year, they opened two more stations north of Masasi, one later destroyed in the Maji-Maji Rebellion (q.v.), and moved on to Ndanda. By 1903 the Benedictine Central School enrolled 150 students, including a paramount chief's son. In 1905, when Bishop Cassian Spiess was traveling from Kilwa Kivinje (q.v.) to Peramiho, he was attacked and killed by Maji-Maji rebels who harbored grievances against the Germans and made no distinctions among government officers, private settlers, and missionaries. The rebels also killed two brothers and two sisters in Spiess's party.

In 1906 the Benedictine Vicariate was renamed the Vicariate Apostolic of Dar es Salaam. After the Maji-Maji Rebellion was suppressed, a period of peace lasted for eight years, until World War I (q.v.) forced all German missionaries to leave what was to become TT. In 1920 the western half of the Benedictine sphere of influence, now the Diocese of Iringa, was handed over to the Consolata Fathers of Italy. The remainder was transferred to the Swiss Capuchin Fathers (q.v.). These orders amalgamated during the 1950s to form the Tanganyika Episcopal Conference (TEC) (q.v.).

BERLIN EVANGELICAL MISSIONARY SOCIETY. In 1887 this German Lutheran group began missionary work in Dar es Salaam (q.v.). The following year, the society opened a mission at Kisarawe and founded another at Maneromango in 1895. In 1903 the society transferred these stations to the Berlin Mission (q.v.).

BERLIN MISSION (LUTHERAN). Organized by 1870, the Berlin Mission entered the southern mainland in September 1891. Welcomed by the Nyakusa chiefs as traders, the Berlin missionaries settled among them as well as among the Bena, Kinga, and Hehe (q.v.) and formed what was later to be called the Synod of Southern Tanzania. The 1891–1898 Hehe uprising and the 1905–1907 Maji-Maji Rebellion (q.v.) disrupted the mission's work. World War I (q.v.) also affected the Berlin missionaries, and many, as enemy aliens, were compelled to leave their stations. Despite such setbacks, the mission built churches, schools, hospitals, dispensaries, and a trade school. By 1913 more than 2,000 Africans had been converted. Because of this rapid expansion, the mission created a second synod for the Ulanga/Kilombero region. By this time, African clergy had been afforded leadership positions in the southern synods. By the late 1970s this branch of the mission accounted for nearly 200,000 adherents, four hospitals, 18 dispensaries, one medical training center, 56 African clergy, and 789 evangelists.

In 1903 the Berlin Evangelical Missionary Society transferred responsibility for the Dar es Salaam (q.v.) and Zaramo areas to the Berlin Mission. Proselytizing was difficult along the heavily Muslim coast, however, and by 1913 the mission had attracted only 382 converts. Despite these difficulties and the dislocations of World War I and World War II (qq.v.), this branch of the mission eventually became the Synod of Eastern Tanzania and Coast Region. In 1970 Rev. E. E. Sendoro became its first African president, presiding over approximately 27,000 members and 36 churches, two dispensaries, 22 African clergy, and 52 evangelists.

BETHEL MISSION. German Bethel missionaries founded the Lutheran Church of Vuga/Usambara and Tanga (q.v.). In 1890 Bethel missionaries arrived at Tanga and started missions at Mlolo, Vuga, Lutindi, Bumbuli, and Irete among other places. In 1912 they began printing books at Vuga. Eventually Bethel missionaries established a Northeastern Diocese and a Northwestern Diocese.

In 1946 Bible training started at Mlolo and continued until 1954, when it was moved to Makumira, near Arusha (q.v.). In 1952 a medical training school opened at Bumbuli. By now known as the Northeastern Diocese, Bethel missions expanded after independence until they claimed approximately 45,000 members, 39 African clergy, 75 evangelists, one bible school, three hospitals, and five dispensaries.

In 1910 some of the early Bethel missionaries decided to move on to Ruanda, where their colleagues had already taken up residence. Reaching Bukoba (q.v.), they encountered Church Missionary Society (CMS) (q.v.) African converts. The CMS had influenced people living in this area from their base in Uganda but had not been able to place their own missionaries in Bukoba. The Bethel missionaries accepted a CMS invitation to remain there and opened mission stations at Kigarama, Kashasha, Gubulanga, Kanyangereko, and Ndologe. As German nationals, the Bethel missionaries were interned during World War I (q.v.), and African clergy assumed their duties until the Germans were permitted to return. A few were allowed to remain in educational and medical positions during World War II (q.v.), after which they were joined by missionaries from the United States, Sweden, and Denmark. Together they built churches, schools, hospitals, dispensaries, and an agricultural training school. This complex became known as the Diocese of Northwestern Tanzania, comprising about 100,000 adherents, 270 worship centers, more than 300 pastors and evangelists, and a variety of educational and medical establishments.

BEY, MIRALE. A Turkish pirate who by 1585 was conducting raids on coastal towns claimed by the Portuguese. In 1588 he captured Mombasa Island and held it against a mainland assault by the marauding Zimba in 1589. Eventually a Portuguese fleet from Goa defeated him. With Portuguese consent, the Zimba then crossed to the island and devastated it, only themselves to meet defeat and near-annihilation at Malindi by the Portuguese and the warlike Segeju.

BIBLE SOCIETY OF TANZANIA. This organization was originally part of the British and Foreign Bible Society. In 1965 the society was renamed the Bible Society of East Africa, with headquarters in Nairobi, Kenya. After Uganda's withdrawal from the society in 1968, the Tanzanian branch was again reorganized under the laws of Tanzania. On 31 January 1971 it was officially installed at Luther House in Dar es Salaam (q.v.) but has since been moved to the new capital at Dodoma (q.v.). A member of the Christian Council of Tanzania (CCT) (q.v.), the society's main function is to provide Bibles and other religious materials at low cost to the Tanzanian population.

BILHARZIA (Schistosomiasis). A debilitating infectious disease endemic to many areas of the mainland and the Indian Ocean islands, where slow-moving water is contaminated by human waste. Flatworms (genus *Schistosoma*) are transmitted by aquatic snails and infect blood vessels in the human intestines or bladder. Modern agricultural irrigation projects have further spread the disease. Controlling bilharzia requires health education, snail eradication, and treatment by drugs.

BINNS COMMISSION (1951). This group produced the first comprehensive survey of TT's educational system since the 1924 Phelps-Stokes Commission (q.v.) report. The Binns study group emphasized practical, self-contained educational programs at the primary and secondary levels. It also recommended curricula for African students based more on their own heritage and human environment and less on subjects taught in British schools.

BLOOD CONSTITUTIONAL COMMITTEE. As Zanzibar (q.v.) moved haltingly toward independence in an ethnically divided society, a constitutional committee headed by Sir Hilary Blood, former governor of Gambia, Barbados, and Mauritius, determined that an elected majority should be installed in the colonial LEGCO (q.v.) and that the majority party leader should join the islands' Executive Council as chief minister. On 2 April 1960 the British government appointed Sir Hilary constitutional commissioner. The adoption of a new constitution laid the groundwork for a January 1961 parliamentary election. Contesting the election were the Afro-Shirazi Union (ASU), the Zanzibar National Party (ZNP) (q.v.), and the Zanzibar and Pemba People's Party (ZPPP) (q.v.), which had recently broken off from the ASU. The ASU was then renamed the Afro-Shirazi Party (ASP) (q.v.) and campaigned under this label. Having failed to achieve a LEGCO majority, the government held another election in June 1961. This time the ZNP and ZPPP campaigned together against the ASP. Amid considerable ethnic strife, the ZNP-ZPPP coalition gained a slim majority of three out of 23 contested seats, which paved the way toward Zanzibari internal self-government in June 1963 and full independence on 10 December 1963. The Zanzibari Revolution followed in January 1964.

BOMA. The Swahili word for fort or fortress. The term carries two meanings: (1) a bush enclosure to contain and protect domestic livestock; and (2) a colonial and postcolonial district administrative office housing the district (now area) commissioner and his/her district team of administrative and technical specialists.

BOMANI, ERNEST EMMANUEL (b. 1930). Born in Musoma, Ernest Bomani was educated at Ikizu Teacher Training Centre, Bwiru Government Secondary School, and St. Mary's Roman Catholic School at Tabora (q.v.). In 1953 he joined TT's Cooperative Development Department as an inspector. After completing a commercial course of study in Kenya, he joined the Victoria Federation of Cooperative Unions (VFCU) (q.v.) in 1956 as acting secretary of the organization's Mwanza (q.v.) headquarters. After two years as an apprentice manager at one of the VFCU's cotton ginning stations, Bomani entered Northwestern Polytechnic in London, where in 1960 he earned a diploma in business administration. After returning to TT, he became general manager of the VFCU and president of the government-supported Cooperative Supply Association of Tanzania (COSATA). He also served as a director of the British Trading Company Smith MacKenzie, Tanganyika, of Tasini Textiles, and of the Tanganyika Sisal Marketing Association. Bomani also served as a Lint and Seed Marketing Board member and a councillor of Makerere University (q.v.).

BOMANI, MARK (b. 1932). Born in Musoma, Mark Bomani was educated at Bwiru and Tabora (q.v.) Government Schools. He studied at Makerere University (q.v.) from 1953 to 1957 and received the B.A. (Lond.) degree. Bomani also earned a diploma in social studies from The Hague. He studied law in the Netherlands and then at London University, from which he received the LL.B. degree in 1961. During the same year Bomani became a Barrister at Law in Lincoln's Inn. In 1962 he was appointed deputy solicitor general for Tanganyika and in 1965 promoted to attorney general, a post he held until 1976, when he was assigned to the UN Institute for Namibia, headquartered in Lusaka, Zambia. In 1995 he was appointed chancellor of the University of Dar es Salaam.

BOMANI, PAUL LAZARO (b. 1925). Born in Musoma, Paul Bomani was educated at Ikizu Teacher Training Centre and, for a time, at Tabora Government School. Instead of pursuing a teaching career, he took an accounting job in 1945 at Williamson Diamond Mine. In 1947, at age 22, Bomani became secretary of the Mwanza African Traders Co-operative; five years later, he helped to organize the Lake Province Growers' Association. In 1953/54, Bomani undertook a correspondence course offered by Loughborough Co-operative College, England, from which he earned a higher certificate in co-operative accounts.

He then continued in what was to become a significant career in the private and public sectors. In 1955 he became general manager of the Victoria Federation of Cooperative Unions (VFCU) (q.v.). This placed him at the head of Africa's largest agricultural marketing co-operative. By 1965 the federation owned the bulk of Tanzania's cotton ginneries.

Bomani's political career began with his appointment as Mwanza provincial chairman of the Tanganyika African Association (TAA) (q.v.) in 1952. Named by Governor Sir Edward Twining (q.v.) to the LEGCO (q.v.) in 1955, Bomani served until September 1957 as the only spokesman for the TAA's replacement party, TANU (q.v.). In 1959 he returned to the LEGCO as an elected TANU representative.

In 1960 he became minister for agriculture and co-operative development, and in 1961 he was elected to the independence parliament and appointed minister for finance. In 1965 Bomani suffered a political setback when he lost his Mwanza (q.v.) parliamentary seat, but this did not prevent him from filling other important positions, including those of minister for economic affairs, minister of commerce, and Tanzanian ambassador to the United States. Bomani also served as a director of the International Monetary Fund (IMF), as a governor of the International Bank for Reconstruction and Development (World Bank), and as vice chairman of the African Development Bank. In later years, he has served as minister of agriculture (1985–1986), minister of labour and manpower development (1987), minister of local government, co-operatives, and crop marketing (1988), and minister of state in the president's office for "special duties" (1990). In the October 1990 elections Bomani again lost his seat in the Tanzanian National Assembly (q.v.).

BRITAIN-TANZANIA SOCIETY. The Britain-Tanzania Society was established in January 1975 to promote friendly relations between citizens of the two countries. To that end, the society has sponsored mutual educational activities, welcomed visitors, concerned itself with the welfare of students, and encouraged group visits. In November 1975 the society established a charitable trust called the Tanzania Development Trust to collect funds in support of small-scale development projects in Tanzania. In December 1975 the society first issued the *Bulletin of Tanzanian Affairs*. From 1986 onward the *Bulletin* has appeared three times yearly and includes news stories, newspaper clippings, and other pertinent information about Tanzania. According to its constitution, the Britain-Tanzania Society "is independent of any government and of any political party or other organisation devoted to sectarian or sectional purposes." As of 1995, the Society's United Kingdom chapter had about 600 members and the Tanzania chapter approximately 200.

BRITISH ADMINISTRATORS AND GOVERNORS OF TANGANYIKA TERRITORY (1920–1961).

Administrators:
Byatt, Sir Horace Archer (1916–1920)
Governors:
Byatt, Sir Horace Archer (1920–1924)
Cameron, Sir Donald Charles (1925–1931)
Symes, Sir George Stewart (1931–1934)
MacMichael, Sir Harold (1934–1938)

Young, Sir Mark Aitchison (1938–1941)
Jackson, Sir Wilfred Edward (1941–1945)
Battershill, Sir William Denis (1945–1949)
Twining, Sir Edward (1949–1958)
Turnbull, Sir Richard (1958–1961)
Also see entries under each name.

BROWN, ROLAND GEORGE MACCORMACK (b. 1924). Born in London and educated at Ampleforth College, 1938–1942, and Cambridge University, 1942–1943 and 1946–1948, from which he earned an M.A. degree. In 1949 Brown became Barrister at Law in Gray's Inn, London. He first arrived in East Africa in 1953 to help mediate a dispute between the British colonial authorities and Mutesa II, the *kabaka* (king) of Buganda, who had been exiled to the United Kingdom. Brown subsequently advised Chief Minister Julius Nyerere (q.v.) at the March 1961 pre-independence Constitutional Conference in Dar es Salaam (q.v.). He then served as attorney general of Tanganyika (later Tanzania) until 1965, when an African, Mark Bomani (q.v.), replaced him. Brown continued to serve the Tanzanian government as a legal consultant on international and commercial affairs, and in 1966 President Nyerere seconded him to President Kenneth Kaunda of Zambia, where he headed an inquiry into a wave of labor disturbances in the Zambian copper belt.

BRYCESON, DEREK NOEL MACLEAN (1922–1980). Born in China and educated at St. Paul's School, London, and Trinity College, Cambridge, from which he received a B.A. degree. Bryceson served in the Royal Air Force from 1940 to 1943, during which time he was shot down in the Western Desert Campaign of World War II (q.v.). Complications set in from his wounds, which left him permanently handicapped. In 1947 he emigrated to Kenya as a farmer-settler and moved south to TT in 1951, where he acquired a 1,200 acre (480 hectare) farm near Mount Kilimanjaro (q.v.).

In 1957 Bryceson entered politics and served as assistant minister for social services. In the 1958–1959 parliamentary elections, he defeated his United Tanganyika Party (UTP) (q.v.) opponent, John Hunter, and became deputy leader of the opposition and unofficial minister for mines and commerce in the transitional government. He later held the posts of minister for health and labor and minister for agriculture (subsequently agriculture, forests, and wildlife) in the independence government. He was the first European member of TANU (q.v.) and a close friend of Julius Nyerere (q.v.). In 1972 Bryceson became director of national parks, a position he held until his death in 1980. He is survived by his second wife, Jane Goodall (q.v.).

BUKOBA. Town located in a valley of seven hills near Lake Victoria (q.v.). In 1890, Emin Pasha (q.v.) reached Haya- (q.v.) controlled Bukoba, built the town's first rail station, and helped to found the robusta coffee (q.v.) industry. In early 1891 Emin's expedition departed for Karagwe, leaving behind Captain Wilhelm Langheld to consolidate the German sphere of influence here and at Mwanza (q.v.) to the southeast. By 1924 the British assumed control of Bukoba and established a special primary school for the sons of government chiefs. Beginning as a small fishing village on the western shore of Lake Victoria, the town had grown to about 8,000 in 1967 and to 47,009 by 1988.

BUKOBA BAHAYA UNION. In 1924 Clemens Kiiza founded the Bukoba Bahaya Union in western Bukoba (q.v.) to promote "the development of our country and . . . the seeking of a system for a simple way to civilization to our mutual advantage." The union became a major opponent of government-appointed native authorities in Bukoba District. Kiiza also purchased a coffee-hulling machine and, to guarantee a regular coffee (q.v.) supply, organized Bahaya farmers into the Native Growers Association.

In 1937 leaders of the Bukoba Bahaya Union—by now part of the Tanganyika African Association (TAA) (q.v.)—rioted for a paramount chief, more education, and the abolition of *nyarubanja* (estates; powerful chiefs awarded such estates to their most loyal and powerful followers). Although the 1937 coffee riots represented the first challenge to British colonial rule in Bukoba, the authorities quickly restored order by rejecting TAA demands, jailing some of its organizers, and forcing this branch of the association to go underground for several years. In addition, the Native Growers Association collapsed, and Kiiza lost his hulling license.

BUKOBA COOPERATIVE UNION (BCU). In 1950 a group of 48 coffee (q.v.) societies formed the Bukoba Native Cooperative Union, which acted as a single producing, processing, and marketing cooperative. The union sent several members of its staff abroad for training, built a large headquarters building, and operated a coffee-curing plant. In 1960 the union changed its name to the BCU, and by 1966 it had become the best organized and financed organization responsible for promoting one of Tanzania's most important export crops. Like other private cooperative unions, the BCU was disbanded in 1976 by a socialist TANU (q.v.) government ostensibly intent on eliminating corruption and economic exploitation in the rural areas. Critics charged that the real reason for abolishing cooperative unions was to remove the last effective challenges to the party's hegemonic control over the Tanzanian economy. Facing serious declines in crop production and export earnings, TANU's successor party, the CCM (q.v.), reinstated the BCU and other cooperative unions in 1982, albeit under strict political supervision. Nevertheless, these cooperatives eventually challenged government price controls over coffee. In August 1992 more than half of the cooperative societies in Bukoba (q.v.) refused to sell coffee at fixed government prices. Two months later the Tanzanian government announced that major cooperative societies would be free to deal with private traders and sell their coffee directly to foreign purchasers.

BURTON, SIR RICHARD FRANCIS (1821–1890). A British explorer, linguist, and orientalist who, with John Hanning Speke (q.v.), traveled from Bagamoyo to the Lake Tanganyika (qq.v.) region in 1857 and 1858. Born in Hertfordshire, England, Burton joined the British East India Company's military service in 1842. Following his tour in India, he visited Mecca and the Kingdom of Ethiopia before arriving at Zanzibar (q.v.) in 1856. Shortly afterwards, Burton assumed command of an expedition to central Africa, financed by the Royal Geographical Society, to discover the source of the Nile River. In June 1857 he and Speke set out along an Arab caravan route leading to Kazeh, the site of modern Tabora (q.v.). In February 1858 they reached Lake Tanganyika (q.v.), where they discovered that this body of water could not be the source of the Nile because its waters flowed south.

In June 1858 the explorers returned to Kazeh, and Burton, who was ill at the time, consented to Speke's search for another lake to the north of Lake Tanganyika. In August 1858 Speke reached the southern shores of a great lake, which he named Victoria Nyanza (present-day Lake Victoria [q.v.]) and pronounced to be the source of the Nile. Burton refused to accept Speke's claim, but it was later confirmed in another expedition, again funded by the Royal Geographical Society, in which Speke was joined by James Augustus Grant (q.v.). On 28 July 1862 Speke stood at the falls (which he named after the society's president, Sir Roderick Murchison) in what is now northwestern Uganda, where the Nile flows from Lakes Kioga and, ultimately, Victoria.

BUSAIDI DYNASTY (1840–1964). This Arab ruling family originated in Oman, where it replaced the Yarubi dynasty. Throughout the eighteenth century, the Busaidi expanded commercial and political activities along the East African coast. When Seyyid Said (q.v.) died in 1856, he bequeathed his empire to his two sons, Thwain and Majid (q.v.), the former ruling Oman and the latter governing Zanzibar (q.v.). Although they appointed various governors on the East African mainland in the late nineteenth century, the Busaidi only controlled a few coastal towns, such as Dar es Salaam and Mombasa. In 1890 they accepted a British protectorate over Zanzibar. After the islands gained independence, an African revolution brought an end to the Busaidi dynasty.

BUSH SCHOOL. A subgrade of a British colonial-era primary school, providing instruction approximating that offered in Standards I and II of the British-style primary course. Bush schools and their teachers were required to be officially registered by the Education (African) Ordinance of 1954. By 1960 a pupil could be admitted into an orthodox government primary school if a vacancy became available at the appropriate standard and if the student passed an entrance examination. Bush schools received no government grants-in-aid.

BUSHIRI IBN SALIM AL-HARTHI (?–1889). Sometimes referred to as Abushiri, a half-Arab who led an 1888–1889 revolt by mainland coastal subjects of the sultan of Zanzibar (q.v.) against the German East Africa Company (q.v.). A renegade against the sultan (q.v.) and his European allies, Bushiri exploited local fears of losing profits from the slave trade (q.v.) to spread the rebellion up and down the coast and as far west as the Southern Highlands (q.v.), where he gained the support of the powerful Hehe paramount, Chief Mkwawa (qq.v.). In October 1888, after determining that the German East Africa Company was incapable of suppressing the revolt, the German government appointed Hermann von Wissmann (q.v.) to command a force against Bushiri. Bushiri escaped the rout of his rebels by Wissmann's lieutenant, von Gravenreuth, in a battle fought west of Bagamoyo (q.v.) but he was later captured and hanged at Pangani on 15 December 1889. Also, see ABUSHIRI REVOLT.

BWANA HERI IBN JUMA (?–1897). A Zigua-Swahili chief, he succeeded his father as ruler over Sadani during the reign of Zanzibari Sultan Majid (1856–1870) (q.v.). In 1882 Bwana Heri became independent of Majid's successor, Barghash (q.v.), when he and his followers defeated the sultan's troops on the mainland opposite Zanzibar (q.v.). In 1888 he joined the Arab revolt against the Germans led by Bushiri (q.v.). Only loosely affiliated with Bushiri, Bwana Heri was treated by the Germans as an independent African chief rather than as a rebel. After foiling several advances against him, he came to terms with the Germans in 1890. When he tried to rise again in 1894, the Germans defeated his forces and he fled to Zanzibar, where he died three years later.

BYATT, SIR HORACE ARCHER (1875–1933). In December 1916 Byatt arrived from British Somaliland and became civil administrator of the northern sector of GEA during World War I (q.v.). In January 1919 he was appointed administrator of the former German territory mandated to Britain by the League of Nations (present-day mainland Tanzania), and in 1920 he became governor of TT. As a cautious governor, with only about 120 British colonial officers at his disposal, Byatt determined that no sudden innovations should be introduced to disturb TT's African population. He retained the 22 administrative districts established by the Germans and continued to rely on the services of former German *akidas* (q.v.) to help govern TT.

Byatt devoted his efforts to rebuilding a devastated country which also suffered from famine and an influenza epidemic. Despite these and numerous other difficulties, Byatt succeeded in banning forced African labor and increasing hut and poll taxes. Because he believed that TT's economic future depended chiefly on African agricultural production, Byatt tried to discourage plantation farming by European settlers—to the point of refusing to meet with their representatives or visit their estates. He also improved public health by controlling diseases such as sleeping sickness, yaws, plague, smallpox, and cerebrospinal meningitis. In early 1924 Byatt departed TT to become governor of Trinidad and Tobago, in which position he served until 1929.

— C —

CAMERON, SIR DONALD CHARLES (1872–1948). Having earlier served as chief secretary to the colonial government of Nigeria, Cameron became one of TT's most innovative and effective governors. During his tenure he introduced a local government policy that he termed "indirect administration," to become more commonly known as "indirect rule" (q.v). He also defended African human rights and promoted African economic self-determination. Cameron inaugurated TT's LEGCO (q.v.), opposed the expansion of the European settler community and a settler-supported federation of TT with Kenya, enlarged TT's educational system, and participated in the formation of the Tanganyika African Association (q.v.). He supported the adoption of the Native Authority Ordinance of 1927 (q.v.), which revised and extended a 1923 ordinance conferring definite powers on local African leaders under what became known as indirect rule. Ironically, Cameron rejected all attempts to introduce Western-style democracy to TT. He justified this policy by claiming that a political system based on English institutions and concepts would have "created political chaos and anarchy where some order previously existed, with no compensating advantage to the individuals concerned."

In further defense of indirect rule, he went on to maintain that "the Mandatory Power is under a solemn obligation so to train the natives that they may stand by themselves . . . and it seems obvious that in doing the latter, the wise course, if not the only practical course, is to build on the institutions of the people themselves, tribal institutions which have been handed down to them through the centuries. If we set up artificial institutions, these institutions can have no inherent stability and must crumble away at the first shock which they may receive. It is our duty to do everything in our power to develop the native politically on lines suitable to the state of society in which he lives" (Donald Cameron, "Principles of Native Administration and Their Application," *Local Government Memoranda: No. 1* [Dar es Salaam: Government Printer, 1930], p. 1).

After leaving TT, Cameron served as governor of Nigeria from 1931 to 1935.

CAMERON, VERNEY LOVETT (1844–1894). The Royal Geographical Society engaged Cameron to assist David Livingstone (q.v.) in his work. On 27 March 1873 he departed Bagamoyo in charge of the Livingstone Relief Expedition. After learning that Livingstone had already died, Cameron decided to complete Livingstone's work by exploring Lake Tanganyika's southern shores. During his travels Cameron also confirmed that the Lualaba and the Nile were not the same river. On 7 November 1875 he reached Benguela, Angola, thus becoming the first European to cross Africa from east to west.

CAPUCHIN FATHERS. The Swiss Capuchin Fathers received the eastern part of the Benedictine Fathers' area of influence when German missionaries departed East Africa during World War I (q.v.). In 1953 the Vicariate of Dar es Salaam was raised to the rank of an Archdiocese and Metropolitan See of the Ecclesiastical Province of Eastern Tanganyika, led by Archbishop Edgar Maranta. The Capuchins later amalgamated with other orders to form the Tanzania Episcopal Conference (TEC) (q.v.). Also, see BENEDICTINE MISSION OF ST. OTTILIEN CONGREGATION.

CASHEW. The cashew tree originally came from Brazil. In the sixteenth century the Portuguese introduced the tree to India, and East Africa received it sometime during the same century. The cashew tree produces fruit as early as its second year, but it usually takes five to six years before it produces an economically beneficial crop. TT exported 2,669 tons of cashews in 1945 and 63,633 tons in 1965. Cashew nuts are grown primarily in the southern regions of Mtwara and Lindi. By the early 1990s yearly production was about 40,000 tons, and the Tanzanian government hopes to increase annual production to approximately 130,000 tons. To achieve this goal, Tanzania will require foreign investment to rehabilitate all processing facilities.

CASSAVA. Portuguese and other European traders probably introduced cassava, or manioc, into Africa from the Americas during the fifteenth century. The Portuguese later brought the plant to East Africa. John Hanning Speke (q.v.) found cassava in Zanzibar (q.v.) and implied that he also encountered it on his travels to Lake Tanganyika (q.v.). It seems likely, however, that cassava was absent or unimportant in most of East Africa until after 1850, when Arabs and Europeans encouraged its growth as a safeguard against drought and famine.

Cassava remains a major edible root crop, and while it is not as popular as grains, it is Tanzania's major reserve staple. It is easy to plant, cultivate, and harvest; it is resistant to drought, disease, and insects; its growth is vigorous; and its yield is certain. Cassava consists of many sweet and bitter varieties, and both its root and leaves are edible. On the other hand, an overdependence on cassava produces deficiencies in vitamins, especially of the B group, and in proteins.

CENTRAL COMMITTEE (CC). The most powerful agency of TANU (q.v.), the CC was a subordinate organ of the party's National Conference. As part of the larger National Executive Committee (NEC), the CC consisted of approximately 20 senior party officials and presidential appointees, and it met about once a month and oversaw party administration. Like the TANU National Conference and the NEC, the CC was carried over into the organization of the CCM (q.v.). See CHAMA CHA MAPINDUZI.

CENTRAL DEVELOPMENT COMMITTEE. This government body was established in December 1938 to facilitate large-scale development in TT by examining and reporting "on methods whereby the development of the Territory by non-native and native enterprises may be encouraged . . . to make Tanganyika a country." Its main conclusion was that development could not be effected unless communications were much improved. The committee's work was terminated with the onset of World War II (q.v.).

CENTRAL LEGISLATIVE ASSEMBLY. The Central Legislative Assembly was created following World War II (q.v.) as the legislative arm of the East African High Commission (EAHC) (q.v.), which was responsible for managing interterritorial economic and other services for TT, Kenya, and Uganda. A speaker presided over the assembly, which included seven official members appointed ex officio from the EAHC staff; two members of the Arab community appointed by the EAHC; two nominated official members from each territory appointed by its governor; three unofficial members appointed by each governor to represent the African, Asian, and European communities of TT, Kenya, and Uganda; and three representatives elected by the Legislative Councils (q.v.) of each territory.

CENTRAL PLATEAU. Located between the eastern and western branches of the Rift Valley (q.v.), the Central Plateau rises to 5,940 feet (1,800 meters) above sea level. The western part of the plateau covers half of the country and sweeps southeastward into Mozambique. This huge, uplifted basin consists of a hot, dry savanna dotted with granitic outcrops. Humidity is low, and although average rainfall ranges from 20 to 30 inches (500 to 750 millimeters), droughts are common. Most of the Central Plateau is so dry that it is fit only for open-range grazing. The northern area slopes down to 3,700 feet (1,110 meters) to form the depression containing the Lake Victoria (q.v.) basin, where intensive agriculture is practiced. Soils on the plateau vary from yellowish sandy to dark brown clays with low to moderate fertility. More than two-thirds of the region is covered with *miombo*, or open savanna woodlands, which provide a breeding ground for the tsetse fly. Daily temperatures average between 70 and 75 degrees Farenheit (21 and 24 degrees Celsius), although wide variations from these norms are often reported.

CENTRAL RAILWAY. This rail line extends from Dar es Salaam (q.v.) to Kigoma (q.v.) on the eastern shore of Lake Tanganyika (q.v.), a distance of some 772 miles (1,235 kilometers). Work on the Central Railway Line was begun from Dar es Salaam in 1905 and reached Morogoro (q.v.) in 1907, Tabora (q.v.) in 1912, and Kigoma (q.v.) by 1914. Its main feeder line, completed in 1928, runs a distance of 235 miles (376 kilometers) from Tabora (q.v.) to Mwanza (q.v.) on the southern shore of Lake Victoria (q.v.). In 1948 a short spur line was built from Shinyanga (q.v.) to Mwadui to meet the equipment and supply needs of the Williamson Diamond Mine. A more recent feeder line extends 131 miles (210 kilometers) from Kaliua to Mpanda. Another branch from Manyoni to Singida was closed after the Singida gold fields ceased production.

CENTRAL SCHOOL. During the interwar period, central schools were those that taught no fewer than four standards, or grades, of English and offered courses in industrial instruction. Rural primary schools fed students into these urban institutions. By 1930 eight central schools were in operation. Although no tuition was charged, students had to pay a 4 to 10 shilling maintenance fee.

CHAGGA. See PEOPLE.

CHAGULA, DR. WILBERT KUMALIJA (1916–1993). Born near Shinyanga, Wilbert Chagula was educated locally and at the Tabora Government School until 1944. He further studied at Makerere University (q.v.) from 1945 to 1951, where he received his licentiateship in medicine and surgery (L.M.S. [EA]). Following his internship at the Sewa Haji Hospital in Dar es Salaam (q.v.), Dr. Chagula studied at King's College, Cambridge, from 1953 to 1955 and received a B.A. degree with honors in anatomy. After serving as an assistant lecturer in anatomy at the Makerere medical school, he returned to Cambridge University for his M.A. degree, which he received in 1960. Dr. Chagula then studied at the University College of the West Indies in Jamaica (1961) and at the Yale University School of Medicine (1962), at both institutions as a Rockefeller Foundation fellow. Upon his return to Tanzania he became vice president and registrar of the University College of Dar es Salaam (q.v.) in 1963 and subsequently president of the East African Academy and principal of the University College.

In 1970, Dr. Chagula entered politics and became minister of water development and power. He also held the positions of minister for economic and development planning and minister for water, energy, and minerals. In February 1977, he became minister of finance and administration for the East African Community (EAC) (q.v.). Dr. Chagula has also served as a member of the UN Advisory Council on the Application of Science and Technology to Development, as a member of the TANU (q.v.) National Executive Committee, and as chairman of the Tanganyika National Scientific Research Council and of the Tanganyika Society of African Culture.

CHAMA CHA MAPINDUZI (CCM, Revolutionary Party). In 1977 the Afro-Shirazi Party (q.v.) and TANU (q.v.) merged to form the CCM. The CCM, which was the sole legal party until 1992, sought to establish a socialist democratic state by encouraging self-help at all levels of society. The CCM's leadership is composed of a 70-member National Executive Committee (NEC), a 20-member Central Committee (CC) (q.v.), and chairmen and secretaries for each of the country's 25 regions. By the early 1990s the CCM had about one million members and encompassed several affiliated organizations, including the CCM Youth League (*Vijana*), Union of Tanzania Workers (*Juwata*),

Cooperative Union of Tanzania (*Washirika*) (q.v.), United Women of Tanzania (UWT) (q.v.), and Tanzania Parents' Association (*Wazazi*).

Over the years an increasing number of local dissidents and foreign observers have accused the CCM of corruption and incompetence. In 1992, under growing domestic and international pressure, the Tanzanian government authorized the formation of opposition parties. Within months, several new organizations emerged, including the Civic United Front (CUF), Movement for a Democratic Alternative, National Committee for Constitutional Reform, National Convention for Construction and Reform (NCCR), Pragmatic Democratic Alliance, Republic Party, Tanzania Democratic Alliance Party, Tanzanian Democratic Party, United People's Democratic Party, Union for Multi-Party Democracy, and the Zanzibar Special Committee Towards Multi-Party Democracy. Also, see OPPOSITION POLITICAL PARTIES.

CHESHAM, LADY MARION (1903–1973). American-born, Marion Chesham was married to Lord John Chesham, a member of the British nobility, who in 1936 was granted a 110,000-acre (44,000-hectare) concession in the grasslands of the Sao Hill area south of Iringa. Intending to start a cattle ranch and to attract European settlers to Iringa District, he had the land cleared and surveyed, roads built, and a clubhouse constructed near Mafinga, complete with golf and tennis courts. Some 200,000 acres (80,000 hectares) were eventually involved in Chesham's Southern Highland Estates, but the scheme never increased European settlement, largely because soil conditions were inadequate to support large-scale ranching. In 1939, at the outset of World War II (q.v.), the Cheshams returned to England, where Lord Chesham joined the Royal Air Force Fighter Command and Lady Chesham took up war work in London. Lord Chesham died in 1952.

In 1956 Lady Chesham returned to TT, introduced coffee (q.v.) growing at Mafinga and managed a farm at Rungemba, north of Sao Hill. Supporting the Tanganyikan independence movement, she stood as an independent candidate, backed by TANU (q.v.), in the 1958–1959 multiracial elections to the LEGCO (q.v.). Lady Chesham joined TANU before independence and assumed Tanganyikan citizenship in 1962. In return for her political support, Julius Nyerere (q.v.) made her a nominated member of the National Assembly (q.v.), a position she retained until soon before her death in 1973.

One of Lady Chesham's most significant achievements remains the Community Development Trust Fund, which she founded in 1962. Aided by donations from domestic and international contributors, the Trust Fund sponsored, with matching self-help labor, the construction of wells, health facilities, community and daycare centers, and similar projects in the less-developed rural parts of Tanzania and especially in the south. In poor health, Lady Chesham resigned as director of the Trust Fund in 1971, but the fund continued its work and by the early 1990s was still widely considered to be the strongest organization of its type in Tanzania. Lady Chesham died in London on 6 September 1973.

CHEYO, JOHN MOMOSE (b. 1944). After completing his primary and secondary education, Cheyo attended Leeds University in the United Kingdom (1969–1973). He holds the B.Sc. degree in textile technology, an advanced diploma in communications and social development, and an advanced diploma in agriculture. In 1966 and 1967 Cheyo served as TANU (q.v.) youth secretary for Mwanza Region. From 1973 to 1975 he worked as a production manager at Mwanza Textiles, and in 1978 he joined Trexi International, a Swiss-based textile firm. He served Trexi until 1983 as a regional technical manager for East Africa. After being nominated as the United Democratic Party (UDP) presidential candidate in the early 1990s, Cheyo pledged to encourage self-reliance and to end Tanzania's reputation as a "nation of beggars." More specifically, he promised to scrap all laws that made land either state or village property and to allow farmers freely to use their land and sell their crops. Cheyo also said that he would open Tanzania to foreign investors and establish large farms to provide employment for Tanzania's youth. He failed to win the country's 1995 presidential election. Also, see ELECTIONS, TANGANYIKA TERRITORY, TANGANYIKA, TANZANIA; and OPPOSITION POLITICAL PARTIES.

CHIEF JUSTICE. Head of the judicial branch of government, the chief justice is a presidential appointee and consults with the president concerning the appointment of eight or more associate judges to the Tanzanian High Court. The chief justice also serves as an appointed member of the Judicial Service Commission. He has the constitutional power to declare Tanzanian presidents unable to discharge their duties, and he certifies their resignations if they decide to leave office before the expiration of their full five-year terms.

CHIEFS' ORDINANCE OF 1953. This ordinance, officially named the African Chiefs' Ordinance, was enacted to make clear government's intention that the passage of the Local Government Ordinance of 1953 would not lead to the abolition of the office of chief. It also provided for selected chiefs to be sent overseas for further education or to the newly created Local Government School at Mzumbe, near

Morogoro, for training in court procedures, accountancy, and local government finance and administration.

CHRISTIAN COUNCIL OF TANGANYIKA (TANZANIA) (CCT). Formed in 1934, the CCT replaced the Tanganyika Missionary Council, which had coordinated most of the activities of the Protestant churches. Until all schools were nationalized in 1970, the CCT's education secretary-general served as liaison between the Education Department (later Ministry) and schools managed by private voluntary agencies. After the Tanzanian government assumed principal responsibility for education, the CCT remained active in several other areas through its Departments of Relief, Finance, Literature, Urban Christian Service, Family and Social Welfare, and Development Planning and Relief Service.

CHUMA, JAMES (1850–1882). Also known as Juma, Chuma was a former slave who, along with Abdullah David Susi (q.v.), accompanied David Livingstone (q.v.) on his travels throughout eastern and central Africa. In 1873 he helped to carry the missionary explorer's body back from central Africa to Bagamoyo (q.v.) for transfer to Zanzibar (q.v.) and ultimately to its final resting place in Westminster Abbey. After Livingstone's death, Chuma led a Universities' Mission to Central Africa (UMCA) (q.v.) caravan from Zanzibar to Masasi in 1877 and Joseph Thomson's (q.v.) caravan from Zanzibar to Lake Nyasa and Lake Tanganyika in 1879. He died of tuberculosis at the UMCA hospital in Zanzibar.

CHURCH MISSIONARY SOCIETY (CMS). The CMS was formed as part of the Anglican Church's missionary effort. In 1844 Dr. and Mrs. Johann Ludwig Krapf (q.v.) were the first CMS missionaries sent to East Africa. In 1846 Rev. Yohannes Rebmann (q.v.) settled in Rabai, near Mombasa, where he and Krapf established a mission station. In early 1848 Rebmann set out overland and reached Mount Kilimanjaro (q.v.) in May. The following July Krapf traveled from Mombasa to Usambara and received a friendly reception from the paramount chief, Kimweri (q.v.). In 1852 Krapf again visited Usambara. In 1876 other missionary explorers arrived at Bagamoyo (q.v.) and made a number of stops through what is now mainland Tanzania en route to Uganda. By 1878 a mission had been established at Mpwapwa, one of the stopping-over places. This mission was placed under the CMS of Equatorial East Africa, which included stations in present-day Kenya, Tanzania, and Uganda. As the CMS grew, the need arose to divide this jurisdiction into two parts, with Uganda and western Kenya comprising one and Tanganyika together with coastal Kenya the other.

The CMS Diocese of Central Tanganyika subsequently opened six stations and employed more than 200 evangelists. In 1908 a CMS school at Kongwa began training proselytizers and teachers and medical training was offered at Mvumi and Kilimantinde. In 1921 the CMS ordained two African pastors. In 1927 the CMS of Australia assumed control over the Diocese of Central Tanganyika, and the Right Reverend G. A. Chambers was appointed bishop in November 1928. In the period of Bishop Chambers's service, the number of mission stations increased to 15 and of pastors to 28. In 1933 the CMS built and consecrated a cathedral at Dodoma (q.v.). Also located at Dodoma, Mvumi Girls School and the Boys Secondary School developed reputations for outstanding instruction.

In 1947 Bishop Chambers resigned and was succeeded by Bishop Wynn-Jones, who served until his death in 1950. The following year Alfred Stanway became the third bishop of the Diocese of Central Tanganyika. In 1955 the CMS consecrated the first African assistant bishop, Yohana Omari, who served until his death in 1963. A year later Assistant Bishop Yohana Madinda replaced Omari. Because of the CMS's rapid expansion, a Diocese of Victoria Nyanza was created in 1963 under the leadership of Bishop Melvin Wiggins. In 1965 the CMS formed the Diocese of Morogoro under Bishop Gresford Chitemo and in 1966 established the Western Diocese with Bishop Musa Kahurananga in charge. The Africanization (q.v.) of the CMS leadership became virtually complete in 1971, when Bishop Stanway resigned in the Diocese of Central Tanzania and Bishop Madinda took his place as archbishop. Also, see ANGLICAN CHURCH IN TANZANIA.

CITY-STATES. By the tenth century A.D., Arabs and Shirazis (qq.v.) were trading and settling along the East African coast, eventually establishing a string of entrepôts on the mainland and on offshore Indian Ocean islands. These communities depended on the Indian Ocean trade in gold (q.v.) and ivory as well as the slave trade (q.v.), and included Malindi, Lamu, and Mombasa in what is now Kenya, and Mafia, Pemba, Zanzibar, and Kilwa Kisiwani (qq.v.) in present-day Tanzania. As trade increased in the eleventh and twelfth centuries, these centers became self-governing city-states with their own merchant houses, military forces, and civil administrations. Their emerging urban civilization also produced the Swahili (q.v.) language and culture.

Initially, the most important city-state was Kilwa Kisiwani. Between the thirteenth and fifteenth centuries, it gained ascendancy over the entire coastal area, but in the fifteenth century, Kilwa was over-taken by Zanzibar and Mombasa. Portuguese conquest of the coast delayed the further development of the Arab-dominated city-states. By 1506 the Portuguese had taken control, and they maintained their presence until 1729, when a group of Omani Arabs seized all settle-ments north of the Ruvuma River. The powerful Mazrui dynasty of Mombasa later challenged and temporarily localized Omani suzer-ainty, leading to an unstable pattern of competition for control that lasted until the rise of European influence and subsequent colonial domination in the nineteenth century.

CLARKE, EDWARD A.W. (1860–1913). Consul general in Zanzibar. As head of the British Foreign Office's African Department, Clarke traveled to Zanzibar in late 1905 to reorganize the administration of the Zanzibar Protectorate (q.v.) as part of a larger effort to consoli-date British control by reducing the independent powers of the sultan (q.v.). This reorganization strengthened the consul general's office so that it was virtually indistinguishable from that of a colonial governor. Clarke's plan was implemented in 1906, and he was appointed British agent and consul general in early 1909. Later, in declining health, Clarke ignored physicians' admonitions to leave Zanzibar. In 1913 he died while still in office. Having by now eliminated any pretense of Zanzibari independence, the British government marked Clarke's passing by transferring the protectorate from Foreign Office to Colo-nial Office administration and by replacing the consul general with an even more powerful Resident.

CLOSER UNION. In 1924 the colonial secretary, Leopold S. Amery, unveiled a plan to strengthen the British position in East Africa by amalgamating TT, Kenya, and Uganda into a "closer union." This plan would have increased the political influence of local European settlers. It would also have created common services in areas such as railways, harbors, post, telegraphs, aviation, customs, research, and defense. In July 1924 the British government appointed an East Af-rica Commission to consider how to facilitate economic development throughout the region. The commission reported that, despite the common needs of the East African dependencies, the expense of cre-ating a "closer union" was prohibitive. However, the commission suggested that the governors of three territories meet periodically to discuss issues of mutual interest. In 1929 the Hilton-Young Commis-sion (q.v.) recommended that a federation of TT, Kenya, and Uganda was desirable and could best be achieved by the appointment of a high commissioner who would devise native policy for the three terri-tories. The following year a Joint Select Committee of the British

Parliament indicated that "closer union" of a political or constitutional character was out of the question. Sir Donald Cameron (q.v.) played a major role in defeating the "closer union" scheme by advancing his indirect rule (q.v.) policy in TT. Despite the rejection of "closer union," European settlers in TT and Kenya continued to support the concept in the 1930s because they feared that the British government might give TT back to Germany. In 1938 settlers from both territories founded the Tanganyika League (q.v.) to ensure British retention of TT. Also, see ORMSBY-GORE COMMISSION.

CLOVE GROWERS' ASSOCIATION (CGA). The CGA reflected the ethnic and racial foundations of British economic policy in colonial Zanzibar (q.v.). By the late 1920s Arab (q.v.) fortunes in the clove (q.v.) industry were in serious decline. Part of the reason for the problem was market related and would worsen in the world depression of the 1930s. Another factor involved pressure placed on Arab growers from below by an increasing number of African smallholders burdened by comparatively few operating costs and from above by Asian and European (qq.v.) merchants who were officially thought to be profiting excessively from the clove trade. In 1927 the colonial government sought to counter these perceived trends by forming the CGA to organize Arab and African growers along cooperative lines. This would enable them to control their laborers' wages, to provide subsidized storage and marketing facilities, and to receive preharvest loans at reduced interest rates. The authorities further subsidized the CGA by paying members bonuses on clove trees that had been producing since 1923. This subvention was soon ended, but the Agricultural Department continued to lend money to CGA members and to store their crops.

This favoritism failed to rescue the depression-ravaged growers, but it aroused the animosity of Asian and European merchants. They were further incensed in 1933, when an official report on indebtedness recommended that the government segregate Zanzibar's economy along racial lines and that only "a person of Arab or African origin" should engage in commercial agriculture. Subsequent policy shifted an increased share of the protectorate's debt recovery to Asian creditors, disallowed the transfer of Arab and African land to Asians and Europeans without the British Resident's consent, established the CGA as a "privileged corporation," authorized it to levy contributions on clove exports, insured a government guarantee on its profits, and made it the sole authority for allocating clove licenses. A 1937 decree granted the CGA a monopoly over the clove trade by eliminating other dealers.

In response, local Asian traders and their counterparts in India organized a successful boycott of Zanzibari cloves. The colonial government eventually retreated and again permitted non-CGA interests to market and export the crop. In addition to further restrictions placed on CGA trading practices, two Asians were appointed to the association's board of directors and another two to its advisory committee, which set prices. In 1941 the colonial government took over from the CGA on a much wider scale by forming an Economic Control Board with far-reaching powers to set prices and to license both exports and imports.

CLOVES. Cloves have been Zanzibar's single most important export since the abolition of the slave trade (q.v.). More than 80 percent of world production is grown on Zanzibar and Pemba Islands (qq.v.), with approximately 85 percent of the total Zanzibari crop produced on Pemba.

In 1818 Seyyid Said (q.v.) had large areas of bushland cleared, dispossessing many African smallholders, to plant cloves, which were in great international demand. He also compelled plantation owners to forsake coconut growing in favor of cloves. By the end of Said's life in 1856, Zanzibari plantations were producing three-fourths of the world's supply of cloves. In 1872 a hurricane destroyed most of the islands' clove trees, but they were immediately replaced.

Clove trees grow to about 40 feet (12 meters), normally yield 25 to 35 pounds (11 to 13 kilograms) per year, and have an average life of between 50 and 60 years. Their fruit is exported to North America, Europe, and Asia and is used primarily as a food spice. On Zanzibar and Pemba more than six million trees are cultivated on approximately 80,000 acres (32,000 hectares). Cloves and clove oil form more than half of Zanzibari exports and account for about 90 percent of export earnings. Between 1982 and 1994, the clove price dropped from more than US$9,000 a ton to less than US$2,000 a ton. Nevertheless, on 14 August 1994 the cash-poor Zanzibari government sought to increase production by raising the prices for cloves by 17.6 percent. In 1993 Tanzania produced a total of about 10,000 tons of cloves.

COAL. Large deposits of high-quality and easily exploitable coal exist near Songea in southern Tanzania, where there are also significant iron ore deposits. The Ruhuhu River basin to the east of Lake Malawi (q.v.) also contains 285 million tons of good quality non-coking coal and 116 million tons of lesser grade fuel. The Kiwira-Songea field near the northwestern shores of Lake Malawi has reserves of another 20 million tons. After the completion of the TAZARA Railway (q.v.) in 1975, the problem of transporting coal was greatly reduced, and

850 tons were mined and transported in 1976. By the early 1990s Tanzania produced about 50,000 tons of coal annually.

COCONUTS. By 500 A.D., coconuts had been introduced to Africa from Southeast Asia. Many new coconut plantations had appeared on Mafia Island (q.v.) by 1890 and multiplied along the coast until the end of the century. Today coconuts are grown mainly in Mtwara, Coast, and Tanga regions on the mainland, and on Mafia and Zanzibar (q.v.) Islands. By the early 1960s more than five million palms were in production, and 14,000 tons of copra (dried kernels of coconut) and 2,400 tons of coir (coconut fiber) were exported in 1967. Local consumption exceeded 50,000 tons. In recent years coconut production has stagnated because of ageing trees. In mid-1989 the World Bank's (q.v.) International Development Association (IDA) provided a US$25 million credit to Tanzania to double coconut and cashew (q.v.) production in 10 years. The project included research into improved tree varieties and hybrids, training, and credit for farmers. In the early 1990s Germany also funded the National Coconut Development Programme, which sought to produce hybrid seeds by crossing them with coconut dwarf seeds imported from Malaysia. When this project failed, researchers turned their attention to improving the East African tall plant, which lives up to 100 years. The outcome of these efforts remains to be seen.

COFFEE. In the mid–nineteenth century, explorers John Speke and James Grant (qq.v.) found robusta coffee varieties already growing in Bukoba (q.v.). Over the coming decades European settlers, government workers, and missionaries introduced coffee in many parts of GEA and TT. In 1893, for example, Roman Catholic missionaries successfully introduced coffee as a smallholder crop at Kilimanjaro. It became so popular with local Chagga (q.v.) growers that by 1907 European planters protested against the danger of plant disease and the threat that smallholder production posed to their labor supply.

Indigenous to the West Lake region, robusta had ceremonial significance to the Haya (q.v.) and originally could only be grown by chiefs. The first exports of Haya robusta occurred in 1898. About the same time, European missionaries introduced arabica coffee in Morogoro. A European settler brought this variety to Sukumaland, and it became a popular cash crop by 1911. Most of the seed bought at that time was acquired from Java.

At the start of World War I (q.v.), Chagga growers owned about 14,000 coffee trees on the slopes of Mount Kilimanjaro (q.v.). Major (later Sir) Charles Dundas (q.v.), the first postwar British administrator at Moshi (q.v.), encouraged the Chagga in this endeavor, and the number of trees increased dramatically. Production for export grew from slightly more than 1,000 tons in 1913 to more than 10,000 tons by 1928. Coffee had become so popular among Chagga growers that, with Dundas's support, they formed the Kilimanjaro Native Coffee Planters' Association in 1925 "to protect and promote the interests of the native coffee growers on the mountain side." In 1928 the colonial government enacted a Coffee Ordinance that required the registration of all plantations and dealers and empowered the Agricultural Department to inspect plantations for plant disease. Subsequent regulations permitted strong action against diseased estates. In 1933 the Kilimanjaro Native Coffee Planters' Association was reorganized as the Kilimanjaro Native Cooperative Union (KNCU) (q.v.).

Arabica coffee is modern Tanzania's leading export crop, and three-fifths of it is grown by the Chagga in Kilimanjaro Region. In July 1989 the International Coffee Organization suspended international quotas, which caused an immediate 50 percent drop in world coffee prices. As a result, Tanzania's coffee export earnings declined from more than US$84 million in 1989 to about US$58 million in 1991/92. Despite a 1994 increase in world coffee prices, Tanzania continues to work for the introduction of new international coffee quotas. In July 1994 the Tanzanian government also sought to stimulate the industry by allowing private traders to buy coffee directly from producers. By the mid-1990s Tanzania produced about 1 percent of total world coffee production.

COLONIAL DEVELOPMENT AND WELFARE ACT OF 1945. Enacted by the British government, this act differed from its 1929 and 1940 predecessors in that it introduced the concept of socioeconomic development in the interests of the colonized to a greater extent than of the colonizing power. The act authorized large expenditures in raising the standards of economically lagging regions within individual colonies and mandated territories, including TT, which constituted a unique policy conception at the time. The act also implied a British recognition of the rapid approach of colonial internal self-governance and eventual independence, brought forth by the economic burden of the empire on post–World War II (q.v.) Britain and the rising forces of anticolonial nationalism in Asia and Africa.

COMMON MARKET OF EASTERN AND SOUTHERN AFRICAN STATES (COMESA). On 5 November 1993 the Preferential Trade Area for Eastern and Southern African States (PTA) (q.v.) transformed itself into the COMESA. Fifteen of the 22 eligible member states (Tanzania, Eritrea, Ethiopia, Kenya, Lesotho, Madagascar, Malawi, Mauritius, Mozambique, Namibia, Rwanda, Sudan, Swaziland,

Uganda, and Zambia) signed the treaty that created COMESA. The new organization seeks to establish a common market that will embrace customs, trade, monetary cooperation, transport and communications, industry, legal, administrative, and budgetary matters. COMESA expects to initiate a fully functioning common market by the year 2000 and a monetary union by the year 2020.

COMMUNITY DEVELOPMENT TRUST FUND. See CHESHAM, LADY MARION.

CONSOLATA FATHERS. Originating in northern Italy, this Roman Catholic order was allocated the western half of the German Benedictine Mission of St. Ottilien Congregation (q.v.) when the Germans were compelled to leave what was to become TT during World War I (q.v.). The Consolata mission later became the Diocese of Iringa and then amalgamated with other groups to form the Tanzania Episcopal Conference (TEC) (q.v.).

CONSTITUTIONS. Since independence, there have been six constitutions: (1) The Constitution of Tanganyika, 1961, adopted at independence, which provided for a parliamentary form of government; (2) the Constitution of the Republic of Tanganyika, 1962, which changed the country's governing structure from a parliamentary to a presidential form of rule; (3) the Constitution of Zanzibar, 1963, adopted at independence, which created a parliamentary government under the strong authority of the sultan (q.v.) and which lasted barely a month before the Zanzibar Revolution (q.v.) of January 1964; (4) the Interim Constitution of the United Republic of Tanzania, 1965, which acknowledged the union of Tanganyika and Zanzibar and the concept of a one-party state, but which also allowed considerable governmental autonomy for Zanzibar and provided that TANU (q.v.) would represent the mainland politically while the Afro-Shirazi Party (q.v.) would represent the Zanzibari islands; (5) the Permanent Constitution of the United Republic of Tanzania, 1977, which asserted single-party supremacy over the entire country under the recently created CCM (q.v.), but which also recognized Zanzibar's distinct status by authorizing a separate cabinet and ministerial system for the islands; (6) the Zanzibari Constitution, 1979, which confirmed this semiseparate governing arrangement by providing for an elected House of Representatives with legislative jurisdiction over Zanzibar and Pemba (qq.v.).

COOPERATIVE SOCIETIES. The Cooperative Societies Ordinance of 1932, which provided for the registration of agricultural marketing societies for cash crops, established the legal foundation for the cooperative movement. The ordinance also required an annual auditing of cooperative accounts and official supervision of registered societies' affairs. The first cooperative, the Kilimanjaro Native Cooperative Union, Ltd. (KNCU) (q.v.), was registered on 1 January 1933 and included 11 primary affiliated societies for the marketing of coffee. By 1939 the KNCU had grown to incorporate 27 primary societies with 25,728 members. In that year its coffee sales exceeded £70,000, and the union also collected and marketed other African produce, including hides and maize. The KNCU remained Tanzania's most important cooperative until 1976, when the authorities disbanded all cooperative unions.

Other major cooperatives registered during the 1930s included the Matengo Cooperative Marketing Union with three affiliated societies, registered at Songea in 1936 for the sale of tobacco, and the Buguti Coffee Cooperative Society, also registered in 1936, at Ngara. Although the colonial government appointed one of its senior officers as cooperative consultant in 1935, no appreciable expansion of the movement occurred until 1949. In that year the Mwakaleli Coffee Growers Association, forerunner of the Rungwe African Cooperative Union, was registered in the Southern Highlands (q.v.), and the Bukoba Native Cooperative Union, later the Bukoba Cooperative Union (BCU) (q.v.), was officially recognized. It grew rapidly to some 60 primary societies and became the principal organization responsible for coffee sales in the West Lake area. The Lake Province Growers Association was formed in 1951 as TT's most important organizer of cotton sales. It was subsequently renamed the Victoria Federation of Cooperatives Unions, Ltd. (VFCU). From this point the pace of registration quickened, so that by 1957 462 marketing societies and five consumer societies were officially in existence, up from a total of 62 marketing societies in 1948. On the eve of independence, in 1960, the number had risen to 579 marketing societies with 326,000 members. This growth continued well into the 1960s.

In 1962 the Tanzanian government sought to gain control over this important source of economic power by creating the Cooperative Union of Tanzania (originally Tanganyika) (CUT) (q.v.) as a "mass organization" of the ruling party. The CUT's secretary-general also served on TANU's National Executive Committee (NEC) and required all cooperatives to become affiliated with his organization. Led by the KNCU and the VFCU, the number of societies thus co-opted reached 1,600 by 1966, with a membership of 500,000. The Cooperative Supply Association of Tanzania (COSATA), another TANU affiliate, also sought to wrest control over retail marketing from the Asian community. Consisting of 41 societies at its formation, it supplied agricultural inputs to cooperatives and producers and managed retail sales. By 1966 all of COSATA's branches were operating at a loss, and in 1967 COSATA was amalgamated with several export-import firms, nationalized under the Arusha Declaration (q.v.), into the State Trading Corporation.

In another movement toward state-managed socialism, the Tanzanian government abolished all cooperative societies in 1976 because they were judged to be inefficient, corrupt, and biased toward larger and more prosperous cash-crop farmers. Their local organizational functions were turned over to village councils, recently established under the Villages and *Ujamaa* Villages (q.v.) Act and their wholesale marketing, storage, and processing services were transferred to parastatal organizations, including the National Milling Corporation. Neither the villages nor the parastatals adequately fulfilled these responsibilities. Consequently, the Cooperative Societies Act of 1982 reinstated cooperative societies under the CCM's (q.v.) supervision, through an umbrella organization representing the reconstituted cooperative unions. In 1990 the National Assembly (q.v.) passed an amendment to the Cooperative Societies Act of 1982, which stipulated that only economically viable cooperatives could be registered. Supposedly, this action underscored the fact that "cooperative societies must be created out of economic merits and not just to appease the people politically." The Cooperative Societies Act of 1991 sought further to afford cooperatives autonomy from the government and the CCM, thus ending the role of cooperative societies in further efforts at state-managed development. Also, see UJAMAA VILLAGES; VILLAGIZATION.

COOPERATIVE UNION OF TANZANIA. See COOPERATIVE SOCIETIES.

COTTON. In 1902 the German colonial government declared that cotton should be developed as a cash crop in southern GEA. Each *jumbe* (q.v.) managed a communal plot, and his village was compelled to work it in rotation, employing seeds and tools supplied by the government. A cotton project located near the Rufiji River failed because of poor organization, inadequate soils, a mixture of fertile and infertile seeds, and crop disease. This scheme and its forced-labor component likely contributed to the Maji-Maji Rebellion (q.v.) of 1905–1907. In 1905 the German authorities established a cotton cultivation school at Mpanganya and, from 1906 to 1914, opened several European cotton estates. A European settler introduced cotton into Sukumaland on an African sharecropping basis. By 1911 90 percent of all production came from the Lake Victoria (q.v.) region, from which it was transported north and exported to Europe via the Uganda Railway and the port at Mombasa, Kenya. Cotton production rose further in British-administered TT, so that by 1949 annual export income from the crop had reached more than £1.4 million.

After independence cotton production grew from 161,200 bales in 1961/62 to 434,400 bales in 1966/67. This was a peak production year, in which cotton products moved to first place among Tanzanian exports. By the 1970s more than TShs.300 million in annual foreign exchange earnings were still being recovered from sales of cotton lint and seed cake, but yields had dropped each year, to 250,000 bales by 1975. In 1973 the Tanzanian government had established the Tanzania Cotton Authority to manage production and sales. Its inefficiencies and other producer disincentives generally associated with state-controlled agriculture partly account for this production shortfall, but insects and weather also played their parts. Major enemies of cotton include blackarm, jassids, stainers, red bollworm, pink bollworm, budworm, aphids, and helopeltis. Accompanying an increasingly underfunded attempt to control these pests, a campaign was launched in 1975 to raise exportable output after several years of drought. In 1984 the Tanzania Cotton Marketing Board replaced the Tanzania Cotton Authority. During the late 1980s cotton production increased, largely because the Netherlands funded a major rehabilitation project for ginneries and transportation.

COX COMMISSION. This body was headed by Christopher Cox, former education adviser to the British secretary of state for the colonies. It drew up educational proposals for inclusion in a 10-year development plan, introduced in 1946, which sought to expand African education and increase the literacy rate of colonial subjects in TT as well as to enable an increasing number of primary school-leavers to attend secondary and higher educational institutions. Accordingly, the plan stressed primary and secondary education to prepare the African community for greater involvement in the cash economy of TT.

CURRENCY. In recent times a coin of Egypt's Ptolemy VIII (116–80 B.C.) was found in association with a dagger not far from Dar es Salaam (q.v.). More than 170 Chinese coins, dating from the seventh to the thirteenth centuries, have also been found in Zanzibar (q.v.). The first currency to have originated in Tanzania probably dates to 1300 A.D., when Kilwa Kisiwani (q.v.) captured the gold (q.v.) trade from Sofala and, together with Zanzibar, began minting its own coins.

The right to issue paper currency was first conferred on the German East Africa Company (q.v.) by the sultan (q.v.) of Zanzibar in 1888. The Deutsch Ostafrikanische Bank was created in 1905, with head offices in Berlin. The bank issued its first notes in the five rupee denomination, equivalent in value to one-third of a British pound. Following World War I (q.v.) an East African Currency Board was established to provide a common currency for the region now under British jurisdiction, and the denomination was changed from rupees to shillings. In 1921 the British government enacted the Metallic Currency Ordinance and adopted the East African shilling as a subsidiary coinage. In 1923 the colonial authorities redeemed German silver coins and withdrew them from circulation. Two years later coins other than East African shillings ceased to be legal tender. From this time until after independence the East African shilling was backed by the British pound, at the rate of 20 shillings to the pound.

By independence, the East African shilling was stably valued at seven to the US dollar. In 1964 the Tanzanian government created a separate Tanzanian currency, the Tanzanian shilling (TSh.). After Kenya and Uganda followed suit, the East African Currency Board was dissolved in 1966. A period of rapid inflation followed, which prompted a modest devaluation in 1975 to a ratio of eight Tanzanian shillings to one US dollar. The Tanzanian government also removed the currency from the dollar standard of valuation and transferred it to the International Monetary Fund. These actions failed to halt the shilling's decline, prompting further devaluations of 12 percent in 1982, 20 percent in 1983, and 26 percent in 1984. Between 1984 and 1986, however, the official value of the Tanzanian shilling had fallen to 18 to the US dollar, and the unofficial (black-market) value was far less, at more than 100 to one. Between 1986 and 1988 the shilling's official value dropped by 80 percent against the dollar, from US$0.05 to US$0.01. Beginning in 1986, the government reluctantly agreed to further limited devaluations demanded by the International Monetary Fund, the World Bank, and bilateral foreign-aid donors. Nevertheless, the average official value of the Tanzanian currency fell from 40 shillings to the US dollar in 1986, to 95 to one in 1988, and to about 200 to one in 1990, 300 to one in 1992, and 500 to one in 1994, with no major recovery anticipated. Also, see BANK OF TANZANIA.

— D —

"DAILY NEWS." Succeeding the privately owned *Tanganyika Standard* and *Tanganyika Weekly Standard* in 1972, the *Daily News* is a government-owned and managed newspaper, published in Dar es Salaam, and it is Tanzania's only English-language daily with a circulation of less than 50,000. It covers national news and international events reported from international wire services and carries feature articles and editorials, some of which are critical of local politicians and government policy. Its Letters to the Editor section is also a popular forum for political debate. The newspaper's Sunday edition, the *Sunday News*, offers a wider range of features and photographs and sells about 60,000 copies per week. Also, see PERIODICALS AND NEWSPAPERS.

DAR ES SALAAM. Capital of GEA, TT, Tanganyika, and Tanzania, the name of this city is Arabic for "Haven of Peace." Dar es Salaam is also Tanzania's chief international port and largest city. It is located on the East African coast about 45 miles (72 kilometers) southwest of Zanzibar (q.v.). The city originally consisted of a natural deepwater lagoon on the Indian Ocean coast bordered by bushlands and plantations of cassava (q.v.), millet, maize (q.v.), and sesame. Dar es Salaam featured a safe anchorage for dhows (q.v.) and smaller fishing vessels, and its central village was named Mzizima ("Place of Health").

Intending to move his capital from Zanzibar to the mainland, Sultan Majid ibn Said (q.v.) took control of the area in 1862 and ruled through the *jumbes* (q.v.) of Mzizima. In 1866 Majid began to build a new port on the banks of the lagoon, which he named Dar es Salaam. He died in 1870 before his plans reached fruition. Majid's brother and successor, Sultan Barghash ibn Said (q.v.), discontinued the construction work, but he did manage to abolish the rule of the local *jumbes* and substitute that of Zanzibar. In 1887 the German East Africa Company (q.v.) assumed control over Dar es Salaam. In 1891 the Germans transferred their capital from Bagamoyo (q.v.) to Dar es Salaam. The construction of the railway in 1907 enhanced the city's economic importance.

After Germany lost GEA in World War I (q.v.) the British continued to employ Dar es Salaam as the capital of TT. On 1 January 1949 the colonial authorities created the Dar es Salaam Municipal Council and elected a mayor each year from its membership. On 10 December 1961 one day after independence, Dar es Salaam received city status.

Since the late nineteenth century there has been a steady growth in the city's population (q.v.). By 1894, the number of residents had risen from about 900 in 1867 to more than 10,000. In 1928 Dar es Salaam's non-African population consisted of approximately 800 Europeans, 4,500 Asians, and 20,000 Arabs (qq.v.). From this point the total number of inhabitants increased exponentially to about 35,000 in 1930, 67,000 in 1945, 129,000 in 1957, 275,000 in 1967, 517,000 in 1975, 609,000 in 1977, 1,360,850 in 1988, and 1.9 million in 1993. During this time the city's boundaries increased to encompass an area of 32 square miles (83 square kilometers).

In November 1974 Julius Nyerere (q.v.) announced that the national capital would be moved to Dodoma (q.v.); however, a lack of resources has prevented the Tanzanian government from completing the relocation. As a result, Dar es Salaam continues to serve as the focus of governmental, industrial, and commercial activity, and, as the terminus of the Central and TAZARA (q.v.) railway lines, it remains the country's main port.

In 1986 several bilateral and multilateral donors and lenders funded a US$150 million project to increase the capacity of Dar es Salaam's port facility. An expansion of docking and storage space was badly needed to accommodate an increased flow of exports and imports on the TAZARA Railway, which was causing serious bottlenecks at the port. As a result of these improvements, turnaround times between Dar es Salaam and TAZARA's western terminus at Kapiri Mposhi, Zambia, were reduced from about 26 days in 1982 to an average of 14 days by late 1988. Previously favoring other routes, Zambia now began shipping 80 percent of its exports and 45 percent of its imports through Dar es Salaam. By the early 1990s the port handled approximately 25 percent of southern Africa's shipping. It also services most of Tanzania's manufacturing industries, which produce a variety of products, including metal goods, clothing, foodstuffs, soap, paint, furniture, pharmaceuticals, glassware, and cigarettes.

Dar es Salaam's mean daily maximum and minimum temperatures are about 86 degrees Fahrenheit (30 degrees Celsius) and 65.6 degrees Fahrenheit (18.6 degrees Celsius), respectively. The city's relative humidity, averaging 85 percent, approaches 100 percent on nearly every night of the year and rarely drops below 55 percent during the day. Dar es Salaam's average annual rainfall ranges between 35 inches (875 millimeters) and 44 inches (1,100 millimeters).

DAR ES SALAAM TECHNICAL COLLEGE. This college was founded in 1958 as a secondary-level technical institute to offer commercial and technical courses. In 1964 the technical curriculum was transferred to the Ifunda Technical Secondary School, and in 1965 the Technical College was founded to provide technician training. It offered an Ordinary Technician diploma to Form IV graduates and an Engineering diploma (in civil, electrical, and mechanical engineering) after the Ordinary Technician course and several years of working experience. The college also offered an education option in cooperation with the Dar es Salaam College of National Education.

DECENTRALISATION OF GOVERNMENT ADMINISTRATION ACT OF 1972. This legislation authorized the transfer of governmental authority and personnel from Dar es Salaam (q.v.) to regional and district headquarters. Under the act, the number of regions and districts was increased to create smaller and more manageable administrative units. Regional and area commissioners, who were made responsible to the prime minister's office and aided by regional and district development directors, also received greater autonomy. Development directors supervised technical specialists, who were grouped into regional and district development teams.

In 1976 the Tanzanian government amended the act, in conformity with the Villages and *Ujamaa* Villages Act of 1975 and the Urban Wards (Administrative) Act of 1976, to provide for the advisory representation of villages, *Ujamaa* villages (q.v.), and urban wards on advisory district development councils. These bodies submitted suggestions for development projects to their appointed regional development committees, which in turn devised annual development plans and submitted them to district and regional TANU (q.v.) executive committees. The plans would then be transmitted to central party and government agencies for final approval and funding. The amendment abolished existing local governmental organizations in favor of this new system, which placed most decision-making power in the hands of regional and area commissioners (who were also local TANU leaders), development directors, and party committees.

Capacity for administrative efficiency may have been improved by the Decentralisation of Government Administration Act, but meaningful local political participation suffered. Funds and technical services continued to be centrally allocated, and local self-determination was all but eliminated in a structure that confined village and urban ward residents to a purely advisory role. In effect, the act produced more of a deconcentration of administration than a devolution of real power. It remained in effect until 1982. After President Julius Nyerere (q.v.) admitted that the legislation's emasculation of local decision-making power had been a mistake, the TANU leadership agreed to reinstate elected district councils.

DELIMITATION COMMISSION. Great Britain, France, and Germany created this commission in 1885 "for the purpose of enquiring into the claims of the Sultan of Zanzibar to sovereignty over certain territories in East Africa, and of ascertaining their precise limits." The Germans already had obtained territories in the hinterland of what was to become GEA, but lacked suitable access to the Indian Ocean. The territories in question were therefore the coastal areas claimed and occupied by the sultanate of Zanzibar, now ruled by Sultan Barghash ibn Said (q.v.). The sultan was not invited to join the commission, to which each of the other three powers appointed one delegate.

In January 1886 the commission commenced its investigations

along the coast from Tungi, south of Cape Delgado, to Kisiju, near Dar es Salaam (q.v.). Finding that the sultan's government was firmly entrenched along the southern coast, the commission proceeded from Kisiju to Zanzibar (q.v.) and then back to the mainland, where its members visited Pangani, Tanga (q.v.), and Vanga along what is now the Tanzanian-Kenyan border. Here too the commissioners found the sultan strongly represented and learned that the Arab governor of Tanga regularly collected taxes from villages located three days' march inland. At this point the British delegate, Colonel H. H. (later Field Marshal Earl) Kitchener, proposed that the commission push inland as far as Mount Kilimanjaro (q.v.). His German counterpart, Lieutenant Schmidt, opposed this suggestion, thus widening differences of jurisdictional interpretation that were already apparent between the German and his British and French colleagues. The British and French governments had instructed their emissaries that only unanimous findings would be taken seriously, but the German commissioner argued that the sultan should rule a coastal strip only 10 miles (16 kilometers) wide, whereas the British and French commissioners would have given the sultan 40 miles (64 kilometers) inland from the coast.

In the end, the German government prevailed. In the Anglo-German Agreement of 1886 (q.v.), the sultan's government was given sovereign rights to Zanzibar, Pemba, and Mafia Islands (qq.v.) and to a 10-mile-wide strip of mainland extending from Mikindani Bay to Kilwa Kivinje (q.v.) on the southern mainland. Farther north, the sultan was granted radii of 10 miles around Kikunya, Kisiju, and Dar es Salaam, and a 3-mile (5-kilometer) strip between Dar es Salaam and Sadani. At Sadani and Pangani, the sultan was allotted territorial radii of 5 miles (8 kilometers), and between these towns the sultan's coastal belt reverted to 10 miles, reduced to 3 miles between Pangani and Vanga.

The agreement also confirmed Germany's colonial rights to territories inland from the Ruvuma to the Umba Rivers and British rights to inland territories from the Umba to the Tana Rivers. Britain also agreed to seek a friendly solution to rival claims between the sultan and the Germans to the Kilimanjaro region.

All of these complicated determinations were made without consulting Sultan Barghash, and all were later abrogated as the Germans and British assumed control over the mainland area claimed by the sultanate and over Zanzibar itself. Also, see ANGLO-GERMAN AGREEMENT, 1890.

DEVELOPMENT PLANS. Since 1945, there have been six major development plans:

Ten-Year Development Plan, 1947–1956. The colonial authorities intended this plan to further the socioeconomic development of post–World War II (q.v.) TT and to help stimulate the faltering, war-weary British economy. Of the plan's £19 million in estimated costs, 65 percent was to be raised from territorial sources. The Ten-Year Plan incorporated a large number of local schemes for African agricultural development on behalf of increased export-crop production, and for the first time stressed primary and secondary education to prepare the African community for greater participation in the cash economy. Real expenditures were revised downward on several subsequent occasions in light of rising costs, a lack of local revenues, and other factors, but in 1955 a supplemental plan was published that promised and, to some extent, delivered increased funding for African commercial agriculture.

Development Plan for Tanganyika, 1961/62–1963/64. In 1960 the colonial government announced this follow-up plan to extend earlier planning into the post-colonial period. This plan sought to implement an agricultural "improvement approach" recommended in that year by the World Bank (q.v.). Like its earlier counterpart, this last colonial plan represented not a detailed program of phased investment but rather a broad declaration of intent to be refined, budgeted, and implemented on a project-by-project basis. Nevertheless, the 1961–1964 plan departed from previous planning efforts in two important respects: It focused on African productivity increases in agriculture, and it replaced coercion with persuasion and incentive as the primary means of gaining mass compliance. Yet the plan's benefits never appreciably extended beyond export agriculture to TT's long-neglected majority of subsistence farmers and pastoralists.

Five-Year Plan for Economic and Social Development, 1st July, 1964–30th June, 1969. By 1964 a marginally productive and largely subsistence-oriented rural sector still dominated the Tanzanian economy. The First Five-Year Plan sought to end this economic stagnation by implementing a World Bank-supported agricultural "transformation approach." According to the World Bank's recommendation, the plan rested on "intensive [economic modernization] campaigns in settled areas, involving a variety of co-ordinated measures, [and] through planned and supervised settlement of areas which are at present uninhabited or thinly inhabited." Projecting total expenditures of £246 million, half of which was drawn from foreign aid and investment, the plan focused on capital-intensive agricultural, manufacturing, and infrastructural programs. A 6.7 percent annual economic growth rate was targeted for the life of the plan, but actual growth averaged only 5.3 percent because of population increases, bad weather, falling export prices, shortfalls in foreign aid and investment, and inadequate research and administrative capacity. The plan's most noteworthy attempt at rapid agricultural development was a highly capitalized village settlement program, which was intended to fulfill President Julius Nyerere's (q.v.) goal of grouping dispersed subsistence producers into modern, communally organized, and easily accessible village communities engaged in fully mechanized agriculture. By 1966 Nyerere judged this program to be a failure because of its excessive costs (approximately £250,000 per settlement scheme), and also because of its tendency, anathema to Nyerere, to promote socioeconomic inequality between assisted and unassisted rural dwellers. Nyerere decided that in the next five-year plan rural transformation should be politically rather than economically motivated.

Second Five-Year Plan for Economic and Social Development, 1st July, 1969–30th June, 1974. This plan aimed to achieve the socialism and self-reliance goals set forth in the 1967 Arusha Declaration (q.v.). Its urban component stressed import substitution and capital-goods production in a mainly nationalized industrial sector. In the rural areas, the plan focused on villagization (q.v.), including the creation of communal *Ujamaa* villages (q.v.), a policy later reinforced in the Villages and *Ujamaa* Villages Act of 1975. Politically activated self-help became the key ingredient of plan implementation; only 1 percent of estimated expenditures were allocated to manufacturing and processing and less than 6 percent to agriculture. Infrastructural development accounted for more than 70 percent of proposed spending and was concentrated on the development of socialist villages and parastatal corporations. The Second Five-Year Plan projected an annual economic growth rate of 6.5 percent. In fact, real per capita gains averaged only about 1 percent when measured against population growth. Per capita food production also fell (partly because of the dislocations associated with villagization), and the cost of living rose by more than 50 percent. Tanzania's fledgling industries remained dependent on imported fuels, materials, and concessional funding, virtually erasing profit increases and compromising the plan's commitment to economic self-reliance. The country became generally more dependent on foreign aid, as import costs exceeded export values by US$771 million to US$414 million in 1974 and as the balance-of-payments deficit reached US$286 million.

Third Five-Year Plan for Economic and Social Development, 1st July, 1976–30th June, 1981. Following a two-year "interim strategy" to attempt recovery from the economic losses of the preceding years, the Third Five-Year Plan sought further to achieve price and wage stability, reductions in external trade and payments deficits, and economic growth rates of 5 to 6 percent. Although the villagization campaign ended in 1977, it had taken its toll on food production. Marketed output had fallen by more than 7 percent while population growth had peaked at more than 3 percent. Flooding, drought, and falling world prices also wreaked havoc on the export-crop sector. Tanzania continued to import large quantities of grain, primarily destined for the urban areas, and required large infusions of foreign financial assistance to help it manage debt while persisting with its now-problematic strategy of socialism and self-reliance. By 1979 68 percent of the country's development budget was financed by foreign aid, the balance-of-payments deficit had risen to nearly US$500 million, and the external debt now stood at more than US$1 billion. In 1980 export earnings financed only 44 percent of imports, the remainder being paid from international loans and grants. By 1981 the Ugandan-Tanzanian War (q.v.) and occupation had drained nearly US$1 billion from domestic revenues. Agriculture continued to decline, nationalized industries operated at an average of about 30 percent of capacity, and foreign lenders and aid donors expressed increasing discontent with Tanzania's socialist economy.

Fourth Five-Year Plan for Economic and Social Development, 1st July 1981–30th June 1986. Preceded by a vaguely stated *Long-Term Perspective Plan 1981–2000*, the Fourth Five-Year Plan retained earlier commitments to long-term infrastructural development but at least acknowledged the need for investments in short-term economic growth. Nevertheless, both it and subsequent five-year planning were soon superseded by economic recovery and reform programs that progressively moved Tanzania away from its 15-year experiment in socialism.

In 1981 the CCM (q.v.) leadership published its National Economic Survival Programme (NESP), which sought to preserve the political and economic status quo. However, major reversals of development policy were embodied in the Structural Adjustment Programme (SAP) begun in 1982 and in the Economic Recovery Programme (ERP) launched in 1986 (q.v.). A 1990/91 Economic and Social Action Programme (ESAP), which replaced the ERP, emphasized the improvement of social services. Despite all of these efforts, most economists agreed that significant improvements in the Tanzanian economy would require considerable time and sound growth policies.

DHOW. A galleonlike, lateen-rigged Arabian sailing ship of the basic type that still trades along the East African coast and, with the aid of monsoon winds, traverses the Indian Ocean. Historically, dhows brought salt, metal goods, beads, furniture, tools, and cloth from Arabia and beyond. They carried away slaves and local products such as ivory, dried fish, tortoise shells, and wooden building materials. Along with the *ngalawa* (a small outrigger canoe), the dhow also has been used for fishing off the mainland and Zanzibari coasts.

DIAMONDS. Lodged in a 3,500-foot (1,050-meter) by 5,000-foot (1,500-meter) bed of superimposed gravels, diamonds were first discovered near Mabuki, south of Mwanza (q.v.), before World War I (q.v.) but were exploited only after the war. This short-lived source yielded 23,000 carats in 1929, which quickly fell to 13,107 carats in 1930, 7,790 carats in 1931, and 1,387 carats by 1932. In 1940 Dr. John T. Williamson came upon a more promising deposit at Mwadui to the northeast of Shinyanga. Paying a royalty of 15 percent to the TT Treasury, the Williamson mine earned £12,600 in 1940 and £638,383 by 1945. In 1948, annual output reached £1 million. From 1951 to 1954, TT produced 840,420 carats (791,206 from Williamson), worth more than £8.5 million, and from 1954 to 1956, the Mwadui mine yielded nearly £3 million per year. During the same period a smaller mine at nearby Alamasi contributed diamonds valued at another £300,000. By 1960 TT's total diamond output brought about £4.65 million (Shs.93 million or US$13.3 million), £700,000 (Shs.14 million or US$2 million) of which contributed to the Tanganyika Treasury.

Tanganyikan diamonds were sent to London for processing and grading and were then resold to individual companies for cutting. In 1966 the Tanzania Diamond Company Ltd. commenced operations at Iringa and became a chief buyer, with annual sales of approximately Shs.60 million from a daily output of about 5,200 cut stones. Since the mid-1970s, however, Tanzania's source of diamonds has become progressively exhausted. By this time average annual sales totaled £150,000, lowering diamonds from 90 percent to 88 percent of total income derived from minerals.

In recent years, diamond production has continued to fall, from a peak of 120,200 carats in 1986 to a low of 11,577 carats in 1990. Although output recovered to 92,206 carats in 1991, it fell to 67,303 carats in 1992 and to 40,847 carats in 1993. Similarly, exports declined from US$8.3 million in 1992 to US$5.3 million in 1993. Tanzania's diamond industry faces a bleak future. Estimated reserves are about 3.9 million carats, which means that the life of the industry could be less than 10 years.

DIRIA, AHMED HASSAN (b. 1937). Born in Zanzibar (q.v.), Diria attended Gulioni Primary School, Zanzibar, and later studied in the former Soviet Union (1858/59), and at the Kwame Nkrumah Ideological College at Winneba, Ghana (1960/61), and Jawaharlal Nehru University, India (1970/71). From 1954 to 1958 Diria began his government career by working as a labor inspector. In 1959 and 1960 he served as deputy secretary general of the Zanzibar and Pemba Federation of Labour, and from 1959 to 1963 he was a member of the Central Committee of the Afro-Shirazi Party (q.v.). After Abeid Karume (q.v.) seized control of the Zanzibari government in 1964 Diria became governor of Pemba (q.v.) and assistant administrator-general of Zanzibar. Following the unification of Zanzibar with the mainland in 1964 he was appointed as Tanzania's ambassador to Egypt, and in 1969 to Zaire. Over the next two decades, Diria served in a variety of diplomatic and domestic posts, including acting director of Africa/ Middle Eastern Affairs in the Ministry of Foreign Affairs, assistant secretary to the Ministry of Regional Administration, high commissioner to India, ambassador to Japan and the Philippines, and ambassador to the former West Germany. In March 1989 he was appointed minister of state in the president's office. On 20 September 1990 Diria became minister of information and broadcasting, and following the October 1990 elections he replaced Benjamin Mkapa (q.v.) as foreign minister.

DISTRICT SCHOOLS. The British colonial government developed these educational institutions after World War II (q.v.). For the most part, they consisted of Standards V and VI attached to existing local primary schools teaching Standards I–IV or of newly created boarding schools covering only Standards V and VI. Other district schools were attached as preparatory courses to secondary schools and teacher training centers. Toward the late 1950s middle schools (q.v.) with Standards V to VIII housed in single institutions replaced district schools. Also, see AFRICAN EDUCATION, TANGANYIKA TERRITORY.

DOCKWORKERS' UNION. A trade union organized in 1947 on the docks of Dar es Salaam (q.v.). Initially operating in secret, this union issued anonymous demands, which were ignored by employers and the colonial government. To further its claims, the Dockworkers' Union organized a strike and gained official recognition. After a brief period of existence as a registered African association, the union became inactive in 1950. Its reorganization in 1952 marked the beginning of TT's independent trade union movement. Also, see NATIONAL UNION OF TANGANYIKA WORKERS; TANGANYIKA FEDERATION OF LABOUR.

DODOMA. A city located 250 miles (400 kilometers) northwest of Dar es Salaam (q.v.) on Tanzania's Central Plateau (q.v.) at an altitude of

3,700 feet (1,110 meters) above sea level. After the Central Railway's (q.v.) arrival in 1910, Dodoma evolved as an important station settlement intersecting the Great North Road. During World War I (q.v.) a famine brought about by the appropriation of grain and cattle by German and British soldiers caused the death of at least 30,000 inhabitants of the Dodoma area. During the 1920s commercial aircraft traveling from Cape Town to Cairo landed at Dodoma. When a Church Missionary Society (q.v.) cathedral was dedicated there in 1933, the community was raised to town status. In 1955 the Dodoma Town Council commenced operations.

Situated in a semiarid region prone to drought and occasional famine, Dodoma's population stood at only 9,144 in 1948. By 1952 this number had risen to 12,217 and by 1959 to about 13,000. In addition to employment gained from its being a railhead, until 1974 the city's main industries involved rice and flour milling and soap manufacturing. European missionaries introduced wine production, and Dodoma wines eventually became famous throughout East Africa. Dodoma's demographic and, to a lesser extent, employment situations began to change after November 1974, when Julius Nyerere (q.v.) selected it as Tanzania's new capital city. The prime minister's office and CCM (q.v.) party headquarters were the first official agencies to move from Dar es Salaam, but financial problems, construction delays, and other logistical difficulties have prevented the complete relocation of government to Dodoma. Nevertheless, Dodoma's new status has contributed to the city's dramatic growth in population. From 37,000 in 1975, the number of residents rose to 41,000 in 1977 and to 180,000 in 1988. By the early 1990s it had become increasingly clear that the plan to move the capital to Dodoma was moribund, largely because of a lack of money to build the city and pressure from the International Monetary Fund and the World Bank (q.v.) to abandon the project.

DUNDAS, SIR CHARLES (1884–1956). Major (later Sir) Charles Dundas became the first British administrative officer assigned to Moshi (q.v.) following World War I (q.v.). During the East African Campaign (q.v.), he served on the British Political Staff because of his fluency in the German language, acquired during 17 years of living in Hamburg as the son of a British consular official. As the war progressed, he was placed in charge of Wilhelmstal (Lushoto) and was then assigned to Pangani before being appointed Moshi district administrator. During this tour of duty Dundas became concerned with a high infant mortality rate among the Chagga (q.v.). He also introduced coffee (q.v.) to Chagga growers as a cash crop. In 1925, with Dundas's assistance, the Chagga formed the Kilimanjaro Native

Planters' Association (KNPA), TT's first African agricultural cooperative society.

In 1926 Dundas became Tanganyika secretary for native affairs. As such, he represented African interests in early LEGCO (q.v.) sessions. He later became governor of the Bahamas and of Uganda before his death in 1956.

— E —

EAST AFRICA ASSOCIATION. Established in 1964 to promote economic development and foreign investment in Tanzania, Kenya, Uganda, Mauritius, Seychelles, and Madagascar. Headquartered in London, the association is an independent, nonpolitical body financed from the subscriptions of its members and its own investment income.

EAST AFRICA EXAMINATION COUNCIL. In postcolonial Tanzania, Uganda, and Kenya, this organization administered the East African version of the Cambridge Overseas Examinations leading to the Cambridge School Certificate. Beginning in 1968, the document was known as the East African Certificate of Education. After Tanzania nationalized all of its educational institutions in 1970, it withdrew from the council so that it could devise its own examinations more in keeping with the Arusha Declaration's (q.v.) ideological and policy commitments to primary and secondary education.

EAST AFRICAN AIRWAYS. See AVIATION.

EAST AFRICAN CAMPAIGN (1914–1918). See WORLD WAR I.

EAST AFRICAN COMMON SERVICES ORGANIZATION (EACSO). On 9 December 1961 the Colonial Office replaced the East African High Commission (EAHC) (q.v.) with the EACSO to carry on regional cooperation in postcolonial Kenya, Tanganyika, and Uganda. The British intended that this action would internalize interterritorial economic and infrastructural cooperation by shifting its management from the colonial authorities to the African chief ministers of the three newly independent countries.

The EACSO Authority included elected representatives from Kenya, Tanganyika, and Uganda, who also sat as ex officio members in the organization's Central Legislative Assembly. A secretary-general and a legal secretary oversaw a permanent Secretariat, charged with implementing Assembly measures concerning civil aviation, customs and excise revenues, income taxes, interterritorial research, university education, communications, and public service.

From the outset, EACSO suffered a basic problem that had also affected its predecessor. By deliberate colonial design, Kenya's economic performance had consistently outpaced that of TT and Uganda, and the distribution of trade, tax, and investment revenues under EACSO merely reinforced this trend and threatened further to entrench an increasingly unbalanced economic relationship between Kenya and its less-favored partners—thus threatening the collapse of regional cooperation. Accordingly, in 1965 the specially appointed Philip Commission examined the future of East African economic relations. The commission recommended that an East African Community (EAC) (q.v.) be created to address problems of economic imbalance while preserving and extending regional common services. The Philip Commission report led to the Treaty for East African Cooperation, concluded by the Kenyan, Tanzanian, and Ugandan governments on 1 December 1967. This treaty authorized the EAC to assume control over EACSO's economic services. An East African Common Market (EACM) was also instituted to manage a common external tariff, and it specified restraints on regional trade, termed "transfer taxes," that Tanzania and Uganda could impose on imports from Kenya. An East African Development Bank was likewise formed and mandated to make 80 percent of its investments in Tanzania and Uganda.

EAST AFRICAN COMMUNITY (EAC). This organization was preceded by the East African High Commission and the East African Common Services Organization (qq.v.). On 6 June 1967 Tanzania, Kenya, and Uganda signed a treaty establishing the EAC "to strengthen and regulate the industrial, commercial and other ties among [Kenya, Tanzania, and Uganda] with a view to bringing about accelerated, harmonious and balanced development." Within this context, its main objectives were to establish and maintain a common customs and excise tax, gradually to abolish trade restrictions among partner states, to coordinate economic planning and transport/communications policies, and eventually to develop a common agricultural policy. The three heads of state or their representatives comprised the East African Authority, EAC's highest executive organ, which featured a rotating chairmanship. EAC headquarters were located at Arusha (q.v.), but the head offices of its various components were in major towns and cities throughout East Africa. An East African Assembly reported to the Authority and presided over five councils; the Common Market Council, the Communications Council, the

Finance Council, the Economic Consultation and Planning Council, and the Research and Social Council.

To manage regional economic and infrastructural cooperation, several East African corporations, administrations, and departments were brought under the jurisdiction of the authority and the assembly. The largest of these was the East African Railways Corporation; others included East African Airways, Harbours, Cargo Handling Services, Posts and Telecommunications, External Communications, Development Bank, Court of Appeal, Fishery-Marine-Freshwater, Malaria and Medical Research-TB-Leprosy-Sleeping Sickness, Customs and Excise, Meteorology, Literature Bureau, Statistics, Veterinary Research, Educational Examinations Council (localized after 1973), Inter-University Commission, and Community Training Centre for Secretariat Staff.

The EAC collapsed in 1977 because of a number of factors, including Idi Amin Dada's January 1971 military coup d'état in Uganda and its aftermath of increasing tensions among Uganda, Tanzania, and, to a lesser extent, Kenya. More basic difficulties centered on the divergent development strategies of socialist Tanzania and mercantile-capitalist Kenya, the different and mutually antagonistic leadership styles of Presidents Julius Nyerere (q.v.) and Jomo Kenyatta, and the disproportionate share of trade, investment, and other EAC benefits perennially reaching Kenya. Following a series of mutual accusations, confiscations of community assets, and repatriations of EAC employees, none of the three countries remitted its 1977/78 financial contribution to the community. Without an operating budget for the coming fiscal year, the EAC was dissolved on 1 July 1977.

Subsequently Tanzania, Uganda, and Kenya periodically discussed the possibility of increasing political and economic cooperation, but these efforts failed to produce tangible results. Finally, on 30 November 1993, the three governments signed a Treaty for Enhanced East African Co-operation. This agreement established a framework for regional cooperation in several areas, including trade, industry, agriculture, energy, transport, communications, law, and security. Tanzanian, Ugandan, and Kenyan leaders hoped that this treaty would eventually lead to revival of the EAC or to the creation of a similar organization.

EAST AFRICAN FEDERATION. See CLOSER UNION.

EAST AFRICAN HIGH COMMISSION (EAHC). By 1927 the British colonial authorities had joined TT, Kenya, and Uganda into a system of common tariffs, duty-free transfers of imported goods, a single currency, and increasingly integrated services, including railroad transportation, customs, posts and telegraphs, railways and harbors administration, civil aviation, and defense. In 1939 the colonial authorities introduced a regional income tax. On 1 January 1948 the EAHC was established to manage these and newer regional activities. Devised by British Colonial Secretary Arthur Creech Jones, the EAHC was led by a multiracial Central Legislative Assembly (q.v.) and immediately began to absorb the regional service organizations that had been created piecemeal over the preceding years. Four months after its inception, for example, it amalgamated the East African Railways, and in 1949 the East African Posts and Telecommunications and the East African Railways and Harbours authorities were formed. The Assembly's portfolio also extended to Makerere University (q.v.) in Uganda, then East Africa's only degree-granting higher educational institution.

The EAHC likewise presided over novel attempts at regional integration. One of the most notable examples was the East African Literature Bureau (EALB), created in 1947. The EALB promoted African writing, advised young authors, published and disseminated literary and cultural works in and about East Africa, supported literacy campaigns in the three member territories, and managed the East African Community's (q.v.) Central Printing Section. The EALB also pioneered the public library movement in East Africa and in 1964 provided the Tanganyika Library Services Board with 11 staff members, 50,000 books, Shs.8,259 (US$1,183) in financial contributions, and assorted equipment. On 9 December 1961 the EACSO (q.v.) replaced the EAHC.

ECONOMIC RECOVERY PROGRAMME (ERP). Launched in 1986, the ERP represented a second official attempt to reverse Tanzania's deepening economic crisis of the late 1970s and 1980s. Its predecessor, the Structural Adjustment Programme (SAP), required large financial contributions from bilateral and multilateral sources, but by late 1985 most donors and lenders had curtailed their aid and refused to negotiate further assistance until the government serviced its US$3 billion debt. Debt-relief credits from the International Monetary Fund (IMF) seemed the only way to end the crisis, and to this end President Ali Hassan Mwinyi (q.v.) announced the ERP in June 1986. This plan involved additional currency devaluations to those made earlier, removal of import restrictions, increases in producer prices for food and export crops, and an intensive anticorruption and efficiency campaign aimed at Tanzania's more than 400 parastatal corporations. In July 1986 the IMF responded by making US$800 million available, and the following year it granted the country another US$90 million structural adjustment facility to help implement the ERP. Meeting in

Paris, bilateral donors agreed to release US$400 million in suspended aid and pledged another US$130 million in new loans and grants.

The CCM (q.v.) party leadership had already attempted to block market-oriented reforms with its National Economic Survival Programme (NESP) of 1981. At the CCM's Third National Congress in October 1987, party hard-liners, reacting to the latest developments, excluded the ERP's chief architect, Finance Minister Cleopa Msuya, from its newly elected National Executive Committee (NEC). Declaring that the "building of socialism and self-reliance is a permanent task," they also ensured that the ERP would not proceed unopposed into the 1990s. Although immediate reductions in the country's 459 parastatal corporations were called for by the international community, for example, few were privatized or abandoned by 1990. Nevertheless, after eight months of negotiations and a further currency devaluation, in November 1988 the IMF approved another standby credit facility. On these terms, the ERP was pursued on a "hesitant to moderate" basis.

In 1990 the Economic and Social Action Programme (ESAP) replaced the ERP and sought to reduce social spending, increase donor support, and intensify local self-help initiatives. Tanzania's economic performance during the ESAP's first two years was generally deemed satisfactory, in spite of floods and drought which reduced the production of cash and food crops and a decrease in world market prices for export commodities such as cloves, coffee, and sisal (qq.v.).

ECONOMIC SABOTAGE CAMPAIGN. On 18 March 1983 Prime Minister Edward Sokoine initiated an "economic sabotage" campaign to fight "detestable social evils" such as black marketeering and bribery, smuggling, cattle rustling, hoarding, and land racketeering. On 22 April 1983 the National Assembly (q.v.) passed an Economic Crimes Bill that authorized special tribunals, party and vigilante searches, property seizures, and arrests. During 1983 and 1984, the government arrested 4,363 people and seized about US$5 million in currency and property. In late 1984 the authorities abandoned the campaign and ordered future cases to be handled through the normal court system. The economic sabotage campaign failed to end corruption in Tanzania, and a parallel economy still flourishes.

ECONOMY. In 1993 Tanzania was the second poorest country in Africa, largely because of the government's failed socialist policies. That year the total economy's GDP was about US$2.1 billion and the mainland's per capita GNP was approximately US$90. Agriculture provides about 56 percent of GDP and perhaps 90 percent of employment. Products associated with the agricultural sector include coffee, tea, cotton, sisal, tobacco, cashew, coconuts, cloves, pyrethrum (qq.v.), and meat. The industrial sector contributes less than 15 percent to the GDP. Major industrial activities include mining, oil refining, textiles, cement, fertilizers, manufactured import substitutes, and processed agricultural commodities.

The economy is heavily dependent on foreign assistance. In the early 1970s the People's Republic of China was Tanzania's largest donor country, providing more than US$400 million in aid. Most of these funds went to building, equipping, and maintaining the TAZARA (q.v.) railway. More recently, major donors have included the International Monetary Fund, the World Bank (q.v.), Sweden, the Netherlands, the United Kingdom, and Germany. Between 1970 and 1992 the United States provided more than US$400 million in aid to Tanzania. Dar es Salaam's present commitment to liberalizing the country's economy will probably ensure a continuation of Western assistance.

Still, Tanzania persists as one of the world's poorest countries. The average annual GDP has remained virtually stationary, at about US$3.1 billion, since 1970. Growth in agricultural production averaged only 0.9 percent between 1970 and 1980, although market-oriented policy reforms facilitated a partial recovery to an annual average of 4.9 percent between 1980 and 1993. This has helped to reduce Tanzania's reliance on purchased food imports, from 399,000 tons in 1980 to 215,000 tons in 1993, and on food aid, from 89,000 tons in 1979/80 to 35,000 tons in 1992/93. Because of an average 3 percent annual population growth rate, however, food production has still been plagued by an average annual per capita growth rate of -1.3 percent.

Because of sectoral inefficiencies and recent policy reforms favoring agriculture, the average industrial growth rate declined from 2.6 percent in the 1970–1980 period to 2.5 percent in the 1980–1993 period. Industrial enterprises have also been adversely affected by high costs for imported inputs and energy, the latter rising from 12 percent of export earnings in 1971 to 40 percent by 1992.

Since the economic adjustments and reforms of the late 1980s and 1990s, the most drastic decline in activity has occurred in state-provided social and economic services, which fell from an average annual growth rate of 9 percent in the 1970s to an average of slightly over 2 percent thereafter. Part of the reason for this spending decrease has involved policies aimed at curbing the country's soaring annual inflation rate, which averaged 24.3 percent between 1980 and 1993.

The Tanzanian economy retains its colonial bias toward the production and export of primary products, to the extent that more than 80 percent of all exports consist of unprocessed agricultural commodities and minerals to which little value has been added. This distortion renders the economy highly susceptible to world market conditions and promotes its continuing dependence on foreign aid. Exports averaged an annual growth rate of -0.4 percent between 1980 and 1993 and earned only US$420 million in 1993. In contrast, imports cost US$1.52 billion in 1993, despite cutbacks induced by austerity measures and by a lack of purchasing power that had produced an average growth rate of -1.1 percent in the previous decade.

Suggestive of Tanzania's future need for foreign economic assistance, the balance-of-payments deficit after official aid transfers increased from US$36 million in 1970 to US$408 million by 1993, while its deficit before official transfers swelled from US$37 million to US$935 million. Receipts of official development assistance totaled US$484 million in 1985; eight years later these contributions had risen to nearly US$1 billion, or more than 45 percent of GDP. As suggested by a total external debt that increased from US$2.49 billion in 1980 to US$6.75 billion by 1993, economic recovery, growth and diversification, and release from the vagaries of foreign aid continued to elude Tanzania in the 1990s. Also, see BANK OF TANZANIA; COMMON MARKET OF EASTERN AND SOUTHERN AFRICAN STATES; COOPERATIVE SOCIETIES; CURRENCY; DEVELOPMENT PLANS; EAST AFRICAN COMMUNITY; ECONOMIC RECOVERY PROGRAMME; EMPLOYMENT; EXPORTS; and GROSS DOMESTIC PRODUCT.

EDUCATION. See AFRICAN EDUCATION, GERMAN EAST AFRICA; AFRICAN EDUCATION, TANGANYIKA TERRITORY; EUROPEAN EDUCATION.

EDUCATION ACT OF 1969. This act placed all public and private schools under the authority of the Director of National Education in the Ministry of Education, with the exception of primary schools, which remained the responsibility of local educational authorities. Most important, NGOs transferred their privately assisted schools to government management, and NGO teachers became public employees. The director was also authorized to approve all fees set by private schools. Adult and higher educational institutions were likewise brought under the director's administrative supervision.

EDUCATION ACT SUPPLEMENT NO. 62 OF 1968. This law gave the Director of National Education the power to establish boards of governors for private schools, thus enabling the extension of official control over nongovernmentally supported educational institutions.

This extension of authority was formalized in the Education Act of 1969 (q.v.).

EDUCATION (AFRICAN) ORDINANCES OF 1927, 1933, AND 1950s AMENDMENTS. These colonial ordinances arose from the conclusions of the Education Conference of 1925, convened shortly after Governor Sir Donald Cameron (q.v.) arrived in TT. Attended by government and missionary educators, this conference proposed to join private and public schools under one educational system, supported by a system of official grants-in-aid and administered as part of a single, coherent educational policy for TT. Following upon the recommendations of the conference, the 1927 ordinance instructed that all schools be registered in areas of secular instruction; that teachers be registered by government if their schools received public assistance; that freedom of religious instruction be guaranteed; that at least one Grade I teacher be registered at a school before the English language could be taught; and that official grants-in-aid be provided to mission schools if they met the requirements of the ordinance.

The Education (African) Ordinance of 1933 established standards of governance for schools administered by local governments authorized under the Native Authority Ordinances of 1923 and 1927 (qq.v.). Amendments passed during the 1950s required the registration of teachers in native authority schools, authorized supervisory Native Authority Education Committees to be formed, set maximum and minimum enrollments in primary schools, and authorized the director of education to censor textbooks for educational quality and to close schools providing inferior instruction.

EDUCATION ORDINANCE OF 1961. This act superseded all previous legislation governing primary and secondary education in Tanganyika. It provided for a uniform, integrated, and decentralized system of instruction. Under its provisions, the minister of education controlled school staffing, admissions policy, syllabus adoption, secular instruction, standards of discipline and internal school organization, and the opening and closing of NGO-supported as well as government schools. NGO ownership of private schools was retained, although the government now shared in school administration. Local Education Authorities also received more powers than the former Native Authority Education Committees established under the Education (African) Ordinance of 1933 (q.v.), as amended, and a governing board for postprimary institutions was created to provide for greater managerial efficiency and to ensure the integration of these institutions within their local communities. Finally, under this legislation a single advisory council replaced four existing educational advisory councils.

EDUCATION SECRETARIES GENERAL. Two of these private organizations were originally formed in TT, one for Protestant religious denominations and the other for Roman Catholic orders. The Protestant Education Secretary General represented the interdenominational Christian Council of Tanganyika (CCT) (q.v.), and its Catholic counterpart acted on behalf of the Tanganyika Episcopal Conference (TEC) (q.v.). Both organizations coordinated and administered missionary education in accordance with government policy and managed communications between the official and nongovernmental parts of TT's educational establishment.

Following independence three additional Education Secretaries General were formed; one for His Royal Highness the Aga Khan's Education Department, another for the East African Muslim Welfare Society, and a third for the Tanganyika African Parents' Association (TAPA). After the Tanzanian government nationalized all schools in 1970, the Education Secretaries General became official coordinating bodies for the educational activities of their respective school systems.

ELECTIONS, TANGANYIKA TERRITORY, TANGANYIKA, TANZANIA. There have been nine major post–World War II elections in TT, Tanganyika, and Tanzania:

Election of 1958–1959. By 1955 the UN and the Colonial Office had requested that TT hold national elections for the selection of unofficial members to the LEGCO (q.v.). Anticipating these elections, Governor Sir Edward Twining (q.v.) encouraged TT's European and Asian communities to form the United Tanganyika Party (UTP) (q.v.) to confront TANU (q.v.) with an organized political opposition. Attempting to enlist support for the UTP from Africans loyal to the colonial administration, Twining excluded native authority chiefs from an existing ban on political activities by public officials. Under a franchise tightly restricted by education and wealth, 60,000 voters of all races registered to participate in TT's first territory-wide election, held in two phases during 1958 and 1959. Ten of the 30 available seats were reserved for Europeans and another 10 for Asians, which at first prompted TANU to boycott the elections. The party later reversed itself on this issue and then was subjected to the Twining government's harassment of Julius Nyerere (q.v.) and other TANU candidates. In the midst of the campaign, the more moderate Sir Richard Turnbull (q.v.), replaced Twining as governor and the election was held as scheduled. When the returns were tallied, TANU and TANU-supported candidates had won all 30 elected LEGCO seats, paving the way for another election in 1960 and for internal self-government and independence in 1961. In the meantime, the UTP quietly disbanded.

Election of 1960. In this last election to be held during the British administration of TT, the franchise was expanded to include nearly one million, largely African, voters. Of 71 contested LEGCO seats, 50 could be contested by candidates of any race, 11 were reserved for Asians, and ten for Europeans. TANU candidates ran unopposed in 58 contests and lost only one of the remaining 13 seats. Julius Nyerere was appointed chief minister and formed a cabinet of 10 unofficial ministers drawn from the TANU elected majority. Joined by an official delegation consisting of the deputy governor and two other senior colonial officers, this cabinet presided over a short transition from internal self-government, which began on 15 May 1961, to full independence on 9 December 1961.

Election of 1962. The main purpose of this election was to accommodate the constitutional changes that converted the Tanganyika government from a parliamentary to a presidential form of rule. Julius Nyerere ran unopposed for the new presidency and received overwhelming public support. He then appointed his friend and TANU colleague Rashidi Kawawa (q.v.) as vice president of the republic.

Elections of 1965. After the adoption of the Interim Constitution of the United Republic of Tanzania (q.v.), single-party National Assembly (q.v.) and presidential elections were held in September 1965. More than three million voters registered, and two-thirds of them participated in the elections. Under an arrangement permitting TANU candidates to compete against each other, single candidates ran in only 6 of 107 local constituencies. Julius Nyerere ran unopposed for reelection as president. Of the incumbent members of parliament, 31 opted not to run again, 12 failed to be nominated by the party, and 17 lost their seats in the voting—including two ministers and nine junior ministers. President Nyerere received a "yes" vote from more than 95 percent of those casting ballots.

Elections of 1970 and 1975. Extending a trend begun in 1965, the 1970 parliamentary election offered Tanzanians an opportunity to register their dissatisfaction with the government's inability to raise their standards of living in postcolonial Tanzania. More than half of the incumbents seeking reelection were either rejected in local and/or national TANU nominating processes or defeated at the polls. President Nyerere received a 95 percent vote of approval. The 1970 voting pattern was repeated in 1975. With over 10 percent more registered voters than in 1970, 82 percent actually voted and more than 90 percent of these reelected President Nyerere. On the other hand, 2 of

14 ministers lost their seats and only half of 86 incumbents seeking reelection were returned to the National Assembly.

Elections of 1980. Occurring after the formation of the CCM (q.v.) in 1977 and the adoption of Tanzania's permanent constitution in the same year, these were the first all-union elections. By now seven million voters were registered, four million more than for the 1965 election. Nearly six million went to the polls, and again more than half of the National Assembly was rejected in apparent protest against the country's worsening economic situation. President Nyerere was returned with a 93 percent "yes" vote, and, according to constitutional provisions governing the union, Zanzibaris confirmed Aboud Jumbe (q.v.) as president of Zanzibar and first ("union") vice president of Tanzania. Nyerere already had replaced Rashidi Kawawa as second vice president and prime minister. Kawawa's successor, Edward Sokoine, was elected to the National Assembly, and Nyerere reappointed him to both executive posts.

Elections of 1985. President Nyerere had already decided to retire from the presidency in 1985, and the CCM nominated Aboud Jumbe's successor as first vice president, Ali Hassan Mwinyi (q.v.), for the office. With seven million voters casting ballots, Mwinyi was easily elected as Tanzania's second president, although once again a substantial number of incumbent parliamentarians were turned out of office. As a Zanzibari, Mwinyi appointed Joseph Warioba (q.v.), a mainland MP, as first vice president and prime minister, according to the constitutional provision that the presidency and first vice presidency must be shared between a mainlander and a Zanzibari. If the first vice presidency is occupied by a mainlander, the second vice presidency becomes the "union" vice presidency and is filled by the elected president of Zanzibar (q.v.). Under the Mwinyi government, Idris Abdul Wakil (q.v.) assumed this position.

Elections of 1990. These elections took place amid an intense national debate about whether to sanction multiparty politics in Tanzania. In the August 1990 CCM elections, Julius Nyerere relinquished the party chairmanship. Delegates elected Nyerere's chosen successor, Ali Hassan Mwinyi, in his place. In the October 1990 uncontested presidential election, Mwinyi received about 95 percent of the votes. In the National Assembly election, 33 MPs lost their seats, including two regional commissioners and a veteran minister, Paul Bomani (q.v.). Immediately after the elections, President Mwinyi reshuffled his government and replaced Prime Minister Warioba with John Malecela (q.v.).

Elections of 1995. Chaos, controversy, and allegations of fraud plagued Tanzania's first multiparty presidential and parliamentary elections, held during October 1995, both in Zanzibar (q.v.) and on the mainland. The Tanzania Electoral Monitoring Committee, the Commonwealth Observers' Group, Organization of African Unity observers, and a UN observation team all agreed that neither election was properly supervised or fairly conducted. In Zanzibar, the CCM and the Civic United Front (CUF) both demanded that the elections be declared null and void. On the mainland, opponents of the incumbent CCM petitioned the courts for an annulment of the elections. After a judge rejected this appeal, 10 opposition parties withdrew from the electoral process. In spite of these disputes, the electoral commissions in Zanzibar and on the mainland confirmed the results of both polls.

In Zanzibar, the incumbent CCM president, Salim Amour (q.v.), won 165,271 votes (50.2 percent of the total), while the CUF's candidate, Seif Sharif Hamad, received 163,706 votes (49.8 percent). In the parliamentary election, the CCM won 26 seats (52 percent) as against 24 seats for the CUF, and the CUF won all 21 seats in Pemba (q.v.) as well as 3 in Zanzibar.

On the mainland, the CCM's presidential candidate, Benjamin Mkapa (q.v.), received 4,026,422 votes (61.8 percent of the total), thereby becoming Tanzania's third president. His nearest rival was Augustine Lyatonga Mrema (q.v.), representing the National Convention for Construction and Reform (NCCR), who won 1,808,616 votes (27.8 percent). Other major opposition candidates included the CUF's Ibrahim Harun Lipumba (q.v.), who received 418,973 votes (6.4 percent), and United Democratic Front (UPD) representative John Momose Cheyo (q.v.), who secured 258,734 votes (4 percent). In the parliamentary election, the CCM won 186 seats in the 232-seat parliament (80.2 percent), while the combined opposition shared the remaining 46 seats, with the CUF winning 24 seats, the NCCR 16 seats, the UDP 3 seats, and the Party for Democracy and Development 3 seats. Also, see OPPOSITION POLITICAL PARTIES.

ELECTIONS, ZANZIBAR. Major elections in Zanzibar have included:
Election of 1957. From its inception in 1926, the Zanzibari LEGCO (q.v.) included an unofficial minority of members appointed mainly from the Arab community. The 1957 election sought to fulfill the colonial government's desire to accommodate increasing political activity within and among all ethnic and racial groups by expanding the LEGCO's unofficial minority. The British also hoped that the election would facilitate an orderly transition to independence under the continued leadership of the sultan (q.v.). To this end, the colonial authorities added six elected unofficial seats to the existing 12 appointed seats. By this time, Zanzibar's leading political parties were the Zanzibar National Party (ZNP) (q.v.) and the Afro-Shirazi Union (ASU),

the former dominated by Arabs and the latter enjoying strong African support. In the 1957 election Africans won five of the six contests, but the ASU secured only three seats and the ZNP none. The remaining three seats were won by independent candidates backed by non-party ethnic associations, revealing that ethnic loyalties ran at least as deep as political party identification in Zanzibari politics.

First Election of 1961. After the 1957 election, factional conflicts divided the ZNP. Similarly, the ASU's African leadership failed to strengthen its relatively weak base of support in the Shirazi (q.v.) ethnic community. In 1959 Pemba Shirazis formed their own Zanzibar and Pemba People's Party (ZPPP) (q.v.), and Zanzibari Shirazis rallied around Abeid Karume (q.v.) under the banner of the renamed Afro-Shirazi Party (ASP) (q.v.). Having enlarged the LEGCO to create an unofficial majority of 22 contested seats, the British scheduled an election for January 1961. This time the ASP won more than 40 percent of the popular vote and 10 seats, while the ZNP won 9 seats with 36 percent of the vote and the ZPPP 3 seats with an electoral share of 17 percent. These results placed the ZPPP in a position to determine a majority coalition, but this possibility evaporated when two of its elected representatives sided with the ZNP and one with the ASP. A frustrated colonial government added one more seat to the LEGCO and scheduled another election for June 1961.

Second Election of 1961. In this election the ZNP and the ZPPP campaigned together against the ASP, pitting Arabs and Pemba Shirazis against a much larger number of native Zanzibari and mainland Africans. Ethnic violence broke out after the ZNP-ZPPP alliance gained a slim majority of three seats, but the winning coalition soon disintegrated over the issue of the sultan's future role in the Zanzibari government. Under the leadership of Ahmad Abdulrahman Babu (q.v.), a radical faction of the ZNP broke off to form the Umma (Masses) Party (q.v.) after the ZNP leadership endorsed the sultan as the proper head of state and government in an independent Zanzibar. Sensing future victory, Abeid Karume and his ASP followers intensified their political recruitment within the African community.

Election of 1963. Finally deciding that Zanzibar should become independent as soon as possible, the British arranged for a period of internal self-government to begin in June 1963. In preparation for independence by December 1963, a LEGCO election was held in July to fill 32 elected seats. The recently formed Umma (Masses) Party fielded no candidates, but the election results were no less threatening to the prospects for political unity in postcolonial Zanzibar. The ASP won more than 54 percent of the vote and 13 seats, but the ZNP-ZPPP coalition captured 18 seats and was invited to form an interim government. Karume and other ASP leaders charged that Arab gerrymandering was responsible for this disparity, but in reality the existing distribution of party support gave the ASP large majorities in eight constituencies while enabling the ZNP and ZPPP to win by smaller margins in more heavily contested races. Upon taking office, the new government reaffirmed its support for the sultan, prompting an ASP response that Zanzibari independence would be nothing more than "*Uhuru wa urabu tu*"—independence only for Arabs.

Later Elections. Following the 12 January 1964 Zanzibar Revolution (q.v.), Abeid Karume and his ASP stalwarts established a hand-picked Zanzibar Revolutionary Council (ZRL), but competitive elections were suspended until the creation of the CCM (q.v.) and the adoption of Tanzania's permanent union constitution in 1977. With more than 40 of 233 elected members, Zanzibaris were now granted nearly 20 percent of the seats in the Tanzanian National Assembly (q.v.), although the Zanzibari population then stood at only 500,000 or 2.5 percent of the union total. This representational incongruity and mainland threats to eliminate it helped to fuel heated debates in the late 1980s and early 1990s, on the retention, reorganization, or elimination of the union government. In 1979 the authorities approved a new Zanzibari constitution, which confirmed the islands' semiautonomous governing status by authorizing an elected House of Representatives to enact laws for Zanzibar and Pemba (qq.v.). Three such elections had taken place by the early 1990s.

Just before the 1990 Zanzibari elections, President Idris Abdul Wakil (q.v.) announced his retirement after five years in office. The CCM then nominated Salim Amour (q.v.) as the islands' sole presidential candidate. He won approximately 98 percent of the vote. Opposition elements claimed that numerous irregularities plagued the election and that Amour received the support of only 65 percent of eligible voters.

Tanzania's first multiparty elections, held in 1995, reflected a decisive contest between political and economic reformers and socialist hard-liners and between those who favored a continuation of the union and those who wanted to terminate it. In the end, pro-union candidates triumphed by a narrow margin. Also, see ELECTIONS, TANGANYIKA TERRITORY, TANGANYIKA, TANZANIA; and ZANZIBAR HOUSE OF REPRESENTATIVES.

ELIUFOO, SOLOMON NKYA (1920–1971). Born at Machame on the southern slopes of Mount Kilimanjaro (q.v.), Eliufoo was educated locally and at Tanga (q.v.) Secondary School. Following the completion of his secondary education in 1940, he studied at Makerere University (q.v.), from which he earned an education diploma in 1943. After remaining at Makerere for a two-year teaching assignment, Eliufoo served as secretary and treasurer to the Lutheran Church from 1946 until 1953, following which he left for the United States for two years of study at Bethany College, Kansas. Before returning to TT, Eliufoo also studied for a time at Bristol University in England. Upon his return, he taught at Marangu Teacher Training Centre near Moshi (q.v.) and also served as education assistant to the Lutheran Church of Northern Tanganyika. Eliufoo's political career began when he won a LEGCO (q.v.) seat in the 1958–1959 territorial election. On 1 July 1958 he was named unofficial minister of health, a post he held until late 1960. Continuing to represent Moshi as an MP, Eliufoo became the first president of the Chagga Council in 1960 and was appointed as Tanganyika's second minister of education in 1962. He held this position until 1968, when failing health forced his resignation.

EMPLOYMENT. By 1910 more than 70,000 Africans were in formal employment, and the number working for Europeans, Asians, and Arabs (qq.v.) increased to about 172,000 by 1913. Of these, some 80,000 worked on plantations, 20,000 as porters, 21,000 for railway companies, 10,000 for commercial firms, 9,000 in domestic service, and 6,000 for the police. By 1945 about 340,000 Africans were engaged in regular employment, many as migrant laborers, and by 1961 this number had risen to about 500,000. Wages remained low, however, so that in 1961 97 percent of all formal-sector workers earned less than Shs.700 (US$100) per month.

By 1965 only 3.5 percent of Tanzania's labor force had jobs paying salaries or hourly wages, and despite a proliferation of parastatal corporations following the Arusha Declaration (q.v.), job creation remained low. In 1978, for example, the working-age population (those in the 15- to 64-year-old group) comprised 48.5 percent of the total population and was estimated to be growing at an average annual rate of 3.5 percent, adding about 380,000 people to the labor force each year. Between 1983 and 1986, however, only 43,342 new jobs were created in the formal employment sector. This lack of opportunity gave rise to considerable growth in Tanzania's informal, "second" economy, including all production and exchange, legal and illegal, not accounted for in national statistics and not officially regulated or taxed. According to some estimates, in 1986 the informal economy accounted for Shs.39 billion (US$975 million) or about 31.4 percent of the Tanzanian GNP. By 1988 economically active Tanzanians numbered an estimated 10.5 million, of whom 703,684 (or 7 percent) were engaged in formal wage employment. In the early 1990s the World Bank (q.v.) estimated that the labor force totaled 14 million people, more than 80 percent of whom worked in the agricultural sector, primarily as subsistence farmers.

ETHNIC GROUPS. See PEOPLE.

EUROPEAN EDUCATION. Before World War II, most European children were sent to the United Kingdom or to continental Europe for their education. During the war the colonial government established a temporary school at Mbeya, and students also attended European schools in Kenya, Rhodesia, and South Africa. After World War II new settlers, traders, and government employees demanded a local secondary educational facility and paid a per capita annual property tax of £20 to finance a new school. The authorities also allocated one-fifth of the money collected as German war reparations to build the St. Michael's and St. George's Grammar School near Iringa (q.v.). In June 1957 TT's special representative to the UN promised that the school would eventually become nonracial, and in 1960 the first African and Asian students were enrolled.

After independence European enrollments fell, and the property tax was no longer available to finance the school. The Tanzanian government took control of St. Michael's and St. George's and then closed it in 1963 because of its failure fully to integrate the student body as well as for financial reasons. Since then new waves of expatriate workers in Tanzania have given rise to several international primary schools to service this community. Expatriates typically send their children back to their home countries for secondary and higher education.

EUROPEANS. The Germans intended the GEA to serve as a haven for European settlement. By 1907 the number of Europeans (loosely defined as Caucasians, from whatever parts of the world) had reached 2,772. Germans constituted 70 percent of this early population, which included 303 missionaries, 168 professional soldiers, 319 government officials, and the remainder settlers, traders, and company officials. In 1905 200 Afrikaners migrated from South Africa and acquired farms averaging 2,500 acres (1,000 hectares) per family. New settlement continued to increase, so that by 1912 4,744 Europeans resided in GEA, including a new influx of Greek, Dutch, and Danish plantation owners. Still, by the outbreak of World War I (q.v.), Europeans and European companies occupied less than 1 percent of the land.

After the war Britain consolidated its rule in East Africa. TT was a Mandated Territory of the League of Nations and later a UN Trust Territory, rather than an outright British colonial possession. As such, it was less attractive to European settlers and business interests than were the politically more secure and temperate Kenya highlands, mineral-rich Rhodesia, and semi-independent South Africa. As a British Protectorate superimposed upon and preserving a local Arab dictatorship, Zanzibar proved even less hospitable to large-scale European settlement, which never reached more than a few hundred people. On the mainland, the European population totaled about 8,000 in 1930 and reached 10,648 in the census year of 1948, or 0.1 percent of TT's population. Rising to 20,534 in 1957, the number of Europeans reached an all-time high of about 22,700 (0.2 percent of the total population) at independence. From that time, Europeans have formed a shrinking community of increasingly diverse and largely temporary residents in Tanzania, heavily represented by foreign-aid workers and, more recently, by business representatives.

EVANGELICAL LUTHERAN CHURCH IN TANZANIA (ELCT). In 1963 the various Lutheran Church groups in Tanzania amalgamated and formed this organization. The ELCT consists of the Synods of the South, Central, Eastern and Coast, Kenya, Arusha Region, Mbulu, and Ulanga Kilombero, and the Dioceses of the North, Northwest, and Pare. Each synod is led by a prescient and each diocese by its bishop. These heads confer in executive committees and in conference. The ELCT is a member of the Lutheran World Federation and the World Council of Churches. In Tanzania, it created its own magazine, *Uhuru na Amani* (Freedom and Peace), a radio station, "Voice of the Gospel," the Makumira Theological College, a training seminary, and a medical school. Until Tanzanian schools were nationalized in 1970, ELCT churches managed about one-sixth of the country's educational services. Operating 15 hospitals and 71 dispensaries, the ELCT also provided approximately 10 percent of Tanzanian medical services. In 1975 ELCT churches included 380 African pastors, 47 missionaries, 2,242 evangelists, and more than 700,000 adherents. By the early 1990s Bishop Samson Mushemba led a membership of about 1.5 million.

EVERY HOME EVANGELISM, TANZANIA. See CHRISTIAN COUNCIL OF TANGANYIKA (TANZANIA).

EXECUTIVE BRANCH OF GOVERNMENT, GERMAN EAST AFRICA. Following an 1890 agreement to end the rule of the German East Africa Company (q.v.), the German Reich in 1891 accepted administrative responsibility for GEA. Having already represented the German chancellor as Reich commissioner, Hermann von Wissmann (q.v.) hoped to become the colony's first governor. He was disappointed, however, as Governors Julius von Soden and Friedrich von Schele (qq.v.) created a framework for German administration between 1891 and 1895. Wissmann finally served as governor in 1895 and 1896.

At the head of the German administration was a governor, who had the power to issue decrees and was responsible for enforcing German laws (*Gesetze*), imperial edicts (*Verordnungen*), and the chancellor's instructions. In a departure from standard German practice at home, the governor's authority was almost unilaterally extended to the determination of when and how to deploy the colony's *Schütztruppe* (q.v.) (Protective Forces). The civil administration consisted of individual departments, including Finance, Surveying and Agriculture, Public Works, Justice, and Medicine. German-managed local government evolved from a reliance on treaties with local African notables and on military posts established at centers of European interest, into a three-tiered arrangement of European officials supervising indigenous *akidas* and *jumbes* (qq.v.). This system persisted through the administrations of Governors Wissmann, Eduard von Liebert, and Count Adolf von Götzen (qq.v.), from 1895 to 1906.

The Maji-Maji Rebellion (q.v.) occurred in southern GEA between 1905 and 1907. The physical devastation, loss of life, and financial reversals caused by the uprising and its suppression created a public outcry in Germany, which led to the creation of a colonial office in Berlin and to the appointment in 1906 of Baron Albrecht von Rechenberg (q.v.) as GEA's first civilian governor. This professional diplomat and former German consul in Zanzibar also had served as a judge in GEA and quickly established himself as an able administrator and champion of African over European socioeconomic interests in the colony. He instituted educational, health, and labor reforms—all of which were opposed by the settler community—on behalf of his goal of developing GEA as an African-oriented commercial enterprise and not as a settler-dominated plantation economy. Rechenberg also lost the support of local military officers when he proposed a reduction in the size of the *Schütztruppe*. He was finally replaced in 1912 by GEA's last German governor, Heinrich Schnee (q.v.), who restored harmonious relations between the government and the settlers, and who served until the British removed him and other German administrative officers in 1916, during the East African Campaign of World War I (q.v.).

EXECUTIVE BRANCH OF GOVERNMENT, TANGANYIKA AND TANZANIA. TT's last two colonial governors, Sir Edward Twining and Sir Richard Turnbull (qq.v.), heavily influenced the configuration of Tanganyika's post-independence government. Twining attempted to fashion a "multiracial" government patterned after what was also being sought in Kenya Colony and in the Federation of Rhodesia and Nyasaland. This effort failed in the election of 1958–1959, which confirmed the overwhelming popular support enjoyed by TANU (q.v.) and its leader, Julius Nyerere (q.v.). Turnbull, on the other hand, made it clear that his predecessor's insistence on multiracialism was a temporary expedient and that, after the attainment of internal self-government, the Executive Council and LEGCO (qq.v.) would consist primarily of Africans. Accordingly, the colonial government created the Council of Ministers after the 1960 election, an executive agency based for the first time on an unofficial majority of African members.

After independence the government initially accepted a British-devised constitution. It provided for a parliamentary system modeled after Britain's and presupposed a permanent civil service designed to influence policy formulation and implementation. A cabinet replaced the Council of Ministers, and some Europeans were appointed to ministerial and other senior administrative posts until suitable African replacements could be recruited. In 1962 Nyerere resigned from the prime ministership and began the process of Africanizing the civil service. In November 1962 Tanganyika changed its governing system from a parliamentary to a presidential form and withdrew as a British Dominion, although it remained within the Commonwealth of Nations. On 9 December 1962 Nyerere easily won a presidential election and became the Republic of Tanganyika's first president.

In 1964 Nyerere appointed a presidential commission to investigate the formation of a one-party state in Tanganyika. The commission's report led to the adoption in 1965 of the Interim Constitution of the United Republic of Tanzania. This basic law, which remained in effect until 1977, recognized the union of Tanganyika and Zanzibar (q.v.) and acknowledged Tanzania as a de jure one-party state under TANU's leadership on the mainland and Afro-Shirazi Party (ASP) (q.v.) control in Zanzibar. Before and after the Arusha Declaration (q.v.) of 1967, the scope of the party-government's executive hegemony was progressively widened to include formerly autonomous trade unions, rural cooperative societies, and private business firms. Eventually most of the latter were organized into more than 400 parastatal corporations, resulting in the rapid growth of the country's central bureaucracy. In 1972 governmental authority was further expanded and centralized with the abolition of semiautonomous regional, district, and local government organizations.

With the 1977 merger of TANU and ASP into the CCM (q.v.), the Permanent Constitution of the United Republic of Tanzania replaced the Interim Constitution. This document reasserted single-party rule and enabled Zanzibaris for the first time to elect representatives to the National Assembly (q.v.). Real legislative as well as executive authority, however, was concentrated in the CCM Central Committee (CC) (q.v.), exercising power through a cabinet of more than 20 ministerial posts and through its own regional and district executive and working committees. Some local autonomy was returned in 1982 with the reinstatement of district councils and cooperative societies; and in 1992, the government amended the Permanent Constitution to allow for the creation of competing political parties. Yet by the early 1990s the Tanzanian presidential republic remained highly centralized and was still dominated by its CCM-led executive branch.

EXECUTIVE BRANCH OF GOVERNMENT, TANGANYIKA TER-RITORY. In 1919, at the end of World War I's (q.v.) East African Campaign, Sir Horace Byatt (q.v.) became administrator of GEA. On 22 July 1920 a Tanganyika Order in Council changed Byatt's position from administrator to governor and commander in chief, with the power to make policies for the renamed territory, subject to the approval of the British colonial secretary. The following year, the Belgian government accepted a League of Nations Mandate over the western region of Ruanda-Urundi (q.v.), and in July 1922 Great Britain accepted a similar mandate over Tanganyika. Both territories were to be administered in the interests of "peace, order and good government" and of "the material and moral well-being and social progress of the inhabitants." In fact if not in actual ownership, Britain had gained another colonial possession and now governed all of what is now Tanzania.

Byatt established a civil administration for TT, which included an Executive Council consisting of a chief secretary, attorney-general, treasurer, and principal medical officer, along with a criminal and civil High Court, and a temporary Special Tribunal to deal with cases arising before the Order in Council was adopted. The British at first retained the German system of local administration, although British local government officers were granted wide latitude in the development of their own policies.

In 1921 and 1923 the colonial government enacted two Native Authority Ordinances (qq.v.) that presaged the indirect rule (q.v.) policy introduced early in the governorship of Sir Donald Cameron (q.v.) and codified in the Native Authority Ordinance of 1927 (q.v.). In December 1927 Cameron also presided over the creation of TT's first LEGCO (q.v.). Although the European settler community pressed for an administrative union with Kenya and the Ormsby-Gore and Hilton-Young Commissions (qq.v.) recommended a closer union of Britain's East African colonial entities, Cameron managed to retain TT as an independently administered territory. This autonomy did not preclude TT's subsequent participation in the East African High Commission (EAHC) (q.v.) and still later in the East African Common Services Organization (EACSO) (q.v.). In all other respects, TT was governed essentially as Byatt and Cameron had intended until after World War

II (q.v.), under the administrations of four short-term governors—Sir George Stewart Symes , Sir Harold MacMichael, Sir Mark Aitchison Young, and Sir Wilfred Edward Jackson (qq.v.).

On 13 December 1946 TT's League of Nations Mandate was transferred to the UN, converting it into a UN Trust Territory with Britain as the administering power. The office of governor now headed an expanded executive, assisted by an Executive Council (q.v.) composed of nine official and seven unofficial members. Ex officio official members included the chief secretary, attorney-general, and financial secretary/minister for finance and economics. Nominated official members were the ministers for constitutional affairs, natural resources, local government and administration, lands and mineral resources, social services, and communications and works. The Executive Council's unofficial members consisted of two Europeans, two Asians, and three Africans. TT's laws were enacted by the governor with the advice of the Executive Council and the limited advice and consent of the LEGCO. Central government was further divided into 32 administrative and technical departments, including the Provincial Administration, central government's chief link to provincial, district, and native authority administrations. Provincial commissioners administered eight provinces while district commissioners and district officers governed 54 districts and Dar es Salaam, all responsible to the governor. District officers supervised the affairs of the Native Authorities, many of which by the late 1940s comprised "chiefs-in-council" with commoner representation on the councils.

By the late 1950s TT's executive branch of government was staffed by a nonracial civil service consisting of about 2,800 Europeans, 1,500 Asians, and 23,000 Africans (the latter still primarily confined to subordinate posts). Also participating in law enforcement was a system of Local (formerly Native) Courts, District Courts, and Her Majesty's High Court. Further recourse from the High Court was to the Court of Appeal for Eastern Africa.

EXECUTIVE BRANCH OF GOVERNMENT, ZANZIBAR PROTECTORATE. After the declaration of the Zanzibar Protectorate (q.v.) in the Anglo-German Agreement of 1890 (q.v.), the British agent and consul-general, Sir Charles Bean Euan-Smith, explained to Seyyid Ali ibn Said (q.v.) that under its terms, the sultan would transfer control over foreign relations to the British government in exchange for a British guarantee that the sultanate would be protected and passed on to future generations. Euan-Smith failed to mention the limited extent of the sultanate's future control over Zanzibari domestic affairs, but his successor, Sir Gerald Portal, reacted against what he considered to be a slave-owning Arab despotism by seizing control of the sultanate's finances and administration. Portal appointed Europeans to head the treasury, the army and police, public works, and the post office and customs. He also appointed Sir Lloyd W. Mathews (q.v.) as the sultan's "first minister," to coordinate domestic affairs. This regime continued into the consul generalship of James Rennell Rodd, who also rejected Seyyid Khalid ibn Barghash's (q.v.) traditional claim to the sultanate following Seyyid Ali's death and instead installed a contender professing pro-British sentiments, Seyyid Hamed ibn Thwain (q.v.). In a subsequent attempt to regain some power, Seyyid Hamed created a large personal bodyguard which, under British military threat, he quickly disbanded. Seyyid Hamed died in 1896, and Seyyid Khalid made another bid for the throne by seizing the sultan's palace. The Royal Navy bombarded the palace, forcing Seyyid Khalid to take refuge in the German consulate. The British agent and consul general at the time, Sir Arthur Henry Hardinge, appointed another Anglophile, Seyyid Hamoud ibn Muhammad (q.v.) as sultan. Hardinge easily controlled him because Seyyid Hamoud's friendliness toward the British earned him scant Arab support. From this point until Zanzibari independence, the sultan's sovereignty amounted to little more than a polite legal fiction.

In 1913 the Foreign Office transferred administrative responsibility of Zanzibar (q.v.) to the Colonial Office (CO), which created the post of British resident to replace the offices of agent, consul general, and first minister. The CO also placed the new position under the general oversight of the governor of the East Africa Protectorate, later Kenya Colony. In addition, the CO established a Protectorate Council to advise the sultan, with the resident serving as vice president. The British chief secretary, attorney general, treasurer, and three unofficial members drawn mostly from the local Arab community also served on the council. These arrangements remained in place until 1925, when the Resident replaced the governor of Kenya as Zanzibar's direct link to the CO. An Executive Council was also established in that year, composed of the sultan and senior members of the central administration.

During the depression of the 1930s the CO dispatched Sir Alan Pim to Zanzibar with instructions to recommend reforms on how to reduce the protectorate's costs and increase its revenues. Part of Pim's recommendations involved the establishment of a cost-saving indirect rule (q.v.) system of local government similar to that adopted in TT. Accordingly, in 1934 the colonial authorities organized Zanzibari local government into administrative districts, each presided over by a *mudir* (headman). *Mudirs*, in turn, were supported by *shehas* (magistrates) selected by village *wazee* (elders). Local councils, consisting of *mudirs* and *wazee* chosen by their villages, had the power to spend monies collected from hut taxes. Zanzibar town also received its own governing board with official and unofficial representation. Between 1944 and 1947 other town and rural councils were established to facilitate popular participation in government at the local level. At the central level, the Zanzibari LEGCO (q.v.) gradually expanded to include representatives of the African majority.

The most significant change of the 1940s concerned the establishment of His Highness's Zanzibar Service for the training of a Zanzibari administrative cadre to supplement and eventually replace British officers in a modernized Sultanate. Until anti-Arab nationalism finally overtook Zanzibar, African demands were mostly limited to more employment opportunities in the Sultan's government, rather than to self-government based on majoritarian principles.

EXECUTIVE COUNCIL. Established on 31 August 1920 to advise and to assist the governor in administering TT. The Executive Council initially consisted of four ex officio members, but by the last years of colonial rule this number had increased to eight ex officio and nominated official members. The ex officio members were the chief secretary, attorney general, and financial secretary. Nominated official members included representatives from the Departments of Social Services; Local Government; Lands and Mines; Agricultural and Natural Resources; and Communications, Works, and Development Planning.

In 1939 the governor supplemented the council's official representation by appointing four unofficial members (three Europeans and one Asian) to offer responsible criticism of government policy. The colonial government reorganized the Executive Council three subsequent times (in 1948, 1954, and 1959), to change its composition or to alter its powers. As of 1 October 1960 a newly created Council of Ministers assumed all functions of the Executive Council, which then ceased to exist.

EXPORTS. Agricultural products always have contributed the largest share of Tanzania's exports. In 1958 sisal (q.v.) accounted for 27 percent of total export value, coffee (q.v.) for 19 percent, and diamonds (q.v.) for 11 percent. At independence in 1961 sisal exports continued to lead other commodities at 29 percent of total value, with coffee and cotton (q.v.) each contributing 14 percent and diamonds 12 percent. By 1964 these top four exports together claimed more than 70 percent of the country's export earnings, but drastically falling world prices for sisal dropped it to third place, behind cotton and coffee, in 1966. By 1975 nearly 70 percent of Tanzania's export value was earned by six major primary commodities: coffee (19 percent), cotton (12 percent), Zanzibari cloves (q.v.) (12 percent), sisal (12 percent), diamonds (7 percent), and cashew (q.v.) (7 percent). In 1986 coffee export earnings totaled about US$185 million but were sharply reduced by the suspension of the International Coffee Agreement quota system, and in 1991 totaled only US$77 million. An upswing in world coffee prices in 1994 promised to increase the value of Tanzania's coffee exports.

Manufactured exports grew from US$39 million in 1986 to more than US$70 million in 1991. Mineral exports also registered a significant increase, rising from US$13 million in 1986 to nearly US$42 million in 1991. Other exports reflected similar trends. Cotton (US$30 million in 1986 to US$63 million in 1991); tea (q.v.) (about US$14 million in 1986 to almost US$22 million in 1991); tobacco (q.v.) (US$15 million in 1986 to approximately US$17 million in 1991); cashew (US$15 million in 1986 to about US$17 million in 1991); and petroleum products (less than US$5 million in 1986 to approximately US$7 million in 1991).

In the early 1990s the main destinations of Tanzanian exports included Germany, the United Kingdom, India, the Netherlands, Japan, Portugal, and Belgium-Luxembourg. In 1993 the value of these exports totaled US$420 million.

— **F** —

FATUMA, QUEEN. In the late seventeenth century, she came to the throne of Zanzibar (q.v.) and reigned intermittently until 1711. Fatuma married Abdullah, "king" of Utondwe (an Arab settlement, influenced by Mombasa, located south of Sadani on the mainland coast), to whom she bore a son, Hassan. She remained loyal to the Portuguese claimants to the coastal region at a time when all other East African Arab rulers had joined the rising Omani challenge to Portuguese rule. During the Omani attack on Fort Jesus at Mombasa in 1696, Fatuma arranged for food to be sent to the besieged fortress. In retaliation, Omani Arabs raided Zanzibar, forcing the queen and her followers to flee into the bush. When Fort Jesus fell to the Arabs in 1698, the retreating Portuguese left her behind in Zanzibar. The victorious Arabs captured her and her son and transported them as prisoners to Oman. Fatuma was permitted to return to Zanzibar in 1709, and she died there sometime between 1711 and 1728.

FIRST WORLD WAR. See WORLD WAR I.

FISHING. By the middle to late 1950s, Lakes Tanganyika, Rukwa, and Victoria (qq.v.) yielded an annual fish catch of about 50,000 tons, most of which consisted of *dagaa* and several varieties of *Tilapia* consumed mainly in TT. The total value of the catch was approximately £2 million (US$5.7 million) annually. At independence, most of the deepwater fisheries of Lakes Victoria and Tanganyika remained untouched and contained an estimated 30,000-ton yearly crop if exploited on an ecologically sustainable basis. Marine fisheries in Zanzibar and Pemba (qq.v.) yielded an additional 2,000 tons of fish each year, valued between £100,000 and £150,000 (US$286,000 and US$428,000). Supported by the Nyegezi Fisheries Institute near Mwanza (q.v.), by 1974 Lake Malawi (q.v.) fisheries produced more than 5,000 tons of fish, valued at Shs.6.6 million (US$825,000). In 1976 the parastatal Nyanza Fishing and Processing Company opened a large factory to process fish meal from the small Lake Victoria fish *Haplochromis*, but its full capacity of 3,500 tons per year, worth Shs.10.5 million (US$1.3 million), was never reached. In more recent years the Tanzania Fisheries Corporation has devised numerous plans to facilitate the greater exploitation of marine life. However, a lack of resources has prevented the corporation from achieving this goal. In the early 1990s many ecologists and scientists warned that pollution posed an increasing threat to Tanzania's lakes and rivers. By 1995 the Tanzanian government had yet to develop a policy to resolve this problem.

FLAMINGO. A tall, long-necked wading bird of the family *Phoenicopteridae*. One of the largest concentrations of flamingos is found at Lake Manyara in the Mbulu District of Arusha Region. At certain times of the year their numbers are so great that they form a line of shimmering pink stretching for several miles.

FOREIGN RELATIONS. After independence, Tanzanian foreign relations focused on three major goals: the establishment of majoritarian rule in southern Africa, the preservation of a friendly but politically nonaligned relationship with both major power blocs, and the encouragement of political and economic cooperation among African and other Third World countries. In its ultimately successful pursuit of the first objective, Tanzania served as headquarters of the Organization of African Unity's (OAU) African Liberation Committee and also hosted national liberation organizations committed to the independence of Mozambique, Namibia, South Africa, and Zimbabwe. Tanzania was also instrumental in the founding of the Front-Line African States for southern African liberation, the Southern African Development Coordination Conference (SADCC) (q.v.), and SADCC's successor, the Southern African Development Community (SADC). The country was likewise a member of the now defunct Preferential Trade

Area for Eastern and Southern African States (PTA) (q.v.), and, with brief interruptions, it has maintained generally friendly relations with its closest neighbors in the eastern African region. As one of Africa's leading senior statesmen, Julius Nyerere (q.v.) has served as chairman of the Front-Line African States and the OAU and has played a prominent role in the more broadly based Non-Aligned Movement of Third World states.

Although recording successes on all three fronts, Tanzanian foreign policies have not always produced positive results. SADC and the PTA's successor, the Common Market of Eastern and Southern African States (COMESA) (q.v.), remain somewhat fragile collaborative organizations. Moreover, the close economic cooperation that characterized relations among Tanzania, Kenya, and Uganda during the immediate postcolonial period never fully recovered from the 1977 collapse of the East African Community (EAC) (q.v.). Tanzania's politically nonaligned status has also been compromised by chronic foreign-aid dependency and by donor interventions into the domestic policy process, which have continued into the post–cold war period. Tanzania is among Africa's largest recipients of international economic assistance, including bilateral aid from countries represented in the Organization for Economic Cooperation and Development (OECD), and multilateral transfers from the International Bank for Reconstruction and Development (IBRD) (World Bank) (q.v.), the World Bank's International Development Association (IDA), and the International Monetary Fund (IMF). In addition, many reforms and structural adjustments introduced into the economy during the 1980s—embodied, for example, in the Structural Adjustment Programme (SAP) and the Economic Recovery Programme (ERP), (q.v.)—resulted more from donor mandates than from internal initiatives. Discontentment with these influences played a role in Julius Nyerere's decisions to step down as president in 1985 and to retire as CCM (q.v.) chairman in 1990.

From the early 1990s, Tanzania joined with other developing countries in supporting the establishment of an international order more favorable to the interests of small and weak national economies. Its policy position has advocated the stabilization of international prices for primary commodities, balance-of-payments relief for countries suffering from unfavorable trade balances, and gradually paced international debt settlements, together with domestic economic reforms and structural adjustments and improved access to developed countries' markets and technologies. Also, see CURRENCY; and ECONOMY.

FORESTRY. More than two-fifths of Tanzania's land area, some 160,000 square miles (400,000 square kilometers), is forested. Most of these tracts consist of open savanna woodlands, termed *miombo,* which are the main source of locally consumed fuel wood, charcoal, and building poles. The country also contains about 3,600 square miles (9,000 square kilometers) of high-altitude rain forests and 600 square miles (1,500 square kilometers) of coastal mangrove swamps. In the late 1970s all rain forests and approximately 48,000 square miles (120,000 square kilometers) of the remaining forested land were protected in about 500 government reserves, including about 6,400 square miles (16,000 square kilometers) set aside as catchment areas at the headwaters of major rivers and seasonal streams.

Although the colonial government began a limited forest plantation program in the late 1950s that was continued after independence, Tanzania's commercial forest-products industry has remained small. During the 1970s about 17.5 million cubic feet (500,000 cubic meters) of fuel and building materials were produced for domestic use, and, with the addition of a new paper and pulp industry, a period of slow expansion was projected for the 1980s and beyond. To ensure sustainability of resource use, the government also introduced afforestation and reforestation measures to village communities by providing their residents with seedlings and technical assistance.

FRANCISCAN FRIARS. These were the first Christian missionaries to reach what is now mainland Tanzania. In 1505 they established a mission at Kilwa Kisiwani (q.v.), at the start of Portugal's brief occupation of this Arab city-state. In 1513 the Franciscan mission failed when the Arabs retook Kilwa, ending further missionary activity along the coast until the second half of the nineteenth century.

FUNDIKIRA, CHIEF ABDULLAH SAID (b. 1921). Fundikira was born in Tabora of the ruling family of the Nyamwezi, the country's second largest indigenous society. His predecessors included Said, who amassed a large trading empire during the reign of Zanzibari Sultan Said ibn Seyyid (q.v.), and Mgalula, whose flamboyant governing style at first epitomized and later compromised the indirect rule policy of Sir Donald Cameron (qq.v.). He received an education at the Tanga School (q.v.) in 1938 and 1939, and at Makerere University (q.v.) in Uganda between 1940 and 1944. In 1953 and 1954, he also studied agriculture at Cambridge University in Great Britain.

After returning to TT, Fundikira served as the country's first African agricultural officer in Lake and Southern Provinces. In 1957 he succeeded his brother as chief of Unyanyembe. Bearing responsibility for about 150,000 subjects, he held this office until 1962. In 1958 Fundikira was elected unopposed to the LEGCO (q.v.), and the following year he was appointed minister of land and surveys. In 1960 he was reelected to the LEGCO, and in April 1961 became minister of legal affairs and subsequently minister of justice. In 1963 Fundikira was named chairman of the Tanganyika Development Corporation. Before his retirement in 1973, Fundikira's subsequent public service included the presidencies of the Tanganyika Red Cross and the Tanganyika Society for the Prevention of Cruelty to Animals, and the chairmanship of the Board of Directors for East African Airways (EAA).

After Julius Nyerere (q.v.) decided to institute a permanent one-party state, Fundikira resigned as minister of justice and withdrew his membership from the CCM (q.v.). For nearly two decades, Fundikira played no further role in Tanzanian politics. In 1991 he reemerged as the leader of an opposition party, the Union for Multi-Party Democracy (UMD). Among other goals, this party called for the establishment of a free market economy and an end to the Tanzanian military's participation in politics.

— G —

GABACHOLIS. A pejorative term used to describe Tanzanians of Indian or Pakistani origin.

GAME RESERVES. Nine percent of Tanzania's land area, some 33,380 square miles (83,450 square kilometers), is set aside for 17 game reserves in which hunting is by limited permit only and human settlement generally prohibited. They complement 11 national parks and one conservation area in which hunting and settlement are generally prohibited, and 50 game-controlled areas in which settlement and licensed hunting are allowed, to form Tanzania's considerable range of wildlife-protected areas. More than 16,000 square miles (40,000 square kilometers) are claimed by national parks and conservation areas, and a further 49,200 square miles (123,000 square kilometers) by game-controlled areas, bringing to 28 percent the proportion of the country's mainland area wholly or partly devoted to wildlife protection. Also, see individual National Parks: ARUSHA, GOMBE, KATAVI, LAKE MANYARA, MIKUMI, MOUNT KILIMANJARO, RUAHA, RUBONDO ISLAND, SERENGETI, TARANGIRE, UDZUNGWA MOUNTAINS, AND NGORONGORO CONSERVATION AREA.

GENERAL ENTRANCE EXAMINATION. Before and immediately after independence, successful completion of this examination was required for entry into Standard VIII, the highest level of presecondary formal education. The Ministry of Education's examinations officer devised the test and administered it on a regional basis. The examination was given in English and consisted of papers written in mathematics, English, and "general knowledge." In 1967 the government changed the name of the test to the Primary School Leaving Examination, in anticipation of a change in Tanzanian policy toward universal education with more localized content and with Swahili as the primary medium of instruction.

GEORGES, PHILIP TELFORD (b. 1923). Born in the West Indies, Georges served as chief justice of Tanzania during the first decade of independence. From 1942 to 1947 he attended Canada's McGill University and the University of Toronto, from which he received a B.A. (Honours) degree in law. In 1949 he entered the Middle Temple, London, and in the same year opened a private practice in Trinidad. In 1962 Georges was appointed as Judge of the Supreme Court of Trinidad and Tobago and in 1965 was seconded to Tanzania to assume the position of chief justice. Before returning to Trinidad in 1971, he was awarded an honorary doctorate of law by the University of Dar es Salaam (q.v.) and an earned doctorate of law from the University of Toronto.

GERMAN ADMINISTRATION. Unlike the British indirect rule (q.v.) system, a kind of direct rule was practiced in GEA. Under the latter scheme, the Germans divided the colony into 19 civil and two military districts, each under a district administrator or *Bezirksamtmann*. Within each district, central government officials known as *akidas* (q.v.) administered groups of villages, and *jumbes* (q.v.) oversaw individual villages. Under this highly centralized administrative arrangement, the indigenous population was excluded from participation in local government.

GERMAN ADMINISTRATORS, COMMISSIONERS, MILITARY COMMANDERS, AND GOVERNORS OF GERMAN EAST AFRICA (1885–1918).

Administrators:
Peters, Carl (1885–1888)
Commissioners:
Wissmann, Captain Hermann von (1888–1891)
Military Commanders:
Wissmann, Captain Hermann von (January–February 1891)
Governors:
Soden, Julius von (1891–1893)

Schele, Colonel Friedrich von (1893–1895)
Wissmann, Captain Hermann von (1895–1896)
Liebert, General Eduard von (1896–1901)
Götzen, Count Adolf von (1901–1906)
Rechenberg, Baron Albrecht von (1906–1912)
Schnee, Heinrich (1912–1918)

Also, see entries under each name.

GERMAN EAST AFRICA (*Deutsch Ostafrika*). From 1890 to 1918, this was the name applied to all of what is now mainland Tanzania, Rwanda, and Burundi.

GERMAN EAST AFRICA COMPANY (*Deutsch-Ostafrikanische Gesellschaft*). The Society for German Colonization (*Gesellschaft für Deutsche Kolonisation*) began the German colonization of East Africa. In 1884 it dispatched an expedition led by Carl Peters (q.v.) and two other agents, who signed access treaties with local African leaders in the hinterland between the coastal towns of Pangani and Kingani. In February 1885 the German government granted the society a charter permitting the exploitation of these territories. Sultan Barghash ibn Said (q.v.) protested that these "possessions" lay in his jurisdiction and sent troops to confirm his presence. In response, the Germans mounted a naval demonstration off Zanzibar (q.v.), which compelled the sultan to recognize the society's inland claims. In a treaty concluded in December 1885 between the sultan and the German government, Barghash also agreed to German trading rights at Dar es Salaam (q.v.) and Pangani and duty-free passage through the sultan's coastal lands to the interior.

To further German commercial interests against continuing Arab resistance, Peters helped to transform the Colonization Society into the German East Africa Company. Incorporated in 1887/88, the company inherited a precarious financial position along with 10 stations consisting of trading posts and European agricultural estates. Count Otto Pfeil, another company director, visited these sites and concluded that all were economically untenable. Peters decided that, for the German East Africa Company to exploit the resources of the interior, it would have to secure control over the coastal area ruled by the sultan. Accordingly, in 1888 the company raised its flag and began collecting customs duties at several coastal towns. This prompted a popular Arab revolt, led by Bushiri ibn Salim al-Harthi and Bwana Heri ibn Juma (qq.v.), which threatened to overwhelm the sultan's troops and the German East Africa Company's *askaris* (q.v.). At this point, German Chancellor Otto von Bismarck appointed Captain Hermann von Wissmann (q.v.) as Reich commissioner and authorized him to assemble a force to put down the rebellion. By early 1891 Wissmann had suppressed the Arab revolt.

In the meantime, Peters, two of his colleagues, and Emin Pasha (q.v.) had managed to establish German East Africa Company stations as far west as Bukoba (q.v.). On the other hand, the Anglo-German Agreement of 1886, the Anglo-German Agreement of 1890 (qq.v.), and Wissmann's suppression of the Arab revolt had already persuaded the German government to strip the German East Africa Company of any governing authority it might claim and to limit the company to commercial activities. This decision was confirmed in an agreement reached on 20 November 1890 and implemented on 1 January 1891. The company retained many privileges, however, including first rights to upcountry lands and railway concessions, and the right to establish its own bank, to issue currency, to raise loans in Germany, and to be compensated at no less than 600,000 marks per year from customs revenues.

By April 1888 the German East Africa Company, operating from the ports of Pangani and Dar es Salaam, has established 18 trading posts in the interior. In addition, the *Deutsch-Ostafrikanische Plantagengesellschaft* (German East African Plantations Society), a German East Africa Company subsidiary, had established a tobacco (q.v.) plantation near Pangani. On 1 January 1891 the German East Africa Company relinquished control of GEA to the German Reich.

GERMAN-PORTUGUESE AGREEMENT OF 1886. This treaty fixed the southern German boundary along a line proceeding southwestward from the mouth of the Ruvuma River, which today forms the border between mainland Tanzania and Mozambique. It should be noted, however, that the area south of the Ruvuma was not formally ceded to the Portuguese by the Zanzibari sultanate until after World War I (q.v.).

GOGO. See PEOPLE.

GOLD. Historically, gold was mined over a wide area in what is now mainland Tanzania. In 1922 prospectors discovered substantial deposits in the northwestern districts of Mwanza and Musoma and along the Lupa River near Lake Rukwa. Within a few years, there were operational gold mines in Geita and Musoma districts of Lake Province, others in the Kahama District and the Singida District of Central Province, and the Lupa gold fields in the Chunya District of the Southern Highlands (q.v.) Province. Alluvial gold was also found in the region of the Ruvu River in the Morogoro District of the Eastern

Province, in the Mpanda area of Kigoma District, and at Madengi near Dodoma (q.v.).

In 1938 gold output peaked at more than 100,000 ounces (2.8 million grams), and in 1939 export earnings from gold reached nearly £1 million, an amount exceeded only by sisal earnings. Gold production subsequently declined. By 1966 two of the three major mines became depleted and were closed, and by 1970 two others were nearing exhaustion. Although two new mines were scheduled to become operational during the 1970s, only 84 ounces (2,400 grams) were sold in 1975. In more recent years the Tanzanian government has sought to increase gold production, but a lack of investment resources has thwarted its efforts.

GOMBE NATIONAL PARK. Gazetted in 1968, this park, only 3 miles (5 kilometers) wide and 9 miles (15 kilometers) long, is located about 15 miles (24 kilometers) north of Kigoma (q.v.) on Lake Tanganyika's (q.v.) eastern shore. Gombe is one of the few areas in Africa that harbors chimpanzees. Since 1964 Jane Goodall (q.v.) has operated a research station in Gombe. Her Jane Goodall Institute for Wildlife Research supports wildlife conservation, research, and education, and is particularly concerned with chimpanzees.

GOODALL, JANE (b. 1934). After attending Uplands School, the University of Cambridge, and Oxford University, Goodall accepted a position as an assistant secretary to paleontologist Louis Leaky and worked in Olduvai Gorge (qq.v.). In 1964 Goodall moved to Gombe Stream Game Reserve (now Gombe National Park [q.v.]), and devoted herself to preserving the area for chimpanzees. In 1986 Goodall founded the Committee for Conservation and Care of Chimpanzees, which soon developed an international following. Well-known in part for her numerous publications, Goodall has also received awards from several institutions, including the National Geographic Society and the New York Zoological Society. She also manages the Jane Goodall Institute for Wildlife Research, headquartered in Tanzania.

GORDON, GEORGE BERNARD (b. 1924). Gordon was one of the few senior British civil servants retained after independence. Born in Brighton, England, he joined the British army in 1942 and was seconded to the King's African Rifles (q.v.) from 1944 to 1946. He was appointed an administrative officer in the Tanganyika civil service in 1946 and served as a district commissioner (1949–1952), a community development officer (1953–1955), an establishments (personnel) officer (1956–1960), and chief establishments officer (1961–1962). He became principal of the Civil Service Training Centre, Dar es

Salaam (q.v.), in 1963 and worked there and in other posts until his retirement in the mid-1970s.

GÖTZEN, COUNT ADOLF VON (1866–1910). Supported schemes to establish Afrikaner refugees from the South African Boer War and poor Germans from Russia on the foothills of Mount Meru. Götzen refused to allow European settlers to buy their farms until the land had been cultivated. He is best remembered for his brutal suppression of the Maji-Maji Rebellion (q.v.). While fighting the rebels, Götzen implemented a scorched-earth policy in southern GEA which caused the destruction of a region the size of Germany. During this campaign more than 100,000 men, women, and children died as a result of famine and disease.

GRANT, JAMES AUGUSTUS (1827–1892). An Indian Army officer who served as second in command on John Hanning Speke's (q.v.) 1860–1863 expedition to Lake Victoria (q.v.). During this trip, Grant established a reputation as a botanist by collecting some 750 plant species, which he subsequently presented to the Hookerian Herbarium in England. After Speke's death, Grant published his account of the expedition, titled *A Walk Across Africa*.

GREAT UHURU RAILWAY. See TAZARA RAILWAY.

GROSS DOMESTIC PRODUCT (GDP). Defined as a country's total output of goods and services, TT's GDP was about US$500 million in 1958. Approximately 61 percent derived from commercial and subsistence agriculture (including crops, livestock, forestry, hunting, and fishing), 18 percent from industry (mainly mining, manufacturing, and construction), and 21 percent from public and private services. Tanzania's First Five-Year Plan for Economic and Social Development projected an average annual GDP growth rate of 6.7 percent over the life of the plan, from 1964 to 1969. In fact, however, GDP growth averaged 5.3 percent, and this shortfall was repeated during the second and third plans. Projected growth rates of 6.5 percent (1969–1974) and 6 percent (1976–1981) were matched with actual growth rates of 4.8 percent and 5.9 percent, with per capita GDP growth considerably smaller because of rapid population growth. This uneven but generally downward trend continued as Tanzania faced severe economic hardships throughout the 1980s and into the 1990s, with GDP growth averaging 3.1 percent between 1980 and 1992. During this period agriculture recovered from a dismal 0.7 percent growth rate during the 1970s to an average rate of 3.8 percent, but growth in industry and services slumped from 2.6 percent and 9.0 percent, respectively, to slightly over 2 percent in each sector.

In 1970 Tanzania's GDP stood at US$1.2 billion in current dollars, 40 percent of which was contributed by agriculture, 17 percent by industry, and 42 percent by services. By 1992 the GDP had risen to $2.3 billion, but an average annual inflation rate of over 25 percent acted as a powerful GDP deflator. Following the economic policy reforms of the late 1980s, agriculture's contribution to GDP now totaled 61 percent, with 12 percent contributed by industry and 26 percent by services. This sectoral distribution of GDP was very similar to that recorded in 1958 during the late colonial period. Also, see DEVELOPMENT PLANS; and ECONOMY.

GROUNDNUT SCHEME. This ill-fated agricultural project originated in a suggestion by TT's director of agriculture to the managing director of the United Africa Company, that 20,000 acres (8,000 hectares) of land be planted with groundnuts (peanuts) to help alleviate Britain's post-1945 shortage of margarine fats, and also to provide jobs for thousands of African agricultural workers. Outlined in *A Plan for the Mechanized Production of Groundnuts in East and Central Africa*, the project envisioned the clearing and planting of more than 3 million acres (1.2 million hectares). In 1946 an investigative team sent from Britain proposed three sites, at Urambo in Western Province, Kongwa in Central Province, and Nachingwea in Southern Province.

As the result of a favorable decision taken by the British government, the Groundnut Scheme was implemented in great haste and under the direction of the inexperienced Ministry of Food instead of the Colonial Office. Little research was conducted into local agricultural conditions, and the scheme was implemented as a mechanized endeavor utilizing refurbished war-surplus equipment not well suited to its newly assigned tasks. The British established a target of 150,000 acres (60,000 hectares) for 1947, the first year of operations, but a lack of advance preparation, machinery, and other resources prevented this goal from being attained. By 30 June 1954 local officials had allocated a total of 150,000 acres (60,000 hectares) in Central Province, 180,000 acres (72,000 hectares) in Western Provinces, and 154,000 acres (61,600 hectares) in Southern Province to groundnut production. The British government had already officially abandoned the Groundnut Scheme in 1951, however, after an expenditure of approximately £35 million, £24 million of which was irretrievably lost.

During the late 1950s and early 1960s operations were briefly resumed under the auspices of the Tanganyika Agricultural Corporation

(TAC), but the same logistical and financial problems soon ended this attempt at large-scale, capital-intensive agricultural development.

— H —

HA. See PEOPLE.

HADIMU. One of the African ethnic groups in Zanzibar. The name, meaning "slave," is unfounded because the Hadimu were neither conquered nor enslaved by the dominant Arabs. The Hadimu are of very mixed ethnic origin, consisting of immigrants from different parts of the East African mainland who arrived in Zanzibar (q.v.) at quite different times. Their one common link, providing them a sense of unity, was their loyalty to a single authority figure, the Hadimu *Mwenye Mkuu* (Chief).

After Sultan Said (q.v.) moved his capital to Zanzibar in the first part of the nineteenth century, the general trend was for the Hadimu to be displaced from more fertile areas in the western portion of the island to the less fertile eastern and southern regions. When the *Mwenye Mkuu* himself moved from Zanzibar town, the exodus gained momentum. The final result was a settlement pattern resembling that of a colonial "native reserve," in which the Hadimu could conduct their own affairs while still held subject to the poll tax and other demands of the sultanate. This arrangement changed in 1865, when Sultan Majid (q.v.) forced a merger between the Hadimu and another group, the Tumbatu. Although the Tumbatu resisted subordination to the Hadimu, the uneasy union persisted until after Zanzibar had become a British protectorate in 1890. During the world economic recession of the 1930s, the Hadimu began to gain some economic parity with the Arabs by acquiring land from financially distressed Arab plantation owners.

HAMED IBN THWAIN, SEYYID (c. 1853–1896). Sixth Busaidi (q.v.) ruler of Zanzibar from 1893 to 1896, he fought off two other claimants to the throne. The youngest was Khalid ibn Barghash, son of Seyyid Barghash, and the eldest was Hamoud ibn Muhammad, whose father was Seyyid Said's (qq.v.) second eldest son. The British supported Seyyid Hamed because he acknowledged Queen Victoria as his suzerain, accepted five British officers into his government, and took advice from the British agent and consul general in all matters relating to the slave trade and the government and administration of the Sultanate. In 1895 relations between Seyyid Hamed and the British deteriorated, largely because the British suspected him of providing aid to Omani rebels who opposed the Sultan of Muscat. After Seyyid Hamed's death, Seyyid Khalid launched an unsuccessful rebellion against the British to gain the throne.

HAMERTON TREATY. Signed on 2 October 1845 by Atkins Hamerton, the British consul at Zanzibar (q.v.) from 1841 to 1857, and Seyyid Said (q.v.). This treaty, which came into effect on 1 January 1847, restricted the slave trade to Seyyid Said's East African possessions and outlawed slavery north of Mogadishu. Although it was doomed by numerous vagaries such as whether the treaty permitted trade by sea in Abyssinian slaves, implementation of the Hamerton Treaty began to erode Seyyid Said's power.

HAMOUD IBN MUHAMMAD, SEYYID (1851–1902). Seventh Busaidi (q.v.) ruler of Zanzibar (1896–1902). After thwarting Khalid ibn Barghash's (q.v.) attempt to gain the throne, the British installed Hamoud ibn Muhammad as sultan. Because his position depended on continued British support, Seyyid Hamoud supported all British policy initiatives, including a 6 April 1897 decree that abolished slavery in the Zanzibar Protectorate (q.v.). In exchange for his loyalty, the British awarded Seyyid Hamoud the Grand Cross of (the Order) of St. Michael and St. George (GCMG) and recognized his son, Ali ibn Hamoud (q.v.), as his successor. Seyyid Hamoud is remembered largely for his many reforms and for his determination, in this manner, to Europeanize Zanzibar.

HAYA. See PEOPLE.

HEALTH CARE. Tanzania has a national health care system that offers primary health care at an affordable cost. By the early 1990s, the country had 3,000 rural health facilities, 17 regional hospitals, and three national medical centers. The local pharmaceutical industry consisted of four manufacturers producing about 10 percent of Tanzania's essential drug requirements. The Pharmaceutical Board, acting under the authority of the Pharmaceuticals and Poisons Act of 1978, imported the rest of the country's drug and pharmaceutical needs.

In recent years numerous problems, including foreign exchange shortages, debt service, and a growing population, have created budgetary constraints that in turn have reduced the effectiveness of the health care system. The morale of medical workers has also suffered because of declining real wages, various management and operational problems, and equipment shortages. The lack of foreign exchange has prevented the rehabilitation of medical facilities and the repair of existing medical equipment. The Tanzanian government has no plans to expand the medical sector until the budget situation improves. Also, see MEDICAL SERVICES.

HEHE. See PEOPLE.

HELIGOLAND TREATY. See ANGLO-GERMAN AGREEMENT (1890).

HILTON-YOUNG COMMISSION (1927–1928). Second attempt by the British government to determine whether an East African Federation (q.v.) should be established between TT, Kenya, and Uganda. In its final report, published in 1929, the Hilton-Young Commission claimed that the time was "not yet ripe" for establishing a federation. The commission did recommend an eventual union between the three territories, largely because its members wanted to introduce an inter-territorial policy to assure the future development of the region's African population and its relations with non-African communities. The Hilton-Young Commission maintained that these objectives could be achieved by appointing a high commissioner. In the commission's view, the governors of TT, Kenya, and Uganda could advise the high commissioner, who would have sole power to formulate policy for Africans in the three territories. Apart from the fact that Sir Donald Cameron (q.v.) opposed the commission's proposals, the League of Nations Permanent Mandates Commission doubted that a federation would benefit TT economically or improve the position of Tanganyikan Africans. Also, see CLOSER UNION.

HOROMBO, CHIEF. Chief Horombo (also known as Orombo) was the first leader who united the Chagga (q.v.) people. Although he had no hereditary claim to leadership (many believed he was of Maasai origin), Horombo rose to power in about 1800 and used slave labor to build a capital at Keni. During the late 1830s and early 1840s he gradually extended his authority from his Chimbii chiefdom to about two-thirds of Chagga country. To defend his conquests, he ordered his followers to build a network of stone forts, some of which were several hundred yards long with walls six feet thick. In each conquered area he appointed a local leader to represent him. When Horombo was killed in a battle against the Maasai (q.v.), other chiefs, including Rengwa and Masaki, tried to preserve Chagga unity but failed largely because they lacked Horombo's military and political skills. As a result, the Chagga empire disintegrated into small, local chiefdoms. It was not until the emergence of Chief Rindi (q.v.) in the 1860s that the Chagga again began to unite.

HUMAN RIGHTS. Historically, Tanzania has enjoyed a relatively positive human rights record, especially in comparison with other East African countries, such as Uganda, Ethiopia, Sudan, and Somalia. The judiciary is normally free from government interference except in some political cases. On the other hand, the Preventive Detention Act (q.v.) allows the government to detain indefinitely without bail persons considered to be a threat to national security. Political criminals may also be internally exiled under the provisions of the Deportation Act.

As to press and other collective freedoms, in recent years the Tanzanian media has become more open, but the president may still terminate any publication that is not "in the interest of the people." In order to prevent mass migration to the cities, the Tanzanian government maintains internal travel controls such as residency and employment requirements. The authorities also restrict the right of association and assembly by requiring opposition parties to be registered and groups to have permission before staging public rallies. Labor unions must belong to the officially controlled Organization of Tanzanian Trade Unions.

— I —

IBN BATTUTA (1304–1377). An Arab adventurer and geographer who was born in Tangier and spent 30 years traveling in Europe, the Middle East, Asia, and Africa. In 1331 he visited Kilwa (q.v.), Mombasa, and Mogadishu. His diaries, which have been published in Arabic, French, and English, are essential for understanding the early history of these towns.

IMPERIAL BRITISH EAST AFRICA COMPANY (IBEAC). Originally known as the British East African Association. In 1887 Seyyid Barghash ibn Said (q.v.) leased his mainland possessions between the Umba River and Kipini to this association for a period of 50 years. In exchange for full political and judicial rights, the association agreed to provide Barghash with revenues at least equal to existing customs collections. On 18 April 1888, Sir William Mackinnon (q.v.) and a group of Manchester investors reorganized the association into IBEAC, and on 3 September 1888 this company received a royal charter. Like its predecessor, the IBEAC's purpose was to develop British economic and political interests throughout East Africa.

The IBEAC proved to be a failure because it lacked adequate financing. Moreover, East Africa lacked easily accessible sources of wealth; company officials could not compete with Asian (q.v.) merchants from the coast; and agricultural development was impossible without a railway, which the company could not afford to build. As a result, the IBEAC sold its concession, rights, and assets to the British government for £250,000. On 1 July 1895 the IBEAC formally transferred its territory to the British Crown.

INDIAN ASSOCIATION (IA). The IA was formed in 1918 at Dar es Salaam to safeguard and promote the interests of TT's Asian (q.v.) population. This association, which had branch offices in most towns, patterned its political tactics after those of Mahatma Gandhi. In March 1923, for example, it supported a 54-day *hartal,* or shop closure, which forced the colonial authorities to repeal a discriminatory Profits Tax Ordinance. The IA also opposed "closer union" (q.v.) and collected funds to support Gandhi's civil disobedience campaign in India. The Asian Association (q.v.) eventually replaced the IA.

INDIAN NATIONAL ASSOCIATION (INA). In 1909 the Asian community in Zanzibar (q.v.) established the Committee of Indians, which they renamed the INA in 1914. Over succeeding decades the INA provided political representation for the islands' Asians (q.v.). In 1937, for example, the INA instituted a boycott against the clove industry after the colonial authorities adopted legislation that required Asian merchants to buy all cloves (q.v.) for export from the Clove Growers' Association (CGA) (q.v.) at fixed prices. The INA also sought and received the support of Mahatma Gandhi's Indian National Congress, which organized a consumer boycott of cloves in India. Eventually, the colonial government and the Asian community concluded the "Heads of Agreement," which provided that the CGA would not export cloves and that Asian exporters would buy a fixed percentage of all cloves for export from the CGA.

After India gained independence in 1947, Muslim Asians withdrew from the INA and formed the Muslim Association while Hindu Asians remained loyal to the INA. Both organizations continued to defend Asian rights in Zanzibar.

INDIANS. See ASIANS.

INDIRECT RULE. Sir Donald Cameron (q.v.) was the chief architect of indirect rule in TT. In his view, colonial administration should be based on traditional, precolonial political authority, in which a chief or a native council ruled individual villages. Under this system, the British divided TT into 11 (eventually eight) provinces, each administered by a commissioner who reported to the central government. Provinces were composed of districts governed by provincial commissioners. In each district the colonial government established native authorities (chiefs or chiefs-in-council) who managed local affairs.

Scholars have criticized indirect rule for ignoring the fact that most precolonial Tanzanian societies had never developed powerful chiefdoms and that in others chiefly institutions had been destroyed in the initial phases of colonization. According to this interpretation, by creating chiefdoms where none had existed, the British in fact established a local administrative system similar to that which existed in GEA, in which locally alien *akidas* (q.v.) governed groups of villages.

INVESTMENT PROMOTION CENTRE. This organization was established in July 1990 "to provide an effective framework for the implementation of investment policy and to act as a focal point for the promotion, co-ordination and monitoring of local and foreign investments." According to the Tanzanian government, the Investment Promotion Centre will facilitate the quick acquisition of all necessary permits, licenses, and certificates required by investors. It is administratively located in the president's office.

IONIDES, CONSTANTINE JOHN PHILIP (1901–1968). Known as the "Snakeman of Tanzania," Ionides was educated at Rugby and Sandhurst public schools in England. In 1925 he was seconded to the Sixth (Tanganyika) Battalion, King's African Rifles (KAR) (q.v.). In 1933 he joined the Tanganyika Game Department as a temporary ranger, subsequently serving as the game ranger for the southern range, which included an area that later became Selous Game Reserve (q.v.). In 1943, Ionides began working with snakes and eventually became a noted authority on the subject. During his career as a herpetologist, he supplied snakes to museums throughout the world, including the Coryndon Museum (now the National Museum) in Nairobi, Kenya. Several snake species and subspecies are named after him.

IRAQW. See PEOPLE.

IRINGA. The Germans founded this town, which is located halfway between Morogoro and Mbeya and 157 miles (253 kilometers) south of Dodoma (q.v.), on the Great North Road from Zambia to Kenya. In 1894 Chief Mkwawa (q.v.) built a military fortification at Kalenga as a stronghold against the Germans, who were attempting to suppress his insurgency. In 1896 Mkwawa's opponent, Captain Tom von Prince (q.v.), established a military *boma* (q.v.) at Iringa and defeated Mkwawa in 1898. Today Iringa is a beginning point for tourists visiting Ruaha National Park (q.v.).

— J —

JACKSON, SIR WILFRED EDWARD (1883–1971). As a private advocate, Jackson favored the encouragement of European settlement in TT, but as governor from 1941 to 1945 he maintained that settlement should be conditioned "by a scrupulous regard for the rights and interests, as well as the future needs, of the African population." Jackson also wanted the colonial government to allow for the potential development of new types of African land settlement.

JAMAL, AMIR HABIB (1922–1995). Jamal was born in Dar es Salaam and educated in Mwanza (qq.v.) and at Calcutta University in India where he obtained a B.A. degree in politics and economics in 1942. Upon his return to TT Jamal joined his family's business. During the early 1950s he became one of Tanganyika's most politically active Asians (q.v.) on the side of African nationalism and TANU (q.v.). Jamal was elected to TT's penultimate LEGCO (q.v.) in 1958 and was appointed in 1959 as unofficial minister for urban local government and works. In the transitional period before and immediately after independence, Jamal served as minister for communications, power, and works.

Perhaps Jamal's most influential periods in office occurred between 1965 and 1975, when he served as minister of state in the president's office in charge of the Directorate of Development and Planning (1965–1967), and as minister of finance (1972–1975). Before he retired from public life Jamal further served as minister for commerce and industries, minister of finance and planning, and minister for communications and transport. He died in Canada.

JAMSHID IBN ABDULLAH, SEYYID (b. 1930). Eleventh and last Busaidi (q.v.) ruler of Zanzibar (1963–1964). He assumed power after the death of Seyyid Abdullah ibn Khalifa (q.v.). Unlike his predecessors, he lacked political experience and demonstrated little interest in his African subjects. As a result, Seyyid Jamshid's brief tenure was characterized by increasing rancor, especially among Africans who resented his support of the pro-Arab Zanzibar National Party (ZNP) (q.v.). He also had little liking for the British, largely because he had unpleasant memories of his service as a midshipman in the Royal Navy. After the Zanzibar Revolution (q.v.), he fled to Great Britain, where he lived in exile on a British government pension.

JOHNSTON, SIR HARRY HAMILTON (1858–1927). British explorer, naturalist, and administrator who led the 1884 British Association and Royal Society expedition to Mount Kilimanjaro (q.v.). Although his mission was to study the mountain's flora and fauna, Johnston concluded several jurisdictional treaties with local Chagga (q.v.) rulers which the British government refused to recognize because of their support for the sultan (q.v.) of Zanzibar's claims to the area.

JUDICIARY. During German colonial rule, district courts were established at Dar es Salaam, Tanga, Mwanza, Moshi, and Tabora (qq.v.). These courts exercised jurisdiction only over Europeans, and the Supreme Court, located in Dar es Salaam, heard all appeals. District officers and officers in command of military stations had jurisdiction over Africans and other non-Europeans. Appeals in such cases went to the colonial governor, who then referred them to the Supreme Court.

In TT, Courts of Justice were established in 1920 and carried out the administration of British colonial law. These courts consisted of the High Court of Tanganyika; a Special Tribunal, which decided civil claims caused by World War I (q.v.); Subordinate Courts, which exercised criminal and civil jurisdiction; and Native Courts, which were responsible for hearing cases involving Africans accused of civil and minor criminal crimes. The Court of Appeals for Eastern Africa decided all appeals.

At independence, the Tanzanian government established an independent judiciary composed of the High Court, which consists of a chief justice and 14 judges; a Court of Appeal presided over by a chief justice and four judges; District and Resident Magistrates' Courts; and about 900 Primary Courts. The president appoints all judges in consultation with the chief justice or the Judicial Service Commission. The mainland judiciary is based largely on British common law, with modifications to accommodate traditional and Islamic law in civil cases. In 1985 Zanzibari courts were integrated into the mainland's legal system, but Islamic courts continue to hear cases involving only Muslims, dealing with marriage, divorce, inheritance, and child care.

JUMBE. In GEA, *jumbes* were officially appointed headmen who governed individual villages under the authority of *akidas* (q.v.). *Jumbes* exercised both executive and judicial powers in their local jurisdictions.

JUMBE, ABOUD MWINYI (b. 1920). A former academic who became a moderate Zanzibari political leader and led the Zanzibar National Union (q.v.), which unsuccessfully sought to establish a multiracial Arab-African national movement. In 1960 he joined the Afro-Shirazi

Party (ASP) (q.v.) and served as a member of the Zanzibari legislature from 1961 to 1984. He also held various ministerial posts in the mainland government between 1964 and 1972. In 1972 Jumbe became President of Zanzibar and Pemba after the assassination of Abeid Amani Karume (q.v.).

Jumbe, a staunch supporter of Julius Nyerere (q.v.), cooperated with the mainland government and willingly shared clove revenues with the union. He also conducted an unpopular campaign against corruption and other social and economic crimes in Zanzibar. Jumbe's reputation likewise suffered as a result of widespread food shortages and economic problems caused by the islands' dwindling foreign-exchange reserves. On 29 January 1984 he was forced to resign from the presidency, largely because he was blamed in Zanzibar for implementing mainland reform policies, and on the mainland for tolerating Zanzibari protestors who opposed the Tanzanian union.

— K —

KAMALIZA, MICHAEL (b. 1929). Born in Malawi, Kamaliza rose to power in the trade-union movement and in 1955 helped Rashidi Kawawa (q.v.) found the Tanganyika Federation of Labour (TFL) (q.v.). He then served as general secretary of the TFL's constituent Transport and General Workers Union between 1957 and 1960, and as TFL president from 1960 to 1962. Elected MP for Kilosa, Kamaliza was appointed minister of labor in 1963, and in 1964 was named general secretary of the newly formed National Union of Tanganyika Workers (NUTA) (q.v.), which replaced the TFL. He was also appointed to TANU's Central Committee (CC) (q.v.) and National Executive Committee (NEC). Resigning his ministerial responsibilities in 1967, Kamaliza continued in his NUTA leadership role until 1969, when he was arrested on charges that he conspired to overthrow the government. He was jailed and later released to private life.

KAMBONA, OSCAR SALATHIEL (b. 1928). Kambona attended primary and secondary school in Tabora and Dodoma (qq.v.). A close associate of Julius Nyerere (q.v.), Kambona became general secretary of TANU (q.v.) in 1954, and in 1955 he accepted a scholarship to study law at London University.

After returning to TT, in 1960 Kambona was elected MP for Morogoro and was appointed interim minister for education. From 1961 to 1965 he held the posts of minister for home affairs, minister for external affairs, and minister for defense. In 1964 he resigned the latter post because of ill health, but in 1965 he became chairman of the

OAU's African Liberation Committee. Also in 1965, Kambona was appointed minister of regional administration and in 1967 minister of local government and rural development.

Kambona resigned from government in 1967, again for health reasons, but also because of an increasing rift that had developed between him and Nyerere's TANU government. Entering voluntary exile in England, during 1970 Kambona was charged in absentia for treason. He continued to live in England and Uganda until 1992, when he returned to private life in Tanzania.

KARUME, ABEID AMANI (1905–1972). Prior to his political career, Karume worked as a merchant seaman for 17 years. In 1938 he founded the Syndicate for Dockers and Sailors, a Zanzibari trade union. In 1954 Karume became leader of the African Association (q.v.), and in 1961 he served as Zanzibar's minister of health. Three years later Karume became leader of the Afro-Shirazi Party (ASP) (q.v.) and, following the Zanzibar Revolution (q.v.), the first president of Zanzibar and Pemba with the honorific title of Sheikh (Muslim leader).

Although he helped to negotiate the subsequent union with Tanganyika, Karume remained an advocate of Zanzibari autonomy and refused to share the islands' revenue from clove exports with the rest of the country. He was also a despot who ruthlessly eliminated political opponents and enacted a law that required forced interracial marriages between Arabs and Africans. His regime became a grim version of Julius Nyerere's (q.v.) African socialism; indeed, his critics maintained that Karume wanted to turn Zanzibar and Pemba into a Soviet-styled people's republic. Karume's dictatorial policies resulted in several political murders, a ruined economy, and an exodus of Zanzibari expertise. On 7 April 1972 an assailant, never since identified, assassinated Karume at ASP headquarters.

KATAVI NATIONAL PARK. Gazetted as a game reserve in 1951, Katavi became a national park in 1974. It covers an area of 869 square miles (2,250 square kilometers) and lies between the Ugalla River and Lake Tanganyika's (q.v.) southeastern shores. Noteworthy fauna include elephant, buffalo, zebra, topi, hippopotamus, sable and roan antelope, eland, leopard, lion, and crocodile. Other attractions in the park are Lake Katavi, Lake Chanda, and the Katuma River, which connects these two lakes.

KAWAWA, RASHIDI MFAUME (b. 1929). Born in Songea District in southern Tanzania, Kawawa attended Liwale Primary School, Dar es Salaam Junior Secondary School, and the Government Secondary

School, Tabora. After completing his education, Kawawa secured a clerical position in the colonial Public Works Department. In 1951 he was transferred to the Social Welfare Department, where he operated a mobile cinema, established a film library, and starred in at least three popular films.

Kawawa later joined the Tanganyika Federation of Labour (TFL) and TANU (qq.v.). After attending a trades union course in Great Britain in 1956, he won a seat in the Tanganyika LEGCO (q.v.). In September 1960 Kawawa became minister for local government and housing in the transitional independence government, and the following year he was appointed minister without portfolio.

When Julius Nyerere (q.v.) resigned as prime minister of the independent government in January 1962, Kawawa assumed the vacated position until December, when he became vice-president under the newly adopted presidential constitution. In 1964, however, he agreed to accept the position of second vice president in order to satisfy the terms of a merger agreement between Tanganyika and Zanzibar (qq.v.), which stipulated that a Zanzibari would be appointed first vice president. Over the next decade, Kawawa served as prime minister (1972–1977) and minister of defense (1977–1981). In 1982 he became the CCM's (q.v.) secretary-general and on 24 February 1983 he was appointed minister without portfolio in the president's office.

Many Tanzanians believed that Kawawa would succeed Nyerere after the latter relinquished the Tanzanian presidency in 1985, but Kawawa's unwavering commitment to a state-controlled economy caused him to lose popular support to the more pragmatic Ali Hassan Mwinyi (q.v.), who eventually became Tanzania's second president. In October 1987 the CCM's Third Party Congress reelected Kawawa as secretary-general, and three years later he became CCM vice-chairman. In recent years Kawawa has continued to play a significant role in Tanzanian politics. At the 22 July 1995 CCM congress, for example, he supported Nyerere's move to have Nyerere protégé Benjamin Mkapa (q.v.) nominated as the CCM's 1995 presidential candidate.

KHALID IBN BARGHASH (1875–1927). After the death of Seyyid Hamed ibn Thwain (q.v.), Barghash seized the palace and proclaimed his own succession. The British Resident opposed his sultanate and ordered the Royal Navy to bombard the palace. This action resulted in the death or wounding of about 500 of Barghash's followers and crushed Arab resistance to British colonial rule. Meanwhile, Barghash sought refuge in the German consulate. The British then selected Hamoud ibn Muhammad (q.v.) as sultan. Until the outbreak of World War I (q.v.) in 1914, Barghash lived in GEA. In 1917 British forces captured him and exiled him to St. Helena. Four years later the British sent Barghash to the Seychelles. In 1925, after promising to refrain from political activities, Barghash moved to Mombasa, where he lived in retirement until his death.

KHALIFA IBN HARUB, SEYYID (1879–1960). Ninth Busaidi (q.v.) ruler of Zanzibar (1911–1960). He was perhaps the most well-liked sultan in Zanzibar's history. Apart from his popularity with the Arab community, Seyyid Khalifa gained the support of Africans who lived in Zanzibar (q.v.) and the mainland because of his fluency in Swahili (q.v.) and his commitment to improving the lives of all his subjects. The British supported him because of his commonsense approach to the islands' political, economic, and social problems. In 1947, for example, Seyyid Khalifa sought to improve his government by establishing "His Highness's Zanzibar Service." The purpose of this professional civil service was to encourage young, educated Zanzibaris to embark on government careers. Seyyid Khalifa also established the Clove Growers' Association (q.v.) to stimulate to island's clove industry. His reputation for evenhandedness also helped to offset the impact of the radical, divisive, and anti-African Zanzibar National Party (q.v.). Seyyid Khalifa's death marked the end of whatever social unity had been achieved in Zanzibar.

KHALIFA IBN SAID, SEYYID (1854–1890). Khalifa, the fourth Busaidi (q.v.) ruler of Zanzibar (1888–1890), was a weak sultan who demonstrated little understanding of public affairs. In late 1888 Seyyid Khalifa relinquished his control over the East African coast to the Imperial British East Africa Company (IBEAC) (q.v.) and the German East Africa Company (q.v.). A few days after the German East Africa Company assumed control of its portion of the coast, the local population, which remained loyal to the sultan, launched the Abushiri revolt (q.v.). In response to this uprising, Germany persuaded Britain to institute a joint blockade of the coast to prevent the import of arms and the export of slaves. On 13 October 1889 Seyyid Khalifa signed an agreement that gave Britain and Germany the right to search all Arab dhows (q.v.) for slaves. In return, the two European powers lifted the blockade. Seyyid Khalifa never made public the terms of the slavery agreement.

KHERI, MWINYI (1820–1885). Using Ujiji (q.v.) as a base, this Arab trader supervised a large slave and ivory caravan trading network. In 1876 his wealth included 120 slaves, 80 guns, and 9 canoes. In 1881 he became governor of Ujiji under the suzerainty of Zanzibar's Sultan

Barghash (q.v.); however, Mwinyi Kheri continued to enjoy considerable autonomy over local affairs until his death.

KIGOMA. A town on the eastern shore of Lake Tanganyika (q.v.) about 773 miles (1247 kilometers) from Dar es Salaam (q.v.), Kigoma lies at the end of the Central Railway (q.v.). A ferry service operates from Bujumbura, Burundi, to Kigoma, and then south to Mupulungu, Zambia. Long-distance overland truckers also travel through Kigoma. The town's 1988 population was 84,647.

KILIMANJARO NATIONAL PARK. This park was officially created in 1973 with a total area of 454 square miles (756 square kilometers). The park includes Mount Kilimanjaro (q.v.) and is noted more for its scenic beauty than for its proliferation of wildlife.

KILIMANJARO NATIVE COOPERATIVE UNION (KNCU). See CO-OPERATIVE SOCIETIES.

KILWA. Three towns bear the name Kilwa. Kilwa Kivinje (Kilwa of the casurina trees) lies on the Indian Ocean coast some 150 miles (241 kilometers) south of Dar es Salaam (q.v.). According to Richard Burton (q.v.), Kilwa Kivinje was founded in about 1830 when the inhabitants of Kilwa Kisiwani migrated there to avoid British ships seeking to suppress the slave trade (q.v.). During the 1860s Kilwa Kivinje was the terminus for the southern caravan route from Lake Malawi (q.v.) and exported about 20,000 slaves annually. The town was also the site of the GEA's southern administrative headquarters.

Kilwa Kisiwani (Kilwa on the island), or Quiloa, as it was known to the Portuguese, is located 18 miles (29 kilometers) south of Kilwa Kivinje. Throughout its earlier history, Kilwa Kisiwani was the site of numerous Arab and Shirazi Persian trading settlements. At the zenith of its power in the thirteenth to the fifteenth century, Kilwa Kisiwani's economic influence extended to Mafia, Pemba, Zanzibar (qq.v.), the Comoros, Mozambique, and Madagascar. Today, it is nothing more than a small African village.

Kilwa Masoko (Kilwa of the markets) is a thriving, relatively new market town opposite Kilwa Kisiwani. The town boasts an airport, jetty, timber mill, college, bank, and hotel. The discovery of natural gas deposits at nearby Songo Songo Island will undoubtedly stimulate Kilwa Masoko's growing economy.

KIMWERI ZA NYUMBAI (?–1868). Ruler of the Kilindi empire. In the early nineteenth century, he became leader of Usambara in today's northeastern Tanzania. During his 60-year reign, Kimweri extended Kilindi influence from his capital at Vuga to the Arab and Swahili (qq.v.) towns along the Indian Ocean coast. During the early 1850s he clashed with Seyyid Said (q.v.) over control of these towns. In 1853 the two leaders agreed to a joint government along the coast. After Kimweri died, a civil war broke out in Usambara, which ended only when the Germans occupied the region.

KING'S AFRICAN RIFLES (KAR). On 1 January 1917 the British government authorized the creation of the KAR, a regiment of African troops commanded by British officers and noncommissioned officers seconded from the regular army. During World War I (q.v.), 22 KAR battalions participated in the East African Campaign. In March 1919 a newly constituted Second Battalion, KAR, was stationed at Tabora (q.v.), where it remained until 1933. At approximately the same time, the British authorities also constituted the Sixth (Tanganyika) Battalion, KAR, with headquarters at Dar es Salaam (q.v.). Authorized personnel strength for the KAR in TT was set at 2,000 African *askaris* (q.v.) and 72 British officers and noncommissioned officers. During the 1929–1931 period, the KAR was reorganized into a Northern and a Southern Brigade, the latter unit maintaining its headquarters in Dar es Salaam.

In 1939 the British War Office assumed control over the KAR, and in World War II (q.v.) units of the Sixth (Tanganyika) Battalion took part in various campaigns in East Africa, Madagascar, and southeast Asia. In February 1950 the battalion deployed to Mauritius for garrison duty. Several companies also participated in the Mau Mau emergency in Kenya. At independence the KAR became known as the Tanganyika Rifles (q.v.), and in 1964 it was reorganized as the Tanzania People's Defence Force (TPDF) (q.v.).

KIRK, SIR JOHN (1832–1922). British official who served in Zanzibar as vice-consul (1867–1873) and consul general (1873–1887). Throughout much of this period, Kirk maintained such a close relationship with Sultan Barghash (q.v.) that he became known as Zanzibar's "unofficial prime minister." Kirk used his influence with Sultan Barghash to suppress the East African coastal slave trade and to argue for an Anglo-Arab partnership in Zanzibar and the East African interior. In mid-1887 Kirk retired from Zanzibar, largely because his opposition to German colonial expansion in East Africa had become an embarrassment to the British government.

KIVUKONI COLLEGE. This educational institution was authorized in 1958 by TANU (q.v.) and formally established on 29 July 1961 across the harbor from Dar es Salaam (q.v.), as an adult educational and ideological center offering both short-term and long-term courses.

KLERRUU, WILBERT (1932–1971). In 1961 Klerruu became Tanganyika's first Ph.D., earned in political science at the University of California. He then was appointed assistant publicity secretary and later publicity secretary for TANU (q.v.). In 1964 he was named regional commissioner for Mtwara, and later for Iringa, regions. In 1971, while touring an *Ujamaa* village (q.v.) in Iringa region, Klerruu was murdered by a local resident.

KRAPF, JOHANN LUDWIG (1810–1881). Born in Germany, Krapf began in 1837 a six-year period of service as a Church Missionary Society (CMS) (q.v.) missionary in Ethiopia. Arriving at Mombasa in May 1844, Krapf traveled extensively in, and mapping, what was later to become northeastern GEA, eventually establishing a CMS mission station at Tongwe, southeast of Tanga (q.v.). He also published the first transliterated Swahili (q.v.) grammar, and his vivid description of the Usambara Mountains (q.v.) is included in another book, *Travels in East Africa*.

— L —

LAKE MANYARA NATIONAL PARK. Gazetted in 1960, this park covers an area of 125 square miles (325 square kilometers) and is located in the Rift Valley (q.v.) about 74 miles (120 kilometers) southwest of Arusha (q.v.). The park includes the northern and most of the western parts of Lake Manyara, which is famous for its tree-climbing lions and its vast flocks of flamingo (q.v.). Congregations of buffalo, klipspringer, reedbuck, giraffe, hippopotamus, and black rhinoceros also inhabit the park. In addition to flamingos, more than 350 bird species populate Manyara, including egret, ibis, stork, and kingfisher.

LAKE NYSA. With a length of 360 miles (576 kilometers) and an average width of 30 miles (48 kilometers), Lake Malawi is the third largest lake in Africa. It lies 1,645 feet (493 meters) above sea level and has a maximum depth of 2,316 feet (695 meters). The lake contains at least 200 fish species, although in recent years environmentalists have become concerned about the impact of overfishing. Tanzania shares jurisdiction over Lake Malawi with Mozambique and Malawi.

LAKE RUKWA. This lake, which is 2,650 feet (795 meters) above sea level and about 20 miles (32 kilometers) long, is regarded as the southernmost point of East Africa's Rift Valley (q.v.).

LAKE TANGANYIKA. The world's longest freshwater lake, Lake Tanganyika measures 420 miles (677 kilometers) in length, with an average width of 31 miles (50 kilometers) and a total area of 12,703 square miles (32,900 square kilometers). Lake Tanganyika is also the world's second deepest lake, with depths of 4,700 feet (1,433 meters), and the lowest point in Africa, at 1,174 feet (358 meters) below sea level. Tanzania claims 5,150 square miles (13,390 square kilometers) of the lake. The Malagarasi River, which drains the western part of the country's Central Plateau, empties into Lake Tanganyika. Salt in this river causes the lake's waters to be brackish.

Lake Tanganyika has hosted a long human history. In ancient times, various African peoples, including the Ha (q.v.), the Jiji, and the Nyamwezi (q.v.), settled along the lake. Around 1820 an Arab trading caravan crossed Lake Tanganyika. In 1857 Richard Burton and John Hanning Speke (qq.v.) viewed it, and by 1914 the German railway had reached Kigoma (q.v.) along its eastern shore. During the British colonial period, the East African Railways and Harbours Administration operated shipping services on the lake, primarily between Kigoma and ports in what are now Burundi and Zaire.

LAKE VICTORIA. Formerly known as Lake Nyanza, Lake Victoria is the source of the Nile River and is the largest freshwater lake in Africa, with an area of about 27,000 square miles (70,260 square kilometers) and a coastline of more than 2,000 miles (3,200 kilometers). The lake is 3,717 feet (1,115 meters) above sea level and about 220 miles (352 kilometers) in diameter, and it is quite shallow, with a maximum depth of less than 300 feet (90 meters). Average annual inflow from rainfall is an estimated 3,430 billion cubic feet (98 billion cubic meters), and from tributaries about 560 billion cubic feet (16 billion cubic meters). Outflow due to evaporation is approximately 3,255 cubic feet (93 billion cubic meters), and into the Nile River about 735 billion cubic feet (21 billion cubic meters). The soils of the Lake Victoria basin and its islands are suitable for intensive cultivation. As a result, this region features a dense population, which is supported by a variety of rail, road, and shipping services.

In recent years, several problems have brought Lake Victoria to the verge of ecological disaster. Many scientists maintain that the 1962 introduction of the Nile perch (*Lates niloticus*), which experts believed would provide a high-yielding source of protein for Tanzania, Uganda, and Kenya, was a mistake. The proliferation of this fish, a voracious predator that can weigh more than 200 pounds (90 kilo-grams), now poses the greatest threat to Lake Victoria's delicate ecological balance. The species feeds on smaller fish, including *Haplochromis*, which, together with other species such as catfish, eat algae at the bottom of the lake. As the Nile perch has reduced the population of algae-eating fish by at least one-half, the lake's self-cleaning system has collapsed, and oxygen levels in many places have fallen to almost zero.

Another threat to the lake is the South American water hyacinth (*Eichhornia crassipes*), a large free-floating aquatic weed that spreads over still and slow-flowing waters. Since it first appeared in the 1980s this weed has rapidly multiplied and covered vast parts of Lake Victoria with a dense mat that deprives fish and plankton of oxygen essential for their survival.

Lastly, pollution from sewage and runoffs of fertilizers, pesticides, and industrial wastes has caused massive algae blooms. As algae die and fall to the lake's bottom, bacteria decompose them. This process requires large amounts of oxygen, leaving deeper waters too poor in oxygen to support fish. As a consequence, fish seek shallow inshore waters, where they are eaten by Nile perch and caught by fishermen in unsustainable numbers. By the 1990s oxygen levels in shallow waters had also begun to fall because of the introduction of the water hyacinth.

The gradual degradation of Lake Victoria poses a threat to the 30 million people who depend on it for their livelihood. Even with corrective human intervention, this situation is unlikely to change in the near future because the rivers flowing into and out of Lake Victoria are so languid that up to 100 years are required for the lake to clean itself.

On 8 July 1994 Tanzania, Kenya, and Uganda responded to this impending ecological catastrophe by signing an agreement establishing the Lake Victoria Fisheries Organization. This body, which commenced operations in 1995, is intended to implement a $US20 million five-year program to ensure the ecologically sustainable exploitation of Lake Victoria's resources. Despite this action, many scientists and ecologists remain apprehensive about Lake Victoria's long-term well-being.

LAMECK, LUCY (1931–1993). Born in Moshi (q.v.), Lameck was the first Tanganyikan woman to hold a parliamentary and ministerial position in government. Trained as a nurse, she became a Kilimanjaro Native Cooperative Union (KNCU) (q.v.) secretary at Moshi in 1953 and later read economics, history, and political science at Ruskin College, Oxford University, from 1957 to 1959. After returning to Tanganyika, Lameck was elected to parliament and was appointed organizing secretary of the TANU (q.v.) Women's Section and junior minister for community development and cooperatives. She also served on TANU's National Executive Committee (NEC) and Central Committee (CC) (q.v.).

LEAKEY, LOUIS SEYMOUR BAZETT (1903–1972). Apart from his numerous activities in the fields of paleontology, archaeology, and anthropology, Leakey achieved prominence as a naturalist, historian, political analyst, handwriting expert, and administrator. His most notable accomplishment was the discovery of numerous early hominids in Olduvai Gorge (q.v.) and elsewhere in East Africa.

LEAKEY, MARY DOUGLAS (1913–1996). Born in London, she traveled during her early years with her father, an artist, to France, Italy, and Switzerland. Her education was erratic; after being expelled from several Catholic convents for untoward behavior, she briefly studied under private tutors. In 1930 she began auditing archaeology and geology classes at University College, London, and at the London Museum. In 1930, 1931, 1932, and 1934 she also worked as a summer assistant for the Devon Archaeological Exploration Society, which had undertaken a study of neolithic sites in southern England. On 24 December 1936 Mary married Louis Leakey (q.v.), and three weeks later the couple sailed for Kenya.

For more than three decades, Mary and Louis Leakey worked on numerous archaeological sites throughout East Africa. During this time, Mary established a reputation as one of the world's foremost archaeological researchers. Among her accomplishments are discoveries of *Proconsul africanus* (now termed *Proconsul beseloni*) on Rusinga Island in 1948 and a *Zinjanthropus* (q.v.) skull at Olduvai Gorge (q.v.) in 1959. From 1968 to 1972 Mary spent an increasing amount of time at Olduvai Gorge, in part because her marriage to Louis had deteriorated. Following her husband's death in 1972, Mary continued her work at Olduvai until 1975, when she moved her operations to nearby Laetoli. This decision proved to be fortuitous. In January 1978, she announced that her expedition had discovered a series of early hominid footprints that were approximately 3.6 million years old.

In late 1983 Mary Leakey retired from fieldwork and moved to Langata, a suburb of Nairobi, Kenya. Over the years she received many awards for her work, including honorary doctorates from the University of Chicago and from Oxford, Witwatersrand, and Yale Universities. She was also the first woman to win the Golden Linnaean Medal awarded by the Royal Swedish Science Academy, and she received a Gold Medal from the Society of Women Geographers. Mary was also a member of the British Academy and an honorary foreign member of the American Academy of Arts and Sciences. She died in Nairobi in late 1996.

LEGISLATIVE COUNCIL (LEGCO). On 19 March 1926 the Tanganyika (Legislative Council) Order in Council established the LEGCO. This legislation provided for an advisory body that consisted of 13 official members and a maximum of 10 unofficial members, chosen by the governor, who debated colonial policy and public issues. Just before the outbreak of World War II (q.v.), two Africans, Chief Abdiel Shangali of Machame and Chief Kidaha Makwaia of Busiha, received appointments as unofficial members to the LEGCO. Previously, unofficial European members had represented African interests. By 1948 the LEGCO consisted of 14 unofficial members (four Africans, three Asians, and seven Europeans), and 15 official members who preserved a majority for the government. In April 1955 the African, Asian, and European communities each had 10 elected members. An elected speaker also replaced the colonial governor as LEGCO chairman. In a September 1960 pre-independence election, TANU (q.v.) won every LEGCO seat but one. After TT gained internal self-government on 1 May 1961, the LEGCO was renamed the National Assembly (q.v.).

LETTOW-VORBECK, PAUL VON (1870–1964). In 1913 Lettow-Vorbeck became commander of GEA's military, known as the *Schütztruppe* (q.v.) or Protective Forces. During the East African Campaign of World War I (q.v.) he relied on hit-and-run tactics to occupy a huge Allied force for more than four years. On 23 November 1918 an undefeated Lettow-Vorbeck finally surrendered his command at Abercorn, Northern Rhodesia (now Zambia). Military personnel throughout the world still study Lettow-Vorbeck's career and the East African Campaign to enhance their understanding of the principles of guerrilla warfare.

LIEBERT, EDUARD VON (1850–1934). Liebert was cofounder of the German Colonial Society and the Pan-German League, and he served as GEA's fourth governor from 1896 to 1901. He considered Africans to be incapable of developing their own export production capabilities and wanted to turn GEA into a land of German farmers, using military force to counter African resistance to German colonial rule. In 1897 Liebert sought to pacify the Hehe (q.v.) people by offering a 5,000 rupee reward for their Chief Mkwawa (q.v.), dead or alive, and by ordering all captured Hehe warriors to be shot. He also brutally suppressed a series of revolts that occurred after the introduction of a law requiring Africans to pay German-imposed hut taxes in cash.

LIPUMBA, IBRAHIM HARUN (b. 1952). Born at Tabora (q.v.), Lipumba attended Tabora Boys Secondary School (1967–1970) and Pugu Secondary School in Dar es Salaam (1971–1972). Following a brief period at the University of Dar es Salaam (q.v.), he studied at Stanford University, California (1979–1983), where he earned two degrees in economics. From 1991 to 1993, Lipumba served as an economic adviser to President Ali Hassan Mwinyi (q.v.) and eventually persuaded Mwinyi to liberalize and privatize the Tanzanian national economy. Lipumba was also instrumental in the establishment of cordial relations between Tanzania and several international financial institutions, including the World Bank (q.v.) and the International Monetary Fund. From 1993 to 1995 Lipumba taught at Williams College, Massachusetts, and in August 1995 the newly formed Civil United Front (CUF) nominated him as its 1995 presidential candidate. His ultimately unsuccessful campaign focused on economic reconstruction, reduced government spending, and improved welfare services.

LIVINGSTONE, DAVID (1813–1873). Livingstone was a famous Scottish missionary and explorer and the first European to cross Africa from west to east. During his last major expedition (1866–1873) he traveled through much of western Tanzania, resolved questions about the source of the Nile River, attempted to spread Christianity among various African peoples, and worked to stop the slave trade. These activities not only captured the world's attention but also prepared the way for the eventual European colonization of East Africa.

LIWALI. An Arab (q.v.) or Muslim African judge of an Islamic court. *Liwalis* often also exercised executive functions over local Muslim communities. A *liwali* enjoyed greater status than a *kathi*, who presided over an Islamic religious court usually located in one of the coastal districts.

LONDON MISSIONARY SOCIETY. After David Livingstone's (q.v.) death, the London Missionary Society dedicated itself to carrying out his unfinished religious work. In 1877 the society launched its first East African expedition, led by Rev. Roger Price. Harsh climatic conditions and disease forced Price to return to the coast, but two expeditions set out later for the interior. One of these was commanded by Rev. J. B. Thomson and the other by Rev. Arthur W. Dodgshun. In August 1878 the Thomsom party reached Ujiji (q.v.) and six months later, Dodgshun arrived. Both men died shortly thereafter. Edward Coode Hore then assumed control over the mission. During the next five years, the London Missionary Society opened stations at Ujiji, Urambo, Kavala Island, and Mtowa. By 1893 unexpected deaths and resignations forced the London Missionary Society to close all of these stations and to transfer its operations to the British sphere of influence in Northern Rhodesia (now Zambia).

LUSINDE, JOB (b. 1930). Born at Dodoma, Lusinde was educated there, at the Government Secondary School, Tabora, and at Makerere University College (q.v.), where he received a diploma in education. Following a brief career in the colonial local government service, he entered TANU (q.v.) and became the party's deputy provincial secretary for Central Province. After TT's independence, Lusinde held a variety of ministerial positions and established himself as one of the country's most left-leaning politicians in his roles as minister for communications, transportation and labor and later as Tanzanian ambassador to China.

— M —

MAASAI. See PEOPLE.

MACKINNON, WILLIAM (1823–1893). Founder of the Imperial British East Africa Company (IBEAC) (q.v.). In 1878 he leased mainland territory from Seyyid Barghash ibn Said (q.v.). Although this venture came to nothing, his agents laid the groundwork for British imperial rule in East Africa by signing numerous treaties with local leaders in what eventually became Kenya and Uganda.

MACMICHAEL, SIR HAROLD (1882–1969). MacMichael served as TT's fourth governor, from 1934 to 1938. Although a capable administrator, he failed to serve out the full six-year term of his governorship largely because he lacked sympathy with the African population of TT. During his tenure, MacMichael wanted to limit educational expenditures, but on a more positive plane he sought to encourage TT's economic development by repealing the African hut and poll taxes in favor of a system of graduated personal taxation based on wealth. MacMichael also vigorously opposed British politicians who endorsed the eventual return of TT to Germany. One of his lasting contributions was his support for the establishment of *Tanganyika Notes and Records* (later *Tanzania Notes and Records*), a semischolarly journal that remains an essential source of information for anyone interested in Tanzanian history.

MAFIA ISLAND. Mafia is located opposite the Rufiji Delta, 100 miles (160 kilometers) south of Zanzibar. This coral island, 152 square miles (394 square kilometers) in area, is the southernmost and the smallest of Tanzania's main islands. Between the twelfth and the fifteenth centuries, Mafia contained a Shirazi settlement that maintained close links to Kilwa (q.v.). At one time the Portuguese maintained an agent and a small blockhouse on Mafia. In 1890 Germany assumed control of the island; in 1916 Mafia became the responsibility of the Zanzibari government; and in 1922 it became part of TT. The German administrative headquarters was at Chole, but the British evacuated this site because it had a poor harbor. The modern African population, numbering 33,054 in 1988, is heterogeneous because of immigrations from the Middle East, India, and the African mainland. Mafia contains numerous coconut plantations.

MAHALE MOUNTAINS NATIONAL PARK. Gazetted in 1985, this park is also known as Nkungwe. Mahale, whose area is 623 square miles (1,613 square kilometers), lies on the eastern shore of Lake Tanganyika (q.v.) about 90 miles (150 kilometers) south of Kigoma (q.v.). Mahale is comprised of lowland and mountain forests mixed with bamboo. The park is home to 55 mammal species, including chimpanzee, lion, warthog, sable antelope, and Lichtenstein's hartebeest.

MAIZE. Maize, one of Tanzania's main food crops, is grown throughout the country, principally by peasant smallholders. Historically, maize yields have been low because farmers lack modern tools and farming methods, and also because much of the country suffers from either poor or erratic weather conditions. Nevertheless, production has occasionally reached impressive levels. In 1988/89, for example, a bumper crop of 3.1 million tons was harvested, which enabled Tanzania to export small quantities of surplus. Since then, maize yields have averaged about 2.3 million tons annually.

MAJI-MAJI REBELLION (1905–1907). This conflict originated in 1902, when German Governor Count Adolf von Götzen (q.v.) ordered that cotton be grown throughout southern GEA. He also directed every headman to establish a cotton plot, where all villagers would work. By 1905 cotton plots existed in all coastal districts south of Dar es Salaam, including Morogoro (q.v.) and Kilosa. This project caused considerable hardship because the land was unsuitable for cotton cultivation and the work was poorly organized and badly managed. Consequently, profits were nearly nonexistent and Africans forced into the scheme decided to rebel.

On the evening of 31 July 1905 the revolt began when the Matumbi people drove all foreigners from their hills. Unrest quickly spread to most areas in the cotton belt, the regions around the middle and lower Rufiji River, Uluguru, the Mahenge Plateau, and the Lukuledi and Kilombero valleys. Rebel leader Abdullah Mapanda enjoyed considerable support because he gave his followers a magic potion that supposedly made them impervious to German bullets. German colonial forces responded to this revolt by unleashing a reign of terror against the rebels and their supporters. Using European, New Guinean, Papuan, and Melanesian troops, the Germans killed between 75,000 and 120,000 Africans in a population of two million. Such devastation ended African resistance to German colonial rule in the south.

MAJID IBN SAID, SEYYID (1834–1870). The second Busaidi (q.v.) ruler of Zanzibar from 1856 to 1870, Seyyid Majid depended on the British to protect him from his half-brother, Thwain, who ruled Oman. In 1859 the British Navy thwarted Thwain's plans to invade Zanzibar. Two years later the British resolved the dispute between the two brothers by recognizing Zanzibar's independence from Oman, and also by requiring Seyyid Majid to make annual payments to Thwain as compensation for their unequal inheritance. During Seyyid Majid's reign, the Busaidi made their first serious attempt to establish Zanzibar's control over the Tanzanian mainland. Seyyid Majid likewise began to develop Dar es Salaam as a future capital, but he died before completing the project. His brother Barghash (q.v.) succeeded him.

MAKERERE UNIVERSITY. One of Africa's oldest educational institutions, Makerere University was opened in Kampala, Uganda, in 1921 as a technical school. Many notable Tanzanians, including Julius Nyerere (q.v.), studied at Makerere, which in 1949 became a university college associated with the University of London. During the late 1970s and early 1980s, warfare and instability throughout Uganda all but destroyed the institution. After a new government, headed by Yoweri Museveni, seized power in January 1986, Makerere University began the long, slow process of rebuilding and rehabilitation. By the mid-1990s, however, the university had yet to regain its earlier stature.

MAKONDE. See PEOPLE.

MALACELA, JOHN SAMUEL CIGWIYEMISI (1934–   ). Born in Dodoma (q.v.), Malacela received his primary education at a local mission school. He then attended St. Andrew's College, Minaki, and Bombay University, India, where he earned a bachelor of commerce degree in 1959. During 1961/62 he studied administration at Cambridge University. Malacela began his government career as Tanganyikan consul to the United States and third secretary of the Tanganyikan Mission to the UN. From 1964 to 1968 he continued his UN sojourn as Tanzanian ambassador, where he also served as chairman of the UN Committee on Decolonization. In May 1968 Malacela became ambassador to Ethiopia. In January 1969 he was appointed minister of research and social services in the East African Community (EAC) (q.v.), and he later became the EAC's minister for finance and administration. In February 1972 Malacela was named Tanzanian foreign minister and later served as minister of agriculture (1975–1980), minister of mines (1980–1982), and minister of communications and transport (1982–1985). After being defeated in the October 1985 parliamentary election, he devoted his energies to bringing a peaceful end to apartheid in South Africa. In November 1990 President Ali Hassan Mwinyi (q.v.) named Malacela prime minister.

MATHEWS, SIR LLOYD W. (1850–1901). Mathews was one of the most important and effective British officials who ever served in Zanzibar. Over a period of 26 years, he worked for five successive sultans. As a Royal Navy lieutenant, Mathews trained an army for the sultan. In 1881 he retired from the Royal Navy and accepted a post in the sultan's service, with the rank of brigadier general, as commander in chief of Zanzibar's 1,300-man army. Ten years later Mathews became the sultan's first minister, in charge of supervising the islands' administration. Although the government he presided over consisted of only a few departments run by a handful of British officials, Mathews earned the respect and admiration of his colleagues and much of the local population for his efficiency and evenhandedness. On 11 October 1901 Mathews died of malaria. He was buried with full naval and military honors in the English cemetery outside Zanzibar town.

MBEGA, CHIEF. The semimythical leader who founded the Kilindi kingdom in Usambara. According to the oral traditions of the ruling Kilindi clan, Mbega entered Usambara from Ngulu country to the south and settled among the Shambala people. Because he was an excellent hunter, he shared his meat with the Shambala, killed the wild pigs that were destroying their crops, and helped people to settle their disputes. In gratitude, the Shambala provided Mbega with wives and made him king of all Usambara. He appointed his sons as district governors, established a military force, and began to expand his kingdom. After Mbega's death, his son Bughe ascended to the throne.

MBEYA. The town of Mbeya was founded in 1927 when gold (q.v.) was discovered in the neighboring mountains. During the 1930s gold mining brought a degree of prosperity to Mbeya, but by 1956 the gold fields were abandoned. The construction of the Great North Road connecting Tanzania with Zambia saved Mbeya from becoming a ghost town, and the arrival of the TAZARA (q.v.) railway line in the early 1970s soon transformed it into a modern transportation and communication center. Mbeya is located 529 miles (853 kilometers) southwest of Dar es Salaam (q.v.). The town's 1988 population was 152,844.

MEDICAL SERVICES. On 1 April 1891 the German colonial authorities established a Medical Department with five doctors and 14 workers. In 1893 the Sewa Haji Hospital opened in Dar es Salaam (q.v.). Prior to World War I (q.v.), professionally trained German doctors staffed GEA's Medical Department while German and British physicians worked in the colony's few mission hospitals. The German colonial authorities maintained a network of 12 general hospitals, a sanitorium, a mental hospital, and several leprosy segregation camps. During the war, medical officers from the Royal Army Medical Corps, the Indian Medical Service, the East and West Africa Medical Service, and the Nyasa-Rhodesia Force replaced German doctors.

Following the armistice, the British established a civil medical service in TT. In October 1919 Dr. John B. Davey became TT's first chief medical officer with Dr. J. O. Shircore as his deputy. After the latter became chief medical officer in 1924, 19 medical officers joined TT's medical service. Shircore also doubled the number of medical personnel by developing training programs for African dispensers, tribal dressers, and rural sanitary inspectors. By 1934 there were 100 registered and 58 licensed physicians in the country.

During World War II (q.v.), the Medical Department lost staff at all levels to the army. The conflict also revealed the poor state of TT's public health record; one-third of African army recruits were unfit for service and another third were unfit for active duty. During the immediate postwar period, the British emphasized the development of rural dispensaries, the training of an African staff, and the need for greater cooperation between mission and government medical personnel.

During the last years of British colonial rule, the Medical Department sought to train a cadre of Africans who could assume responsibility for operating the country's health care system. As a result of these efforts, independent Tanzania possessed a nationwide network of medical services that operated through the cooperation of the government, local authorities, missions, and volunteer agencies. In 1975 the government began to nationalize all hospitals, and five years later all private medical practice ended.

During the 1980s Tanzania operated more than 3,000 hospitals and dispensaries with more than 1,000 physicians. In more recent years, the Tanzanian medical establishment has become increasingly concerned about the AIDS (q.v.) epidemic and its impact on the country's well-being. To the extent that it is available, medical treatment is free for Tanzanian citizens or is subsidized by local businesses. Also, see HEALTH CARE.

MEMBAR, MUSA. See TANZANIA YOUTH DEMOCRACY MOVEMENT.

MERU LAND CASE. A complex legal case that helped to arouse African political consciousness throughout TT. The dispute concerned Engare-Nanyuki, a rich pastoral area on the slopes of Mount Meru. Between 1925 and 1939 the Meru people purchased two farms in Engare-Nanyuki, which the British colonial authorities had seized after World War I (q.v.) as ex-German property. According to the Meru, the government had assured them that these lands would remain Meru property forever. In 1947, however, the Wilson (a judge on the High Court of Tangenyika) Report authorized the displacement of the Meru from Engare-Nanyuki in order to turn these lands over to European settlers. As compensation, the Wilson Report allowed the Meru to settle in Kingori, a region on the slopes of Mount Kenya in Kenya Colony. The Meru also received some European-owned farms in the Usa River area of TT.

Between June 1949 and September 1951, the Meru repeatedly asked the colonial authorities to rescind the decision taken in the Wilson Report. When this tactic failed to achieve any results, the Meru implored the UN to intervene and prevent the government from executing the resettlement scheme. Notwithstanding this request, the Meru were evicted from Engare-Nanyuki. Although continued Meru complaints failed to secure the return of their land, their numerous petitions to the UN hastened the emergence of African nationalism in TT. Within a few years of independence, Engare-Nanyuki was back in Meru hands.

MIKUMI NATIONAL PARK. Gazetted in 1964, Mikumi was previously a controlled hunting area. Located 183 miles (294 kilometers) from Dar es Salaam, Mikumi is 550 square miles (3,230 square kilometers) in area. In spite of its small size, the park contains nearly all species of game animals found in Tanzania, including elephant, zebra, lion, giraffe, wild pig, wolf, buffalo, wildebeest, impala, hippopotamus, antelope, warthog, and large cats.

MINING. In the early 1990s minerals accounted for only about 1.5 percent of Tanzania's GDP. The country still possesses a rich supply of untapped mineral resources, including diamonds, gold, coal (qq.v.), nickel, phosphates, copper, lead, and salt. Mineral exports declined from US$53.24 million in 1992 to US$41.49 million in 1993. This shortfall occurred because of low gold purchases, reduced diamond production, and a salt market weakened by continuing unrest in the Zairean, Rwandan, and Burundian markets.

Better to exploit the country's mineral resources, by late 1994 Tanzania's Investment Promotion Centre (q.v.) had approved 21 projects for investors from the United States, Canada, Australia, South Africa, Japan, and Britain. In addition, the De Beers Corporation of South Africa concluded an agreement with Tanzania to manage the Williamson Diamond Mine at Mwadui. By the year 2000, Tanzania hopes to become a major mineral-producing country.

MIRAMBO, CHIEF (c. 1840–1884). Mirambo was a military leader who transformed a minor Nyamwezi chiefdom into a powerful empire that dominated most of Tanzania's important trade routes. Between 1871 and 1875 Mirambo enjoyed a string of military successes that established his reputation as one of future GEA's most effective African rulers. After 1875 Mirambo received numerous European administrators, traders, and missionaries, most of whom came quickly to be impressed with his organizational abilities. In 1883 and 1884 Mirambo's army suffered a series of defeats at the hands of the northern Ngoni and the southern Nyamwezi. After Mirambo's death, the Nyamwezi empire collapsed because of poor leadership and the advance of German imperial forces.

MKAPA, BENJAMIN WILLIAM (b. 1938). Tanzania's third president. Born on 12 November 1938 at Ndanda, Masasi District, in Mtwara Region, Mkapa attended primary school at Lupaso from 1945 to 1948. From 1949 to 1956 he received his secondary education at Ndanda Secondary School, Kigonsera Seminary, and St. Francis College, Pugu. In 1962 he graduated with a B.A. degree in education from Makerere University College, Kampala, Uganda. In 1962 and 1963 Mkapa studied diplomacy and international relations at Columbia University in New York.

In 1962 Mkapa was employed as a district officer in Dodoma and Dar es Salaam (qq.v.). In 1963 he joined the Tanganyika foreign service. From 1966 to 1972 he served as a managing editor of the TANU's (q.v.) two newspapers, *Nationalist* and *Uhuru*. During the 1972–1974 period, Mkapa served as founding editor of the government newspaper, *The Daily News*. In 1974 Mkapa became press secretary to President Julius Nyerere (q.v.), and two years later he was appointed director of the Tanzania News Agency. In November 1976 he received a diplomatic post as Tanzanian high commissioner to Nigeria, which he relinquished three months later when he was recalled and made minister of foreign affairs. Mkapa then served in a variety of positions, including ambassador to Canada (1982–1983), ambassador to the United States (1983–1984), minister of foreign affairs (1984–1990), minister for information and broadcasting (1990–1992), and minister of science, technology and higher education (1992–1995). He has also held numerous other offices such as chairman of the Front-Line States Foreign Ministers' Committee and vice chairman of the Science and Technology Ministerial Council of the South. In 1989 he became a member of the CCM's (q.v.) National Executive Committee.

On 22 July 1995 Mkapa won 686 (51 percent) of 1,331 votes cast in the second round of voting at a CCM party congress in Dodoma (q.v.), convened to select the party's presidential candidate. His running mate was Omar Ali Juma. Mkapa's platform emphasized self-reliance and continued public ownership of the economy. He also pledged to promote modern production methods, increases in national income and public revenue, and some degree of economic privatization.

After being sworn in as Tanzania's third president on 23 November 1995, Mkapa sought to heal the political divisiveness that had arisen during the election campaign by promising not to discriminate against opposition politicians. He also attempted to address Tanzania's problem with public corruption by declaring his personal assets and ordering other members of the government to do likewise. In the area of foreign policy, Mkapa quickly established a reputation as a political moderate and a supporter of regional cooperation in Africa. One of his earliest triumphs involved his role in helping to bridge the longstanding rift between Kenya and Uganda, by helping to create the Permanent Tripartite Commission. After months of delay, and largely at Mkapa's urging, Kenya agreed to name a secretary-general to the Arusha-based Commission, an organization that may succeed the defunct East African Community (q.v.).

Though encouraging, such positive measures have done little to resolve Tanzania's chronic economic difficulties. Many bilateral and multilateral donors were still alienated by the country's many tax evasion and corruption scandals, and as a result, foreign aid levels remained low as of early 1996. Mkapa's ultimate success may depend on his ability to maintain distance in policy selection from his mentor, Julius Nyerere, who continues to support some of the failed socialist policies he pursued during his presidency and CCM chairmanship.

Also, see ELECTIONS, TANGANYIKA TERRITORY, TANGAN-
YIKA, TANZANIA.

MKWAWA, CHIEF (?–1898). Ruler of the Hehe people (1879–1898)
who led the most protracted East African resistance to German colonial rule. Mkwawa organized a well-disciplined Hehe army that conquered much of southern Tanzania. During the 1880s Mkwawa,
whose father was Chief Munyigumba (q.v.), began expanding his empire eastward just as Germany was moving inland. In 1891 Mkwawa
opened hostilities against the Germans by destroying three-quarters
of their expeditionary corps. After this victory Mkwawa became
known as the "Black Napoleon." Over the next several years he survived another German military expedition in 1894, harassed trading
caravans, and punished Africans who collaborated with the Germans.
In July 1898 he committed suicide rather than surrender to German
military authorities. Soldiers severed his head and sent it to Germany.
In 1954 the German government returned the skull to the Hehe people. Also, see PEOPLE.

MORESBY TREATY. Signed on 21 September 1822 by Captain Fairfax
Moresby, governor of Mauritius, and Seyyid Said (q.v.). This treaty,
which was the first British move against the Arab slave trade (qq.v.),
prohibited the trade outside the sultan's dominions from Cape Delgado to a point 60 miles (96 kilometers) east of Socotra and from
there to Diu Head. The Moresby Treaty also allowed the British to
capture Arab slavers trading in non-Muslim states. In addition, the
treaty outlawed the sale of slaves to Christian merchants, but not to
Muslims, and provided for the appointment of a British consul or
agent in Zanzibar(q.v.). Lastly, the treaty recognized the sultan's
claims to the East African coast.

MOROGORO. A town located 126 miles (203 kilometers) west of Dar
es Salaam (q.v.) and situated at the foot of the Uluguru Mountains
(q.v.). Morogoro is an important transportation and communication
center and lies on the Central Railway (q.v.). The town is also situated
at a road junction that links Iringa, Dar es Salaam, and Tanga (qq.v.),
and it is a starting point for tourists visiting the Selous Game Reserve
and Mikumi National Park (qq.v.). The town's 1988 population was
117,760.

MOSHI. A town located in the foothills of Mount Kilimanjaro (q.v.)
474 miles (758 kilometers) northwest of Dar es Salaam (q.v.). Prior
to the arrival of the Germans, Moshi was the capital of Chief Rindi
(q.v.), who was one of the most important and influential rulers in

northern Tanzania. The town was the terminus of Tanga Railway (q.v.) until 1929, when the line was extended to Arusha (q.v.). Moshi, which lies at an altitude of 2,900 feet (870 meters), is also the center of an important coffee (q.v.) growing region. In addition, agricultural processing facilities are located in and around Moshi, including saw-mills, a textile factory, canning factory, soap works, candy factory, and a sugar refinery situated about 14 miles (22 kilometers) outside town. In 1988 Moshi's largely Chagga (q.v.) population was 96,838.

MOUNT KILIMANJARO. Located along the Tanzanian-Kenyan bor-der, Mount Kilimanjaro is the highest peak in Africa at 19,340 feet (5,896 meters). The mountain began to form about 750,000 years ago as a result of lava spewing out of Shira, Kibo, and Mawenzi volcanic vents. Although previously thought to be extinct, Mount Kilimanjaro is dormant and may have the capacity to erupt again, as it did in 1940–1941 and 1954–1955.

The mountain features a cold, dry climate, low humidity, and con-siderable extremes in temperature. The southern slope faces the pre-vailing winds from the Indian Ocean and receives more than 45 inches (1,125 millimeters) of annual rainfall, while the northern slope receives less than 30 inches (750 millimeters). Mount Kilimanjaro may be divided into five ecological zones. The lower slopes, between 2,624 and 5,905 feet (800 and 1,800 meters), are used for cultivation and livestock grazing. Human encroachment has changed this area's environment from what was once scrub, bush, and lowland forest into grass and crop land. The second zone, from 5,905 to 9,187 feet (1,800 to 2,800 meters), consists of a forest on the southern slope. Zone three, from 9,187 to 13,120 feet (2,800 to 4,000 meters), contains heath and moorland. Zone four, from 13,120 to 16,400 feet (4,000 to 5,000 meters), is a highland desert in which about 50 species of hardy plants live. The last zone, above 16,400 feet (5,000 meters), is a sum-mit characterized by arctic conditions.

Mount Kilimanjaro has always fascinated humans. The Chagga used the mountain for religious purposes, and early Greek and Chi-nese geographers mentioned the existence of a snow-covered peak near the equator. On 11 May 1848 Johannes Rebmann (q.v.) was the first European to sight Mount Kilimanjaro, and in 1889 Hans Meyer, a German scientist, became the first European to ascend the mountain. Over the next century Mount Kilimanjaro became a popular tourist attraction, and by the early 1990s ecologists expressed concern that an increasingly large number of climbers, coupled with a growing human population at the lower altitudes, posed a serious threat to the mountain's environment.

MOUNT KILIMANJARO NATIONAL PARK. Gazetted in 1973, this park is located 24 miles (40 kilometers) north of Moshi along the Tanzanian-Kenyan border and covers an area of 720 square miles (1,864 square kilometers). Not surprisingly, its greatest attraction is Mount Kilimanjaro (q.v.), although small numbers of elephant, buffalo, rhinoceros, eland, duiker, and leopard live within park boundaries.

MOUNT MERU. Meru is a volcanic mountain formed an estimated 20 million years ago. Located in Arusha National Park (q.v.) and rising to 14,990 feet (4,566 meters), it is the second highest peak in Tanzania. A tropical rain forest ranges from 4,600 to 6,000 feet (1,380 to 1,800 meters). The southern slope faces the Indian Ocean's prevailing winds and receives more than 40 inches (1,000 millimeters) of annual rainfall, while the northern slope obtains less than 30 inches (750 millimeters). In 1876 the Austrian Count Teleki von Szek was the first European to sight Mount Meru.

MREMA, AUGUSTINE LYATONGA (b. 1944). Born in Kiraracha, Moshi District, Mrema attended Makomu Primary School (1956–1959) and Makomu Middle School (1960–1963). Following Form IV study, he entered Kivukoni College (q.v.), Dar es Salaam (1970–1971), and later the University of Sofia, Bulgaria (1980–1981), where he received a diploma in social sciences and management. From 1966 to 1974 he worked as a school teacher, head teacher, and ward education secretary. From 1974 to 1979 Mrema served as CCM (q.v.) party district political commissioner for Bunda, Serengeti, and Hai districts. In 1982 he became an assistant to the Dodoma regional security officer, and in 1983 he was appointed assistant secretary to the CCM Commission for Defence and Security, a post he held until 1985.

In 1985 and again in 1990, Mrema was elected MP for Moshi (q.v.). During his second term he became minister for home affairs. Until 1993 he also served as deputy prime minister. In November 1994 Mrema was transferred to the Ministry of Labour, Community Development, and Youth, but in February 1995 President Ali Hassan Mwinyi (q.v.) fired him for criticizing the alleged embezzlement of public funds by a foreign businessman. Mrema then resigned from the CCM and joined the newly formed National Convention for Construction and Reform (NCCR). In March 1995 he received the NCCR's presidential nomination, with Sultan Ahmed Sultan as his running mate. During his campaign Mrema charged that the government had allowed the country's resources to be looted and had failed adequately to collect taxes. He promised to reduce Tanzania's poverty and welcomed international investors under better regulated terms.

Mrema also vowed to end official corruption, to increase the number of Tanzanian universities, to reduce youth unemployment, and to revamp the agricultural sector. These pledges were insufficent for him to win the 1995 presidential election. Also, see ELECTIONS, TANGANYIKA TERRITORY, TANGANYIKA, TANZANIA; and OPPOSITION POLITICAL PARTIES.

MTWARA. Bearing the name of the administrative region of which it is the capital, Mtwara is located near the Tanzania-Mozambique border about 90 miles (144 kilometers) south of Kilwa (q.v.). Mtwara's importance stems from its natural harbor, which has two deepwater berths capable of handling large ships. The town's 1988 population was 76,632.

MUNYIGUMBA, CHIEF (?–1879). Sometime between 1855 and 1860, Munyigumba became chief of the Muyinga clan, one of fifteen ruling clans among peoples who later became known as the Hehe. Throughout the 1860s and 1870s he asserted his control over these clans and unified the Hehe people. In order to achieve these goals, Munyigumba adopted the military tactics of the neighboring Ngoni people (tactics originally developed by the southern African Zulus) and used them against his enemies. His state lacked civil institutions and a governing bureaucracy, although he appointed local leaders, known as *munzaliga,* to every conquered region. These individuals possessed wide political and military powers but owed their positions to Munyigumba. After his death, his son Mkwawa (q.v.) eventually gained the loyalty of the Hehe, employed his father's governing techniques, and led Hehe resistance against the Germans. Also, see PEOPLE.

MUSOMA RESOLUTION. This 1974 TANU (q.v.) resolution adopted a policy of universal primary education. It also provided that, before entering into higher educational programs, students would first have to work for two years. A 1976 amendment to the Musoma Resolution partially exempted female students from this work requirement.

MWALIMU. Swahili (q.v.) word for teacher. Normally, the word is used as a title of respect or in reference to former President Julius Nyerere (q.v.).

MWANZA. Tanzania's second largest city, located on the shores of Lake Victoria (q.v.). Originally, Mwanza was a center for dhow (q.v.) building. In later years the city became an agricultural marketing hub for the maize, cassava, and cotton (qq.v.) grown by the Sukuma people, Tanzania's largest ethnic group. Despite its location in Tanzania's interior, Mwanza is fairly cosmopolitan, with a large Asian population, good links to Kenya and Uganda, and rail service to Dar es Salaam.

MWINYI MKUU. Dynastic title held by the rulers of Zanzibar's Hadimu people. Prior to the invasion of the Omani sultanate of Seyyid Said (q.v.) in 1840, the Mwenyi Mkuu was the main political authority in Zanzibar. Thereafter, the Mwenyi Mkuu reigned as a vassal of Seyyid Said and his successors until 1873, when the last holder of the title died.

MWINYI, ALI HASSAN (b. 1925). President of Tanzania from 1985 to 1995. Mwinyi was born on the mainland but moved as a child to Zanzibar (q.v.), where he trained as a teacher, after which he received advanced education at Newcastle and Hull Universities in Great Britain. Returning to Zanzibar, Mwinyi taught at and later directed the Zanzibari Teacher Training College. He then served in Zanzibar as a permanent secretary in the Ministry of Education and as an executive with the Zanzibari State Trading Corporation. Mwinyi's service to the union government included appointments as minister for health, minister for home affairs, ambassador to Egypt, and minister of state in the vice president's office.

Immediately before becoming the union president, Mwinyi held the twin positions of president of Zanzibar and Pemba and first vice president of Tanzania (1984–1985). After succeeding President Julius Nyerere (q.v.) in 1985, Mwinyi sought to repair the damage caused by Nyerere's failed socialist policies by liberalizing the economy, ending some state monopolies, and encouraging private enterprise. In the political arena, he supported, albeit reluctantly, the democratization process and also a more pragmatic foreign policy. In 1990 Mwinyi became chairman of the CCM (q.v.) after Nyerere resigned that position. Deciding not to run in the 1995 presidential election, Mwinyi was replaced by Benjamin Mkapa (q.v.), Tanzania's third president.

MZIZIMA. Traditional local name for Dar es Salaam (q.v.), meaning "Healthy Town."

— N —

NATIONAL ASSEMBLY. Preceded by the LEGCO (q.v.), this institution is the Tanzanian government's central legislative body. On 1 May 1961 the LEGCO was renamed the Tanganyika Parliament; after independence it was designated as the National Assembly. Under the provisions of 1992 constitutional amendments, the National Assembly includes 101 elected members from the mainland, up to 55 elected members from Zanzibar and Pemba (qq.v.), and 75 ex officio and nominated members. In addition, 15 percent of National Assembly seats are reserved for women. The number of electoral constituencies is subject to revision by the Electoral Commission. The country's second vice president is selected from among the elected members of the National Assembly and also serves as prime minister, head of government, and leader of the National Assembly. The constitution guarantees the National Assembly's legislative supremacy and states that the president has no power to legislate without its approval. The National Assembly has numerous standing committees, including Finance and Economic Affairs, Political Affairs, Public Accounts, Social Services, Standing Orders, and General.

NATIONAL INVESTMENT (PROMOTION AND PROTECTION) ACT. On 19 June 1990 the National Assembly (q.v.) enacted this legislation to stimulate local and foreign investment by establishing an Investment Promotion Centre (q.v.) and adopting rules to govern domestic and foreign investment in Tanzania. To encourage investment, the act provides for a five-year tax holiday and allows for up to 50 percent of retained foreign exchange receipts (i.e., up to 25 percent of export earnings) to be used to effect overseas remittances. Although this act improved Tanzania's investment climate, the country must still improve its economic infrastructure, labor practices, and efficiency if it is to attract significant investment.

NATIONAL PARTY OF THE SUBJECTS OF THE SULTAN OF ZANZIBAR (NPSS). The NPSS was the first nationalist political party in Zanzibar. In mid-1955 a small group of peasants from the village of Kiembe Samaki created the NPSS, which advocated a multiracial ideology and independence for Zanzibar. The lack of strong political leadership doomed the NPSS, which eventually evolved into the Zanzibar National Party (q.v.).

NATIONAL SERVICE. In 1963 the government established a voluntary national service. The National Service Act of 1966 made service compulsory for secondary, technical college, and university graduates. In October 1966 University College, Dar es Salaam (q.v.), students demonstrated against the act, and Second Vice President Rashidi Kawawa (q.v.), under the direction of President Julius Nyerere (q.v.), retaliated by expelling some 400 of the protestors. After a year, most were reinstated.

National Service was for a two-year period. After a three-month basic training course, changed in 1975 to six months, trainees could volunteer to join the army, police force, or village development programs. In these positions, National Service personnel received a basic allowance and supposedly 40 percent of the wages they would have received had they held regular jobs.

NATIONAL UNION OF TANGANYIKA WORKERS (NUTA). In February 1964 the National Assembly (q.v.) approved the dissolution of Tanganyika's trade unions organized under the aegis of the Tanganyika Federation of Labour (TFL) (q.v.). In their place, NUTA was installed as the sole body authorized to represent the country's workers. NUTA was organized into numerous administrative subdivisions, including designated units for agricultural workers, transport and general workers, domestic and hotel employees, the East African Community (EAC) (q.v.), dockers, miners, central and local government workers, and teachers. By the late 1960s NUTA included more than 230,000 dues-paying members. Membership in NUTA was not compulsory, but organizations with over 50 percent of their workers in the union could seek government assistance in requiring all others to join.

In 1977 the Union of Tanzania Workers (JUWATA) replaced NUTA, and by the early 1990s this union claimed approximately 500,000 members divided into eight sections (central and local government and medical workers; agricultural workers; industrial and mine workers; teachers; domestic, hotels, and general workers; commerce and construction workers; communication and transport workers; and railway workers). Like NUTA before it, JUWATA was intended more to exert CCM (q.v.) party control over the Tanzanian labor force than to represent workers' interests in the largely nationalized economy. In December 1991, however, the Organization of Tanzanian Trade Unions (OTTU) replaced JUWATA. For the trade union movement this action reflected the government's larger desire to grant greater autonomy to mass organizations in order "to further democratise the country's political system."

NATIVE AUTHORITY ORDINANCE OF 1923. This colonial ordinance established a local government system that employed supposedly traditional African leaders as administrators. The ordinance replaced a German system that had employed *akidas* and *jumbes* (qq.v.) as local agents of central rule. It conferred powers on European administrative officers and African chiefs and headmen to issue orders and regulations providing for local "peace, order and good government." In administrative districts where there were strong chieftainships, the ordinance empowered native courts to hear petty cases.

NATIVE AUTHORITY ORDINANCE OF 1927. This amendment to the Native Authority Ordinance of 1923 (q.v.) reflected Sir Donald Cameron's (q.v.) determination to establish and empower grassroots African governmental institutions in TT. The main difference between this ordinance and the 1923 policy was that the 1927 version created a hierarchy of native authorities with greater powers. These new authorities enjoyed full power of arrest for crimes committed in their jurisdictions. They could also issue orders regulating the manufacture and sale of liquor, possession of weapons, theft, and gambling. They were likewise authorized to administer enterprises requiring considerable manpower, for example, projects concerned with conservation, public works, and recovery from natural disasters.

NEW, CHARLES (1840–1875). In 1863 New became a missionary with the United Methodist Free Church in Mombasa. In 1871 he journeyed to Mount Kilimanjaro. Until his return to England in 1872 he worked among the Nyika, Galla, and Chagga (q.v.) peoples. During his stay in England, New became a celebrity because of his missionary work, his antislavery activities, and his explorations in East Africa. In June 1874 New arrived in Zanzibar, hoping to open a mission station among the Chagga. He died on 15 February 1875, after having made an initial contact with Chief Rindi (q.v.), the Chagga chief.

NGORONGORO CONSERVATION AREA. Gazetted in 1959, this area covers 2,500 square miles (6,475 square kilometers) and includes the Ngorongoro Crater, one of the most spectacular wildlife habitats in Africa. The crater has a diameter of 11 miles (16 kilometers) with a floor area of 102 square miles (163 square kilometers). Ngorongoro dates back 2.5 million years, and its collapsed volcanic peak may have rivaled Mount Kilimanjaro's (q.v.) in height. In 1951 the colonial government included Ngorongoro in the Serengeti National Park (q.v.). Five years later Ngorongoro was detached from the Serengeti because of a conflict between park authorities and local Maasai (q.v.) herdsmen who opposed the withdrawal of their grazing rights from the crater. Ngorongoro thus became a conservation area for the benefit of wildlife and pastoralists alike. Although the wildlife population has diminished as a result of hunting and human population pressure, Ngorongoro still contains lion, elephant, rhinoceros, buffalo, and many plains herbivores such as wildebeest, Thomson's gazelle, zebra, and reedbuck. A large flamingo (q.v.) concentration also thrives at Lake Magadi, a soda lake in the crater.

NYALALI COMMISSION. President Ali Hassan Mwinyi (q.v.) appointed this commission in 1991 to determine whether the Tanzanian people favored the introduction of a multiparty political system. According to the Nyalali Commission's findings, some 77 percent of the people surveyed favored the continuation of a one-party system. Advocates of a multi-party state charged that fear of government retribution influenced these results, and in any case the commission recommended that the Tanzanian constitution be amended to permit multiple political parties. This recommendation was accepted. By early 1994 12 parties had been registered, each with its own ideology and development strategy.

NYAMWEZI. See PEOPLE.

NYERERE, JULIUS K. (b. 1922). Father of Tanzanian independence and known as *Mwalimu* (q.v.) to his followers, Nyerere was born in Butiama, Musoma District, in the vicinity of Lake Victoria (q.v.). After completing primary schooling at the Busegwe Maryknoll mission school, Nyerere received his secondary education during the 1930s at St. Mary's School in Tabora (q.v.) and at St. Francis School, Pugu. From 1943 to 1945 he attended Makerere University (q.v.) in Kampala, Uganda. Nyerere then returned to Tabora to teach in a Catholic school. Between 1949 and 1952 he undertook graduate studies at the University of Edinburgh, Scotland.

In 1953 Nyerere began his political career when he was elected president of the Tanganyika African Association (TAA) (q.v.). One year later he transformed the TAA into the Tanganyika African National Union (TANU) (q.v.) and became this political party's founding president. Nyerere and TANU then led TT to independence on 9 December 1961.

After independence Nyerere became Tanganyika's first prime minister in 1961 and its first president in 1962. During this period he refined his philosophy of *ujamaa* (q.v.) into a governing ideology, which was officially announced in the Arusha Declaration (q.v.) of 1967. Again under Nyerere's leadership, TANU and the Zanzibari Afro-Shirazi Party (ASP) (q.v.) were merged as the CCM (q.v.) in 1977. At the first CCM party congress, he was elected chairman, a position to which he was reelected in 1982 and 1987. In 1985 Nyerere decided not to campaign again for the Tanzanian presidency, although he continued to serve as CCM chairman until his 1990 resignation. Since then Nyerere, who has become an honored elder statesman throughout Africa, has continued to speak out on matters affecting Tanzania and the continent as a whole.

Under Nyerere's rule, Tanzania became an increasingly rigid and ineffective one-party state. In particular, application of his socialist ideology all but destroyed the country's economy. In foreign policy

Nyerere's most notable accomplishments include his decision to depose dictator Idi Amin Dada by invading Uganda in 1979, and his long-standing leadership in opposition to the apartheid system of racial discrimination in South Africa. During the early 1990s he reluctantly approved efforts to convert the Tanzanian political system into a multiparty democracy.

After his retirement from political life, Nyerere has enhanced his reputation as an African and Third World philosopher-statesman. One of his earliest accomplishments in this regard occurred in 1987, when he became chairman of the South Commission. The Non-Aligned Movement of Third World States had established this organization to review the post-1945 development experiences of colonies and former colonies and to recommend future development strategies. In the commission's first report, *The Challenge to the South,* Nyerere argued for greater South–South cooperation. To achieve this goal, he advocated the creation of a Group of Developing Countries (also known as the Group of Fifteen), which would act as an international forum on matters affecting Third World states. Nyerere has also strongly advocated greater African political and economic collaboration through organizations such as the Southern African Development Coordination Conference (SADCC), the Southern African Development Community (SADC), and the Common Market of Eastern and Southern African States (COMESA) (qq.v.).

In the early 1990s the emergence of a pro-democracy movement in Tanzania marked another turning point in Nyerere's long political career. Initially skeptical of demands for an open political system, he reluctantly approved efforts to turn the country into a multiparty state. As the 1995 national elections approached, Nyerere again became more active in Tanzanian politics. In particular, he accused the government of his successor, President Ali Hassan Mwinyi (q.v.), of corruption. Mwinyi responded by claiming that when Nyerere was president he pursued a self-defeating economic and political agenda and suppressed or harassed people who disagreed with him and his policies. Nyerere then intervened in the CCM's deliberations to ensure that one of his disciples, Benjamin Mkapa (q.v.) would receive the ruling party's 1995 presidential nomination. Most observers agreed that Nyerere would continue to play a significant behind-the-scenes role in Mkapa's government.

NYUNGU YA MAWE (c. 1840–1884). An African ruler who unified the Kimbu people by conquering and consolidating more than 30 of their autonomous chiefdoms in what is now Chunya District north of Mbeya (q.v.). By the end of Nyunga's career, his army, known as the *Ruga Ruga* (q.v.), had acquired approximately 20,000 square miles

(50,000 square kilometers) of territory. He ruled this empire by re-placing traditional chiefs with loyal governors. In the late 1870s Ny-ungu attempted to seize control of northern Tanzania's trade routes by harassing Arab (q.v.) trading caravans. When he died in late 1884, Nyungu bequeathed one of Tanzania's most stable empires to his daughter, Mugalula. After Mugalula committed suicide, another woman, Msavila, assumed control of the empire. In 1895 Msavila submitted to German colonial rule and renounced all claims to sover-eignty over the Kimbu people.

— O —

OKELLO, JOHN (1937–). Although Ugandan by birth, Okello became the "Field Marshal" of the 1964 Zanzibar Revolution (q.v.). In 1959 he moved to Zanzibar (q.v.) and then to Pemba (q.v.), where he worked for several years as a mason, painter, and occasional laborer. During this time Okello served as secretary to the Afro-Shirazi Party (ASP) (q.v.) youth wing for Pemba. In early 1963 he moved back to Zanzibar and eventually led the revolution and commanded its "free-dom fighters." Okello left the island in early 1964 and was then ex-pelled from Tanganyika and Kenya. He subsequently returned to Uganda and claimed that he would devote his energies to liberating South Africa and Mozambique. Ugandan authorities soon jailed him for alleged security violations.

OLDUVAI GORGE. This narrow gorge, 31 miles (50 kilometers) long, cuts across the Serengeti and Salei Plains in an east-west direction and is located between the Ngorongoro Conservation Area and the Serengeti National Park (qq.v.). Known as the cradle of humanity, Olduvai is the site of some of the most important fossil hominid finds of all time.

In 1931 Louis Leakey (q.v.) started his first dig at Olduvai. Over the next 28 years Leakey and his wife, Mary (q.v.), uncovered hun-dreds of fossils and bones. In 1959 they discovered the remains of an early man, which they called *Zinjanthropus* (q.v.), later known as *Australopithecus boisei*. The two also discovered *Homo habilis,* which became the focal point of Leakey's highly contentious theory that the genus *Homo,* which evolved into modern man, existed to-gether with *Australopithecus* but was not a direct descendent. In 1979 Mary Leakey discovered hominid footprints at Laetoli, near Olduvai, which she claimed were those of a man, woman, and child. Since these 3.7 million year old prints were made by creatures that walked upright, Mary Leakey's findings seemed to confirm that direct human ancestors existed at a much earlier time than had previously been supposed.

OPERATION MADUKA. A plan devised in the early 1970s by Prime Minister and Second Vice President Rashidi Kawawa (q.v.), to close private shops (*dukas*) held to be in unfair competition with government cooperatives. Hundreds of largely Asian (q.v.) private shops were subsequently closed, creating considerable hardship for the country's peasants, who had to travel longer distances to government shops, pay higher prices, and tolerate frequent shortages of commodities. In May 1976 Julius Nyerere (q.v.) intervened in this situation by charging that anyone who ordered the closure of private shops was "an enemy of Tanzania's policy of socialism and self-reliance." Shortly thereafter, Operation Maduka was terminated and Rashidi Kawawa demoted from prime minister and second vice president to minister of defense.

OPERATION TANDAU. This policy initiative involved a scheme, devised in early 1976 by Minister of Agriculture Alfred Tandau, to dismiss 20 percent of all public service workers. The opposition of the National Union of Tanganyika Workers (NUTA) (q.v.) eventually forced the abandonment of Tandau's proposal, which would have resulted in the release of 9,000 to 10,000 workers.

OPERESHENI KILA MTU AFANYE KAZI (Operation Every Person Must Work). In June 1976 Julius Nyerere (q.v.) initiated this policy, which held that "all able-bodied persons must be productively employed." His goal was to provide jobs for everyone who wanted employment and to compel so-called "work-shy" urban dwellers to return to the rural areas and take up employment in agriculture. The government attempted to begin implementation of this policy by rounding up the unemployed of Dar es Salaam (q.v.) and resettling them in the countryside. The roundup, known as Operation Rwegasira (named for the regional commissioner for Dar es Salaam), was a total failure. Those who were resettled quickly returned to the city. The operation was criticized as socially unpopular and economically disruptive, and the government press claimed that the policy was doomed because the unemployment problem had not been attacked in a humanely socialist context. Within months, Nyerere quietly abandoned the entire scheme.

OPPOSITION POLITICAL PARTIES. After the ruling CCM (q.v.) and the Tanzanian National Electoral Commission approved the establishment of a multiparty political system in March 1992, opposition political parties proliferated. By the eve of the October 1995 presidential and parliamentary elections, the National Electoral Commission had endorsed 1,311 candidates from 13 parties. Apart from the CCM, these parties included the National Convention for Construction and Reform (NCCR), Civic United Front (CUF), United Democratic Party (UDP), National Reconstruction Alliance, Party for Democracy and Development, National League for Democracy, Popular National Party, Tanzania Democratic Alliance, Union for a Multi-Party Democracy, United People's Democratic Party, Tanzania People's Party, and Tanzania Labour Party.

The three strongest opposition parties were the NCCR, the CUF, and the UDP, the others being underfunded, disorganized, and lacking in support. During pre-election campaigning, each major opposition party outlined a fairly comprehensive policy platform. The NCCR's major promises included eliminating corruption, reducing government spending, curbing youth unemployment, and improving the agricultural sector. In addition to supporting greater autonomy for Zanzibar (q.v.), the CUF pledged to improve educational standards, to revise the country's economic policies, and to reduce the size of government. The UDP committed itself to eliminating state control over agricultural land, ending youth unemployment, encouraging foreign investment, and allowing farmers to market their crops in the absence of government controls and interference. Also, see ELECTIONS, TANGANYIKA TERRITORY, TANGANYIKA, TANZANIA.

ORMSBY-GORE COMMISSION (1924). This commission represented the first attempt by the British government to determine whether an East African Federation (q.v.) should be established between TT, Kenya, and Uganda. The Ormsby-Gore Commission (named after the Secretary of State for the Colonies at the time) visited East Africa to report on how to accelerate the economic development of Britain's East African dependencies as well as to secure closer cooperation in several areas, including transport, cotton cultivation, general agriculture, and medicine. The commission was also to investigate the improvement of social conditions within the African population and African relations with non-Africans. The commission rejected the "closer union" (q.v.) concept but recommended regular meetings of officials from TT, Kenya, and Uganda to discuss issues of mutual interest. It also supported the establishment of a common customs union; the adoption of uniform commercial laws in areas like bankruptcy, patents, designs, and trademarks; and the opening of an interterritorial soil research station at Amani in northeastern TT.

OWEN, JOHN (1912–1995). Apart from serving as director of national parks between 1960 and 1970, Owen worked with the Serengeti Research Institute at Seronera, which conducted a series of pioneering scientific studies of the Serengeti and its ecosystem. Also, see SERENGETI NATIONAL PARK.

— P —

PAN-AFRICAN FREEDOM MOVEMENT OF EAST AND CENTRAL AFRICA (PAFMECA). In 1958 TANU (q.v.) sponsored an All African People's Conference, convened at Mwanza (q.v.), which created PAFMECA to counter Britain's multiracial policy for the region. The organization sought to coordinate and promote independence movements throughout East and Central Africa. PAFMECA included African nationalists and trade unions from the Congo (now Zaire), Kenya, Nyasaland (now Malawi), Northern Rhodesia (now Zambia), Southern Rhodesia (now Zimbabwe), Ruanda-Urundi (now Rwanda and Burundi), Uganda, TT, and Zanzibar.

PASHA, EMIN (1840–1892). Born to a Jewish family as Eduard Schnitzer at Oppeln, Silesia. He studied medicine at Breslau and Berlin and entered practice at Scutari, Albania. Schnitzer eventually converted to Islam and assumed the name Emin, meaning "faithful one."

In 1876 Emin entered the Egyptian administrative service at the relatively low rank of effendi, and quickly rose to the ranks of bey and finally pasha. General Charles Gordon hired him first as chief medical officer and in 1878 as governor of Equatorial Province in southern Sudan. Emin held this post until 1889, in the interim surviving the Mahdist revolt of 1883 and becoming a skilled linguist and authority on the anthropology, zoology, botany, and meteorology of the southern Sudanese region. The revolt had cut Emin off from the outside world, and in 1887 a British rescue mission was organized under Henry M. Stanley (q.v.). Having rescued Emin, the Stanley party crossed East Africa to Bagamoyo (q.v.) by way of Lake Edward, Ankole, and Karagwe. On the day of his arrival, Emin was seriously injured when he fell out of a window at the Bagamoyo Boma (q.v.). After several months of recovery, he joined the German colonial service under Imperial Commissioner Hermann von Wissmann (q.v.).

In 1890 Wissmann sent Emin to the Lake Victoria (q.v.) region to forestall the consolidation of British influence over the area and, upon hearing of it en route, to enforce the Anglo-German Agreement of 1890 (q.v.). He met Carl Peters (q.v.) during an extended stopover at Mpwapwa. Proceeding then to Tabora (q.v.), Emin established German authority over local African and Arab communities and, with his lieutenant, medical officer Franz Stuhlmann, helped to suppress the last vestiges of the Arab slave trade (q.v.) in an area extending between Tabora and Sukumaland to the north. In October 1890 Emin crossed Lake Victoria by canoe and established a German station on Bukoba Bay in Buhaya country. Leaving another officer, Captain Wilhelm Langheld, in charge at Bukoba (q.v.), Emin crossed the Anglo-German border into Uganda in early 1891 and, ignoring a recall order from Wissmann, pushed on into the Congo. In October 1892 local Africans, at the instigation of Arab slave traders, murdered Emin.

Emin Pasha had been a pioneering, if a somewhat unorthodox and undisciplined, extender of German administration into the East African interior. He brought more territory and peoples under German rule through peaceful and conciliatory means than Carl Peters had ever achieved through his violent *Schrecklichkeit* ("frightfulness," or scorched-earth) tactics.

PEMBA ISLAND. Located 31 miles (50 kilometers) north of Zanzibar (q.v.), Pemba has an area of 380 square miles (984 square kilometers) and is 42 miles (68 kilometers) long and 14 miles (23 kilometers) wide. Pemba's townships include Wete (the regional capital), Chake Chake, and Mkoani. The island is fertile and features a varied topography with small, steep hills and valleys. The average annual rainfall is 73 inches (1,825 millimeters). The mean maximum temperature is 86.3 degrees Farenheit (30 degrees Celsius) and the mean minimum temperature is 76.1 degrees Farenheit (25 degrees Celsius). Pemba produces about 85 percent of Zanzibari cloves (q.v.). Coconuts also serve as an important export, and fishing is the island's leading industry. A few rubber plantations are located on the island.

Africans from the mainland initially settled on Pemba. In about the tenth century, Persian settlers arrived there and unified the island's previously autonomous villages. In 1508 the Portuguese attacked Pemba and extracted tribute from the islanders until most fled to Mombasa. A century later, Omani Arabs (q.v.) expelled the Portuguese, and in 1882 Seyyid Said (q.v.) conquered the island. In 1890 Pemba and Zanzibar became a British protectorate.

After the Zanzibar Revolution (q.v.) of January 1964, Abeid Karume (q.v.) closed the island to tourists and other foreigners because of considerable antigovernment sentiment on the island. Although Pemba became less isolated during the 1980s, many islanders remained opposed to the Zanzibari government and to the union with the mainland. The island's 1988 population was 265,039.

PEOPLE. More than 120 ethnic groups reside in Tanzania, and most are of Bantu–language group origin. Each has its own unique culture, social organization, and language. Unlike the situation in most of Africa, no group is large enough to claim dominance. As a result, the level and intensity of ethnic conflict in Tanzania is lower than elsewhere on the continent. Swahili (q.v.), spoken by 96 percent of the population, has also helped to unify the Tanzanian people. The majority of Tanzanians live in the rural areas and engage in farming and/or pastoral pursuits. The following 10 ethnic groups form about 50 percent of the country's population.

Chagga (Bantu-speaking). Originally organized under a system of local chiefs, the Chagga people constitute Tanzania's third largest ethnic group. They live on the slopes of Mount Kilimanjaro (q.v.). To farm the mountainside, the Chagga have developed an irrigation system that carries water up to 600 feet (180 meters) above river level. The Chagga have also used cooperative farming to their advantage. On 15 January 1925 they formed the Kilimanjaro Native Planters Association to organize coffee (q.v.) marketing. In 1931 the Kilimanjaro Native Cooperative Union (KNCU) succeeded this association and eventually became a model of African progress for people throughout the country. Reliance on cooperative farming and the widespread cultivation of coffee have enabled the Chagga to become one of the most prosperous ethnic groups in Tanzania.

Gogo (Bantu-speaking). At some point the Gogo people moved eastward from Unyamwezi and Uhehe into the region southwest of the Masasi Steppe near Dodoma (q.v.). Despite their recently acquired agricultural proficiency, the formerly pastoral Gogo still raise cattle. In past times they also possessed a high degree of military organization under chiefly governing institutions. During the 1830s they halted the southward expansionism of the Maasai (q.v.). In the nineteenth century the Gogo exchanged ivory for slaves to cultivate their land. Because of a lack of water, the Gogo have historically suffered from periodic drought and famine. During the 1953–1955 period, for example, one of the worst droughts in history decimated Gogo society. To make matters worse, the now-impoverished Gogo were compelled themselves to pay for a large-scale government rescue campaign.

Ha (Bantu-speaking). The Ha people originate in small lineage-based communities along the Burundi border between Lake Victoria and Lake Tanganyika (qq.v.). In this region, which is infested with tsetse (q.v.) flies, the Ha have traditionally tended their long-horned cattle, grown tobacco, and harvested honey. In the period between the two world wars, the British colonial government unsuccessfully sought to establish cash crops in Buha (meaning "country of the Ha"). As a result of this failure, some British officials applied the labor-reserve concept to the Ha people by promising European settlers that Buha would be used to supply laborers to plantations and estates throughout TT. In recent years, the Ha have also resisted government attempts to move them from their homeland to better watered areas.

Haya (Bantu-speaking). Originally organized into chiefly clans, the Haya live along the western shore of Lake Victoria (q.v.). Long before the arrival of Europeans, they grew and sold coffee (q.v.). Local coffee and tea (q.v.) processing plants enable the Haya to export both crops and have helped them to attain a level of prosperity rivaling that of the Chagga (q.v.).

Hehe (Bantu-speaking). The Hehe formed a centralized kingdom in response to an 1840s Ngoni invasion from southern Africa. Settled on a plateau in the Iringa (q.v.) highlands, during the nineteenth century the Hehe established an impressive military reputation by resisting the colonizing Germans. Today the Hehe sustain this military legacy by supplying a large proportion of the recruits to the Tanzania People's Defence Force (TPDF) (q.v.). The Hehe practice a mixed economy combining farming and pastoralism.

Maasai (Nilotic-speaking). The Maasai people live in north-central Tanzania in an area known as the Maasai Steppe. Maasai unity and, to some extent, political organization are based on an age-set (q.v.) system that requires a person pass go through five or six phases in adult life, from *moran* (warrior) to elder. The *laibon* functions as a Maasai spiritual leader. The Maasai, who never established an organized state, still live in pastoral, patrilineal communities and believe, according to Maasai tradition, that God created cattle for their exclusive benefit. Among rural Maasai, the size of a man's cattle herd reflects his wealth, prestige, and standing in society. Cattle breeding and cattle raiding thus lie at the heart of Maasai life and culture. In recent years wandering Maasai herds have placed increasing pressure on areas such as the environmentally fragile Ngorongoro Conservation Area (q.v.). Although government attempts to encourage the Maasai to adopt a settled lifestyle have met with some success, many Maasai remained committed to their seminomadic traditions.

Nyamwezi (Bantu-speaking). Comprising one of Tanzania's largest ethnic groups, the Nyamwezi live near Tabora (q.v.). They are known as the "people of the moon," because of their propensity to wander in many parts of East Africa. Between 1700 and 1800, the Nyamwezi established a reputation as important traders. Organized under chiefly but surprisingly democratic principles, entire clans traveled as far west as the Congo rain forest to collect copper, wax, ivory, and slaves, journeying then to the coast to exchange these items for cloth, metal tools, pots, and cowrie shells, which they used as money. During the nineteenth century the Nyamwezi became the most important African traders and the most powerful ethnic group in the interior. Today the Nyamwezi are largely cultivators and cattle herders.

Sukuma (Bantu-speaking). Ethnically related to the Nyamwezi (q.v.), the Sukuma ("people to the north") constitute Tanzania's largest tribal grouping and live in the vicinity of Lake Victoria near Mwanza (qq.v.). Organized into several chiefdoms, the Sukuma remained isolated from missionary influence, Western education, and the cash-crop economy until the twentieth century. In more recent decades the Sukuma have become prosperous thanks especially to the introduction of cotton into Sukumaland during the British colonial period. The port of Mwanza has also prospered because of the Sukuma's commercial influence, as reflected in the success of the cotton-based Victoria Federation of Cooperative Unions (VFCU).

Makonde (Bantu-speaking). The Makonde live in small, informally governed communities on the Makonde Plateau, which extends along the southern Indian Ocean. Because of their isolation, the Makonde have been relatively unaffected by colonial and postcolonial developments. The conservative Makonde also have a reputation for resisting external change and defending their traditional way of life. Makonde wood carvings are famous throughout the world.

Iraqw (Cushitic-speaking). The Iraqw homeland lies in the central highlands of Mbulu District west of Arusha (q.v.). These people, who live in relatively isolated communities, practice mixed farming and cattle raising. Commercial dealings with the outside world have been based largely on necessity rather than on a desire to gain wealth, although in recent decades private and government-sponsored agricultural development projects have partially drawn the Iraqw into the cash economy.

PEOPLE'S LIBERATION ARMY (PLA). In early 1964 Zanzibari revolutionaries established the 2,000- to 3,000-man PLA, whose mission was to defend the islands and to preserve internal self-government. Brigadier Yusuf Himid commanded the PLA, which was trained and armed by a Soviet mission of 40 to 60 advisers. In late 1964 Colonel Ali Mahfoudh, a Cuban-trained Arab revolutionary who was second-in-command of the PLA, and a small number of troops deployed to the mainland town of Mtwara (q.v.). From this location near the Mozambique border, Mahfoudh provided assistance to the insurgent *Frente de Libertaçao de Moçambique* (FRELIMO) to free Mozambique from Portuguese colonial rule. In March 1966 the government announced that the PLA had joined the the Tanzania People's Defence Force (TPDF) (q.v.).

PEOPLE'S REPUBLIC OF ZANZIBAR. This state came into existence on 12 January 1964 following the Zanzibar Revolution (q.v.) and was disbanded on 26 April 1964, when Zanzibar united with the mainland to form the United Republic of Tanganyika and Zanzibar, which later that year became the United Republic of Tanzania (qq.v.).

PERIODICALS AND NEWSPAPERS. The following alphabetical listings include some of the former and current journalistic and other periodical materials published in GEA, TT, Tanganyika, and Tanzania.

Newspapers:
  Afrika Kwetu, 1947–1963
  Al Falaq, 1929–1963
  Amtlicher Anzeiger für den Bezirk Mische, 1908–1915
  Amtlicher Anzeiger für Deutsch-Ostafrika, 1900–1916
  Anzeiger für Tanga, 1902–1904
  Daily News, 1972-present
  Dar es Salaam Times, 1919–1926 (thereafter *Tanganyika Times*)
  Das Hochland, 1930–1937
  Der Pflanzer, 1905–1914
  Deutsch-Ostafrikanische Rundschau, 1908–1912
  Deutsch-Ostafrikanische Zeitung, 1899–1914
  Habari za Mwezi, 1895-?
  Kipanga, ?-present
  Kwetu, 1937-?
  Majira, 1993-present
  Mambo Leo, 1923–1962
  Msimulizi, 1891-?
  Mwongozi, 1942–1963
  Mzalendo, 1972-present
  Nuru, 1992-present
  Pwani na Bara, 1910-?
  Rafiki Yangu, 1910-?
  Sunday News, 1954-present
  Tanga Post and East Coast Advertiser, 1919–1925
  Tanganyika Standard, 1930–1972 (thereafter *Daily News*)
  Tanganyika Times, 1926–1930 (thereafter *Tanganyika Standard*)
  Tanganyika Weekly Standard, 1930–1972
  Uhuru, 1961-present
  Usambara Post, 1904–1916
  Weekly Mail, 1993-present
  Zanzibar Voice, 1922–1963
Periodicals:
  The African Review, 1971-present
  Azania Youth, 1985-present

Bulletin of Tanzanian Affairs, 1975-present
Business Times, 1988-present
Dar es Salaam Medical Journal, 1969-?
Dar es Salaam University Law Journal, 1966-?
East Africa Journal, ?-present
East African Agricultural and Forestry Journal, 1935-present
East African Medical Journal, 1923-present
Eastern Africa Law Review, 1967-present
Elimu Haina Mwisho, ?-present
Family Mirror, 1988-present
Gazette of the United Republic, ?-present
Government Gazette, 1964-present
Habari za Washirika, ?-present
Jenga, ?-present
Journal of International Relations, 1976-?
Kiongozi, 1950-present
Kweupe, ?-present
Maji Maji, 1971-present
Maji Review, 1974-? *Mbioni,* ?-present
Mfanyakazi, ?-present
Mlezi, 1970-present
Mambosasa, 1988?-present
Miombo, 1988?-present
Mwenge, 1937-present
Nchi Yetu, 1964-present
Nuru, 1992-present
Safani, ?-present
Samachar, 1902–1963
Sauti ya Siti, 1988-present
Sikiliza, ?-present
Swara, 1978-present
Taamuli, ?-present
Thanganyilea (later *Tanzania*) *Notes and Records* 1938–present
Tanzania Education Journal, 1972-present
Tanzania Medical Journal, 1984?-present
Tanzania Zamani, 1967-present
TNR, 1936-?
Uhuru na Amani, ?-present
Ukulima wa Kisasa, 1955-present
University Science Journal, 1975-?
Urusi Leo, 1968-present
Weekend Magazine, 1989-present

"PERIPLUS OF THE ERYTHRAEAN SEA." This volume is a trader's handbook, written by a Greek merchant sometime between 120 and

130 A.D. It was intended to provide a guide to ports and markets on the Indian Ocean coast, including those of East Africa. The *Periplus* reveals how Red Sea merchants sent Arab (q.v.) trading agents to East Africa, where they settled among the coastal African communities, intermarried, learned local languages, and established a trade in ivory, tortoise shell, and rhinoceros horn. It also indicated that it was possible to buy slaves along the East African coast. The *Periplus* discussed Rhapta (q.v.), the island of Menouthias (probably present-day Zanzibar [q.v.]), and Mtepe, a settlement presumably located south of Dar es Salaam (q.v.). This source remains essential for those seeking to understand the early history of the East African coastal area and offshore islands.

PETERS, DR. CARL (1856–1918). Founder of the German East Africa Company (q.v.). In November and December 1884, Peters signed a *schutzbrief* (q.v.) with chieftains and village elders in Useguha (Uzigua), Nguru, Usagara, and Ukami, which placed 56,000 square miles (140,000 square kilometers) of land under German protection. On 27 February 1885 the German government proclaimed a protectorate over these territories and empowered Peters to acquire additional concessions along the frontier of the Congo Free State. Two years later the German government dismissed Peters from imperial service for his brutality toward Africans and Arabs (q.v.).

PETROLEUM. No significant oil discoveries have been made in Tanzania, but by the early 1990s several international companies were exploring for oil. These include Shell and Esso, Elf Aquitaine, Petrofina, PetroCanada, AGIP, Amoco, Exxon, Statoil of Norway, BP, Texaco, Broken Hill (Pty) Company, Oil and Natural Gas Commission of India, and the Swiss-based International Energy Development Corporation. By late 1994 these efforts had been unsuccessful, although some natural gas deposits had been found in the Songo Songo Island area south of Dar es Salaam (q.v.) and in Kimbiji southwest of the city. In early 1994 the World Bank (q.v.) announced that it would finance a US$200 million project to exploit these deposits. The Tanzania Petroleum Development Corporation, the Tanzania Electric Supply Company, and two Canadian firms, Ocelct and TransCanada, were to implement this scheme.

PHELPS-STOKES COMMISSION (1924). An American educational foundation chaired by Jesse Jones, formerly of the Hampton Institute of Virginia, that investigated the state of African education in TT. The commission praised the progress the colonial government had made in reorganizing the African school system after World War I (q.v.) and noted that "a genuine effort has been made to relate the school work to the condition and needs of the people, especially as regards health and agriculture." The commission also criticized the authorities for their refusal to provide grants-in-aid to mission schools. In 1926/27, the colonial government reversed this policy, which enabled various mission societies to play a greater role in African education.

POLICE. During the German colonial period, the army performed all police duties in GEA. In 1919 the British established TT's first police force. British personnel served as officers, Asians filled the middle ranks, and Africans were employed in the lower ranks. The police usually confined operations to towns, with local chiefs held responsible for maintaining law and order in rural areas. Provincial police chiefs also provided protection to European settler farms and plantations. In April 1964 the independent government created a single police force for Tanzania and Zanzibar under the inspector general of police, who also still serves as a member of the CCM's Central Committee (qq.v.). Below him are three commissioners, each commanding an operational division. One of these units is responsible for Zanzibar, one for the mainland, and one for the 700-person Criminal Investigation Department (CID), which is responsible for intelligence gathering, countersubversion, and the investigation of political offenses. There also are 26 regional subdivisions, which correspond to the mainland's 20 administrative regions and the six offshore island regions. To provide a socialist orientation to law enforcement, Julius Nyerere (q.v.) established the People's Militia (*Jeshila Mgambo*), each member of which has arrest powers similar to those of a constable. A Police Field Force Unit is responsible for preserving law and order in regional and district capitals; a marine police patrols the coastline and the inland lakes; and a paramilitary force is used for riot control and emergencies. Police recruits are selected from the National Service (q.v.).

POPULATION. Since independence, the government has conducted an official census three times, in 1967, 1978, and 1988. The results showed a dramatic population increase from 12,313,469, to 17,512,610, and to 23,174,336 over the two decades. According to World Bank (q.v.) estimates, by 1993 the Tanzanian population had further grown to about 28,000,000. In 1992 the United Nations Fund for Population Activities (UNFPA) launched a US$21 million four-year program to help reduce Tanzania's 3 percent average annual population growth rate, which was then among the 10 highest in the world. The UNFPA program focused on educational research and promoting the participation of women in family planning activities.

Population densities on the mainland average 26 people per square kilometer and in Zanzibar densities about 260 people per square kilometer. Actual mainland population distributions are uneven, varying from one person per square kilometer in semiarid locations to more than 70 people per square kilometer in the wetter and more fertile rural areas.

POSTS AND TELECOMMUNICATIONS. The Germans established East Africa's first postal and telegraphic system. In 1893 the colonial government issued postage stamps, and until the outbreak of World War I (q.v.) postal facilities steadily improved. This was largely because of the development of railway service between Dar es Salaam and Kigoma (qq.v.) and between Tanga and Moshi (qq.v.). The railway and post office also built a telegraph network that linked GEA's major cities and townships.

After World War I the British sought to rebuild and reorganize the communications infrastructure. In 1920 the colonial government established a Department of Posts and Telegraphs, and on 1 January 1933 this department was amalgamated with the Kenya and Uganda departments. After the creation of the East African High Commission (EAHC) (q.v.) on 1 January 1948, posts and telegraphs became a High Commission service. During the last years of colonial rule, 151 post offices in TT were operated by a a staff of 1,600. Telegraph services were available at 128 post offices, 43 postal agencies at railway stations, and six railway stations where no post offices were located. Fifty-nine telephone exchanges were also in service.

After independence, the country's Posts and Telecommunications Administration operated postal, telegraph, and telephone services. By 1967 275 post offices operated throughout Tanzania, with modern telegraph and telephone systems available in much of the country. Beginning in the 1970s, postal and telecommunication services gradually deteriorated throughout the country, and by the early 1990s the telephone had become all but useless for local communications. In October 1991, however, the inauguration of a direct-dialing system improved international telephone connections. The replacement of a satellite earth station at Mwenge with a new installation supplied by an Italian company provided Tanzania with access to Atlantic and Indian Ocean satellites. In early 1994 Japan's Mitsubishi Corporation initiated work on the second phase of a rehabilitation project for the Dar es Salaam (q.v.) telephone system. To improve all services, the Tanzanian government divided the Tanzanian Posts and Telecommunications Corporation into separate posts and telecommunications companies.

PREFERENTIAL TRADE AREA FOR EASTERN AND SOUTHERN AFRICAN STATES (PTA). The PTA was established on 21 December 1981 and dissolved on 5 November 1993. This organization sought to establish a regional common market, to liberalize trade, and to encourage cooperation in industry, agriculture, transport, and communications. On 1 July 1984 the PTA adopted a common list of 209 trade items, and by 1991 this list had increased to 319 items. Member states used the PTA monetary unit of account (the *utapa*) to settle interstate debts every two months. Outstanding balances were payable in US dollars. The PTA was constrained by "rules of origin," which allowed preferential treatment only for goods produced by companies in which citizens of member nations managed operations and owned at least 51 percent of company equity. By the early 1990s this regulation impeded regional trade, and, as a result, intra-PTA commerce accounted for only about 6 percent of PTA members' total transactions. Before its demise, the organization's members included Tanzania, Angola, Burundi, Comoros, Djibouti, Eritrea, Ethiopia, Kenya, Lesotho, Madagascar, Malawi, Mauritius, Mozambique, Namibia, Rwanda, Somalia, Swaziland, Uganda, Zambia, and Zimbabwe. On 5 November 1993 the PTA was replaced by the Common Market of Eastern and Southern African States (COMESA) (q.v.).

PREVENTIVE DETENTION ACT. Patterned after the colonial Deportation Ordinance of 1921, this act was introduced in 1962. It allows the president to detain, indefinitely and without trial, anyone whom he deems to be "dangerous to peace and good order." The existence of this law inevitably draws criticism from Tanzanian dissidents, international human rights organizations, and Western governments. In 1985 the government amended the Preventive Detention Act to provide some measure of protection for detainees.

The act did not originally extend to Zanzibar, but in 1964 the Zanzibari government proclaimed its own Preventive Detention Decree. Although in 1985 the Preventive Detention Act was extended to include Zanzibar, Zanzibari authorities continued to invoke the Preventive Detention Decree, especially against individuals who opposed the union with the mainland. In 1990, for example, police arrested more than 100 people and held 15 in detention for advocating termination of the union.

PRINCE, TOM VON (1866–1914). Along with Emil von Zelewski (q.v.), Tom von Prince was one of the most significant military personalities in GEA. Although he was the son of an English police officer, he attended military school in Kassel (1886) with his future commander, Paul von Lettow-Vorbeck (q.v.). To gain quick promotions, he went to GEA and enlisted in the *Schütztruppe* (q.v.). After participating in the campaigns against Bushiri ibn Salim al-Harthi and Bwana Heri (qq.v.), he became station commander at Mikindani. He also earned the African nickname *"Bwana Sakkarani,"* which meant a warrior in a state of reckless exaltation. In February 1891 Prince fought a successful campaign against Chief Sina of Kibosho, who had rejected German protection. Next, he commanded a small force that defeated Sultan Sikki of Tabora (q.v.). Prince then spent several years campaigning against Chief Mkwawa (q.v.), who was finally defeated in 1898. During World War I (q.v.), he led a European company that consisted of planter volunteers from Usambara and a field company of African *askaris* (q.v.). On 4 November 1914 Prince was killed while fighting to defend Tanga (q.v.).

PRISONS SERVICE. Until the coming of the Europeans, prisons were unknown in Tanzania. Instead, indigenous societies punished or exacted compensation from offenders according to local custom. The Germans built the first prisons in what is now mainland Tanzania, and they typically sentenced convicted criminals to hanging, beheading, flogging, or hard labor. The British built more prisons but curtailed the use of especially brutal punishments. In 1931 the colonial authorities established the Tanganyika Prisons Service. Today the Prisons Service is a police force agency headed by the Commissioner of Prisons, which manages approximately 50 prisons. Types of prisons include remand prisons, maximum-security prison farms, prison farms, a maximum-security prison, and a prison for the mentally ill. There also are temporary detention facilities that adjoin major police stations in regional capitals. Juvenile prisoners are segregated, but women prisoners are not. Most prisons offer vocational courses.

PYRETHRUM. Pyrethrum is a plant that stands about 28 inches (70 centimeters) tall and bears white, daisylike flowers that are used in the production of insecticides. By 1938 pyrethrum had become an established crop in the Dabaga and Mufindi areas of Southern Province. The following year, the crop was introduced to Uwemba, and in 1940 planting started on Mount Meru (q.v.). Today the two main pyrethrum growing areas are located in the Southern Highlands and in Arusha and Kilimanjaro regions. In the early 1990s Tanzania produced an annual crop of about 2,000 tons. The rehabilitation and further development of pyrethrum processing facilities is required to reach a total annual market capacity of 4,000 tons.

— R —

RADIO TANZANIA. Radio Tanzania was established in 1951 as the Voice of Dar es Salaam, later known as the Tanganyika Broadcasting

Corporation and the Tanganyika Broadcasting Service. On 1 July 1965 the government dissolved this corporation and incorporated it into the Ministry of Information and Tourism as a its Radio Tanzania division. Radio Tanzania broadcasts an array of news, educational, and entertainment programs in English and Swahili (q.v.). On the mainland, Radio Tanzania maintains five shortwave transmitters and broadcasts three programs simultaneously for a total of 165 hours a week. In 1994 Radio Tanzania ordered a South African short-range automatic transmitter to serve the Dar es Salaam (q.v.) audience with music, advertisement, and entertainment programs on the FM system. The station also broadcasts from Zanzibar in Swahili for approximately 50 hours a week.

In April 1993 the National Assembly (q.v.) endorsed a bill allowing privately owned radio and television stations to operate in the country. The law also created the Tanzania Broadcasting Commission, which assumed responsibility for the issuing of licenses to private investors, who must be Tanzanian nationals. Prospective investors are required to pay about US$3,225 and US$1,720, respectively, to establish television and radio stations. Within months several private television stations had appeared, including Coastal Television Network and Independent Television.

REBMANN, JOHANNES (1820–1876). Rebmann was a member of the Church Missionary Society (CMS) (q.v.) who, with fellow traveler Johann Ludwig Krapf (q.v.), explored vast parts of the East African interior. On 11 May 1848 Rebmann became the first European to see Mount Kilimanjaro (q.v.). Rebmann's various journeys in East Africa inspired Richard Burton (q.v.), who sought Rebmann's advice before setting out on his 1857–1858 journey to discover Lake Tanganyika (q.v.).

RECHENBERG, BARON ALBRECHT VON (1861–1935). After serving as a provincial magistrate in Tanga, an official in Germany's Zanzibar consulate, and a diplomat in Russia, Rechenberg returned to GEA as governor. He was a linguist, speaking Swahili (q.v.), Arabic, and Gujarati. Although an excellent administrator, he alienated many German settlers and officials by his adamant defense of African rights and interests.

To stabilize GEA after the Maji-Maji Rebellion (q.v.), Rechenberg sought to implement reconstruction and economic policies that benefited GEA's African peasant farmers. To achieve this goal, he advocated an expansion of African health and education services and championed the development of scientific agricultural practices to benefit African cultivators. Rechenberg also relied on the support of the German colonial secretary, Bernhard Dernburg, who wanted to make GEA financially autonomous, to encourage rail construction, and to facilitate African participation in the colony's economic development.

Although Rechenberg opposed European settlement and plantations, the number of European settlers more than doubled during his tenure. Rechenberg eventually resigned his governorship because of political difficulties with GEA's European settler community and growing opposition in Germany to his policies. His governorship was considered a success, however, not least because trade between GEA and Germany had tripled between 1906 and 1911.

REFUGEES. Since independence, Tanzania has provided asylum to hundreds of thousands of refugees from eastern and southern Africa. Although Dar es Salaam has forbidden refugees from using Tanzania as a base to mount subversive activities against their home countries, there are reports that Rwandan and Burundian refugees have occasionally ignored this restriction. In 1992 approximately 6,500 Burundians returned home because of political reforms in their country. During the same year, Tanzania repatriated about 6,000 South African refugees, which led to the closure of several refugee camps that had been operated by the African National Congress (ANC). In October 1992 the ANC admitted that it had detained prisoners at Mazimbu and Dakawa refugee camps. Amnesty International documented that ANC personnel had beaten and tortured prisoners at these camps. As a matter of policy, Tanzania refuses to provide asylum to all Kenyan refugees.

In early 1994 Tanzania hosted an estimated 480,000 refugees from Burundi, 50,000 from Rwanda, 60,000 from Mozambique, 15,000 from Zaire, 3,000 from South Africa, and 1,200 from Somalia. By late June 1994 at least 436,500 additional refugees had moved into western Tanzania from Rwanda because of genocidal ethnic warfare in that country.

REGIONAL COMMISSIONER. Regional commissioners function as head government officers in Tanzania's 25 regions plus Dar es Salaam. During the colonial period, provincial commissioners filled this post as chief local government officers.

REGIONS. For purposes of local government, Tanzania is divided into administrative regions. These include Arusha, Coast, Dar es Salaam, Dodoma, Iringa, Kigoma, Kilimanjaro, Lindi, Mara, Mbeya, Morogoro, Mtwara, Mwanza, Pemba North, Pemba South, Rukwa, Ruvuma, Shinyanga, Singida, Tabora, Tanga, West Lake, Zanzibar Central/South, Zanzibar North, Zanzibar Urban/West, and Ziwa Magharibi. A regional commissioner (q.v.), appointed by the central government, administers each region. Regions are subdivided into 60 districts on the mainland and nine in Zanzibar (q.v.), each administered by an area commissioner.

RELIGION. There are no precise figures regarding the religious affiliations of Tanzanians. Scholars have maintained that approximately one-third of the country's population professes to be Christian (Roman Catholic and various Protestant denominations), another third adheres to the Islamic faith, and the remaining third practices one or another of the country's numerous indigenous religions. It should also be noted that many Christian and Muslim Tanzanians also follow tenets of traditional religions, such as praying to ancestors and other spirits, employing magic to achieve personal goals and settle disputes, and relying on the advice and guidance of diviners.

Christianity first appeared in Tanzania when Roman Catholic Franciscans established a mission at Kilwa Kisiwani (q.v.) during the Portuguese occupation of this coastal city-state in the 1505–1513 period. In the late 1840s Catholic and Protestant missionaries also established themselves along the coast. During Tanzania's period of formal colonization, the most active missionary societies included the Africa Inland Mission, Augustana Lutheran Mission (q.v.), Benedictine Fathers, Berlin Mission (q.v.), Bethel Mission (q.v.), Capuchin Fathers (q.v.), Church Missionary Society (q.v.), Fathers of the Holy Ghost, Italian Fathers of the Consolation, Leipzig Mission, London Missionary Society (q.v.), Moravian Mission, Neukirchen Mission, Seventh-Day Adventists, Universities' Mission to Central Africa (q.v.), and White Fathers (q.v.). Since independence most Christian denominations have operated under an umbrella organization, the Christian Council of Tanzania (q.v.), established in 1934. In addition, much of Tanzania's Christian clergy has been Africanized.

Islam first appeared in Tanzania during the late medieval period when Arab traders established stations in Zanzibar and along the mainland coast. Arab slave traders also helped to spread Islam to the country's interior. Unlike their Christian counterparts, Muslims did not establish missionary societies. Nevertheless, Islam gradually spread throughout Tanzania, and the subsequent appearance of a now mostly Sunni Islamic Asian (q.v.) minority added to the Tanzanian Muslim population. Today most of the country's Muslims are concentrated in Zanzibar and Pemba (qq.v.), in and around the cities and towns of Dar es Salaam, Kigoma, Tabora, Tanga (qq.v.), Kondoa, and Singida, and also along the Ruvuma River. The National Muslim Council of Tanzania, founded in 1969, supervises Islamic affairs on the mainland, while the Supreme Muslim Council, formed in 1991, administers Islamic activities on the islands.

Along with Christianity and Islam, the Hindu, Sikh, and Buddhist faiths are represented in small groups belonging to the Asian community. The National Spiritual Assembly, which propagates the Baha'i religion, is also represented in some 2,300 localities throughout Tanzania.

REPUBLIC OF TANGANYIKA. This mainland Tanganyikan republic existed between 9 December 1962 and 26 April 1964. It ceased to exist on 26 April 1964, when Tanganyika united with the People's Republic of Zanzibar (q.v.) to form the United Republic of Tanganyika and Zanzibar and, later that year, the United Republic of Tanzania (qq.v.).

RHAPTA. This was the most important pre-Islamic trading town on the East African coast. Although its exact location is unknown, the *Periplus of the Erythraean Sea* (q.v.) claimed that Rhapta was located along the present-day Tanzanian coast. Modern geographers believe that the town was sited either near the mouth of the Pangani River or on the Rufiji Delta. Arab merchants settled in Rhapta, intermarried with the local inhabitants, learned their language, and grew rich by exporting ivory and importing iron tools and weapons. *The Geography of Ptolemy* described Rhapta as a metropolis.

RIFT VALLEY. The Rift Valley, also known as the Great Rift Valley, forms a large depression in the earth's surface that extends from Jordan in the Middle East south to the Zambezi River in central Mozambique. The Rift Valley contains a series of geological faults that resulted from ancient volcanic activity. The Tanzanian portion, which runs north to south through the middle of the country, includes the lowest (Lake Tanganyika [q.v.]) and the highest (Mount Kilimanjaro [q.v.]) points in Africa. An eastern branch of the Rift Valley runs through central Tanzania and the country's Southern Highlands. The western Rift Valley forms the borders between Tanzania and Uganda, Rwanda, and Burundi. It also serves as the western edge of Tanzania's Central Plateau and Lake Victoria (q.v.) basin. The eastern Rift Valley divides the central and eastern plateaus that comprise most of Tanzania's broad reaches of savanna country.

RINDI, CHIEF (?–1891). Also known as Mandara, Rindi portrayed himself as the paramount Chagga (q.v.) chief in the Mount Kilimanjaro (q.v.) region when the Europeans arrived. In fact, Chief Sina of

Kibosho dominated much of the area although Rindi maintained a capital at Moshi (q.v.).

Around 1860 Rindi assumed the throne of the Moshi chiefdom. Rather than to use military force to prevent threats to his power, Rindi relied on diplomacy and made several carefully chosen alliances to isolate his main rival, Sina of Kibosho. For example, in 1885 Karl Jühlke, a companion of Carl Peters (q.v.), concluded a treaty with Rindi, according to which Rindi placed himself under German protection and ceded sovereignty over his domain to the German East Africa Company (q.v.). This treaty negated several agreements that Rindi had earlier concluded with the British.

In February 1891 Rindi welcomed a 500-man German military expedition that sought to destroy Sina. To ensure German success, Rindi ordered 1,000 of his own men armed with spears and 400 guns to join the expedition. Sina escaped, but eventually he concluded a peace agreement with the Germans in which he gave over two districts to Rindi and released the chief of Uru, whom he had imprisoned.

Despite his machinations, Rindi never became the paramount Chagga chief. After Rindi's death, his son, Meli, opposed German colonial rule. A military expedition led by Colonel Friedrich von Schele (q.v.) defeated Meli, and the Chagga people never again challenged the Germans.

RIVERS. Tanzania's three largest rivers are the 450-mile (720-kilometer) Ruvuma, the 429-mile (431-kilometer) Kagera, and the 175-mile (280-kilometer) Rufiji. The Ruvuma rises in southern Tanzania, flows east, forming the boundary between Tanzania and Mozambique, and empties in the Indian Ocean north of Cape Delgado. The Kagera flows north along the Tanzanian-Rwandan border, turns east along the Ugandan border, and empties into Lake Victoria near Bukoba (qq.v.). It forms the longest headstream of the Nile River. The Rufiji rises in south-central Tanzania and flows east into the Indian Ocean opposite Mafia Island (q.v.). The Rufiji River basin, which includes one of Tanzania's most agriculturally productive regions, covers almost one-fourth of the country's total area. The Rufiji has great potential for irrigation and hydroelectric power development.

Smaller Tanzanian rivers include the Great Ruaha, a tributary of the Rufiji, which drains the Usagara Mountains; the Grummeti, which flows from eastern Mara Region into Lake Victoria; and the Malagarasi, which flows into Lake Tanganyika near Kigoma. There are also the Mara, which marks the border between South Mara and Tarime Districts and flows into Lake Victoria; the Mkomazi, which is located in the Maasai Steppe and is bounded by the Pare and Usambara (q.v.) mountain ranges; and the Pangani, which rises in Mount Kilimanjaro (q.v.) and in the Pare and Usambara (q.v.) Mountains and flows into the Indian Ocean south of Tanga (q.v.). The Ruhuhu drains the Ungoni Highlands into Lake Malawi; the Rungwe drains the basin of Lake Rukwa; the Ruvu begins in the Uluguru Mountains and has its mouth near Bagamoyo; and the Wami, which rises south of Kilosa and empties into the Indian Ocean opposite Zanzibar (q.v.).

ROADS. Since independence, most of Tanzania's major roads have fallen into poor condition because of either inadequate construction or a lack of maintenance. The country's road network totals approximately 52,800 miles (88,000 kilometers) and accounts for more than 60 percent of all internal traffic flows. The network consists of about 2,280 miles (3,800 kilometers) of paved trunk roads, 3,900 miles (6,500 kilometers) of unpaved trunk roads, 10,638 miles (17,730 kilometers) of regional roads, some 18,000 miles (30,000 kilometers) of district and feeder roads, and approximately 18,000 miles of unclassified roads that are mainly managed by village councils, national park administrations, and parastatal corporations.

By the mid-1980s prolonged inadequate maintenance had caused damage to all roads. According to World Bank (q.v.) estimates, only about 15 percent of the trunk roads and 10 percent of the rural roads were then in good condition. In 1990 the Tanzanian government sought to address this problem by launching an internationally funded Integrated Roads Project. As a result, by early 1994 the percentage of trunk roads in good condition had more than doubled, and the proportion of improved rural roads had increased by at least 50 percent.

There are six main trunk roads. The north-south route originates at Namanga on the Kenyan border and extends to Arusha, Moshi (qq.v.), Korogwe, Chalinze, and Dar es Salaam (q.v.). The Great North Road also begins at Namanga and proceeds to Arusha, Dodoma, and Iringa (qq.v.), where it joins the Tanzania-Zambia Highway. The Tanzania-Zambia Highway links Dar es Salaam with Morogoro, Iringa, Mbeya (q.v.), and Kapiri Mposhi in Zambia. The east-west road runs from Dar es Salaam to Dodoma, Singida, and Shinyanga, branching off there to Mwanza and Bukoba (qq.v.). The southern road serves Nanganga, Masasi, Tunduru, Songea, and Makambako. The Dar es Salaam-to-Mtwara route passes through Kibiti.

ROBERT, SHAABAN (1909–1962). Robert was a distinguished East African writer and Tanganyika's greatest poet. Son of a Yao clerk, he spent most of his life in Tanga (q.v.) and Pangani. His work encompassed several different forms, including the short story, political allegory, autobiography, essay, translation, poem, and novel. He also served as chairman of TT's Swahili Committee. Robert was also a political activist who protested the inequities of British colonial rule. In 1932 he wrote his first poetry. His first major prose works include *Pambo la Lugha* (The Embellishment of Language) and a self-portrait entitled *Masiha Yangu* (My Life). One of his finest books is *Kusadikika, Nchi iliyo Angani* (Faith for the Country of the Sun). Robert's last work was a novel, *Siku ya Watenzi Wote* (Day of All Hardworking People).

RUAHA NATIONAL PARK. Gazetted in 1964, this park lies between the Njombe and Ruaha Rivers and covers an area of 5,000 square miles (12,950 square kilometers). It lies 70 miles (112 kilometers) west of Iringa (q.v.). Although noted for its elephant and greater kudu herds, the Ruaha National Park also contains large numbers of sable and roan antelope, hippopotamus, and crocodile.

RUANDA-URUNDI. A former Belgian mandate that covered an area of about 21,234 square miles (55,208 square kilometers) between contemporary Tanzania, Uganda, and Zaire. In 1899 Germany made Ruanda-Urundi part of GEA. Belgium ruled the region as a mandated and trust territory from 1923 until 1962, when it was divided into the independent states of Rwanda and Burundi.

RUBONDO ISLAND NATIONAL PARK. This park extends over an area of 93 square miles (240 square kilometers) and is located northwest of Mwanza (q.v.). The island's major attraction is the presence of many sitatunga, which are found nowhere else in Tanzania except in the Selous Game Reserve (q.v.). Other park animals include hippopotamus, crocodile, giraffe, elephant, rhinoceros, and chimpanzee.

RUETE, EMILY (1844–1924). Born Salme Binte Said al-Bisaidi in Zanzibar (q.v.), she was a daughter of Seyyid Said (q.v.). During the reign of her brother, Seyyid Majid ibn Said (q.v.), she became involved with a German trader named Heinrich Reute. After becoming pregnant, she fled to Aden, where she converted to Christianity and married Reute. She then accompanied her husband to Germany and became a German citizen. After her husband died in 1870, leaving her with three children and little money, she returned to Zanzibar, appeared before the sultan, Seyyid Barghash ibn Said (q.v.), and petitioned him for a share of her father's inheritance. He eventually agreed to pay her compensation, and with it she returned to Germany. In subsequent years she wrote *Memoirs of an Arabian Princess from Zanzibar* and *An Arabian Princess between Two Worlds: Memoirs, Letters, Sequels to the Memoirs,* both of which are autobiographical classics.

RUGA RUGA. The *Ruga Ruga* was a formidable late–nineteenth century Kimbu army under the command of Nyungu ya Mawe (q.v.).

— S —

SAID IBN SEYYID (1791–1856). Founder of the Busaidi (q.v.) dynasty. Under his leadership, Zanzibar (q.v.) became the center of Omani commercial and political activity and the main entrepôt for the East African slave trade (q.v.). He adopted the name Seyyid, traditionally an honorific Islamic title for a learned man, as a dynastic title for the Busaidi. In 1840 Seyyid Said moved his capital from Oman to Zanzibar, thereby establishing himself as a middleman between mainland traders and American and European merchants who visited the coast. Seyyid Said financed his administration through customs duties and taxes collected on the slave trade.

SALIM, AHMED SALIM (b. 1942). After Julius Nyerere (q.v.), Salim is one of Tanzania's most effective and internationally recognized leaders. He was educated at Mkoani Primary School, Pemba (q.v.), Lumumba College, Zanzibar, and Columbia University, New York City. In 1960 Salim began his political career when he became secretary-general of the Zanzibar Youth Movement. In 1963 he joined the Zanzibar National Party (q.v.) as its publicity secretary. Salim then served as Tanzania's ambassador to Egypt (1964–1965), high commissioner to India (1965–1968), and director of African and Middle East Affairs in the Ministry of Foreign Affairs (1968–1969). During the 1970s he worked in a variety of diplomatic posts, including the chairmanship of the UN Committee on Decolonisation (1972–1979). From 1980 to 1984 he served as Tanzania's minister of foreign affairs. In 1984, he became prime minister and a leading candidate to succeed Julius Nyerere (q.v.) as president. He failed to gain the presidency, probably because his political and economic views clashed with the more radical philosophies of the CCM (q.v.). In 1985, Salim became deputy prime minister and minister of defense. He also served as the CCM's vice chairman. On 26 July 1989 Salim was confirmed as secretary-general of the Organization of African Unity (OAU).

SCHELE, COLONEL FRIEDRICH VON. Upon assuming the governorship of GEA, Schele launched several punitive expeditions to pacify the interior. In August 1893 he defeated Chief Meli of Moshi and crushed all Chagga resistance in the Kilimanjaro area. On 30 October 1894 his 600-man force routed Hehe Chief Mkwawa's (q.v.) army by surrounding and then sacking his fortress at Iringa. Mkwawa managed to escape and continued to fight the Germans. Schele's harsh tactics earned the wrath of German liberals, who insisted on the primacy of civilian authority in GEA. In 1895 Schele, a military officer, refused to submit to the authority of the German Foreign Office's Colonial Department and resigned in protest.

SCHNEE, HEINRICH (1871–1949). German colonial administrator and last governor of GEA, who introduced legislation for the protection of African laborers against exploitation and ill-treatment. Schnee also supported the improvement and extension of schools for Africans. His relatively benevolent governorship kept the peace between 1906 and 1914. With the outbreak of World War I (q.v.), Schnee, who wanted to declare East Africa neutral, found himself at odds with General Paul von Lettow-Vorbeck (q.v.), who wanted to continue military operations against the British. The two also disagreed on the treatment of Africans, with Schnee arguing against the press-ganging of African carriers and the abrupt requisitioning of food and other supplies from local villages. From 1930 to 1933 Schnee headed the Deutsche Kolonialgesellschaft (German Colonial Society), an organization that worked for the restoration of the German colonies in Africa and for the rights of German residents in former colonies of the Reich.

SCHUTZBRIEF. German term for a treaty of protection between an African chief and German colonial authorities.

SCHÜTZTRUPPE. Established in 1891 as GEA's "Protective Forces." German authorities intended the *Schütztruppe* to be used primarily against Africans rather than other European colonial powers, and so the *Schütztruppe* participated in many campaigns of conquest and punitive expeditions against GEA's African communities. On the eve of World War I (q.v.), the *Schütztruppe* included 2,760 troops (260 Europeans and 2,500 Africans) organized into 14 field companies and one signal company. After the outbreak of hostilities between Germany and England, General Paul von Lettow-Vorbeck (q.v.) battled allied forces for more than four years. His surrender to British forces on 25 November 1918 marked the end of the *Schütztruppe*. Also, see ABUSHIRI REVOLT; MAJI-MAJI REBELLION; MKWAWA; PRINCE, TOM VON; VON SCHELE, FRIEDRICH; and ZELEWSKI, EMIL VON.

SECOND WORLD WAR. See WORLD WAR II.

SELOUS GAME RESERVE. This reserve was gazetted in 1951 and named after the noted big game hunter and explorer Frederick Courtney Selous. Forming the southern extension of the Mikumi National Park (q.v.) and covering some 21,000 square miles (54,490 square kilometers), the Selous is located primarily in the Rufiji River basin, southwest of Morogoro. Although mainly an elephant reserve, Selous contains a wide array of other fauna, including hippopotamus, buffalo, wildebeest, hartebeest, sable antelope, greater kudu, eland, lion, and leopard.

SERENGETI NATIONAL PARK. Originally created as a game reserve in 1929, this northwestern savanna country was made a closed reserve in 1950 and gazetted in 1951 as TT's first national park. Including the Ngorongoro Crater until the Ngorongoro Conservation Area (q.v.) was established in 1959, Serengeti is still the largest national park in Tanzania, covering an area of some 5,600 square miles (14,763 square kilometers). The park stretches from the Ngorongoro Plateau in the south to the mountainous slopes of Isuria in the north and as far west as Lake Victoria. In 1966 the Trustees of the National Parks established the Serengeti Research Institute at Seronera to study the largest migratory concentration of wildlife in the world. During the annual May/June migratory trek, millions of wildebeest, zebra, and antelope move in search of grass and water. The park is also home to lion, elephant, rhinoceros, buffalo, cheetah, eland, topi, giraffe, and hyena.

SEYYID. Originally an Arab (q.v.) term for scholar, Seyyid serves as another name for Sultan in Zanzibar (qq.v.). See references to Zanzibar's Sultans by their names.

SHINYANGA. Shinyanga is a town located on the Central Railway (q.v.) halfway between Tabora and Mwanza (qq.v.). Shinyanga has been important because of its proximity to the Williamson Diamond Mine at Mwadui and the east-west trunk road from Dar es Salaam (q.v.).

SHIRAZI ASSOCIATION. This interest group was formed in Pemba (q.v.) in 1939 and later became active in Zanzibar where it sought to safeguard the rights of the indigenous African population. In early 1957 the Shirazi Association of Zanzibar merged with the African Association (q.v.) to form the Afro-Shirazi Union (ASU), although the two associations maintained their separate identities. The Pemba Shirazi Association opposed this merger and remained committed to Arab rights, even at the expense of the African majority.

SHIRAZIS. During the late twelfth century Shirazis from the southern Somali, or Banadir, coast immigrated to East Africa. A Shirazi leader

named Ali bin al-Hassan settled in Kilwa (q.v.) and subsequently
founded a dynasty that presided over one of the region's most powerful commercial empires. His brothers established themselves at various places along the coast, including Pemba and Mafia (qq.v.), both
of which became important gold trading centers. In the mid-thirteenth
century a conflict developed between Kilwa and Shanga, which was
supposedly located on the island of Sanje ya Kati, a few miles south
of Kilwa Kisiwani. The rivalry, which was probably economic in nature, resulted in the temporary occupation of Kilwa by invaders from
Shanga. Kilwa finally triumphed over its neighbor, but by the late
fifteenth century it was increasingly hard pressed to maintain its commercial dominance because of the increasing wealth and influence of
Mombasa, a major port located in what is now Kenya. In 1505 the
Portuguese stormed Kilwa and built a military garrison on the island.
This action severely curtailed the power of the Shirazis, who sought
to preserve their wealth by establishing commercial relations with the
mainland. Although Shirazi economic activity later flourished, the
Shirazis preserved their non-African heritage and remained aloof
from mainland culture.

SISAL. In 1893 this crop was introduced into GEA from Mexico. By
1912 61,877 acres (24,751 hectares) had been planted and in the following year exports totaled 20,834 tons. During World War I (q.v.)
farmers neglected their plantations, causing annual exports to fall
under 1,000 tons. After the war, crop production recovered, and during the interwar period sisal became TT's premier industry. At the
beginning of World War II (q.v.) the colonial government restricted
sisal production to one-quarter of capacity because of low demand in
Europe. After Japan captured the Dutch East Indies and the Philippines, two important sources of hard fiber, TT resumed full production. By the early 1950s TT produced approximately 145,000 tons of
fiber and each year, less than 10 percent of which was grown by
African smallholders.

   After independence, the sisal industry continued to expand, producing an annual average of about 180,000 tons during the 1960s.
After the introduction of synthetic fibers into the world market during
the 1960s, and after the Tanzanian government nationalized more than
one-half of the country's sisal estates in 1976, annual production
crashed in the 1980s to less than 30,000 tons. In recent years the sisal
industry has somewhat recovered. In 1992 government-run estates
produced only 6,300 tons, but in the following year output increased
to 10,200 tons. Overall production also grew from 30,200 tons in
1986 to 36,000 tons in 1992. On 7 September 1994 the parastatal

Tanzania Sisal Authority announced that its marketing monopoly would be competitively privatized within three years.

SLAVE TRADE. As early as the second century A.D., slaves from East Africa were exported to Egypt. In later centuries East African slaves were sold in Persia, Arabia, India, and China, where they became soldiers, domestic servants, and laborers. By the tenth century A.D., Arab traders had established themselves at numerous trading centers along the East African coast including at Kilwa (q.v.), and on offshore islands such as Zanzibar (q.v.). These traders trafficked in slaves as well as in ivory, amber, and iron. Beginning with the explorations of Vasco da Gama (q.v.) in 1498, the Portuguese gradually established control over most of East Africa's strategic coastal cities and ports. Under Portuguese rule, the commercial importance of the slave trade declined. Portugal's Indian possessions teemed in cheap labor, creating little demand for African slaves. In addition, there is no evidence to suggest that the Portuguese carried on a slave trade with the Muslim Middle East. Even after a 1645 law authorized the exportation of slaves from East Africa to Brazil, the trade failed to prosper because of the great distances involved. During the seventeenth century, Portugal's East African empire gradually disintegrated, prompting the Dutch, English, Germans, French, and Omani Arabs (q.v.) to compete with one another to fill the vacuum left by the Portuguese.

France and the Omani Arabs eventually dominated the East African slave trade. On 14 September 1776 the sultan of Kilwa agreed to provide the French with an annual supply of 1,000 slaves for 100 years. The French exported slaves to several of their Indian Ocean possessions, including Madagascar, the Seychelles, Mauritius, and Reunion. Omani Arabs also sold slaves to the Persian Gulf countries, to Egypt, and to India from markets in Kilwa and Zanzibar. More important, Arab and, later, coastal Swahili traders established a presence in the East African interior. Although the concept of slavery was integral to some African societies, the Arabs gave the slave trade a new impetus by putting it on a commercial basis. From the hinterland, slaves traveled to Bagamoyo (q.v.), a major transshipment point located north of Dar es Salaam (q.v.), and thence to markets in Kilwa or Zanzibar.

Throughout the 1800s Britain and Germany worked to end the East African slave trade. The British sought to achieve this goal by concluding the Moresby Treaty (q.v.), the Hamerton Treaty (q.v.), and the Kirk Treaty with local Arab officials. In January 1889 the German Reichstag voted two million marks to suppress the slave trade in GEA. In late 1894 Governor Hermann von Wissmann (q.v.) authorized German station and district officers to examine all caravans traveling to the coast and to free any slaves they found. The Germans, like the British, also conducted antislavery naval patrols along the East African coast. The German colonial government issued a decree that all children born after 31 December 1905 of slave parents were automatically to be freed. In spite of these efforts, the slave trade continued in many parts of East Africa. Indeed, it was not until 1922 that the British abolished all forms of slavery on what is now the Tanzanian mainland.

SMUTS, JAN CHRISTIAN (1870–1950). On 6 February 1916 Lieutenant-General Smuts became commander in chief of British Allied forces in East Africa. Until his appointment, little military progress had been made against the Germans in East Africa. Smuts enhanced Allied military capabilities by improving intelligence, logistics, and lines of communication. These efforts weakened the Germans and drove them from one sanctuary to another. In March 1917 he relinquished his command, joined the War Cabinet in London, and played a role in the creation of the British Royal Air Force. Smuts served as Prime Minister of South Africa, 1919–1924 and 1939–1948.

SODEN, JULIUS VON (1846–1921). Soden served as GEA's first official governor. He sought to practice a strict colonial economy and to confine German administration to the Indian Ocean coast. In order to achieve these goals, he advocated a form of indirect rule through the Swahili-speaking coastal peoples. Soden also tried to encourage trade and to maintain amicable diplomatic relations with the inland African communities. Unrest in the interior disrupted these plans. In June 1891 he authorized an unsuccessful punitive expedition against the Hehe (q.v.). Additional military disasters elsewhere in GEA eventually forced Soden to resign his governorship.

SONGEA MBANO (c. 1836–1906). An Ngoni military commander who played a significant role in the Maji-Maji Rebellion (q.v.). After spending his early years among Ngoni living south of the Zambezi River, he settled in present-day Songea District of southern Tanzania. By the late 1860s Songea had become a subchiefdom in the Njelu Ngoni kingdom. Songea Mbano eventually commanded a major part of the Njelu army and assumed the position of an autonomous ruler. When they arrived in Ngoni country in 1897, the Germans ignored the titular Ngoni ruler and instead negotiated an agreement with Songea. For the next seven years he cooperated with the Germans. In 1905 Songea joined the Maji-Maji uprising and launched several attacks against the Germans. In 1906 he surrendered to the Germans and was subsequently hanged.

SOUTHERN AFRICAN DEVELOPMENT COORDINATION CON-FERENCE (SADCC). In April 1980 Tanzania, Angola, Botswana, Lesotho, Malawi, Mozambique, Swaziland, Zambia, and Zimbabwe formed SADCC. Namibia joined SADCC shortly after its independence in 1990. The organization's goals included a reduction of economic dependence on South Africa, encouragement of regional integration, and support for national and regional development. Each member state was responsible for coordinating projects in particular sectors. For example, Tanzania was placed in charge of coordinating regional industrial development.

At its 12th annual conference in 1992, SADCC placed a new emphasis on the role of the private sector in economic development and acknowledged that, because of ongoing political changes, South Africa would soon be asked to join the organization. By the early 1990s the SADCC "Programme of Action" included 559 locally and donor-supported development projects valued at US$8.5 billion. In 1993 SADCC was reorganized as the Southern African Development Commmunity (SADC), with a more ambitious mandate to work toward the establishment of a full-scale common market in the region.

SOUTHERN HIGHLANDS. This area, which has a dense population and is conducive to agriculture, is roughly composed of Iringa and Mbeya Regions. Tobacco (q.v.), vegetables, fruit, cattle, dairy products, pyrethrum (q.v.), and tea (q.v.) are produced around Iringa. Wheat, barley, cotton, wool, and coffee (q.v.) are cultivated in Mbeya.

SPEKE, JOHN HANNING (1827–1864). Speke was an English African explorer who accompanied Richard Burton (q.v.) on several trips throughout East Africa between 1856 and 1859. Speke and Burton were the first Europeans to view Lake Tanganyika. Speke was also the first European to discover Lake Victoria, which he correctly identified as the source of the Nile River. In 1860 Speke returned to East Africa with James Augustus Grant (q.v.) to confirm the connection between Lake Victoria and the Nile.

STANLEY, SIR HENRY MORTON (1841–1904). Born John Rowlands, Stanley was an African explorer and journalist who led expeditions that "found" David Livingstone (q.v.) at Ujiji (q.v.) in 1871, traced the southern sources of the Nile River, surveyed Lake Tanganyika between 1874 and 1877, and circumnavigated Lake Victoria in 1875, thereby proving that it was the true source of the Nile. Stanley is also credited with rescuing Emin Pasha (q.v.) in an 1887–1889 expedition to the southern Sudan.

SUKUMA. See PEOPLE.

SULTAN. A ruler, sometimes called Seyyid (q.v.) or Sayyid. See references to Zanzibar's sultans by their names.

SUSI, ABDULLAH DAVID (?–1891). An African companion of David Livingstone (q.v.) on his various expeditions. After Livingstone died in 1873 Susi and James Chuma (q.v.) carried carry his body from to Ilala to Zanzibar (q.v.). After Livingstone's funeral, the two visited England. On 22 June 1874 they received a Royal Geographical Society bronze medal in recognition of their loyalty and service to Livingstone. In 1875 Susi returned to East Africa as a Universities' Mission to Central Africa (UMCA) (q.v.) caravan leader. On 23 August 1886 he was baptized as David. Susi died on 5 May 1891 after a long illness and increasing paralysis.

SWAHILI. More properly termed Kiswahili, this is Tanzania's lingua franca. Swahili is basically a Bantu language that evolved along the East African coast between Lamu and Kilwa during the years of intensive Arab (q.v.) settlement. With the opening of trade routes in the nineteenth century, the language spread inland. Swahili, or Kiswahili, is now spoken by more than 70 million people in numerous East and Central African countries, including Tanzania, Kenya, and parts of Uganda, Zaire, Burundi, Rwanda, Mozambique, Zambia, Malawi, Comoros, Madagascar, Somalia, and Sudan. During the 1960s Julius Nyerere (q.v.) sought to dismantle the last vestiges of the British colonial past by ordering Tanzania's elementary schools, courts, and government institutions to begin using Swahili instead of English. Secondary schools and universities were to follow suit by the year 2000, the government's target date for the complete "Swahilization" of Tanzanian society. This policy proved disastrous in that it placed an entire generation of Tanzanians at a competitive disadvantage in the international marketplace. In late 1993 the government reversed its stance and embarked on a program to increase English language instruction.

SYMES, SIR GEORGE STEWART (1881–1962). Symes, who became governor of TT during the 1930s economic depression in East Africa, devoted most of his energies to improving TT's economy. He introduced, among other things, a retrenchment program, tax legislation, and a project to increase agricultural production by launching "grow-more-crops" campaigns. By mid-1933 these steps, coupled with an increase in major crop prices, improved TT's economic well-being. On the other hand, Symes failed to end the country's dependence on export crops whose value often fluctuated on the world market. In the political arena, Symes advocated the amalgamation of TT, Uganda, and Kenya but feared that such a union would be dominated by European settlers, who would protect their interests at the expense of the African and Asian (q.v.) populations. Symes also entrenched the indirect rule (q.v.) concept by ordering that the native administration confine its activities to local government rather than encouraging the African population to participate in territorial-level politics.

— T —

TABORA. This town is located 496 miles (800 kilometers) west of Dar es Salaam (q.v.) and lies at 3,943 feet (1,202 meters) above sea level. In 1820 Arab (q.v.) traders established a settlement at Tabora in the Nyamwezi (q.v.) chiefdom of Unyanyembe. Originally called Kazeh, Tabora became one of East Africa's most important slave and ivory trading centers along the caravan route linking Lake Tanganyika (q.v.) and the Indian Ocean coast. Until his death in 1859, Nyamwezi chief Fundikara maintained good relations with the Arabs. His successor, Msabila, quarreled with the Arabs over a variety of commercial and personal issues, leading the Arabs to ally themselves with Msabila's rival, Mkasiwa. Msabila, who was forced to relinquish power, fought a guerrilla war against Mkasiwa and the Arabs until his death in 1865. To help stabilize the region, Zanzibar (q.v.) appointed Said ibn Salim as its representative in Tabora. Under Chief Mirambo (q.v.), the Nyamwezi regained control of the caravan route. After Mirambo's death in 1884, his kingdom broke up into small competing groups.

During the colonial period, the Germans intended eventually to make Tabora their capital. After independence, Tabora became a regional capital and an important link in the country's transportation infrastructure because of its location at the junction of the railway lines from Kigoma on Lake Tanganyika and from Mwanza on Lake Victoria (qq.v.). The Nyamwezi people still predominate in Tabora and its environs. Tabora's 1988 population was 93,506.

TANGA. Tanga is a coastal town located 136 miles (218 kilometers) north of Dar es Salaam (q.v.) and established in the fourteenth century by Persian traders. During the German colonial period, Tanga grew in size and became an important port because of the construction of a railway line to Moshi and Arusha (qq.v.). Until World War II (q.v.) the export trade from Tanga was double that from Dar es Salaam. Exports through the port of Tanga include sisal, tea, coffee (qq.v.), cocoa, and copra (dried kernels of coconut [q.v.]).

TANGA RAILWAY. In 1893 German engineers initiated construction of the Tanga Railway, which was also known as the Northern Line. The railway's purpose was to open the agriculturally fertile Moshi-Arusha (qq.v.) districts to the outside world. The railway reached Muheza in 1895, Korogwe in 1902, and Moshi (q.v.) in 1911. During World War I (q.v.), fighting destroyed much of the railway, and in 1919 the British civil administration commenced repair work on the Tanga Railway. In December 1930 Sir Donald Cameron (q.v.) opened the entire line, including the recently built Moshi-Arusha extension. In August 1963 the opening of the Mnyusi-Ruvu line linked the Central Railway (q.v.) with the Tanga Railway and thus with the entire railway systems of Kenya and Uganda.

TANGA SCHOOL. Opened in 1892 by Governor Julius von Soden (q.v.), the Tanga School was GEA's first colonial school for Africans. The German Colonial Society initially ran the school, but in 1895 the German colonial government assumed responsibility for the institution. By 1897 86 African students were enrolled in German-language studies. The school later gained a primary section with four years of schooling, a teacher training section, and a crafts section. In 1911 school staff included four European and 41 African teachers. The school was closed after the outbreak of World War I (q.v.), but in 1920 the British reopened it.

TANGANYIKA. Translated as "sail in the wilderness," this name refers to the mainland of the United Republic of Tanzania. On 1 February 1920 the British adopted the name Tanganyika Territory. After independence on 9 December 1961 the word "Territory" was dropped from the country's name. On 26 April 1964 Tanganyika and the People's Republic of Zanzibar (q.v.) joined to form the United Republic of Tanganyika and Zanzibar (q.v.), and on 29 October 1964 the government renamed the country the United Republic of Tanzania (q.v.).

TANGANYIKA AFRICAN ASSOCIATION (TAA). The TAA was founded at Dar es Salaam in 1929 by a group of British colonial officers and members of the African Civil Service Association. This organization, whose leaders included Cecil Matola, Ramadhani Ali, Kleist Sykes Plantan, and Mzee ibn Sudi, sought to express African opinion on the "closer union" (q.v.) issue and "to safeguard the interests of Africans, not only in this territory but in the whole of Africa." During its early years, the TAA's influence rarely extended beyond Dar es Salaam. In March 1939, however, the Zanzibari TAA branch rejuvenated the organization, which then began to mobilize the masses and to press for "a voice in the Government." By 1939 the

TAA had 1,780 members organized into 39 branches throughout TT. In 1953, Julius Nyerere (q.v.) became TAA president, and on 7 July 1954 he announced the transformation of the TAA into the Tanganyika African National Union (TANU) (q.v.).

TANGANYIKA AFRICAN NATIONAL UNION (TANU). After converting the Tanganyika African Association (TAA) (q.v.) into TANU on 7 July 1954, the new party demonstrated its popularity by winning significant victories in the 1958 and 1960 LEGCO (q.v.) elections and by forming independent Tanganyika's first government. TANU also forged links with African movements in other East African countries, including the Kenya Federation of Labour. TANU was also a founding member of PAFMECA (q.v.) and took the lead in implementing a PAFMECA resolution calling for an economic boycott against South Africa. By the early 1960s TANU had a formal membership of 800,000 and employed 2,000 full-time officers. TANU's governing philosophy, as outlined in the 1967 Arusha Declaration (q.v.), called for national self-reliance and a gradual lessening of dependence on foreign aid, adherence to the philosophy of *Ujamaa* (q.v.), common ownership of property, state control of the means of production, and removal of all class distinctions.

On 5 February 1977 TANU merged with the Zanzibari Afro-Shirazi Party (q.v.) to form the Chama Cha Mapinduzi (CCM) (q.v.). The amalgamated party's first National Conference elected Julius Nyerere (q.v.) as chairman and Aboud Mwinyi Jumbe (q.v.) as vice chairman. The National Conference also elects 40 delegates to the National Executive Committee (NEC), which in turn elects 30 members to the Central Committee (CC) (q.v.). The CCM youth league, workers' organization, cooperative societies union, and women's union comprise the CCM's principal affiliated organizations.

Since the CCM's creation, its performance has become increasingly controversial. According to its critics, the party is corrupt and inefficient and has repeatedly interfered in the private lives of ordinary citizens. As a matter of record, under CCM control the Tanzanian economy all but collapsed. Its leadership also initially opposed demands for a multiparty political system, but the political opposition, which finally emerged in the early 1990s, remained fragmented in later years. It is therefore unlikely that the CCM will be compelled to relinquish power in the near future.

TANGANYIKA FEDERATION OF LABOUR (TFL). On 7 October 1955 the British colonial authorities registered the TFL to represent TT's 22 trade unions on matters that affected them collectively. Although colonial regulations prevented collaboration between the TFL and TANU (q.v.), the two organizations initially enjoyed good relations, since several African leaders served as officials of both groups. In effect, the TFL and TANU leadership ignored the ban on cooperation and staged successful boycotts during a 1957 bus strike and a 1958 brewery workers' strike. By 1961 203,000 people, 42 percent of the country's workers, had joined the TFL, which by then included 35 registered unions. After independence, a gulf developed between the worker-oriented TFL and the productionist TANU leadership. As a result, the TFL split into pro- and anti-government factions. When the TFL threatened to call a general strike in support of the January 1964 army mutiny (q.v.), the government dissolved the TFL and detained about 200 of its members. The TANU government also passed legislation that replaced the TFL with the party-dominated National Union of Tanganyika Workers (NUTA) (q.v.).

TANGANYIKA LEAGUE. In 1938 Ferdinand Cavendish-Bentinck, a European settler who lived in Kenya, formed the Tanganyika League to prevent the British government from transferring TT back to Germany. To achieve this goal, the European business and professional members of the Tanganyika League supported the "closer union" (q.v.) of Kenya and TT. In early August 1939 the Indian Association (q.v.) rejected the unification of the two territories. The controversy between the European and Asian communities over this issue ended after Great Britain declared war on Germany.

TANGANYIKA NATIONAL SOCIETY. On 4 December 1955 the Tanganyika National Society's manifesto appeared in the *Tanganyika Standard*. It was the first multiracial society in TT, and it opposed what its members regarded as TANU's (q.v.) racial nationalism. Many in the colonial administration, including Governor Sir Edward Twining (q.v.), supported the Tanganyika National Society as a counterweight to TANU, whose membership rolls then included only Africans. Under Twining's influence the society was later reorganized as the United Tanganyika Party (UTP) (q.v.).

TANGANYIKA RIFLES. In 1963 the King's African Rifles (q.v.) transferred its two Tanganyika battalions to the newly independent government. By 1964 these units, known as the Tanganyika Rifles, numbered approximately 2,000 personnel. On 19 January 1964 the battalion stationed at Dar es Salaam (q.v.) staged a mutiny against its officers. After the union of Tanganyika and Zanzibar, the government established the Tanzania People's Defence Force (TPDF) (q.v.). Also, see ARMY MUTINY.

TANU. See TANGANYIKA AFRICAN NATIONAL UNION.

TANU YOUTH LEAGUE (TYL). Also known as the "Green Guards," the TYL was established in 1956 as an auxiliary organzation to TANU (q.v.). In the years prior to independence, TYL branches held meetings every Sunday to facilitate the growth of nationalist sentiment among youth. Although interest in the TYL declined after 1961, the organization remained active throughout the country, and many former members moved into regular party posts. After the 1964 army mutiny (q.v.), TYL members formed the majority of the newly established Tanzania People's Defence Force (TPDF) (q.v.). Throughout much of its existence, the TYL has been criticized for interfering in people's ordinary lives by informally and unlawfully assuming police, special investigative, and judicial functions.

TANZAM RAILWAY. See TAZARA RAILWAY.

TANZANIA EPISCOPAL CONFERENCE (TEC). Established in 1957 as the Tanganyika Episcopal Conference, the TEC's name was changed after independence. The TEC is significant in that it united all Catholic orders in the country. Before 1970, when all schools were nationalized, it operated 1,378 primary schools, 44 secondary schools, 8 teacher training colleges, 2 commercial schools, 15 trade schools, 48 handcraft and domestic science centers, and special schools for the hearing, speaking, and sight impaired. In addition, the TEC administered 15 minor and 4 major seminaries and 10 catechist training schools.

TANZANIA FORESTRY ACTION PLAN. On 12 December 1989 the Tanzanian government launched this plan to conserve the country's land resources while "promoting self-sufficiency and export growth in forest based products and services." Tanzania's forestry plan is one of 21 worldwide plans that have been established under the aegis of the international Tropical Forestry Action Plan, which is managed by the UN Food and Agriculture Organisation (FAO). By the early 1990s doubts had arisen as to whether this plan could reverse a deforestation process that annually claims between 750,000 and 1,000,000 acres (300,000 and 400,000 hectares) of Tanzanian woodlands. This pessimism stemmed from the fact that the country's economic well-being depends on an array of activities that cause deforestation, including the clearance of trees for crop production, overgrazing, burning for pasture, and harvesting for fuel wood and charcoal-making. Given Tanzania's poverty, it is unlikely that the government can reverse these trends in the foreseeable future. At current depletion rates,

Tanzania's forest resources will be gone in a little more than a few decades.

TANZANIA NATIONAL ARCHIVES. This government agency was established in 1963 under the supervision of the Ministry of National Culture and Youth. Archives holdings include the records of the German (1885–1917) and British (1919–1961) periods. Beginning in the late 1980s the Archives embarked on a program to acquire the records of the Tanganyika African Association (TAA), TANU (qq.v.), and other, smaller organizations that contributed to the anticolonial struggle. The Archives follows a 30-year rule of closure for public records, after which they may be made available for public inspection.

TANZANIA PEOPLE'S DEFENCE FORCE (TPDF). The TPDF was founded in the aftermath of the 1964 army mutiny (q.v.). The president is commander in chief of the armed forces, and a chief of staff is responsible for the day-to-day operation of the military. In 1994 the armed forces consisted of an army (45,000 personnel), a navy (an estimated 1,000 personnel), and an air force (3,500 personnel). Personnel are recruited through voluntary two-year enlistments. In 1994 paramilitary forces included a 1,400-man police field force and an 85,000-man People's Militia (*Jeshila Mgambo*).

During the early postcolonial period the TPDF received assistance exclusively from Great Britain. After Dar es Salaam broke diplomatic relations with London over Rhodesia's 1965 unilateral declaration of independence, the Soviet Union and the PRC provided weapons and training to the TPDF. The Chinese also built a naval base at Dar es Salaam (q.v.) and a military airfield near Morogoro (q.v.). The TPDF deployed peacekeeping troops to the newly independent and politically unstable Comoros in 1976, a force of regular and paramilitary troops to counter Ugandan aggression against Tanzania in 1979, two other contingents to protect the Seychelles government from South African-inspired coup attempts in 1979 and 1981, and a similar mission to help the Mozambican government survive a South African-supported insurgency in 1987. In the early 1990s the Tanzanian government began downsizing the TPDF and requiring the military to devote more of its resources to civic-action projects.

TANZANIA RAILWAYS CORPORATION. This parastatal organization was formed in 1977 after the collapse of the EAC's (q.v.) East African Railways Corporation. Since its creation the Tanzania Railways Corporation has underperformed in carrying passenger and freight traffic. Revenue difficulties have been exacerbated by a lack of funds for replacing old equipment and improving service. Currency devaluations and high inflation rates have added to the corporation's problems. In 1987 the government, with international financing, initiated a three-year Emergency Recovery Plan, which laid the groundwork for the corporation's rehabilitation. As of early 1993 the railway operated a fleet of 109 diesel locomotives, 100 passenger coaches, and 3,257 freight wagons, in addition to 16 ships on Lake Victoria (q.v.). Two railway lines are managed by the corporation. An 870-mile (1,450-kilometer) central line runs from Kigoma on Lake Tanganyika (qq.v.), with a branch to Mwanza (q.v.) on Lake Victoria. A second line operates from Tanga to Arusha (qq.v.).

A US$276 million Railways Restructuring Project, adopted in 1990, has sought to improve the corporation's performance by rehabilitating these track systems, refurbishing the locomotive fleet, and training new staff. The Tanzanian government has also promised to give the corporation more freedom to operate in a commercially competitive manner. By 1995 the corporation aimed to carry 2.3 million tons of freight and 3.9 million passengers and to reduce its work force from 16,100 in January 1990 to 10,375. Also, see CENTRAL RAILWAY; TANGA RAILWAY; and TAZARA RAILWAY.

TANZANIA YOUTH DEMOCRACY MOVEMENT. This organization was founded in 1979 by Musa Membar, who argued for a more democratic form of government in Tanzania. Membar maintained that the movement had 3,000 members and many sympathizers in the Tanzanian government, though independent observers disputed this claim and argued that the movement had very few members.

Demanding the resignation of President Julius Nyerere (q.v.), Membar and four of his followers hijacked a Tanzanian airliner on 26 February 1982 on an internal flight and forced it to Stansted in England. Two days later they surrendered, thanks to the intervention of Oscar Kambona (q.v.), a former Tanzanian foreign minister who lived in exile in London. A British court subsequently sentenced the five to imprisonment for three to eight years. In September 1990 Membar was released and returned to Tanzania, presumably to facilitate the country's movement toward a multiparty democracy. Tanzanian authorities promptly reimprisoned him, and on 25 May 1991 he died in a Dar es Salaam hospital as a result of an unspecified illness contracted during his confinement. Some human rights advocates maintained that Tanzanian security personnel had murdered Membar.

TARANGIRE NATIONAL PARK. Gazetted in 1970, this park lies about 71 miles (114 kilometers) south of Arusha (q.v.) and covers an area of 1,560 square miles (2,600 square kilometers). Tarangire contains several large mammal species, including elephant, lion, black rhinoceros, eland, oryx, generuk, lesser kudu, waterbuck, giraffe, impala, gazelle, and buffalo.

TAZARA RAILWAY. In April 1970 construction began on this most modern of Tanzania's railways, thanks to a $US166 million loan from the People's Republic of China (PRC). Five years later about 25,000 Chinese, 50,000 Tanzanian, and 15,000 Zambian workers completed construction of the 1,160-mile (1,870-kilometer) railway line, which links Dar es Salaam (q.v.) with Kapiri Mposhi in Zambia. This rail line provided landlocked Zambia with an alternative sea outlet to lines passing through Mozambique and South Africa and provided improved transportation to the Kilombero Valley and to Iringa and Mbeya (qq.v.). Since commencing operations the TAZARA has suffered from financial and technical problems and from a lack of spare parts and equipment. Tanzania has relied on foreign assistance to help resolve these difficulties. In 1987 the US agreed to supply 17 locomotives under a US$46 million grant agreement, and in 1988 the PRC signed a 10-year pact on engineering, managerial, and technical cooperation. Despite such assistance, the TAZARA continues to be plagued by numerous operational problems.

TEA. Historically, tea has been one of Tanzania's most important crops, largely because of its ability to generate foreign-exchange earnings. In the early twentieth century tea cultivation began in the Usambara Mountains (q.v.) west of Tanga (q.v.) and then expanded to the Southern Highlands (q.v.). In the late 1930s nearly 5,000 acres (2,000 hectares) were under cultivation, and by 1966 this area had expanded to more than 25,000 acres (10,000 hectares). Production also increased until, by the early 1990s, Tanzania produced about 1 percent of the world's tea. The Tanzania Tea Authority, established in 1969, accounts for approximately one-quarter of tea production in Tanzania. This government corporation also maintains four tea factories and is building four others. The private firm Brooke Bond Liebig, Tanzania, accounts for about 40 percent of the country's total crop.

In recent years several attempts have been made to increase tea production further. In early 1991, for example, the British Lonrho group of companies announced that it would invest US$5.6 million in a five-year program to double yields at the Mufindi tea estate. Otherwise, old processing equipment and a lack of adequate factory space continue to impede the country's ability to satisfy a growing domestic and international demand for Tanzanian-grown tea.

THOMSON, JOSEPH (1858–1895). Thomson was a British explorer whose first trip to present-day mainland Tanzania (1879–1880) resolved several geographical questions about East Africa's lake system. In 1881 he unsuccessfully searched for coal in the Ruvuma River region for Seyyid Barghash (q.v.). Thomson also led several expeditions throughout Kenya.

TIPPU TIP (c. 1830–1905). Also known as Hamid ibn Muhammad al-Murjebi, Tippu Tip was born in Zanzibar. In the late nineteenth century he was the most powerful Arab-Swahili trader in the East African interior. The basis of Tippu Tip's fortune was trade in slaves and ivory, and by the early 1880s he had extended his trade to what is now northeastern Zambia and eastern Zaire. In 1882 he returned to the coast to negotiate an agreement with Seyyid Barghash (q.v.), through which he became the sultan's agent in Zaire. En route he negotiated an alliance with the Nyamwezi chief, Mirambo (q.v.). In 1890 Tippu Tip departed Zaire for the last time. Shortly thereafter his empire collapsed as a result of Belgian King Leopold II's determination to extend his rule over eastern Zaire. Tippu Tip then retired to Zanzibar and wrote his autobiography, which is widely regarded as a classic in Swahili (q.v.) literature.

TOBACCO. Three types of tobacco are grown in southern, central, and northwestern Tanzania. A flue-cured variety of the Virginia type is used to make cigarettes; fire-cured (heavy western) is processed into pipe tobacco; and aromatic is made into Turkish cigarettes. During colonial times Europeans grew flue-cured tobacco in Iringa District and Africans cultivated fire-cured in Songea District in the Southern Highlands (q.v.) and in the Biharamulo district of Lake Province.

Although expensive and troublesome to produce, tobacco is one of Tanzania's most valuable cash crops. In January 1966 the East African Tobacco Company was reorganized, and the Tanzania section became British American Tobacco Company, Tanzania, which supplied more than 90 percent of the country's tobacco requirements. During the late 1980s and early 1990s Tanzania produced an annual tobacco crop of about 14,000 tons.

TOURISM. During the colonial period, most tourists who visited present-day Tanzania were big-game hunters, although after World War II (q.v.), tourism patterns changed somewhat as more people came to view the TT's flora and fauna. After independence the Tanzanian government discouraged foreign tourism because it was held to be incompatible with socialist development. As a result, the country's tourism infrastructure all but collapsed.

In 1977 this policy was changed, and the Tanzania Tourist Corporation (TTC) launched a vigorous campaign to attract foreign visitors.

As part of this plan the TTC developed two major tourist circuits with hotels and lodges. The Kilimanjaro International Airport, which is located between Moshi and Arusha (qq.v.), links these areas of attraction. The northern circuit comprises Mount Kilimanjaro, Serengeti National Park, Selous Game Reserve, Ngorongoro Conservation Area, Lake Manyara National Park (qq.v.), and some 20 lesser parks and reserves. Along this route, tourists can join hunting, fishing, game viewing, photographic, and mountaineering safaris. The coastal circuit includes Dar es Salaam, Mafia Island, Zanzibar, Mikumi National Park (qq.v.), and the Tanzanian coastline, which is ideal for sunbathing, scuba diving, snorkeling, shell collecting, fishing, and exploring coral reefs. Other tourist attractions include the Rift Valley, Lake Victoria, and Lake Tanganyika (qq.v.).

Although improvements were made in the 1980s on behalf of the tourist industry, it remained constrained by a lack of coastal and up-country hotel space and by a deteriorated road system. In 1994 the Tanzania Tourist Board replaced the TTC and was mandated to make Tanzania a more competitive tourist destination. A Tanzanian government decision to open tourism to private companies and investors has also helped to revive existing lodging facilities and to attract international hotel chains. According to government officials, once fully rehabilitated, tourism could earn Tanzania up to US$500 million per year.

TRAPPE, MARGARET VON. In 1904, she and her husband, Ulrich, walked from the Indian Ocean coast to the interior to take possession of a farm called "Momella," part of which later became Arusha National Park (q.v.). During World War I (q.v.), she served as a mounted courier for General Paul von Lettow-Vorbeck (q.v.), who eventually ordered her to surrender to the British because he was embarrassed by Allied accusations that he was using a female combatant. After the war Margaret became the first woman professional big-game hunter in East Africa.

TRIBES. See PEOPLE.

TSETSE. The tsetse fly transmits trypanosomiasis (sleeping sickness), a brain infection, which, in its various forms, causes drowsiness and eventually death in humans and livestock. The main risk from tsetse is in game parks where the fly is common. Pyrethroid fly spray is the best deterrent to the tsetse fly, which can also be controlled by cutting back bush vegetation, which provides its pupae with essential shade. After decades of successful tsetse control efforts associated with land clearing for agricultural development, in recent years the fly has spread back again into neglected farming areas, including some sisal (q.v.) plantations.

TURNBULL, SIR RICHARD (b. 1909). TT's last governor, Turnbull is noted for maintaining cordial relations with TT's various African communities and for easing the transition from colonial rule to independence. He encouraged the British government and worked with Julius Nyerere (q.v.) to move rapidly through the intermediate stages of responsible government and internal self-government to full independence.

TWINING, SIR EDWARD (1899–1967). Before becoming TT's penultimate governor, Twining was a trained physician who had served in Uganda with the King's African Rifles (q.v.) from 1923 to 1928. During his administration Twining worked to develop TT's economy and infrastructure. Twining also revised the Ten-Year Development and Welfare Plan, 1947–1956, which sought to develop natural resources and to improve communications, social services, public works and township development, roads, ports, and railways. Politically, Twining opposed TANU (q.v.) and tried to restrict Julius Nyerere's (q.v.) pro-independence activities. He also enforced regulations that barred African civil servants from joining political organizations, a policy that he himself breached by allowing native authorities to join the "multiracial" United Tanganyika Party (UTP) (q.v.), which he helped to bring into existence as an alternative to TANU.

— U —

UDZUNGWA MOUNTAINS NATIONAL PARK. Gazetted in 1992 as Tanzania's first forest park, Udzungwa encompassess an area of 770 square miles (1,000 square kilometers). The park is located southwest of Mikumi National Park (q.v.) and contains a modest array of fauna, including elephant, buffalo, bushpig, and hyrax. The World Wildlife Fund for Nature (formerly known as the World Wildlife Fund) pledged to manage Udzungwa for three to five years after it was gazetted.

UGANDAN-TANZANIAN WAR (1978–1979). Charging without proof that Tanzania was fomenting ethnic unrest in Uganda, on 28 October 1978 Ugandan President Idi Amin Dada deployed 3,000 Ugandan army troops into the Kagera region of northwestern Tanzania. After this force reached the Kagera River, Uganda claimed that it had annexed 710 square miles (1,846 square kilometers) of Tanzanian territory. Julius Nyerere (q.v.) then ordered 7,000 Tanzania People's Defence Force (TPDF) (q.v.) and People's Militia soldiers to prepare for a counteroffensive. The TPDF soon recovered the Kagera area, but only after some 10,000 Tanzanian civilians had been killed, kidnapped, or injured.

Over the next few months skirmishes continued along the Ugandan-Tanzanian border. In early February 1979 four TPDF brigades (4,000 soldiers), supported by the People's Militia and 3,000 anti-Amin Ugandan exiles, invaded southwestern Uganda. The allied force, which had grown to 21,000 combatants and support personnel, encountered little resistance from the Ugandan army. However, 2,500 Nubians hastily recruited by Amin from Sudan, together with 2,700 Libyans deployed to Uganda by Libya's Muammar Qaddafi, temporarily slowed the invasion. After a two-day battle for Entebbe in early April 1979, many of the Nubians deserted, and the Libyans departed Uganda. The TPDF and the anti-Amin rebels then moved on the capital, Kampala. On 11 April 1979 they occupied the city, forcing Amin and two Ugandan army battalions (2,000 troops) to flee eastward to Jinja. The following month, the Tanzanians took control of this town, and Amin fled into exile, first to Libya and then to Saudi Arabia. The war cost the TPDF 373 lives, 96 from combat and 277 from accidents. The anti-Amin rebels lost 150; the Ugandan army about 1,000; and Libya approximately 600.

UGWENO. Sometime during the fifteenth century this kingdom in North Pare established a political system controlled by a clan of blacksmiths, the Washana, who traded iron for cattle with the Chagga (q.v.) people. In the early sixteenth century the Wasuya, a commoner clan led by a person called Angovi, revolted against the Washana and seized power. Angovi later relinquished control to his son, Mranga, who centralized the political machinery of his country and established a reputation as one of the most important political reformers in precolonial Tanzanian history. Because of Mranga's reforms, the entire North Pare plateau enjoyed a period of stability that lasted until the nineteenth century.

The undoing of the Ugweno empire resulted from encroachments of hostile chiefs and the destabilizing effects of the slave trade (q.v.). To preserve his power, Ghendewa, chief of Ugweno, built a fortified capital and raised a standing army. Despite these steps, Ghendewa was unable to suppress a rebellion in the southern part of his domain. He therefore invited Chagga warriors to join him in a punitive expedition against the southern rebels. This proved to be a fatal mistake, as the Chagga turned against Ghendewa, killed him, and seized many cattle in and around the capital. The southern district subsequently became independent, while northern Ugweno was torn by a rivalry between Ghendewa's brothers and sons.

UHURU. The Swahili word for freedom. *Uhuru na Umoja, Uhuru na Ujamaa, Uhuru na Kazi,* and *Uhuru na Kujitegemea* (Freedom and Unity, Freedom and Socialism, Freedom and Work, and Freedom and Self-Reliance) became popular slogans during Tanzania's early post-colonial period of the 1960s and 1970s.

UHURU RAILWAY. See TAZARA RAILWAY.

UJAMAA. The Swahili would for familyhood or brotherhood. The term also describes the sense of obligation that people have for the welfare of their fellows. The *Ujamaa* concept took on an ideological connotation during the presidency of Julius Nyerere (q.v.), insofar as he used it to describe an ideal socialist state based on the mutual cooperation and egalitarianism of traditional African society.

UJAMAA VILLAGES. In 1967 Julius Nyerere (q.v.) issued a policy paper, "Socialism and Rural Development," in which he called for "the establishment of *Ujamaa* [q.v.] villages . . . in which people live together and work together for the good of all." After most rural dwellers refused to resettle voluntarily, Nyerere resorted to force in *Ujamaa Vijijini* (Socialism in the Villages) policy implementation. The creation of *Ujamaa* villages turned out to be an economic, social, human-ecological, and political failure. Under President's Ali Hassan Mwinyi's (q.v.) leadership, Tanzania moved away from *Ujamaa* socialism in favor of more freedom of private choice in a market-oriented economy. Also, see VILLAGIZATION.

UJIJI. Ujiji is a town in western Tanzania, located on Lake Tanganyika (q.v.) four miles (six kilometers) south of Kigoma (q.v.). It is one of Tanzania's oldest and most historically significant market centers. In 1845 Arab traders established a settlement here, which eventually became western Tanzania's greatest transshipment point for slaves and ivory. From 1872 until his death in 1885, Mwinyi Kheri (q.v.) served as head of the Arab community at Ujiji. During this period the town prospered as Arabs and Africans cooperated politically and economically to their mutual benefit. Ujiji is also famous for the 10 November 1871 meeting of Henry Morton Stanley and David Livingstone (qq.v.). During much of the twentieth century the town experienced little growth, increasing in population from approximately 7,000 in 1900 to only about 12,000 by 1957.

ULUGURU MOUNTAINS. The Uluguru range is located south of Morogoro (q.v.) about 120 miles (192 kilometers) from the Indian Ocean coast. Its highest elevation is about 8,700 feet (2,646 meters). Like most eastern Tanzanian mountains, the Uluguru Mountains contain forested areas. The mountains bear population densities exceeding 500 per square mile, and extensive cultivation on steep slopes has caused extensive erosion for more than four decades. Colonial and postcolonial governments have attempted to resolve this problem through bench terracing and composting, but such efforts have largely failed because of local opposition to these highly labor-intensive land-use practices.

UMMA (MASSES) PARTY. In early 1964, Ahmad Abdulrahman Muhammad Babu (q.v.) and two other defecting members of the Zanzibar National Party (ZNP) (q.v.) executive committee created this political party. Babu advocated revolutionary socialism as practiced by the PRC and Cuba, and rejected the ZNP's commitment to an Islamic state in Zanzibar. The Umma Party enjoyed the support of many breakaway ZNP factions, and immediately after the 1964 Zanzibar Revolution (q.v.) it merged with the victorious Afro-Shirazi Party (ASP) of Abeid Karume (qq.v.).

UNITED REPUBLIC OF TANGANYIKA AND ZANZIBAR. This is the collective name applied to the union of Tanganyika and Zanzibar from 26 April 1964 until the new country became United Republic of Tanzania on 29 October 1964.

UNITED REPUBLIC OF TANZANIA. The official name of Tanzania since its adoption on 29 October 1964.

UNITED TANGANYIKA PARTY (UTP). The UTP was originally organized as the Tanganyika National Society (q.v.). In early 1956 British Governor Sir Edward Twining (q.v.) encouraged unofficial LEGCO (q.v.) members to convert this interest group into a full-scale political party, thus providing an alternative to TANU (q.v.). In principle, UTP membership was open to all races. In practice, the party sought to preserve European political dominance by supporting a "multiracial" parity system of elections, through which Europeans and Asians would enjoy equal representation with the vastly more numerous Africans in the country's local and central legislative bodies.

UNITED WOMEN OF TANGANYIKA (TANZANIA) (UWT). This constituent organization of TANU (q.v.) was established in 1962 to fight "poverty, ignorance and disease;" to raise the "social, economic and educational status" of women; and "to encourage women to take an active part in promoting family welfare through full participation in the fields of health, education and social development." Led by political activist Bibi Titi Mohammed, the UWT soon established branch offices throughout the country. After the promulgation of the Arusha Declaration (q.v.) in 1967, Mohammed fell from political favor because of her refusal to follow the declaration's leadership code prohibition against private accumulations of wealth by public figures.

The UWT eventually became the national women's organization of the ruling CCM (q.v.), and it has continued to advocate improvements in the economic well-being of women, particularly those who live in rural areas.

UNIVERSITIES' MISSION TO CENTRAL AFRICA (UMCA). In response to an 1857 appeal by David Livingstone (q.v.), a group of English churchmen created the UMCA to establish "centres of Christianity and civilisation for the promotion of true religion, agriculture and lawful commerce" for the peoples who lived along the shores of Lake Malawi (q.v.). In 1863 Bishop William G. Tozer arrived in East Africa and located UMCA headquarters in Zanzibar (q.v.). In 1873, Dr. Edward Steere succeeded Tozer. Under Steere's leadership the UMCA expanded its activities, especially among the Yao. Until the late 1870s the UMCA concentrated its activities on building settlements for freed slaves. In 1869 it opened St. Andrews College, Kingani, for ex-slaves. Over the next several decades the UMCA mainly worked to expand its African school system and to train Africans for the clergy. In 1965 the UMCA merged with the Society for Propagation of the Gospel to form the United Society for the Propagation of the Gospel.

UNIVERSITY COLLEGE, DAR ES SALAAM. In February 1961 the National Assembly (q.v.) passed a Provisional Council Ordinance establishing Tanganyika's first higher educational institution. In October 1961 the University College opened with a Faculty of Law and 14 students. The first degrees were awarded through an affiliation with the University of London, but after the University of East Africa (UEA) (q.v.) opened in 1963 the University College granted its own degrees. By 1970 1,400 students were enrolled at the Dar es Salaam (q.v.) campus, which included faculties in law, arts and social sciences, natural sciences, medicine, and agriculture. The University College also housed specialized programs, including an Institute of Public Administration, Institute of Fisheries, Institute of Swahili Research, Economic Research Bureau, Bureau of Resource Assessment and Land Use Planning, Institute of Education, and Institute of Adult Education. After its nationalization on 1 July 1970, University College was renamed the University of Dar es Salaam (q.v.).

UNIVERSITY OF DAR ES SALAAM. The University of Dar es Salaam, which commenced operations on 1 July 1970, occupies 1,625 acres (650 hectares) on Observation Hill about 8 miles (13 kilometers) north of the city. Organizationally it is similar to its predecessor, University College, Dar es Salaam (q.v.), with the exception that there are no longer formal links to an East African regional institution. During the late 1960s and 1970s the University of Dar es Salaam developed a reputation for political radicalism. In particular, economics, history, and political science courses were often based on Marxist, anti-Western ideological principles. Because of this orientation, the University of Dar es Salaam attracted numerous African revolutionaries. Some of the institution's more illustrious students have include Yoweri Museveni, now president of Uganda, and John Garang, leader of the insurgent Sudanese People's Liberation Army. In more recent years the University of Dar es Salaam has assumed a less doctrinaire approach to education in the social sciences.

UNIVERSITY OF EAST AFRICA (UEA). In 1960 TT, Kenya, and Uganda decided to combine Makerere University (q.v.) in Uganda, the Royal Technical College of Nairobi, and the nascent University College, Dar es Salaam (q.v.). In 1962 the East African Common Services Organization (EACSO) (q.v.) amalgamated these institutions, and on 29 June 1963 the UEA was inaugurated with Julius Nyerere (q.v.) as its first chancellor. This regional university then became the central degree-granting institution for East Africa, but since the UEA was a coordinating rather than a controlling body, its constituent campuses maintained much of their autonomy. The 1967 Treaty for East African Co-operation contained a clause that stipulated that the UEA should continue only until 1970, at which time the development of three or more separate universities would be encouraged. On 1 July 1970 the Tanzanian government nationalized the University College of Dar es Salaam as the University of Dar es Salaam. During the 1970s the University established a separate Faculty of Agriculture, Forestry, and Veterinary Science at Morogoro (q.v.). This campus was later renamed the Sokoine University of Agriculture in honor of recently deceased Prime Minister Edward Sokoine.

USAMBARA MOUNTAINS. Located between Mount Kilimanjaro (q.v.) and Korogwe, the Usambara Mountains are about 70 miles (113 kilometers) long and from 20 to 40 miles (32 to 64 kilometers) wide. Their highest elevation is 7,550 feet (2,300 meters). Large coffee and tea (qq.v.) estates are located in eastern Usambara. In other areas, which are densely populated, maize (q.v.) is the main subsistence crop, with bananas (q.v.) and sweet potatoes forming important dietary supplements. Rice is the main cash crop at lower elevations and is grown in swamps near the base of the mountains. Cattle are grazed in drier lowland areas.

— V —

VASCO DA GAMA (c. 1469–1525). A Portuguese navigator, he was probably the first European to sail around the Cape of Good Hope to Asia. During a 1497–1499 trading voyage to India, da Gama visited Mozambique, Mombasa, and Malindi. In 1502 he returned with a squadron of 20 ships to secure political and economic concessions for Portugal. He subsequently founded the colonies of Mozambique and Sofala, established a loose suzerainty over the Tanzanian coastal area, and forced Kilwa (q.v.) to pay tribute to Portugal. In 1524, a year before his death, Vasco da Gama became Portuguese viceroy to India.

VICTORIA FEDERATION OF COOPERATIVE UNIONS (VFCU). See COOPERATIVE SOCIETIES.

VILLAGE DEVELOPMENT COMMITTEE (VDC). The VDC was a local planning body intended to coordinate village-level development activities in the period preceding the villagization (q.v.) of rural Tanzania during the 1970s. During the 1960s approximately 7,000 VDCs were in operation, each headed by a local TANU (q.v.) chairman. VDC memberships included, in addition to ordinary citizens, grassroots notables such as teachers and local government administrators.

VILLAGIZATION. On 6 November 1973 Julius Nyerere (q.v.) decreed that "to live in a village is an order." The government implemented this policy by rounding up millions of peasants and moving them to *Ujamaa* (q.v.) communal villages. During these resettlement operations, the authorities destroyed much private property and used force against peasants who wanted to remain on their own farms. By 1977 13,506,044 people, or about 80 percent of the total population, had been resettled into 7,373 registered *Ujamaa* villages (q.v.), all of which supposedly contained schools, dispensaries, and clean water. More often, however, peasants had to contend with extremely harsh living conditions, which, because of excessive population densities and insufficient agricultural technologies, also led to extensive resource depletion and soil erosion.

The *Ujamaa* experiment became a rural policy disaster that crippled the agricultural sector and seriously compromised Nyerere's political standing throughout Tanzania. By the late 1980s President Ali Hassan Mwinyi (q.v.) began to encourage reinvestment in individual, privately owned farms.

— W —

WAHEHE WARS (1891–1898). See MKWAWA, CHIEF; PRINCE, TOM VON; SCHELE, COLONEL FRIEDRICH VON; ZELEWSKI, EMIL VON.

WAKIL, IDRIS ABDUL (b. 1925). A Zanzibari who began his career as a teacher and school administrator, Wakil resigned his headship in 1962 and stood for election, subsequently becoming a member of the Zanzibar National Assembly. After the 1964 Zanzibar Revolution (q.v.), Wakil served as a member of the Revolutionary Council and as Zanzibar's minister of education and national culture. After the unification of Tanganyika and Zanzibar (qq.v.) in 1964, he joined the union cabinet and then entered the diplomatic service as Tanzania's ambassador to the former West Germany (1967), The Hague (1969–1973), and the Republic of Guinea (1973–1977).

From 1977 to 1979 Wakil served as director of protocol at the Tanzanian Ministry of Foreign Affairs. In 1980 he became speaker of Zanzibar's House of Representatives (q.v.). On 15 October 1985 he was elected president of Zanzibar and Pemba (q.v.), and subsequently was appointed second vice president of Tanzania. Wakil's political style was reminiscent of Abeid Karume's (q.v.), the islands' first president. His intolerance of opposition provoked a high degree of local animosity toward his regime and the union with the mainland. On 23 January 1988 Wakil accused unnamed ministers and dissidents of conspiring to overthrow his government. To preempt a possible coup, he suspended the Revolutionary Council, dismissed six ministers, and assumed control over the armed forces. Despite these heavy-handed tactics, opposition to Wakil's government continued to grow. As the October 1990 legislative elections approached, he announced his retirement from the Zanzibari presidency.

WARIOBA, JOSEPH SINDE (b. 1940). A lawyer and politician who gained prominence in Tanzania without rising through the ranks of the CCM (q.v.). Warioba was educated at Sarawe and Ikizu Primary Schools, Musoma Middle School, Bwiru and Tabora Secondary Schools, and the University of Dar es Salaam (q.v.). In 1966 he obtained a position in the attorney general's office. Two years later, he became a solicitor for the Dar es Salaam city council. He then served as the director of the Legal and International Organisations Division in the Ministry of Foreign Affairs (1971–1975), as assistant attorney general (1975–1976), and as attorney general (1977–1983). On 24 February 1983 Warioba became minister of justice, and on 5 November 1984 President Ali Hassan Mwinyi (q.v.) appointed him prime minister and first vice president, the second most powerful position in the Tanzanian government. In a government reshuffle in November 1990, Warioba was demoted from the premiership to become minister of local government.

WHEAT. In 1852 Arabs cultivated wheat in Tabora (q.v.) and Karagwe. Approximately 40 percent of Tanzania's wheat is grown on the slopes of Mount Kilimanjaro (q.v.). The National Milling Corporation markets some of the wheat crop, most of which is consumed locally.

WHITE FATHERS. The Society of the Missionaries of Africa (Société de Notre Dame d'Afrique), founded by Cardinal Lavigerie, are called White Fathers because of their white clothes, not because they were once exclusively Caucasian. In 1878 the White Fathers arrived at Bagamoyo (q.v.) and then traveled to Tabora (q.v.), where a few of the missionaries built a village for freed slaves. Others divided into two groups, one moving to Bukumbi near Mwanza (q.v.) and the other settling on the shores of Lake Tanganyika (q.v.). In 1879 the White Fathers reached Ujiji (q.v.), and they subsequently established stations at Unyanyembe in 1881 and at Karema in 1885. During the 1890s the White Fathers occupied Rukwa, Usumbwa, and Buhaya and in the following decade expanded to Ufipa, Buha, Mbulu, and toward Lake Malawi (q.v.). The White Fathers also built seminaries at Rubya in 1903, Tabora in 1908, and Utinta in 1921. In 1917 the order ordained the first two Tanganyikan priests of the Roman Catholic Church. Until joining the Tanganyika Episcopal Conference (q.v.) in 1957, the White Fathers administered a network of primary and secondary schools throughout the country. They also continued to train African priests. Of 303 African priests in 1962, 58 percent had been prepared by the White Fathers.

WILDLIFE. See GAME RESERVES.

WISSMANN, HERMANN VON (1853–1905). Wissmann was a German military officer who is still reputed to be Germany's greatest

African explorer and most efficient colonial administrator. He also is noted for brutally suppressing African communities that resisted German colonial rule. In 1889 he crushed the Abushiri revolt (q.v.) and executed its leader. The following year, he negotiated a truce with the Zigua resistance leader, Bwana Heri (q.v.). Wissmann, who was a morphine addict, ended his East African career by serving as governor of GEA from 1895 to 1896.

WORLD BANK. Tanzania's involvement with the World Bank started in 1959, when the bank sent an economic survey mission "to assess the resources available for future development." In its report, the bank recommended that the country initiate a "transformation approach" that would secure "quicker and higher returns on investment and effort [than through an existing colonial 'improvement approach'] by using selected, sparsely settled areas for planned settlement schemes and cattle ranches." The government began implementing the "transformation approach" by establishing fewer than 30 of a proposed 200 village settlement schemes in the first four years after independence. By 1966 the schemes' high costs and their capitalist approach to agricultural modernization had produced major conflicts with Julius Nyerere's evolving *Ujamaa* (qq.v.) philosophy. Combined with growing tension between farmers and government supervisory staff, these factors caused the Tanzanian authorities to abandon the village settlement program at a loss of approximately Shs.20 million.

This failure set the pattern of Tanzanian–World Bank relations for at least the next 15 years. On 21 July 1994 the extent of this fiasco became known when the World Bank published an internal report acknowledging that it had given "uncritical support" to Tanzania's failed socialist experiment under Julius Nyerere (q.v.). Between the 1967 and 1981 the World Bank made loans of more than US$1 billion to help finance the Arusha Declaration's (q.v.) industrial and rural *Ujamaa* policies. Wholesale nationalization of private enterprises and the forced resettlement of more than 13 million rural dwellers all but destroyed Tanzania's industrial and agricultural capabilities.

Since 1981 the World Bank and other Western financial institutions have encouraged Tanzania to focus its attention on economic privatization and the more effective management of macroeconomic policy instruments, including currency exchange and interest rates, the budget, and the national money supply. The bank has also supported numerous market-oriented development projects in the fields of transportation, industry, education, medicine, agriculture, and finance. Typical of this latter-day policy emphasis is a 1994 US$12.5 million program to improve Tanzania's mining capabilities. In spite of these activities, an increasing number of economists have become skeptical of the World Bank's ability to facilitate lasting social and economic development in Tanzania.

WORLD WAR I (1914–1918). The East African Campaign of World War I developed into one of the most remarkable military adventures of recent history. Initially the colonial government in GEA had no intention of becoming involved in a conflict against the British (contingents from South Africa, Southern Rhodesia [now Zimbabwe], and India also served under British command) and Allied forces (including Belgian and Portuguese contingents). The German governor, Heinrich Schnee (q.v.), wanted GEA to remain neutral, but General Paul von Lettow-Vorbeck (q.v.) believed that by launching a guerrilla war against the British, he could pin down a large number of troops and force the British to divert soldiers destined for the European western front to East Africa. After the Royal Navy shelled a wireless station near Dar es Salaam (q.v.) on 8 August 1914, Lettow-Vorbeck defied Schnee and captured Taveta, a small settlement just inside the border of Kenya.

At the beginning of the campaign, Lettow-Vorbeck's *Schütztruppe* (q.v.) numbered only 218 Germans and 2,542 *askaris* (q.v.) organized into 14 companies. This force eventually totaled 3,007 German troops and 12,100 *askaris*. With this army, for four years Lettow-Vorbeck battled an Allied force that numbered about 70,000 soldiers. Throughout the war several hundred thousand African carriers supported troops on both sides. Relying largely on raids, hit-and-run tactics, and the skillful use of internal lines of communication, Lettow-Vorbeck wrecked havoc upon the British by destroying bridges, blowing up trains along the Uganda Railway, ambushing convoys, and capturing military equipment and other supplies.

The fighting encompassed three phases. In the first two years of the campaign, Lettow-Vorbeck largely succeeded in eluding British forces. During the 1916–1917 period, Jan Smuts (q.v.) fought the *Schütztruppe* to a stalemate. In late 1917 General J. L. van Deventer assumed command of British forces in East Africa and eventually forced the Germans to retreat into Portuguese East Africa (now Mozambique). On 28 September 1918 Lettow-Vorbeck crossed back into GEA, but before he could launch a new offensive, the war ended in Europe.

In more than four years of fighting, German casualties included 439 killed in action and 874 wounded, while British forces suffered 3,443 combat deaths and 7,777 wounded in action. Disease claimed 256 German soldiers and 6,558 British troops. African losses on the German side included 1,290 *askaris* killed in action and about 7,000 carriers dead from disease. Another 3,669 Africans sustained wounds. British forces lost 376 African carriers in combat and 1,645 wounded. A much larger number, 44,911, died of disease. The Belgians and their Congolese troops suffered approximately 3,000 killed and wounded, and among the Portuguese and their African soldiers 1,734 were killed and several hundred wounded.

WORLD WAR II (1939–1945). No fighting occurred in TT during World War II. Even so, the British interned 1,470 German residents of the territory. Some 86,740 Africans served in the King's African Rifles (KAR) (q.v.) and fought against the Italians in Somalia and Ethiopia, the Japanese in Burma, and the Vichy French in Madagascar. Almost half of these troops worked as unskilled laborers in the British Pioneer Corps or in the military labor service.

After 1940 the colonial authorities relied on conscription to satisfy the KAR's manpower needs. The British government also authorized the use of more than 18,000 soldiers on TT's sisal plantations and rubber estates, both of which yielded products essential to the war effort. Although most Africans performed their military service loyally, desertion rates increased as the war progressed, largely because of harsh working conditions on sisal plantations and rubber estates. By 1945 3,861 Africans were absent without leave from the KAR. The economic hardships and physical dislocations associated with World War II helped to lay the groundwork for a postwar nationalist movement that would eventually bring Tanganyikan independence.

— Y —

YOUNG, SIR MARK AITCHISON (1886–1974). Young was an atypically pro-settler governor of TT (1938–1941), who advocated a policy emphasizing the encouragement of European agriculture. This policy led to an increase in the number of white settlers, including Germans, in the territory. With the approach of World War II (q.v.), Anglo-German tension rose as some in this group advocated a plan to help pacify Nazi dictator Adolf Hitler by returning TT to Germany. Young rejected this strategy, arguing that it would betray those Africans who preferred British administration. Young also supported the Tanganyika League (q.v.), an association founded by British settlers but likewise supported by many German farmers, which sought to prevent TT from reverting to Germany.

— Z —

ZANZIBAR AND PEMBA PEOPLE'S PARTY (ZPPP). In late 1959 Ameri Tajo, Mohammed Shamte, and Ali Sharif formed the ZPPP as a splinter party of the Afro-Shirazi Party (ASP) (q.v.). The ZPPP hoped to offer an alternative to the ASP's anti-Arab racism and yet remain devoted to African interests. In June 1961 the ZPPP and the Zanzibar National Party (ZNP) (q.v.) formed a weak coalition government with Shamte as chief minister. The majority of Zanzibar Africans believed that this government was dedicated to preserving the Arab community's political and economic dominance. The coalition government split the ZPPP, caused many of its most effective leaders to join the ASP, and ended its plans of becoming a third force in Zanzibar politics. The coalition managed to survive Zanzibar's final LEGCO (q.v.) election of December 1963, only to fall in the Zanzibari Revolution (q.v.) of January 1964. Also, see ELECTIONS, ZANZIBAR.

ZANZIBAR, BRITISH OFFICIALS. From 1840 to 1963 a series of consuls, consuls general, and Residents maintained British interests in Zanzibar (q.v.). Until 1913 these officials reported to the British Foreign Office; afterward they were responsible to the Colonial Office.

Consuls:
Atkins Hamerton (1840–1857)
Christopher Palmer Rigby (1858–1860)
Lewis Pelly (1861–1862)
Robert Lambert Playfair (1862–1865
Henry Adrian Churchill (1865–1870)
John Kirk (1870–1873)
Consuls General:
John Kirk (1873–1886)
Claude Maxwell Macdonald (1887–1888)
Charles Bean Euan-Smith (1888–1891)
Gerald Portal (1891–1893)
James Rennell Rodd (1893–1894)
Arthur Henry Hardinge (1894–1900)
Charles Norton Edgecumbe Eliot (1900–1904)
Basil Shillito Cave (1904–1909)
Edward A.W. Clarke (1909–1913)
Residents:
Francis Barrow Pearce (1914–1922)
John Houston Sinclair (1922–1924)
Alfred Claud Hollis (1924–1930)
Richard Sims Donkin Rankine (1930–1937)
John Hathorn Hall (1937–1940)
Henry Guy Pilling (1941–1946)

Vincent Goncalves Glenday (1946–1951)
John Daizell Rankine (1952–1954)
Henry Steven Porter (1954–1960)
George Rixson Mooring (1960–1963)

ZANZIBAR HOUSE OF REPRESENTATIVES. On 12 October 1979 the Zanzibar Revolutionary Council adopted a separate constitution that contained provisions for an elected president and a partially elected House of Representatives. On 7 January 1980 Zanzibaris elected 60 members, and the government nominated an additional 55 members. Since its creation the House of Representatives has repeatedly demonstrated a proclivity for contentious behavior. In June 1982, for example, it condemned those who criticized the islands' leadership and called for a repeal of the 1964 union between Zanzibar (q.v.) and the mainland.

According to a new constitution adopted on 12 January 1985, the House of Representatives includes between 45 and 55 members and is elected by secret ballot in constituencies of less than 10,000 voters. This constitution further provides that the House of Representatives also seats Zanzibar's regional commissioners, presidential nominees, and 10 representatives of organizations affiliated with the CCM and the United Women of Tanzania (UWT) (qq.v.). MPs representing Zanzibar in the union parliament are elected from the House of Representatives.

In May 1988 the House of Representatives again became involved in controversy when the CCM expelled the deputy speaker of the House of Representatives, Suleiman Seif Hamad, and two MPs, Shaaban Hamis Mloo and Hai Pandu, for criticizing Zanzibari President Idris Abdul Wakil (q.v.). An ensuing riot resulted in three deaths, several injuries, and 29 arrests. As a result of mainland intervention in the crisis, many Zanzibaris and their MPs maintained that the mainland would eventually "swallow" Zanzibar. Fears of mainland domination have remained a volatile issue in the House of Representatives and have caused many MPs to support, publicly or privately, Zanzibar's separation from the mainland. After the House of Representatives passed a bill endorsing multiparty politics on 14 May 1992, several newly organized political parties also supported a referendum on the terms of the 1964 Tanzania-Zanzibar union.

ZANZIBARI REVOLUTION. On 12 January 1964 "Field Marshal" John Okello (q.v.) and about 700 rebels toppled the Zanzibari government and exiled Sultan Jamshid ibn Abdullah (q.v.). In the chaos that followed, up to 5,000 Zanzibaris lost their lives. Abeid Karume (q.v.), the islands' new president, initially filled his government with Afro-

Shirazi Party (AS) and Umma (Masses) Party (qq.v.) personnel. Kenya, Uganda, the former Soviet Union, Cuba, and the former German Democratic Republic quickly recognized Karume's radical regime. For its part, the Tanganyika government reacted to the revolution by deploying approximately 200 police to Zanzibar in order to help maintain law and order. Further to neutralize the islands' more radical leadership, Julius Nyerere (q.v.) proposed a union of Tanganyika and Zanzibar. After Karume agreed to this plan, the two countries were united on 23 April 1964, with Karume appointed as the new state's first vice president.

ZANZIBAR ISLAND. Zanzibar is a 640 square mile (1,660 square kilometer) coral island that is less than 400 feet (120 meters) above sea level and lies 23 miles (37 kilometers) from the mainland. Approximately 80 percent of its inhabitants is Muslim. Zanzibar town is the island's only urban center. The climate is tropical. Its maximum mean temperature is 84.4 degrees Farenheit (29.1 degrees Celsius) and its minimum mean temperature is 76.6 degrees Farenheit (24.7 degrees Celsius). The island has an average annual rainfall of 60 inches (1,500 millimeters), and its seasons are governed by monsoons. From December to March, winds blow from the northeast, and from June to October from the southwest. Heavy rains normally occur during April and May, and November and December normally bring lighter, "short" rains. Cloves and coconut (qq.v.) products account for more than 90 percent of the value of domestic agricultural exports. Swahili is the most commonly spoken language, although Arabic is also spoken in some Arab (q.v.) circles and for religious purposes. The Asian (q.v.) community speaks either Gujarati or Cutchi. In 1988 the island's population totaled 640,578 inhabitants.

ZANZIBAR NATIONAL PARTY (ZNP). The ZNP was established in 1955, with the support of Arab intellectuals and some African peasants, as an offshoot of the National Party of the Subjects of the Sultan of Zanzibar. The party's president, Sheikh Ali Muhsin Barwani, preached multiracialism but showed favoritism toward Zanzibar's Arab population. Another, more radical faction was headed by Ahmad Abdulrahman Muhammad Babu (q.v.). In the 1957 LEGCO (q.v.) election the ZNP secured none of the 18 available parliamentary seats and polled only a small percentage of the total vote. It improved its showing in the January and June 1961 elections (campaigning with the Zanzibar and Pemba People's Party [ZPPP] in the latter campaign), and after the 1963 pre-independence election, the ZNP and the ZPPP (q.v.) formed a transitional coalition government under the sultan (q.v.). On 12 January 1964, less than one month after

Zanzibari independence, rebel Africans allied under the Afro-Shirazi Party (q.v.) overthrew the ZNP-ZPPP government. Also, see ELECTIONS, ZANZIBAR; and ZANZIBARI REVOLUTION.

ZANZIBAR NATIONAL UNION. In April 1953 Ahmed Lemke, a wealthy Arab, created the Zanzibar National Union. A prototype of the Zanzibar National Party (q.v.), this anticolonial, multiracial organization sought to gain the political support of all racial communities on Zanzibar by emphasizing Zanzibari nationalism and the notion that Islam was a bond of identity that transcended racial divisions. A few months after its creation, the Zanzibar National Union floundered after the colonial government issued a regulation forbidding the participation of African civil servants in politics. Lemke realized that without the support of this educated and influential group, his organization could not speak for all races on Zanzibar. Accordingly, in the summer of 1953 he dissolved the Union.

ZANZIBAR PROTECTORATE. In force between 1890 and 1963, the Zanzibar Protectorate comprised the islands of Zanzibar and Pemba (qq.v.), several adjacent islands, and Latham Island. The Busaidi dynasty (q.v.) ruled the islands with the British government's support and protection. The Busaidi sultan was the protectorate's constitutional ruler, and a British Resident acted as the sultan's chief adviser. The Resident also presided over the Executive Council, which consisted of four ex officio members and three representative members. The sultan appointed all Executive Council personnel on the advice of the British Resident. The British Resident likewise served as president of the islands' LEGCO (q.v.), which included the four ex officio Executive Council members, nine official members who held administrative office, and 12 representative members. Until 1957, when Zanzibaris elected six of the 12 representative members, the sultan appointed all LEGCO members on the advice of the British Resident. The protectorate was divided into three administrative districts (Zanzibar Urban, Zanzibar Rural, and Pemba), each of which was administered by a district commissioner who reported to a senior commissioner. When so requested, a Privy Council also advised the Sultan on the performance of his duties.

ZANZIBAR, SULTANS (1804–1964).

Said ibn Seyyid (1804–1856)
Majid ibn Said (1856–1870)
Barghash ibn Said (1870–1888)
Khalifa ibn Said (1888–1890)

Ali ibn Said (1890–1893)
Hamed ibn Thwain (1893–1896)
Hamoud ibn Muhammad (1896–1902)
Ali ibn Hamoud (1902–1911)
Khalifa ibn Harub (1911–1960)
Abdullah ibn Khalifa (1960–1963)
Jamshid ibn Abdullah (1963–1964)

Also, see entries under each name.

ZELEWSKI, EMIL VON (?–1891). Zelewski assumed command of the *Schütztruppe* (q.v.) after Hermann von Wissmann (q.v.) retired from the post of commissioner. Shortly after, he persuaded the governor, Julius von Soden (q.v.), to authorize a punitive expedition against Chief Mkwawa (q.v.). In June 1891 Zelewski departed Kilwa (q.v.) with a force of 13 Europeans, some 320 *askaris* (q.v.), 170 porters, machine guns, and field artillery. On 17 August 1891, Mkwawa and his followers surprised the Germans in the dense bush near Rugaro. They killed Zelewski, nine European officers, and 250 African soldiers and captured 250 rifles and three guns. Zelewski had badly underestimated Mkwawa and his ability to employ guerrilla tactics against a superior force.

ZINJANTHROPUS. In July 1959 Louis Leakey and his wife Mary (qq.v.), discovered a skull in Olduvai Gorge (q.v.), which they named *Zinjanthropus* (Nutcracker Man) due to its large teeth and cheekbones. The skull, which later was renamed *Australopithecus boisei*, is now in the National Museum in Dar es Salaam (q.v.). According to scientific dating techniques, *Zinjanthropus* lived 1.8 million years ago. Leakey classified this creature as an *Australopithecine* (near man) and claimed that it represented a dead-end branch in the tree of human evolution.

Bibliography

A. Bibliographies and guides
B. History: Precolonial
C. History: German Colonial Period
D. History: British Colonial Period
E. History: Independence Period
F. Military and Security Affairs
G. Economic Affairs
H. General Studies
I. Regional Studies
J. Religion, Missions, and Missionaries
K. Ethnography, Sociology, and Folklore
L. Agriculture, Land Tenure, and Local Administration
M. Foreign Affairs
N. Women's Affairs
O. Arts, Architecture, and Music
P. Education
Q. Environment and Geography
R. Legal Affairs
S. Medicine, Health, and Social Services
T. Literature and Language
U. Communications, Media, and Transport
V. Urban Centers and Urbanization Studies
W. Zanzibar and the Islands

Abbreviations

AA	*African Affairs*
AHS	*African Historical Studies*
AO	*Africa Quarterly*
AR	*Africa Report*
AS	*African Studies*
ASR	*African Studies Review*
AT	*Africa Today*

CH	Current History
CJAS	Canadian Journal of African Studies
CMIR	Church Missionary Intelligencer and Record
CUP	Cambridge University Press
DR	Dietrich Reimer
DUP	Dar es Salaam University Press
EAER	East African Economics Review
EAJ	East Africa Journal
EALB	East African Literature Bureau
EALR	Eastern African Law Review
EAMJ	East African Medical Journal
EAPH	East African Publishing House
EAR	East Africa and Rhodesia
EIHC	Essex Institute of Historical Collections
FAO	Food and Agriculture Organization
GJ	Geographical Journal
GP	Government Printer
HMSO	Her/His Majesty's Stationery Office
IFO	Institut für Wirtschaftsforschung-Africa Studiens-stelle
IJAHS	International Journal of African Historical Studies
JAA	Journal of African Administration
JAH	Journal of African History
JAS	Journal of African Studies
JDA	Journal of Developing Areas
JEARD	Journal of Eastern African Research and Development
JMAS	Journal of Modern African Studies
JRAS	Journal of the Royal African Society
MW	Moslem World
NGM	National Geographic Magazine
OUP	Oxford University Press
ROAPE	Review of African Political Economy
SIAS	Scandinavian Institute of African Studies
STD	Standard
TAR	The African Review
TJH	Transafrican Journal of History
TNR	Tanganyika Notes and Records (later, Tanzania Notes and Records)
TPH	Tanzania Publishing House
UJ	Uganda Journal
UMCA	Universities' Mission to Central Africa
USGPO	United States Government Printing Office
WD	World Development
WP	Westview Press
YUP	Yale University Press

Introduction

The following bibliography provides readers with a general introduction to the field of Tanzanian studies. Most of the available literature is in English, although useful materials also appear in other European languages, including French, German, and Swedish. Comparatively few materials are published in Swahili, Tanzania's lingua franca, or in other indigenous languages. Scholars who desire more comprehensive surveys of writings should refer to the Bibliographies and Guides section of this bibliography, which contains references to the more significant compilations of sources on Tanzania.

Over the past few decades, much scholarship on Tanzania has focused on its history, foreign and military affairs, political and economic development, agricultural capabilities and prospects, and religions. Considerable work is still needed on Tanzanian health and medicine, especially with regard to the quality of rural health care and the impact of Acquired Immmune Deficiency Syndrome (AIDS) and other newly emerging/re-emerging diseases. Additional research is also needed in such areas as Tanzanian prehistory, art and literature, urban affairs, the role and status of women, and the sociopolitical impact of the communications media.

Concerning the German and British colonial periods, books and articles normally fall into two categories. Those written before independence usually extoll the virtues of European rule, while those produced after independence are often highly critical of German and British colonialism. More balanced future assessments of the political, military, economic, and social implications of the colonial experience will undoubtedly offer greater understanding of Tanzania's historical development.

In addition to books and articles, archival data are essential to Tanzania scholars. Most available archival material is limited to the colonial and immediate postcolonial periods and is located on three continents. The Tanzania National Archives in Dar es Salaam and the University of Dar es Salaam library house a variety of documents from the German and British periods of rule. In Europe, records from the German era can be found in the *Deutsches Zentralarchiv,* Potsdam, which contains all former German Colonial Office documents, and the *Bundesarchiv-Militärarchiv,* Freiburg, which contains war diaries and correspondences from German military units participating in the suppression of the Maji-Maji Rebellion. For documentation on the British colonial period, several repositories in the United Kingdom are indispensable. These include the Public Record Office, Kew; Crown Agents for Overseas Government and Administration, Sutton; Foreign and Commonwealth Office, London; House of Lords Record Office, London; Hydrographic Department, Taunton; Post Office, London; Royal Botanic Gardens,

Kew; and India Office Library and Records, London. In North America, archival materials on microfilm are housed at the Consortium for Africa Microfilm Project (CAMP) in Chicago, Illinois. Microfilm copies of full or partial archival files are also located in many major North American universities, including Indiana University, Michigan State University, Syracuse University, the University of Wisconsin at Madison, and West Virginia University. Before visiting any of these archival locations, researchers should inquire as to any special regulations and/or requirements pertaining to the use of specific collections of official documents and other materials.

Apart from items contained in this bibliography, readers interested in recent Tanzanian affairs should examine contemporary periodicals such as *Africa Confidential, Africa Research Bulletin, Focus on Africa,* and *New African* as well as leading scholarly journals including the *African Studies Review, Canadian Journal of African Studies,* and *Journal of Modern African Studies.* The *Economist* Intelligence Unit's quarterly and annual country reports on Tanzania are also useful, especially on economic matters. Lastly, annuals such as *Africa Contemporary Record* and *Africa South of the Sahara* provide valuable sources of continuing information.

A. Bibliographies and Guides

Accessions List for East Africa. Nairobi: Library of Congress Office, Jan. 1968–, six times per year.

African Bibliographical Center. "Arusha: The Politics of Self-Reliance in Tanzania: A Selected and Introductory Bibliographical Guide." *Current Bibliography on African Affairs*, new series, 4 (April 1968): 5–8.

Allen, J.W.T. *Swahili and Arabic Manuscripts and Tapes in the Library of the University College, Dar es Salaam: A Catalogue.* Leiden: Brill, 1970.

Allot, Antony N., ed. *Bibliography of African Law. Part I: East Africa.* London: School of Oriental and African Studies, 1961.

Al-Naqar, Umar. "Arabic Materials in the Government Archives of Zanzibar." *History in Africa* (1978): 377–82.

Araya, R. *Library and Information Services in East Africa: Kenya, Tanzania, Uganda.* Warsaw: University, Institute of Oriental Languages and Cultures, 1986.

Auger, George A. *Tanzania Education since Uhuru: A Bibliography (1961–1971) Incorporating a Study of Tanzania Past and Present and a Guide to Further Sources of Information on Education in Tanzania.* Nairobi: Institute of Education, University of Dar es Salaam, 1973.

Azimio la Arusha: Orodha ya Vitabu na Makala. [Dar es Salaam]: Shirika la Huduma za Maktaba Tanzania, 1977.

Bates, Margaret I. *Study Guide for Tanzania.* Boston: African Studies Center, Boston University, 1969.

Becker, Carl H. "Materialen zur Kenntnis des Islam in Deutsch-Ostafrika." *Der Islam* (1911): 1–48.

———. "Materials for the Understanding of Islam in German East Africa." *TNR* (1968): 31–61.

Beidelman, T. O. "Addenda and Corrigenda to the Bibliography of the Matrilineal Peoples of Eastern Tanzania." *Africa* (1969): 186–88.

———. "Further Addenda to the Bibliography of the Matrilineal Peoples of Eastern Tanzania." *Africa* (1974): 295–96.

Bennett, Norman R. *Arab State of Zanzibar: A Bibliography.* Boston: G. K. Hall, 1984.

Bhargava, S. C. *Bibliography on Crop Production Research in East Africa (with Particular Reference to Crop Research in Tanzania).* Dar es Salaam: Crop Development Division, Ministry of Agriculture, United Republic of Tanzania, 1975.

Bibliography of Economic and Social Material Concerning the Four Lake Regions. Dar es Salaam: University College, Institute of Adult Education, 1967.

Bibliography of Economic and Statistical Publications on Tanzania. Dar es Salaam: Central Bureau of Statistics, 1967.

Blackhurst, Hector, ed. *Africa Bibliography.* Manchester: Manchester University Press, 1984–, annual.

Bridgman, Jon. *German Africa: A Select Annotated Bibliography.* Stanford: Hoover Institution, 1965.

Brown, Walter T. "German Records in the National Archives of Tanzania." *African Studies Bulletin* 2 (1969): 147–51.

Burt, Eugene C. *Annotated Bibliography of the Visual Arts of East Africa.* Bloomington: Indiana University Press, 1980.

Campbell, John, and Valdo Pons. *Urbanization, Urban Planning, and Urban Life in Tanzania: An Annotated Bibliography*. Hull: University of Hull, 1987.

Casada, James A. "British Exploration in East Africa: A Bibliography with Commentary." *Africana Journal* (1974): 195–239.

————. *Sir Richard F. Burton: A Biobibliographical Study*. Boston: G. K. Hall, 1990.

Centre for Development Research. *CDR Library Holdings of Publications (Governmental, Parastatal, Institutional, and Periodical) Published in Tanzania*. Copenhagen: The Centre, 1989.

Cook, Alison. *Soils Bibliography of Tanzania*. Dar es Salaam: Bureau of Resource Assessment and Land Use Planning, 1975.

Dann, Jorgen. *Bibliografi over Tanzania*. Kobenhavn: Mellemfolkeligt Samvirke, 1967.

Dar es Salaam, University College, Library. *Papers of Hans Cory in the Library of the University College Dar es Salaam*. Dar es Salaam: University College, 1968.

Darch, Colin, ed. *Africa Index to Current Periodical Literature*. Munich: K. G. Saur Verlag (Hans Zell), 1977–, annual.

————. *Russian Writings on Tanganyika, Zanzibar, and Tanzania: A Guide to the Published Materials*. Dar es Salaam: Bureau of Resource Assessment and Land Use Planning, University of Dar es Salaam, 1976.

————. *Tanzania*. Oxford: Clio Press, 1985.

Decalo, Samuel. *Tanzania: An Introductory Bibliography*. Kingston: University of Rhode Island, 1968.

East Africana Accessions Bulletin, 1973–. Dar es Salaam: The Library, 1974–, annual.

Energy Resources at the National Central Library: A Select Bibliography. Dar es Salaam: Tanzania National Documentation Centre, 1985.

Finucane, Brendan, Lawrence Rupley, and Tony Killick. "The Economic Literature for Kenya, Tanzania, Uganda, 1974–1980: An Analysis." *African Research and Documentation* 33 (1983): 12–22.

Fleuret, Patrick. *Annotated Bibliography of the Sociology and Political Economy of Somalia, Sudan, and Tanzania*. Binghamton, NY: Institute for Development Anthropology, 1979.

Fosbrooke, Henry A. "Early Exploration of Kilimanjaro: A Bibliographical Note." *TNR* 64 (March 1965): 1–7.

Franz, Eckhart G. and Peter Geissler. *Das Deutsch-Ostafrika Archiv: Inventar der Abteilung "German Records" im Nationalarchiv der Vereinigten Republik Tansania, Dar es Salaam*. 2 Vols. Marburg: Institut für Archivwissenschaft, 1984.

Garver, R. A., ed. *Research Priorities for East Africa*. Nairobi: EAPH, 1966.

Gillman, Clement. "Bibliography on Kilimanjaro," and "Bibliography on Virunga Volcanoes." *The Icecap* (1932): 69–72.

————. "Bibliography of Kilimanjaro, 1944." *TNR* 18 (December 1944): 60–68.

Government Publications Obtainable from the Government Printer. Dar es Salaam: n.p.?, n.d.

Hall, R. de Z. "Bibliography of Ethnographical Literature for Tanganyika Territory." *TNR* 7 (June, 1939): 75–83.

Hannon-Andersson, Carolyn, and Adolfo Mascarenhas. *Domestic Water Supplies in Tanzania: A Bibliography with Emphasis on Socio-economic Research*. Dar es Salaam: Institute of Resource Assessment, 1983.

Heijnen, Johannes Daniel. *River Basins in Tanzania: A Bibliography*. Dar es Salaam: Bureau of Resource Assessment and Land Use Planning, 1970.

Hess, Robert L., and Dalvan M. Coger. *Bibliography of Primary Sources for Nineteenth-Century Tropical Africa*. Stanford: Hoover Institution Press, 1972.

Hill, Patricia J. *Shelf List and Index to Secretariat Archives (Early Series) 1919–1927*. Dar es Salaam: National Archives of Tanzania, 1966.

Holmquist, Frank W., and Joel D. Barkan. *Comprehensive Bibliography: Politics and Public Policy in Kenya and Tanzania*. Iowa City: University of Iowa, Center for International and Comparative Studies, 1984.

Howell, John Bruce. *East African Community: Subject Guide to Official Publications*. Washington, D.C.: Library of Congress, 1976.

———. *Tanganyika African National Union: A Guide to Publications by and about TANU*. Washington, D.C.: Library of Congress, 1976.

———. *Zanzibar's Afro-Shirazi Party, 1957–1977*. Washington, D.C.: Library of Congress, 1978.

Hundsdorfer, Volkhard. *Bibliographie zur Sozialwissenschaftlichen Erforschung Tanzanias*. Munich: Weltforum Verlag, 1974.

Kai-Samba, Ibrahim B., Salum S. Mbwana, and Valley G. Mchomba. *Development for Self-Reliance: A Bibliography of Contribution from the Faculty of Agriculture, Forestry and Veterinary Science, University of Dar es Salaam, 1969–1977*. Morogoro: Faculty of Agriculture, Forestry, and Veterinary Science Library, 1977.

Karugila, J. M. "German Records in Tanzania." *African Research and Documentation* 50 (1989): 12–18.

———. "National Archives in a Developing Country." *TNR* 84/85 (1980): 117–21.

Kasungu, Halima. *Bibliography on Customs, Folklore, and Oral Traditions in Tanzania*. Dar es Salaam: Tanzania Library Service, National Central Library, 1977.

Kaungamno, E. E. "Tanganyika Library Service: 1961–1971." *TNR* 76 (1975): 129–31.

Kikula, I. S., C. G. Mung'ong'o, and R. D. Jengo. *Perspectives on Land Degradation and Conservation in Tanzania*. Dar es Salaam: Institute of Resource Assessment, University of Dar es Salaam, 1990.

Killick, Tony. *Economies of East Africa: A Bibliography: 1974–1980*. Boston: G. K. Hall, 1984.

Kirk Greene, Anthony H.M. *Biographical Dictionary of the British Colonial Service, 1939–1966*. London: Hans Zell, 1991.

Kirkpatrick, B.J.A. *Catalogue of the Library of Sir Richard Burton, K.C.M.G., Held by the Royal Anthropological Institute*. London: Royal Anthropological Institute, 1979.

Kocher, James E., and Beverly Fleischer. *Bibliography on Rural Development in Tanzania*. East Lansing: Michigan State University, 1979.

Kulkarni, H. M. *Periodicals in Tanzania Libraries: A Union List (Excludes University of Dar es Salaam Libraries)*. Dar es Salaam: The Service, 1976.

Kuria, Lucas, and John B. Webster. *Bibliography on Anthropology and Sociology in Tanzania and East Africa*. Syracuse: Maxwell School of Citizenship and Public Affairs, Syracuse University, 1966.

Kurji, Feroz. *Wildlife Ecology: A Bibliography of Some Studies in Tanzania*. Dar es Salaam: Bureau of Resource Assessment and Land Use Planning, University of Dar es Salaam, 1981.

Kurtz, L. S. *Historical Dictionary of Tanzania*. London, and Metuchen, NJ: Scarecrow Press, 1978.

Langlands, Bryan W. "Tanzania Bibliography: 1965." *TNR* 65 (March 1966): 113–22.

———. "Tanzania Bibliography: 1966." *TNR* 66 (December 1966): 231–38; and 67 (June 1967): 79–88.

———. "Tanzania Bibliography: 1966–1967." *TNR* 68 (February 1968): 117–24.

———. "Tanzania Bibliography: 1967." *TNR* 69 (1968): 73–83.

———. "Tanzania Bibliography: 1968." *TNR* 70 (1969): 79–94.

———. "Tanzania Bibliography: 1969." *TNR* 72 (1973): 109–29.

———. "Tanzania Bibliography: 1970." *TNR* 73 (1974): 99–114.

———. "Tanzania Bibliography: 1971." *TNR* 74 (1974): 57–81.

———. "Tanzania Bibliography: 1972." *TNR* 77/78 (June 1976): 135–48; and 79/80 (December 1976): 133–50.

Legum, Colin, ed. *Africa Contemporary Record: Annual Survey and Documents*. New York and London: Africana Publishing Company, 1968/69–, annual.

Ley, Roger Temple. *Litteratur om Tanzania: Annoteret Bibliografi*. Kobenhavn: Mellemfolkeligt Samvirke, 1971.

Library of Congress, African Section. *Africa South of the Sahara: Index to Periodical Literature, 1900–1970*. 4 vols. Boston: G. K. Hall, 1971–, supplements.

Lukwaro, Eliud Lushino Abdallah. *AIDS: A Select Annotated Bibliography*. Dar es Salaam: Tanzania National Documentation Centre, National Central Library, 1988.

———. *List of Practising Librarians, Documentalists, and Archivists in Tanzania*, 3d edition. Dar es Salaam: Tanzania National Documentation Centre, National Central Library, 1985.

McGee, M. Sumar. *National Policies of Tanzania: A Bibliography*. Dar es Salaam: Tanganyika Library Service, 1972.

McHenry, Dean E. *Ujamaa Villages in Tanzania: A Bibliography*. Uppsala: SIAS, 1981.

McKinley, Juanita E. *Education in Tanzania: A Working Bibliography*. Stanford: Stanford University Libraries, 1981.

Maganga, Faustin P. *Background to Environmental Problems in Sukumaland: An Annotated Bibliography*. Dar es Salaam: Institute of Resource Assessment, University of Dar es Salaam, 1987.

———. *Background to Land Use Problems in Mbulu, Hanang, and Babati Districts: An Annotated Bibliography*. Dar es Salaam: Institute of Resource Assessment, University of Dar es Salaam, 1987.

Majaliwa, S. *Bibliography of Hot Springs in Tanzania*. Dodoma: Mineral Resources Division, Tanzania, 1966.

Maro, Paul S., and Valery P. Maro. *Geography of Tanzania's Development: A Bibliography*. Dar es Salaam: Geographical Association of Tanzania, [1982?].

Mascarenhas, Ophelia C. *Preliminary Guide to the Study of Traditional Medicine in Tanzania*. Dar es Salaam: Bureau of Resource Assessment and Land Use Planning, University of Dar es Salaam, 1975.

———. "Tourism in East Africa: A Bibliographical Essay." *Current Bibliography on African Affairs*, new series, 5 (September/October, 1971): 315–26.

———. "Tanzania Bibliography: 1976." *TNR* 84/85 (1980): 159–74.

Mascarenhas, Ophelia C. and Marjorie J. Mbilinyi. *Women and Development in Tanzania: An Annotated Bibliography.* Addis Ababa: African Training and Research Centre for Women, Economic Commission for Africa, United Nations, 1980.

————. *Women in Tanzania: An Analytical Bibliography.* Uppsala: SIAS, 1983.

Mascarenhas, Ophelia C. et al. "Tanzania Bibliography: 1975." *TNR* 81/82 (1978): 171–99.

Matogo, B.W.K. "Public Library Trends in East Africa, 1945–65." *International Library Review* 1 (1977): 67–82.

Mbuligwe, T. M. *Bibliography of Coal in Tanzania.* Dodoma: Mineral Resources Division, Tanzania, 1973.

Mezger, D. and E. Littich. *Recent English Economic Research in East Africa: A Selected Bibliography.* Munich: IFO, 1967.

Mioni, Alberto. "La bibliographie de la langue Swahili: Remarques et supplement à la *Swahili Bibliography* de M. Van Spaandonck." *Cahiers d'Etudes Africaines* 3 (1967): 485–532.

Mkelle, B. *Résumés de vieux manuscrits arabes: Collectés dans l'Ile de Zanzibar.* Zanzibar: Eacrotanal, 1981.

Möller, Ties. *Tansania: Ujamaa und Entwicklungsplanung: Ausgewählte Neuere Literatur.* Hamburg: Deutsches Institut für Afrika-Forschung, 1972.

Molnos, Angela. *Development in Africa: Planning and Implementation: A Bibliography (1946–1969) and Outline with Some Emphasis on Kenya, Tanzania, and Uganda.* Nairobi: East African Academy Research Information Centre, 1970.

————. *Language Problems in Africa: A Bibliography (1946–1967) and Summary of the Present Situation with Special Reference to Kenya, Tanzania, and Uganda.* Nairobi: East African Research Information Centre, 1969.

————. *Sources for the Study of East African Cultures and Development: A Bibliography of Social Scientific Bibliographies, Abstracts, Reference Works, Catalogues, Directories, Writings on Archives, Bibliographies, Book Production, Libraries, and Museums with Special Reference to Kenya, Tanzania, and Uganda, 1946– 1966 (1967–1968).* Nairobi: East African Research Information Centre, 1968.

————. *Die Sozialwissenschftliche Erforschung Ostafrika, 1954–1963 (Kenya, Tanganyika, Sansibar, Uganda).* Berlin: IFO, Springer Verlag, 1965.

Moses, Larry. *Kenya, Uganda, Tanganyika, 1960–1964: A Bibliography.* Washington, D.C.: Department of State, External Research Staff, n.d.

Mwasha, A. Z. *Librarianship in East Africa: A Selected Bibliography.* Dar es Salaam: National Central Library, n.d.

Mwasha, Rabbiel J. *Bibliography of TANU and Afro-Shirazi Party.* Dar es Salaam: National Central Library, 1979.

Mwenegoha, H. A. K. *Mwalimu Julius Kambarage Nyerere: A Bio-bibliography.* Nairobi: Foundation Books, 1976.

Mwinyimvua, E. A. *Directory of Libraries in Tanzania.* Dar es Salaam: Tanzania National Documentation Centre, National Central Library, 1984.

————. *Tanzania Education: A Select Bibliography.* Dar es Salaam: Tanzania Library Service, 1977.

Mwinyimvua, E. A., and Florence M. Nyatta. *Periodicals in Tanzanian Libraries: A Union List.* Dar es Salaam: Tanzania Library Services, 1986.

Nassor, Muhammad H. *Guide to the Provincial (Regional) and District Commissioners' Annual Reports.* Dar es Salaam: National Archives of Tanzania, 1977.

National Central Library. Acquisition Department. *Tanzania National Bibliography, 1974/75–*. Dar es Salaam: Tanganyika Library Service, 1977–, annual.

National Central Library, Cataloguing Section. *Printed in Tanzania: 1969–1973*. 5 vols. Dar es Salaam: Tanganyika Library Service, 1970–1976.

National Policies of Tanzania. Dar es Salaam: Tanganyika Library Service, 1972.

Nikundiwe, Margaret. *Annotated Bibliography of Educational Works Produced by the Institute of Education, Dar es Salaam*. Dar es Salaam: Institute of Education, 1975.

———. *Annotated Bibliography of Educational Works Produced by the Institute of Education, 1975–1977*. Dar es Salaam: Institute of Education, 1977.

Nilsen, Odd. *Bibliography of the Mineral Resources of Tanzania*. Uppsala: SIAS, 1980.

Nimtz, August H., Jr. "Islam in Tanzania: An Annotated Bibliography." *TNR* 72 (1973): 51–74.

Nkya, Ismael E. *Bibliography of Educational Works by the Institute of Education, Tanzania, 1963–1974*. Dar es Salaam: Institute of Education, 1975.

Ofcansky, Thomas Paul. *British East Africa, 1856–1963: An Annotated Bibliography*. New York and London: Garland Publishing, 1985.

———. "Julius Nyerere: A Bio-bibliography." *Africana Journal* (1990): 331–41.

———. "L. S. B. Leakey: A Bio-bibliographical Study." *History in Africa: A Journal of Method* (1985): 211–24.

Owen, D. F., ed. *Research and Development in East Africa*. Nairobi: EAPH, 1966.

Pastorett, Tomma N. *Tanzania-Uganda Conflict, 1978–1979*. Montgomery, AL: Air University Library, 1979.

Pearson, J. D. *Guide to Manuscripts and Documents in the British Isles Relating to Africa*. 2 vols. London: Mansell, 1993, 1994.

Penzer, Norman M. *Annotated Bibliography of Sir Richard Burton, K.C.M.G*. London: A. M. Philpot, 1923.

Periodicals in National Central Library: A List of Newspapers and Journals, 2d edition. Dar es Salaam: Tanzania Library Service, 1978.

Prins, Adriaan H.J. *Swahili-Speaking Peoples of Zanzibar and the East African Coast (Arabs, Shirazi, and Swahili)*. London: International African Institute, 1961.

Publications 1963–1972: An Annotated List. Dar es Salaam: Tanganyika Library Service, 1973.

Roberts, Andrew D. "Bibliography of Primary Sources for Tanzania, 1799–1899." *TNR* 73 (1974): 65–92.

———. "Bibliography of Tanganyika, 1959–1964: Local and Tribal Studies in the Social Sciences." *TNR* 67 (June 1967): 67–77.

Roth, Warren J. "Wasukuma of Tanganyika: An Annotated Bibliography." *Anthropological Quarterly* 3 (July 1961): 158–63.

Rweyemamu, Anthony H. *Government and Politics in Tanzania: A Bibliography*. Nairobi: East African Academy, 1972.

Sachedina, Roshanara. *Bibliography of Asbestos in Tanzania*. Dodoma: Mineral Resources Division, 1966.

Sasscer, R. S. *Tribal Bibliography of Tanzania*. Washington, D.C.: Catholic University of America Libraries, 1969.

Serkkola, Ari. *Rural Development in Tanzania: A Bibliography*. Helsinki: Institute of Development Studies, University of Helsinki, 1987.

Simpson, Donald H. "Bibliography of Emin Pasha." *UJ* (1960): 138–65.

Snell, John P. *Tanzania: An Annotated Bibliography on Population within the Context of Rural Development*. Rome: FAO, 1980.

Subject Index to the "Nationalist," 1964–1972. [Dar es Salaam]: The Service, 1977.

Sumar, M. *Bibliography of Towns in Tanzania*. [Dar es Salaam]: The Service, 1972.

Sumar, M., and E. McGee. *National Policies of Tanzania: A Bibliography*. Dar es Salaam: Tanganyika Library Service, 1972.

"Tanzania National Archives." *TNR* 66 (December 1966): 180–82.

Tanzania National Scientific Research Council. *Bibliography of Agricultural Research in Tanzania*. Dar es Salaam: Tanzania National Scientific Research Council, 1990.

Taylor, Barbara Mary. *Catalogue of Early German Material Relating to Tanzania in the Library of the Mineral Resources Division, Dodoma*. Dodoma: Mineral Resources Division, 1968.

Thurston, Anne. *Guide to Archives and Manuscripts Relating to Kenya and East Africa in the United Kingdom*. 2 vols. London: Hans Zell Publishers, 1991.

———. "Zanzibar Archives Project." *Information Development* (1986): 223–26.

———. "Zanzibar Archives Project and Its Implications for the Preservation of Records in East and Central Africa." *African Research and Documentation* 40 (1986): 16–18.

Townshend, Janet, and Benjamin Wisner. *Bibliography of Dodoma Region*. Dar es Salaam: Bureau of Resource Assessment and Land Use Planning, University of Dar es Salaam, 1971.

Trapps-Lomax, H. R., with the assistance of M. K. Kapinga and A. F. Lwaitama. *Tanzania Applied Linguistics Bibliography, 1960–1980*. Dar es Salaam: Department of Foreign Languages and Linguistics, University of Dar es Salaam, 1982.

Umbima, W. E. *Research in Education on East Africa (Kenya, Tanzania, Uganda): Periodical Articles, Theses, and Research Papers*. Nairobi: University of Nairobi Library, 1977.

Vahtola, Jukka. *Ita-Afrikkaa, Erityisesti Tansaniaa Kasitteleva Pieni Bibliografia*. Helsinki: Kehitysmaamaantieteen Suunta, Maantieteen Laitos, Helsingin Yliopisto, 1975.

Van Spaandonck, Marcel. *Practical and Systematic Swahili Bibliography: Linguistics 1850–1963*. Leiden: E. J. Brill, 1965.

Wadsworth, Gail M. *Women in Development: A Bibliography of Materials Available in the Library and Documentation Centre, Eastern and Southern African Management Institute*. Arusha: ESAMI, 1982.

Walker, Audrey A. *Official Publications of British East Africa. Part III: Kenya and Zanzibar*. Washington, D.C.: Library of Congress, 1962.

———. *Official Publications of British East Africa. Part II: Tanganyika*. Washington, D.C.: Library of Congress, 1962.

Wallenius, Anna-Britta, ed. *Libraries in East Africa*. Uppsala: SIAS, 1971.

Wanzagi, Dorica E. *Maternal Child Health and Family Planning in Tanzania: A Bibliography*, ed. D. Sekimang'a. Dar es Salaam: TANDOC, Tanzania National Documentation Centre, 1986.

Who's Who in East Africa, 1963–1964. Nairobi: Marco Publishers, 1964.

Who's Who in East Africa, 1965–1966. Nairobi: Marco Publishers, 1966.

Who's Who in East Africa, 1967–1968. Nairobi: Marco Publishers, , 1968.

Wield, David, and Carol Baker. "Science, Technology, and Development: A Course Taught at the University of Dar es Salaam, Tanzania." *Social Studies of Science* 3 (1978): 385–95.

Wilding, Richard. *Swahili Culture: A Bibliography of the History and Peoples of the Swahili-Speaking World*. Nairobi: Lamu Society, 1976.

Wright, Marcia. "Tanganyika Archives." *The American Archivist* 4 (October 1965): 511–20.

Zanzibar Museum, Reference Library. *Catalogue of Zanzibar Museum Reference Library, 1955*. Zanzibar: GP, 1955.

B. History: Pre-Colonial

Arundell, R.D.H. "Rock Paintings in the Bukoba District." *Journal of the Royal Anthropological Institute* (1936): 113–15.

Bagshawe, F. J. "Rock Paintings of the Kangeju Bushmen, Tanganyika Territory." *Man* 92 (October, 1923): 46–47.

Bennett, Norman R. "Myinyi Keri." In *Leadership in Eastern Africa: Six Political Biographies*, ed. Norman R. Bennett, 141–64. Boston: Boston University Press, 1968.

Bleek, Doro F. "Hadzapi or Watindega of Tanganyika Territory." *Africa* 3 (July 1931): 273–86.

———. "Traces of Former Bushman Occupation in Tanganyika." *South African Journal of Science* (1931): 423–29.

Brown, Walter T. "Pre-colonial History of Bagamoyo." Ph.D. diss., Boston University, 1971.

Cole, Sonia. *Leakey's Luck: The Life of Louis Seymour Bazett Leakey, 1902–72.* New York: Harcourt Brace Jovanovich, 1975.

———. *Prehistory of East Africa*. New York: Macmillan, 1963.

Culwick, A. T. "Some Rock Painting in Central Tanganyika." *Journal of the Royal Anthropological Institute* (1931): 443–53.

Fosbrooke, Henry A. "Stoneage Tribe in Tanganyika." *South African Archaeological Bulletin* 41 (March 1956): 3–8.

Freeman-Grenville, G.S.P. *Medieval History of the Coast of Tanganyika: With Special Reference to Recent Archaeological Discoveries*. London: OUP, 1962.

Hall, R. de Z. "Pottery in Bugufi, Tanganyika Territory." *Man* 132 (1939): 143–44.

Hartwig, Gerald W. *Art of Survival in East Africa: The Kerebe and Long-Distance Trade, 1800–1895*. New York: Africana Publishing Company, 1976.

Holmes, C. F., and Ralph A. Austen. "Precolonial Sukuma." *Journal of World History* 2 (1972): 377–405.

Horton, M. C. "Asiatic Colonization of the East African Coast: The Manda Evidence." *Journal of the Royal Asiatic Society* 2 (1986): 201–13.

Howell, F. C. "Preliminary Note on a Historic Donga (Maclennan's Donga) in Central Tanganyika." *South African Archaeological Bulletin* (1955): 43–51.

Kappelman, J. "Changement climatique au cours du Plio-Pleistocène dans la Gorge d'Olduvai, Tanzanie." *Anthropologie* 3 (1985): 281–83.

Kimambo, Isaria N. *Political History of the Pare of Tanzania c. 1500–1900*. New York: International Publications Service, 1969.

Koponen, Juhani. *People and Production in Late Precolonial Tanzania: History and Structures*. Helsinki: Finnish Society for Development Studies, 1988.

Leakey, Louis Seymour Bazett. "Archaeological Aspects of the Tanganyika Paintings (with Tentative Notes in Sequences)." *TNR* 29 (July, 1950): 15–19.

———. *Olduvai Gorge: The Cranium and Maxillary Dentation of* Australopithecus (Zinjanthropus) boisei. London: CUP, 1967.

———. *Olduvai Gorge, 1951–61: A Preliminary Report on the Geology and Fauna*. London: CUP, 1967.

Leakey, Mary Douglas. *Africa's Vanishing Art: The Rock Paintings of Tanzania*. London: Hamish Hamilton, 1983.

———. *Disclosing the Past*. Garden City: Doubleday, 1984.

———. "Excavation of Burial Mounds in Ngorongoro Crater." *TNR* 66 (December 1966): 123–25.

———. "Footprints in the Ashes of Time." *NGM* 4 (April 1979): 446–57.

———. *Olduvai Gorge: Excavations in Beds I and II, 1960–1963*. Cambridge: CUP, 1971.

———. *Olduvai Gorge: My Search for Early Man*. London: Collins, 1979.

Leakey, Mary Douglas, and J.M. Harris eds. *Laetoli: A Pliocene Site in Northern Tanzania*. Oxford: OUP, 1987.

Leakey, Mary Douglas, and R.L. Hay. "Pliocene Footprints in the Laetolil Beds at Laetoli, Northern Tanzania." *Nature* 2 (March, 1979): 317–23.

Leakey, Mary Douglas, ed., with Derk Roe. *Olduvai Gorge: Excavations in Beds III, IV and Masek Beds*. Cambridge: CUP, 1994.

Leakey, Richard. *Human Origins*. London: Hamish Hamilton, 1982.

———. *Making of Mankind*. London: Michael Joseph, 1981.

Madokoro, L. "Recent Rockpainting Discoveries in Usandawe." *TNR* 88/89 (1982): 67–81.

Masao, F. T. *Later Stone Age and the Rock Paintings of Central Tanzania*. Wiesbaden: Franz Steiner Verlag, 1979.

———. "Some Common Aspects of the Rock Paintings of Kondoa and Sindiga." *TNR* 77/78 (June 1976): 51–64.

Mutahaba, G. R. *Portrait of a Nationalist: The Life of Ali Migeyo*. Nairobi: EAPH, 1969.

Phillipson, D. W. *Early Prehistory of Eastern and Southern Africa*. London: Heinemann Educational Books, 1977.

Reeve, W. H. "Prehistory in Tanganyika." *TNR* (December, 1938): 49–57.

Roberts, Andrew D., ed. *Tanzania before 1900*. Nairobi: EAPH, 1968.

Sassoon, Hamo. "New Views on Engaruka, Northern Tanzania: Excavations Carried Out for the Tanzanian Government in 1964 and 1966." *JAH* 2 (1967): 201–17.

Schepartz, L. A. "Who Were the Later Pleistocene Eastern Africans?" *African Archaeological Review* (1988): 57–72.

Schmidt, P.R. "Investigation of Early and Late Iron Age Cultures through Oral Tradition and Archaeology: An Interdisciplinary Case Study in Buhaya, Tanzania." Ph.D. diss., Northwestern University, 1974.

Sheriff, Abdul H. "Dynamics of Change in Pre-colonial East African Societies." *African Economic History Review* (Fall 1974): 7–13.

Shorter, Alyward. "Rock Paintings in Ukimbu." *TNR* 67 (June 1967): 49–55.

Shorter, Alyward, and Njelu Mulugala. *Nyungu-Ya-Mawe*. Nairobi: EALB, 1971.

Sutton, John E.G. " 'Ancient Civilizations' and Modern Agricultural Systems in the Southern Highlands of Tanzania." *Azania* (1969): 1–13.

———. "Ancient Dams of Tanganyika Masailand," *Azania* (1973): 105–14.

Tenraa, Eric. "Sandawe Prehistory and the Vernacular Tradition." *Azania* (1969): 91–103.

Tobias, Phillip V. *Olduvai Gorge*, vol. 4, *The Skulls, Endocasts, and Teeth of* Homo habilis. Cambridge: CUP, 1990.

C. History: German Colonial Period

Acker, Pater. "Die Erziehung der Eingeborenen zur Arbeit in Deutsch-Ostafrika." *Jahrbuch über die Deutschen Kolonien* (1908): 117–24.

Arning, Wilhelm. *Deutsch-Ostafrika: Gestern und Heute*. Berlin: DR, 1942.

Axenfeld, K. "Geistige Kämpfe in der Eingeborenenbevölkerung an der Küste Ostafrikas." *Koloniale Rundschau* 2 (November 1913): 647–73.

Bald, Detlef. *Deutsch-Ostafrika 1900–1914: Eine Studie über Verwaltung, Interessengruppen und Wirtschaftlichen Erschliessung*. München: Weltforum Verlag, 1970.

———. "Probleme der Imperialismusforschung am Beispiel Deutsch-Ostafrikas." *Geschichte in Wissenschaft und Unterricht* 10 (1971): 611–16.

Baumann, Oscar. *Afrikanische Skizzen*. Berling: DR, 1900.

———. *In Deutsch-Ostafrika Während des Aufstandes*. Vienna: Hoelsel, 1890.

———. *Usambara und Seine Nachbargebiete*. Berlin: DM, 1891.

Becker, A. *Aus Deutsch-Ostafrikas Sturm und Drangperiode*. Halle: Otto Hendel Verlag, 1911.

Becker, M. "Über Bahnbau in Deutsch-Ostafrika." *Deutsches Kolonialblatt* (1899): 760–63.

Behr, H. F. von. *Kriegsbilder aus dem Araberaufstand in Deutsch-Ostafrika*. Leipzig: Brockhaus, 1891.

Bornhardt, W. *Zur Oberflächengestaltung und Geologie Deutsche-Ostafrikas*. Berlin: DR, 1900.

Braun, K. "Der Reis in Deutsch-Ostafrika." *Berichte über Land-und Forstwirtschaft in Deutsch-Ostafrika* 4 (1906): 167–217.

Bülow, Frieda. *Reisescizzen und Tagebuchblatter aus Deutsch-Ostafrika*. Berlin: Walther und Apolant, 1889.

Bursian, Alexander. *Die Hauser und Huttensteuer in Deutsch-Ostafrika*. Jena: Gustav Fischer, 1910.

Busse, W.K.O. *Bericht über eine im Auftrage des Kaiserlichen Gouvernements von Deutsch-Ostafrika Ausgeführte Forschungsreise Nach dem Südlichen Teile Dieser Kolonie*. Berlin: Mitter und Sohn, 1902.

———. "Berichte über die Expedition Nach den Deutsch-Ostafrikanischen Steppen." *Tropenpflanzer* 4 (1900): 391–402, 579–98; and 5 (1901): 20–32, 105–17, 229–317.

Büttner, Kurt. *Die Anfänge der Deutschen Kolonialpolitik in Ostafrika*. Berlin: Akademie-Verlag, 1959.

Calvert, Albert F. *German East Africa*. London: T. Werner Laurie, 1917; and New York: Negro Universities Press, 1970.

Cana, Frank R. "Frontiers of German East Africa." *GJ* 4 (April 1916): 297–303.

Colln, Daniel. *Bilder aus Ostafrika*. Berlin: Buchhandlung der Deutschen Lehrerzeitung, 1891.

Cornevin, R. "The Germans in Africa Before 1918." In *History and Politics of Colonialism 1870–1914*, vol. 1, *The History and Politics of Colonialism, 1870–1914*, ed. L. H. Gann and Peter Duignan, 383–419. Cambridge: CUP, 1969.

Dalwigk, Egon Frieherrn. *Dernburgs Amtliche Tatigkeit im Allgemeinen und Seine Eingeborenenpolitik in Deutsch-Ostafrika im Besonderen*. Berlin: DR, 1911.

Decken, Carl Claus van der. *Reisen in Ostafrika*. 2 vols. Leipzig and Heidelberg: Winter'sche Verlagshandlung, 1869.

Dempwolff, Otto. *Die Sandawe: Linguistisches und Ethnographisches Material aus Deutsch-Ostafrika*. Hamburg: Friederichsen, 1916.

Dietzel, Karl Heinrich. *Versuch Einer Geographischen Charakterisierung des Ostafrikanischen Zwischenseengebietes*. Weida i. Thür: Druck von Thomas und Hubert, 1917.

Dilthey, Richard. *Der Wirthschaftliche Werth von Deutsch-Ostafrika*. Dusseldorf: A. Bagel, 1889.

Dove, Karl. *Ostafrika*. Leipzig: G.J. Göschen, 1912.

Dundas, C. C. F. *History of German East Africa*. Dar es Salaam: GP, 1923.

Eberlie, R. F. "German Achievement in East Africa." *TNR* 55 (September 1960): 181–214.

Ekemode, Gabriel O. "Fundi: Trader and Akida Kilimanjaro, c. 1860–1898." *TNR* 77/78 (June 1976): 95–101.

———. "German Rule in North-East Tanzania, 1885–1914." Ph.D. diss., University of London, 1973.

Fonck, Heinrich. *Deutsch-Ostafrika: Eine Schilderung Deutscher Tropen Nach 10 Wanderjahren*. 5 vols. Berlin: Voss, 1910.

Förster, Brix. *Deutsch-Ostafrika: Geographie und Geschichte der Kolonie*. Leipzig: F. A. Brockhaus, 1890.

Fulleborn, F. *Das Deutsche Njassa und Ruvuma-Gebiet, Land und Leute*. Berlin: DR, 1906.

Gann, Lewis H., and Peter Duignan. *Rulers of German Africa, 1884–1914*. Stanford: Stanford University Press, 1977.

Götzen, Graf Gustav Adolf von. *Deutsch-Ostafrika im Aufstand 1905/06*. Berlin: DR, 1895.

Great Britain. Naval Staff. Naval Intelligence Division. *Handbook of German East Africa*. London: HMSO, 1923.

Grimm, Dr. *Der Wirtschaftliche Werth von Deutsch-Ostafrika*. 2 vols. Berlin: Walther und Apolant, 1886.

Gunzert, Theodor. "Eingeborenenverbände und Verwaltung Deutsch-Ostafrikas." *Koloniale Rundschau* (1929): 209–14, 241–47.

———. "Memoirs of a German District Commissioner in Mwanza: 1907–1916." *TNR* 66 (December 1966): 171–79.

Gurlitt, Friedrich. *Die Ersten Baujahre in Deutsch-Ostafrika*. Berlin: W. Ernst, 1905.

Henderson, W. O. "German East Africa, 1884–1918." In *History of East Africa*, vol. 2, ed. Vincent Harlow and E. M. Chilver, 123–62. Oxford: Clarendon Press, 1965.

Iliffe, John. "German Administration in Tanganyika, 1906–1911: The Governorship of Freiherr von Rechenberg." Ph.D. diss., Cambridge University, 1965.

————. *Tanganyika under German Rule, 1905–1911.* Nairobi: EAPH, 1969.

Kaerger, Karl. *Tangaland und die Kolonisation Deutsch-Ostafrikas.* Berlin: Herman Walther, 1892.

Karstedt, Oskar. *Hermann v. Wissmann.* Berlin: O. Stollberg, 1938.

Klampen, Erich zu. *Carl Peters: Ein Deutsches Schicksal im Kampf um Ostafrika.* Berlin: H. Siep, [1939].

Klamroth, Martin. "Ostafrikanischer Islam." *Allgemeine Missions-Zeitschrift* (1910): 477–93, 536–46.

Koch, Robert. *Ueber Meine Schlafkrankheits-Expedition.* Berlin: DR, 1908.

Koponen, Juhani. *Development for Exploration: German Colonial Policies in Mainland Tanzania, 1884–1914.* Helsinki and Hamburg: Finnish Historical Society, 1995.

Kurtze, Bruno. *Die Deutsch-Ostafrikanische Gesellschaft.* Jena: Gustav Fischer, 1913.

Leue, Hauptmann A. *Die Besiedlungsfahigkeit Deutsch-Ostafrika.* Leipzig: W. Weicher, 1904.

————. "Die Sklaverei in Deutsch-Ostafrika." *Beiträge zur Kolonialpolitik und Kolonialwirtschaft* (1900/1901): 617–25.

Liebert, E. *Die Deutschen Kolonien im Jahre 1904.* Leipzig: W. Weicher, 1904.

Lindequist, V. *Deutsch-Ostafrika als Siedelungsgebiet für Europaer unter Berucksichtigung Britisch-Ostafrika und Nyassalands.* Leipzig: Duncker und Humblot, 1912.

Lyall, Andrew. "Traditional Contracts in German East Africa: The Transition from Precapitalist Forms." *Journal of African Law*, (Autumn 1986): 91–129.

McCarthy, C. P. "German Plans for Railway Development in East Africa." *GJ* (1918): 314–23.

Mackay, R. *Second (Final) Report of the Malaria Unit, Dar es Salaam, for the Period November 1934 to December 1936.* Dar es Salaam: GP, 1938.

Methner, Wilhelm. *Unter drei Gouverneuren: 16 Jahre Dienst in den Deutschen Tropen.* Breslau: Korn, 1938.

Meyer, Hans. *Das Deutsche Kolonialreich: Band I: Ostafrika und Kamerun.* Leipzig and Wien: Verlag des Bibliographisches Instituts, 1909.

————. *Ergebnisse einer Reise durch das Zwischenseegebiet Ostafrikas, 1911.* Berlin: DR, 1913.

————. *Der Kilimanjaro: Reisen und Studien.* Berlin: DR, 1900.

————. *Ostafrikanische Gletscherfahrten: Forschungsreisen im Kilimandscharo-Gebiet.* Leipzig: Duncker und Humblot, 1890.

Mildbraed, J. "Walter Busse." *Deutsche Botanische Gesellschaft* (1934): 61–71.

Milhalyi, Louis J. "Characteristics and Problems of Labour in the Usambara Highlands of East Africa During the German Period, 1885–1914." *EAJ* 5 (May 1970): 20–25.

Most, Karl. *Die Wirtschaftliche Entwicklung Deutsch-Ostafrika, 1885–1905.* Berlin: W. Susserott, 1906.

Nigmann, Wilhelm. *Die Wahehe.* Berlin: E.S. Mittler, 1908.

————. *Geschichte der Kaiserlichen Schutztruppe für Deutsch-Ostafrika.* Berlin: E. S. Mittler, 1911.

Paasche, Hans. *Im Morgenlicht: Kriegs-, Jagd-, und Reiseer-Lebnisse in Ostafrika.* Berlin: C. A. Schwetschke, 1907.

Paasche, Hermann. *Deutsch-Ostafrika: Wirtschaftliche Studien.* Berlin: C. A. Schwetschke und Sohn, 1906.

Patera, Herbert Viktor. *Bwana Sakkarani: Deutsch-Ostafrika.* Wien: Krystall-Verlag, 1933.

Pentzel, Otto. *Buschkampf in Ostafrika.* Stuttgart: R. Thienemann, 1941.

Perbandt, C. von, G. Richelmann, and R. Schmidt. *Hermann von Wissmann.* Berlin: A. Schall, 1906.

Peter, Chris Maina. "Imperialism and Export of Capital: A Survey of Foreign Private Investments in Tanzania during the German Colonial Period." *Journal of Asian and African Studies* 3/4 (1990): 197–212.

Peters, Carl. *Das Deutsch-Ostafrikanische Schutzgebiet.* Munich: R. Oldenbourg, 1895.

———. *Die Gründung von Deutsch-Ostafrika.* Munich: R. Oldenburg, 1895.

Pierard, Richard V. "Dernberg Reform Policy and German East Africa." *TNR* 67 (June 1967): 31–38.

Poeschel, Hans. *Bwana Hakimu: Richterfahrten in Deutsch-Ostafrika.* Leipzig: Koehler und Voighlander, 1940.

Prince, Magdalene von. *Eine Deutsche Frau im Inneren Deutsch-Ostafrikas.* Berlin: E. S. Mittler, 1908.

Prince, Tom von. *Gegen Araber und Wahehe: Erinnerungen aus Meiner Ostafrikanischen Leutnantszeit 1890–1895.* Berlin: E. S. Mittler und Suhn, 1914.

Raum, O. F. "German East Africa: Changes in African Tribal Life Under German Administration 1892–1914." In *History of East Africa*, vol. II, ed. Vincent Harlow and E. M. Chilver, 163–208. Oxford: Clarendon Press, 1965.

Reichard, Paul. *Deutsch-Ostafrika: das Land und seine Bewohner.* Leipzig: Otto Spanner, 1891.

Reusch, Richard. *Der Islam in Ost-Afrika mit Besonderer.* Leipzig: Adolf Kelin, 1930.

Rodemann, H. W. "Tanganyika, 1890–1914: Selected Aspects of German Administration." Ph.D. diss., University of Chicago, 1961.

Rohrbach, Paul. "Ostafrikanische Studien." *Preussische Jahrbücher* (1909): 82–107, 276–317.

Samassa, Paul. *Die Besiedlung Deutsch-Ostafrikas.* Leipzig: Verlag Deutsche Zukunft, 1909.

Sander, L. *Die Wanderhauschrecken und ihre Bekämpfung in unsere Ostafrikanischen Kolonien.* Berlin: DM, 1902.

Schabel, Hans G. "Tanganyika Forestry under German Colonial Administration, 1891–1919." *Forest and Conservation History* 3 (July, 1990): 130–41.

Scheel, Willy. *Bilder aus Deutsch-Ostafrika.* Berlin: H. Paetel, 1909.

Schmidt, Rochus. *Geschichte des Araberaufstandes in Ost-Afrika.* Frankfurt/Oder: Trowitsch, 1892.

Schmiedel, Hans. "Bwana Sakkarani: Captain Tom von Prince and His Times." *TNR* 52 (March 1959): 35–52.

Schnee, Ada. "Ostafrikanisches Wirtschaftsleben im Kriege." *Koloniale Rundschau* (1918): 9–25.

Schnee, Heinrich. *Deutsches Koloniallexikon.* 3 vols. Leipzig: Quelle und Meyer, 1920).

———. "Die Koloniale Neuordnung der Welt Nach dem Kriege," *Koloniale Rundschau* (1922): 113–16.

———. "Die Ostafrikanische Periode." *Koloniale Rundschau* (1919): 85–89.

———. *German Colonization, Past and Future.* New York: Alfred A. Knopf, 1926.

———. *Unsere Kolonialpolitik in Deutsch-Ostafrika.* Berlin: H. R. Engelmann, 1919.

———. "Zur Frage der Besiedelung Deutsch-Ostafrika." *Deutsches Kolonialblatt* (1913): 260–69.

Scholz, Dr. "Ueber Sälzvorkommen und Salzgewinnung in Deutsch-Ostafrika." *Der Pflanzer* (1913): 226–32.

Schrader, Rudolf. *Das Arbeiterrecht für Eingeborene in Deutsch und Britisch Ostafrika.* Hamburg: L. Friederichsen, 1920.

Schroeder-Poggelow, Richard. *Unsere Afrikapolitik in den Letzen zwei Jahren.* Berlin: Walther und Apolant, 1890.

Seitz, Theodor. *Grundsatze über Aufstellung und Bewirtschaftung des Etats der Deutschen Schutzgebiete.* Berlin: DR, 1905.

Siebenlist, T. *Forsteirtschaft in Deutsch-Ostafrika.* Berlin: Verlag Paul Parey, 1914.

Sigl, Leutnant. "Bericht des Leutnant Sigl, Tabora." *Deutsches Kolonialblatt* (1894): 6–13.

———. "Bericht über den Handelsverkehr von Tabora." *Deutsches Kolonialblatt* (1892): 164–66.

Stentzler, J. *Deutsch-Ostafrika: Kriegs- und Friedensbilder.* Leipzig: W. Weicher, 1906.

Stoecker, Helmuth, ed. *German Imperialism in Africa.* London: C. Hurst and Company, 1986.

Stuhlmann, Franz. *Beiträge zur Kulturgeschichte von Ostafrika.* Berlin: DR, 1909.

———. *Die Wirtschaftliche Entwicklung Deutsch-Ostafrikas.* Berlin: DR, 1898.

———. *Handwerk und Industrie in Ostafrika.* Hamburg: Friederichsen, 1910.

Sunsesi, Thaddeus. "Slave Ransoming in German East Africa, 1885–1922." *IJAHS* 2 (1993): 271–95.

Truschel, Louis W. "German Imperialism in Africa: New Light on Carl Peters." *Studies in History and Society* 2 (1973): 17–33.

Vietsch, Eberhard von. *Wilhelm Solf, Botschafter: Zwischen den Zeiten.* Tübingen: R. Wunderlich, H. Leins, 1961.

Wagner, J. *Geschichte der Gesellschaft für Deutsche Kolonisation und der Deutsch-Ostafrikanischen Gesellschaft.* Berlin: Mitocher und Röstell, 1886.

Weiss, M. *Die Volkerstämme in Norden Deutsch-Ostafrika.* Berlin: Carl Marschner, 1910.

Werth, Emil. *Das Deutsch-Ostafrikanische Küstenland und die Vorgelagerten Inseln.* 2 vols. Berlin: DR, 1915.

Werther, C. Waldemar. *Die Mittleren Hochländer des Nördlichen Deutsch-Ostafrika.* Berlin: Hermann Paetel, 1898.

———. *Zum Victoria Nyanza.* Berlin: Hermann Paetel, 1894.

Wissmann, Hermann von. *Deutschlands Grösster Afrikaner.* Berlin: A. Schall, 1914.

Wright, Marcia. "Chief Merere and the Germans." *TNR* 69 (1968): 41–49.

———. "Local Roots of Policy in German East Africa." *JAH* 4 (1968): 621–30.

Zache, Hans. *Deutsch-Ostafrika, Tanganyika Territorium.* Berlin: Safari-Verlag, 1926.

Zimmerman, Alfred. *Geschichte der Deutschen Kolonialpolitik*. Berlin: E. S. Mittler, 1914.

D. History: British Colonial Period

Alexander, Gilchrist. *Tanganyika Memories*. London: Blackie, 1936.
Austen, Ralph A. "Official Mind of Indirect Rule: British Policy in Tanganyika, 1916–1939." In *Britain and Germany in Africa*, ed. Prosser Gifford and William Roger Louis, 577–606. New Haven: YUP.
Barington, John M. "United Nations and Education in Tanganyika." *Journal of Educational Administration and History* 1 (1988): 60–65.
Basehart, H. W. "Traditional History and Political Change among the Matengo of Tanzania." *Africa* 2 (1972): 87–97.
Bates, Darrell. *Gust of Plumes: A Biography of Lord Twining of Godalming and Tanganyika*. London: Hodder and Stoughton, 1972.
Bates, Margaret L. "Tanganyika." In *African One-Party States*, ed. Gwendolen M. Carter, 395–483. Ithaca: Cornell University Press, 1962.
———. "Tanganyika: The Development of a Trust Territory." *International Organization* 1 (February 1955): 32–51.
———. "Tanganyika under British Administration 1920–1955." D. Phil. thesis, Oxford University, 1957.
Bisset, C. B. *Minerals and Industry in Tanganyika*. London: HMSO, 1955.
Burke, Fred G. *Tanganyika: Preplanning*. Syracuse: Syracuse University Press, 1965.
Bryceson, Deborah Fahy. " 'Tepid Backwater': Bagamoyo District and Its Marginal Commodity Production within the Tanganyikan Colonial Economy, 1919–1961." *TJH* (1982): 1–25.
Byatt, Sir Horace. "Tanganyika." *JRAS* 93 (October 1924): 1–9.
Cairns, J. C. *Bush and Boma*. London: John Murray, 1959.
Cameron, Sir Donald C. "Economic Development of Tanganyika Territory." *East Africa* (27 May 1926): 11, 13.
———. *My Tanganyika Service and Some Nigeria*. London: George Allen and Unwin, 1939.
———. "Position and Prospects in Tanganyika." *JRAS* 104 (July 1927): 315–322.
———. *Principles of Native Administration and Their Application*. Dar es Salaam: GP, 1930.
———. *Recent Progress in Tanganyika*. London: Empire Parliamentary Association, 1931.
———. *Tanganyika*. London: Empire Parliamentary Association, 1927.
———. "Tanganyika Will Remain Part of the Empire As Long As Kenya and Uganda." *East Africa* (20 January 1927): 517–18.
Chachage, C.S.L. "British Rule and African Civilization in Tanganyika." *Journal of Historical Sociology* 2 (1988): 199–223.
Chambers, George Alexander. *Tanganyika's New Day*. London: CMS, 1931.
Chidzero, Bernard T. G. *Tanganyika and International Trusteeship*. London: OUP, 1961.
Clarke, Philip Henry Cecil. *Short History of Tanganyika*. London: Longmans, 1960.

Cliffe, Lionel R. "Nationalism and the Reaction to Enforced Agricultural Change in Tanganyika during the Colonial Period." *Taamuli* 1 (1970): 3–15.

Cohen, Sir Andrew B. *British Policy in Changing Africa*. London: Routledge and Kegan Paul, 1959.

Cory, Hans. "Reforms of Tribal Political Institutions in Tanganyika." *JAA* 2 (April 1960): 77–84.

Coutouvidis, John. "Matsis Papers: A Greek Settler in Tanganyika." *Immigrants and Minorities* 2 (1983): 171–84.

Culwick, A. T., and G. M. Culwick. "What the Wabena Think of Indirect Rule." *JRAS* 143 (April 1937): 176–93.

Datta, Ansu Kumar. *Tanganyika: A Government in a Plural Society*. The Hague: Mouton, 1955.

Dougherty, Mary Imbriglia. "Tanganyika during the 'Twenties: A Study of Social and Economic Development of Tanganyika under British Mandate." *AS* 4 (1966): 197–225.

Dudbridge, J., and J.E.S. Griffiths. "Development of Local Government in Sukuma-land." *JAA* 3 (July 1951): 141–46.

Dumbuya, Peter A. *Tanganyika Under International Mandate: 1919–1946*. Lanham, MD: University Press of America, 1995.

Dundas, Anne. *Beneath African Glaciers*. London: H. F. and G. Witherby, 1924.

Dundas, Sir Charles. *African Crossroads*. London: Macmillan, 1955.

———. *Kilimanjaro and its People*. London: H. F. and G. Witherby, 1924.

Egerö, Bertil. *Colonization and Migration: A Summary of Border-Crossing Movements in Tanzania*. Uppsala: SIAS, 1979.

Ehrlich, Cyril. "Some Aspects of Economic Policy in Tanganyika 1945–1960." *JMAS* 2 (June 1964): 265–77.

Fletcher-Cooke, F. "Some Reflections on the International Trusteeship System, with Particular Reference to Its Impact on the Governments and Peoples of the Trust Territories." *International Organization* 3 (Summer, 1959): 422–30.

———. "Tanganyika and the Trusteeship Council." *TNR* 56 (March 1961): 40–48.

Gailey, Harry A. *Sir Donald Cameron, Colonial Governor*. Stanford: Hoover Institution Press, 1974.

Gillman, Clement. "White Colonization in East Africa, with Special Regard to Tanganyika Territory." *Geographical Review* 4 (October 1942): 585–97.

Graham, James D. "Indirect Rule: The Establishment of 'Chiefs' and 'Tribes' in Cameron's Tanganyika." *TNR* 77/78 (June 1976): 1–9.

Great Britain, British Information Services. *Tanganyika: The Making of a Nation*. London: HMSO, 1961.

Great Britain. Central Office of Information. Reference Division. *Tanganyika*. London: Swindon Press, 1959.

Great Britain. Colonial Office. *Development of African Local Government in Tanganyika*. London: HMSO, 1951.

———. *Report on Tanganyika Territory for the Year 1921*. London: HMSO, 1922.

Griner, Madeline. "Problems of Administration in Tanganyika Territory in the Development of Self-government." Ph.D. diss., New York University, 1956.

Harris, C. C. "Tanganyika Today: The Background." *International Affairs* 1 (January 1960): 35–47.

Harris, Tim. *Donkey's Gratitude*. Edinburgh: The Pentland Press, 1992.

Haule, John James. "Press Controls in Colonial Tanganyika and Post-colonial Tanzania, 1930–1967: A Proposition for Research in African Journalism History." Ph.D. diss., Southern Illinois University, 1984.

Herzog, Juergen. " 'Settlers' Factor' in East Africa and Its Role in the Liberation Movement in Tanganyika (1945–1961)." *Asien, Afrika, Lateinamerika* 1 (1986): 95–105.

Heussler, Robert. *British Tanganyika: An Essay and Documents on District Administration.* Durham, NC: Duke University Press, 1971.

Hill, J. F. R. "Green Branches in Tanganyika." *Corona* (April 1960): 126–28.

Hill, J. F. R. and J. P. Moffett. *Tanganyika: A Review of Its Resources and Development.* Dar es Salaam: Government of Tanganyika, 1955.

Hogendorn, J. S., and K. M. Scott. "East African Groundnut Scheme: Lessons of a Large-Scale Agricultural Failure." *African Economic History* 10 (1981): 81–115.

Ingham, Kenneth. "Tanganyika in the 'Twenties." *TNR* 52 (March 1959): 18–30.

International Bank for Reconstruction and Development. *Economic Development of Tanganyika.* Baltimore: The Johns Hopkins University Press, 1961.

Joclson, Ferdinand Stephen. *Tanganyika Territory (Formerly German East Africa): Characteristics and Potentialities.* London: T. Fisher Unwin, 1920.

Johnston, R. H. "Chagga Constitutional Development." *JAA* 3 (July 1953): 134–40.

Kaniki, M. H. Y., ed. *Tanzania under Colonial Rule.* London: Longman, 1980.

Kirkby, Sir Arthur. "Tanganyika Triumphant." *AA* 243 (April 1962): 114–25.

Knight, John, and H. Stevenson. "Williamson Diamond Mine, De Beers, and the Colonial Office: A Case-Study of the Quest for Control." *JMAS* 3 (September 1986): 423–45.

Lennard, T. J., ed. *How Tanganyika Is Governed.* Nairobi: EALB, 1955.

Leubuscher, Charlotte. *Tanganyika Territory: A Study of Economic Policy under Mandate.* London: OUP, 1944.

Liebenow, Gus J. *Colonial Rule and Political Development in Tanzania: The Case of the Makonde.* Nairobi: EAPH, 1971.

———. "Responses to Planned Political Change in Tanganyika Tribal Groups." *American Political Science Review* 2 (June 1956): 442–61.

———. "Some Problems in Introducing Local Government Reform in Tanganyika." *JAA* 3 (July 1956): 132–39.

———. "Tribalism, Traditionalism, and Modernism in Chagga Local Government." *JAA* 2 (April 1958): 71–82.

Listowel, Judith. *Making of Tanganyika.* New York: Maxwell, 1965.

Lugard, Lord. *Dual Mandate in British Tropical Africa.* London: Frank Cass, 1965.

Lumley, E. K. *Forgotten Mandate: A British District Officer in Tanganyika.* Hamden, CT: Archon Books, 1976.

Mackay, R. *Report on Work Done at Dar es Salaam during the Period January 1932–January 1934.* Dar es Salaam: GP, 1935.

McCarthy, Dennis Michael Patrick. *Colonial Bureaucracy and Creating Underdevelopment: Tanganyika, 1919–1940.* Ames: Iowa State University Press, 1982.

———. "Language Manipulation in Colonial Tanganyika, 1919–40." *JAS* 1 (1979): 9–16.

———. "Organizing Underdevelopment from the Inside: The Bureaucratic Economy in Tanganyika, 1919–1940." *IJAHS* 4 (1977): 576–99.

McHenry, Dean E. "Reorganization: An Administrative History of Kigoma District." *TNR* 84/85 (1980): 65–76.

————. "Study of the Rise of TANU and the Demise of British Rule in Kigoma Region, Western Tanzania." *TAR* 3 (1973): 403–21.

Mackenzie, W.J.M. "Changes in Local Government in Tanganyika." *JAA* 3 (July 1954): 123–29.

Mang'enya, E.A.M. *Discipline and Tears*. Dar es Salaam: University of Dar es Salaam, 1984.

Medger, Ruth. *So Fand ich Deutsch-Ostafrika*. Berlin: F. Schneider, 1940.

Mitchell, Sir Philip. *African Afterthoughts*. London: Hutchinson, 1954.

Moffett, J. P., ed. *Handbook of Tanganyika*, 2d edition. Dar es Salaam: GP, 1958.

————. *Tanganyika: A Review of Its Resources and Their Development*. Dar es Salaam: Government of Tanganyika, 1955.

Montague, F. A., and F. H. Page-Jones. "Some Difficulties in the Democratization of Native Authorities in Tanganyika." *JAA* 1 (January 1951): 21–27.

Morris-Hale, Walter. *British Administration in Tanganyika from 1920 to 1945*. Geneva: Université de Genève, Institut Universitaire de Hautes Etudes Internationales, 1969.

Moule, Malcolm. "British Administration of Tanganyika," Ph.D. Diss., Stanford University, 1947.

Munro, J. Forbes. "Shipping Subsidies and Railway Guarantees: William Mackinnon, Eastern Africa, and the Indian Ocean." *JAH* 2 (1987): 209–30.

Newlyn, W. T. and D. C. Rowan. *Money and Banking in British Colonial Africa*. London: OUP, 1964.

Nindi, B. C. "Labour and Capital in Settler Economy in Colonial Tanganyika." *Journal of Eastern African Research and Development* (1987): 90–96.

Norton, Ian. "Inter-racial Local Council in Tanganyika." *JAA* 1 (January 1956): 26–32.

Nyerere, Julius. "Tanganyika Today: The Nationalist View." *International Affairs* (January, 1960): 43–47.

Osborn, Joyce. "Emergent Tanganyika." *Corona* (November 1961): 422–23.

Peacock, Alan T., and Douglas G.M. Dosser. *National Income of Tanganyika, 1952–1954*. London: HMSO, 1958.

Perham, Margery. *East African Journey*. London: Faber and Faber, 1976.

————. "System of Native Administration in Tanganyika." *Africa* 3 (1931): 302–12.

Pratt, Cranford. "Multiracialism and Local Government in Tanganyika." *Race* 1 (November 1960): 33–49.

Reid, Eric. "Tanganyika Territory." In *Eastern Africa To-day and To-morrow*, ed. F. S. Joelson, 273–81. London: East Africa, 1934.

————. *Tanganyika without Prejudice*. London: East Africa, 1934.

Ross, Alistair. "Capricorn Africa Society and European Reactions to African Nationalism in Tanganyika, 1949–60." *AA* 305 (October 1977): 519–35.

Sayers, G. S., ed. *Handbook of Tanganyika*. London: Macmillan, 1930.

Scotton, James F. "Tanganyika's African Press, 1937–1960: A Nearly Forgotten Pre-independence Forum." *ASR* 1 (1978): 1–18.

Seabrook, A.T.P. "Groundnut Scheme in Retrospect." *TNR* 47/48 (July/September 1957): 87–91.

Shadbolt, K. E. "Local Government Election in Tanganyika District." *JAA* 2 (April 1961): 78–84.

Sharaev, V. A. "Politika Angliskikh Vlastei v Derevne Kolonial'Noi Tangan'iki (1945–1960)." *Narody Azii i Afriki* 6 (1975): 75–88.

Shaw, J. V. "Development of African Local Government in Sukumaland." *JAA* 4 (October 1954): 171–78.

Shivji, I. "Law and Conditions of Child Labour in Colonial Tanganyika, 1920–1940." *International Journal of the Sociology of Law* 3 (1985): 221–35.

Skeffington, Arthur. *Tanganyika in Transition*. London: Fabian Commonwealth Bureau, 1960.

Smith, Charles David. *Did Colonialism Capture the Peasantry? A Case Study of the Kagera District, Tanzania*. Uppsala: SIAS, 1989.

Smith, Daniel R. *Influence of the Fabian Colonial Bureau on the Independence Movement in Tanganyika*. Athens: Ohio University Center for International Studies, 1985.

Sommerville, A. A., et al. "Parliamentary Visit to Tanganyika, 1928." *JRAS* 110 (1929): 122–48.

Spry, J. F. "Some Notes on Land Tenure, Adjudication of Rights, and Registration of Titles with Special Reference to Tanganyika." *JAA* 4 (October 1956): 175–79.

Stephens, Hugh W. *Political Transformation of Tanganyika: 1920–67*. New York: Praeger, 1968.

Symes, Sir Stewart. "Inter-racial Partnership Should Operate Wherever Possible." *EAR* (10 June 1954): 1285–87.

———. *Tour of Duty*. London: Collins, 1946.

Tanganyika. *Tanganyika*. Dar es Salaam: GP, 1957.

Tanner, Ralph E. S. "Belgian and British Administration in Ruanda-Urundi and Tanganyika." *Journal of Local Administration Overseas* 3 (1965): 202–11.

———. "Law Enforcement by Communal Action in Sukumaland, Tanganyika Territory." *JAA* 4 (October 1955): 159–65.

Taylor, J. Clagett. *Political Development of Tanganyika*. Stanford: Stanford University Press, 1963.

Turnbull, Sir Richard. "Disrespect for Law and Contempt for Authority in Tanganyika." *EAR* (26 March 1959): 875–76.

———. "Tanganyika Election in 1960." *EAR* (29 October 1959): 198, 203.

———. "Tanganyika Must Concentrate on Quality and Economy." *EAR* (16 October 1958): 191–92.

———. "Tanganyika's Need of Foreign Capital and Enterprise." *EAR* (2 October 1958): 130–31.

Twining, Lord. "Aims of British Policy in Tanganyika." *EAR* (18 September 1952): 50.

———. "Developing Tanganyika's Many Rich Potentialities." *EAR* (12 July 1951): 1261.

———. "Economic Development Must Precede Political Advancement." *EAR* (19 May 1955): 1273–74.

———. "Folly of Time-Table for Constitutional Advancement." *EAR* (9 May 1957): 1205–6.

———. "Governor's Confidence in the Future of Tanganyika." *EAR* (31 December 1953): 536–37.

———. "Last Nine Years in Tanganyika." *AA* (January 1959): 15–24.

———. "Progress in Tanganyika under British Administration." *EAR* (15 May 1958): 1157–58.

———. "Situation in Tanganyika." *AA* (October 1951): 297–310.

——. "Tanganyika Government Will Not Tolerate Lawlessness." *EAR* (7 November 1957): 302–3, 313.

——. "Tanganyika on the Way to Nationhood." *EAR* (15 December 1955): 539–40.

——. "Tanganyika Today and Tomorrow." In *Rhodesia and East Africa*, ed. F. S. Joelson, 227–31. London: East Africa and Rhodesia, 1958.

——. "Tanganyika Will Not Even Consider Universal Suffrage." *EAR* (16 May 1957): 1238–39.

——. "Tanganyika's Integrated Development Plans." *EAR* (5 July 1951): 1229–30.

——. "Tanganyika's Large-Scale Educational Plans." *EAR* (5 May 1955): 1197–98.

——. "Tanganyika's Middle Course in Racial Relations." *Optima* 4 (December 1958): 211–18.

——. "Tanganyika's Party Formula to be Ten-Ten-Ten." *EAR* (16 December 1954): 483–88.

——. "Tanganyika's Remarkable Economic Progress." *EAR* (26 September 1957): 109–10.

U.N. Trusteeship Council. *Report of the Visiting Mission to the Trust Territory of Tanganyika under British Administration*. Lake Success, NY: United Nations, 1949.

——. "Two Years of Progress in Tanganyika: Council Surveys Developments in Largest Trust Territory." *United Nations Bulletin* (July, 1951): 660–67.

"United Tanganyika Party's Statement of Policy." *EAR* (3 October 1957): 142–43.

Varma, S. N. *Tanganyika: A Background Study*. New Delhi: Africa Publications, 1961.

Wakefield, A. J. "Groundnut Scheme." *East African Agricultural Journal* (January 1948): 131–34.

Williams, J. K. *Black, Amber, White: An Autobiography*. Worthing: Churchman, 1990.

Willis, Justin. "Administration of Bonde, 1920–60: A Study of Implementation of Indirect Rule in Tanganyika." *AA* 366 (January 1993): 53–67.

Wood, Alan. *Groundnut Affair*. London: The Bodley Head, 1950.

E. History: Independence Period

Adam, M. Mlamali. "Nyerere: The Man." *New African* (October 1980): 12–19.

Adedeji, Adebayo. *Tanzania Civil Service a Decade after Independence*. Ile-Ife, Nigeria: University of Ife Press, 1974.

Ake, Claude. "Tanzania: The Progress of a Decade." *TAR* 1 (1972): 55–64.

Babu, A. M. "New Europe: Consequences for Tanzania." *ROAPE* 50 (March, 1991): 75–78.

Barke, M., and C. Sowden. "Population Change in Tanzania 1978–88: A Preliminary Analysis." *Scottish Geographical Magazine* 1 (April 1992): 9–16.

Baynham, Simon. "Tanzania 1990: Economic and Political Developments." *Africa Insight* 4 (1990): 255–62.

Bennett, George. "Outline History of TANU." *Makerere Journal* 7 (1963): 15–32.

Campbell, Horace. "Political Challenges of the Second Mwinyi Administration." *Southern Africa* 3/4 (December 1990/January 1991): 27–29.

Cliffe, Lionel. "Arusha Declaration: Challenge to Tanzanians." *EAJ* 12 (March 1967): 3–9.

Cliffe, Lionel, ed. *One-Party Democracy: A Study of the 1965 General Election in Tanzania.* Nairobi: EAPH, 1967.

Duggan, William Redman, and John Civille. *Tanzania and Nyerere: A Study of Ujamaa and Nationhood.* Maryknoll, NY: Orbis Books, 1976.

Fatton, Robert. "Political Ideology of Julius Nyerere: The Structural Limitations of 'African Socialism.' " *Studies in Comparative International Development* 2 (Summer 1985): 3–24.

Fournier, Gordon W.F. "Tanzania: Neither East nor West." *World Mission* (Summer 1966): 73–84.

Frank, Bernard. "Tanzania Permanent Commission of Inquiry: The Ombudsman." *Denver Journal of International Law and Policy* (1972): 255–79.

Frederick, S. W. "Life of Joseph Kimalando." *TNR* 70 (1969). 21–28.

Freund, W. M. "Class Conflict, Political Economy and the Struggle for Socialism in Tanzania." *AA* 321 (October 1981): 483–99.

George, John B. "How Stable is Tanganyika." *AR* 3 (March 1963): 3–12.

Hartmann, J. "The Arusha Declaration Revisited." *TAR* 1 (1985): 1–11.

Hill, Frances. "Administrative Decentralization for Development, Participation and Control in Tanzania." *JAS* 4 (1979/80): 182–92.

Hodd, Michael, ed. *Tanzania after Nyerere.* London: Pinter Publishers, 1988.

Hopkins, Raymond F. *Political Roles in a New State: Tanzania's First Decade.* New Haven: YUP, 1971.

Horne, David L. "Passing the Baton: The Presidential Legacy of Julius K. Nyerere." *JAS* 3 (Fall 1987): 89–94.

Huddleston, Trevor. "Tanzania's Experiment." *Frontier* 3 (1972): 156–60.

Hydén, Göran. "Public Policy-Making and Public Enterprises in Tanzania." *TAR* (1975): 141–66.

Kambona, Oscar S. *Crisis of Democracy in Tanzania.* London: TDS Ltd., 1968.

Karioki, James N. "Socialism in Africa: The Tanzanian Experience." *Civilisations* 1/2 (1973/74): 31–50.

———. *Tanzania's Human Revolution.* University Park: Pennsylvania State University Press, 1979.

Kimicha, M. "Ombudsman and the Permanent Commission of Enquiry (Tanzania)." *Journal of Administration Overseas* 1 (January 1973): 46–50.

Kjekshus, Helge. *Elected Elite: A Socio-economic Study of Candidates in Tanzania's Parliamentary Election, 1970.* Uppsala: SIAS, 1975.

———. "Ombudsman in the Tanzanian One-Party System." *TAR* 2 (1971): 13–29.

———. "Parliament in a One-Party State: The Bunge of Tanzania, 1965–1970." *JMAS* 1 (March 1974): 19–43.

Kyulule, V. L., and L. Mushokolwa. "Role of the Party in Socialist Construction: The Case of CCM in Tanzania." *Taamuli* (1983): 9–24.

Landor, Alfred. "Close-up of Julius Nyerere." *Contemporary Review* 1367 (December 1979): 281–84.

———. "Nyerere in the Tanzanian Dilemma." *Contemporary Review* 1432 (May 1985): 242–46.

Legum, Colin, and Geoffrey Mmari, eds. *Mwalimu: The Influence of Nyerere*. London: James Currey, 1995.

Leys, Colin. "Tanganyika: The Realities of Independence." *International Journal* (Summer 1962): 251–68.

Linton, N. "Nyerere's Road to Socialism." *CJAS* 1 (1968): 1–6.

Lonsdale, John. "Tanzanian Experiment." *AA* 269 (October 1968): 330–44.

McAuslan, J.P.W.B. "Political Stability and Constitutional Development in Tanzania." *The World Today* 12 (December 1966): 535–44.

McCain, James A. "Ideology in Africa: Some Perceptual Types." *ASR* 1 (1975): 81–87.

MacDonald, Alexander. *Tanzania: Young Nation in a Hurry*. New York: Hawthorne Books, 1966.

McGowan, Pat. *Political and Social Elite of Tanzania: An Analysis of Social Background Factors*. Syracuse: Maxwell School of Citizenship and Public Affairs, Syracuse University, 1971.

McHenry, Dean E. "Leaders' Choices for Members of Parliament Compared with Those of Both High-Level Party Officials and the People in Tanzania, 1965–1975." *JDA* 3 (April 1983): 337–47.

———. *Limited Choices: The Political Struggle for Socialism in Tanzania*. Boulder: Lynne Rienner Publishers, 1994.

Matheson, Alastair. "Notable Year for Nyerere," *AR* 1 (January/February): 64–68.

Mmuya, Max. *Towards Multiparty Politics in Tanzania*. Dar es Salaam: DUP, 1992.

Mohidden, Ahmed. "Reflections on Socialist Tanzania." *EAJ* 11 (November 1972): 26–37.

Morgenthau, Ruth Schachter. "African Elections: Tanzania's Contribution." *AR* 11 (December 1965): 12–16.

Mulei, Christopher. "Predicament of the Left in Tanzania." *EAJ* 8 (August 1972): 29–34.

Mueller, Susanne D. "Historical Origins of Tanzania's Ruling Class." *CJAS* 3 (1981): 459–97.

Mushokolwa, L. "Political Economy of Tanzania." *Maendeleo* 1 (January 1985): 36–65.

Mutahaba, G. R. *Portrait of a Nationalist: The Life of Ali Migeyo*. Nairobi: EAPH, 1969.

Mwaga, D. Z., B. F. Mrina, and F. F. Lyimo, eds. *Historia ya Chama cha TANU, 1954 Hadi 1977*. Dar es Salaam: Chuo cha CCM, Kivukoni, 1981.

Mwakawago, Daudi, and Lionel Cliffe. "Meaning of Tanzanian Elections." *EAJ* 7 (November 1965): 8–13.

Mwalimu Nyerere na Tanzania. Dar es Salaam: Black Star Agencies, 1980.

Mwansasu, Bismarck, and R. Cranford Pratt, eds. *Towards Socialism in Tanzania*. Toronto: University of Toronto Press, 1979.

Nellis, John R. *A Theory of Ideology: The Tanzanian Example*. New York: OUP, 1972.

Ngasongwa, J. "Tanzania Introduces a Multi-Party System." *ROAPE* 54 (1992): 112–16.

Norton, P. M. "Tanzanian Ombudsman." *International Comparative Law Quarterly* 4 (October 1973): 603–31.

Noviki, Margaret A. "Interview With President Ali Hassan Mwinyi." *AR* 1 (January/February, 1988): 27–29.

———. "Julius Nyerere: Former President, the United Republic of Tanzania." *AR* 6 (November/December, 1985): 4–10.

Nyerere, Julius K. *Arusha Declaration Ten Years After.* Dar es Salaam: GP, 1977.

———. *Crusade for Liberation.* New York: OUP, 1978.

———. *Freedom and Development.* Dar es Salaam: OUP, 1973.

———. *Freedom and Socialism.* New York: OUP, 1969.

———. *Freedom and Unity.* London: OUP, 1967.

———. *Our Leadership and Future of the Union.* Harare: Zimbabwe Publishing House, 1994.

———. *Principles and Development.* Dar es Salaam: GP, 1966.

———. *Socialism and Rural Development.* Dar es Salaam: GP, 1967.

———. "Tanzania: Ten Years after Independence." *TAR* 6 (1972): 1–54.

———. "Tanzania's One Party Democracy." *EAJ* 3 (June 1965): 24–26.

———. *Ujamaa: Essays on Socialism.* New York: OUP, 1971.

"Nyerere, Julius K[ambarage]." In *Current Biography Yearbook, 1963,* ed. Charles Moritz, 301–4. New York: The H. W. Wilson, 1964.

O'Barr, Jean F. "Cell Leaders in Tanzania." *ASR* 3 (December 1972): 437–65.

Obichere, Boniface I. "Tanzania at the Crossroads: From Nyerere to Mwinyi." *JAS* 3 (Fall, 1987): 84–88.

Ododa, Harry. "Voluntary Retirement by Presidents in Africa: Lessons From Sierra Leone, Tanzania, Cameroun, and Senegal." *JAS* 3/4 (1988): 94–100.

Othman, Haroub, ed. *State in Tanzania.* Dar es Salaam: DUP, 1980.

Othman, Haroub, Immanuel K. Bavu, and Michael Okema, eds. *Tanzania: Democracy in Transition.* Dar es Salaam: DUP, 1990.

Picard, Louis A. "Attitudes and Development: The District Administration in Tanzania." *ASR* 3 (December 1980): 49–68.

———. "Socialism and the Field Administrator: Decentralization in Tanzania." *Comparative Politics* 4 (1980): 439–57.

Pratt, R. Cranford. *Critical Phase in Tanzania, 1945–1968: Nyerere and the Emergence of a Socialist Strategy.* Cambridge: CUP, 1976.

———. "Nyerere on the Transition to Socialism in Tanzania." *TAR* 1 (1975): 63–76.

Resnick, Idrian N. *Long Transition: Building Socialism in Tanzania.* New York: Monthly Review Press, 1981.

Rigby, Peter. "Local Participation in National Politics: Ugogo, Tanzania." *Africa* 1 (1977): 89–107.

Ruhumbika, Gabriel, ed. *Towards Ujamaa: Twenty Years of TANU Leadership.* Nairobi: EALB, 1974.

Rweyemamu, Anthony H., ed. *Nation-Building in Tanzania.* Nairobi: EAPH, 1970.

Samoff, Joel. "Bureaucracy and the Bourgeoisie: Decentralization and Class Structure in Tanzania." *Comparative Studies in Society and History* 1 (January 1979): 279–306.

———. "Bureaucrats, Politicians, and Power in Tanzania: The Institutional Context of Class Struggle." *JAS* 3 (Fall 1983): 84–96.

———. "Crisis and Socialism in Tanzania." *JMAS* 2 (June 1981): 279–306.

Saul, J. S. "Nature of Tanzania's Political System: Issues Raised by the 1965–1970 Elections." *Journal of Commonwealth Political Studies* 2 (July 1972): 113–39; and 3 (September 1972): 198–221.

Segal, Aaron. "Where is Tanzania Heading?" *AR* 9 (October 1965): 10–17.

Svendsen, Knud Eric, and Merete Teisen, eds. *Self-reliant Tanzania*. Dar es Salaam: TPH, 1969.

Shiviji, Issa G. *Class Struggles in Tanzania*. London: Heinemann, 1976.

———. "Democracy Debate in Africa: Tanzania." *ROAPE* 50 (March 1991): 79–91.

———. *Silent Class Struggle*. Dar es Salaam: TPH, 1976.

Singleton, Seth. "Tanzania since Arusha." *AR* 9 (September 1971): 10–14.

Smith, Philip. "Politics after Dodoma." *AR* 1 (January/February 1988): 30–32.

Smith, William Edgett. *Nyerere of Tanzania*. Harare: Zimbabwe Publishing House, 1981.

———. *We Must Run While They Walk: A Portrait of Africa's Julius Nyerere*. New York: Random House, 1972.

Sperber, K. W. *Public Administration in Tanzania*. Munich: Weltforum Verlag, 1970.

Stein, Howard. "Theories of the State in Tanzania: A Critical Assessment." *JMAS* 1 (March 1985): 105–23.

Tandon, Yashpal. *In Defence of Democracy*. Dar es Salaam: DUP, 1993.

"TANU Guidelines of February 1971." *TAR* 4 (1972): 1–8.

Tanzania Today: A Portrait of the United Republic. Nairobi: University Press of Africa, 1968.

Tordoff, William. "General Elections in Tanzania." *Journal of Commonwealth Political Studies* 1 (March, 1966): 47–64.

———. *Government and Politics in Tanzania*. Nairobi: EAPH, 1967.

———. "Parliament in Tanzania." *Journal of Commonwealth Political Studies* 2 (March 1965): 85–103.

———. "Politics in Tanzania." *The World Today* 8 (August 1965): 351–60.

———. "Regional Administration in Tanzania." *JMAS* 1 (May 1965): 63–89.

———. "Trade Unionism in Tanzania." *Journal of Development Studies* 4 (July 1966): 408–30.

Tordoff, William, and Ali Mazrui. "Left and the Super-Left in Tanzania." *JMAS* 3 (October 1972): 427–45.

Tripp, Aili Mari. "Local Organizations, Participation, and the State in Urban Tanzania." In *Governance and Politics in Africa*, ed. Göran Hydén and Michael Bratton, 221–42. Boulder: Lynne Rienner Publishers, 1992.

United Republic of Tanzania. *Arusha Declaration and Tanganyika African National Union's Policy on Socialism and Self-Reliance*. Dar es Salaam: TANU Publicity Section, 1967.

Van Donge, Jan Kees, and Athumani J. Liviga. "1985 Tanzanian Parliamentary Elections: A Conservative Election." *AA* 350 (January 1989): 47–62.

———. "1982 Elections for Membership of the National Executive Committee of Chama Cha Mapinduzi: A Case Study of Political Recruitment in Tanzania." *Journal of Commonwealth and Comparative Politics* 1 (March 1985): 43–66.

———. "Tanzanian Political Culture and the Cabinet." *JMAS* 4 (December 1986): 619–40.

von Freyhold, Michaela. "Post-colonial State and Its Tanzanian Version." *ROAPE* 8 (1977): 75–89.

F. Military and Security Affairs

Abbott, Peter. *British East Africa: Kenya, Tanganyika, Somaliland, Uganda, and Zanzibar to 1964*. Leeds: Raider Books, 1988.

Abdul Karim bin Jamaliddini. "Gedicht von Majimaji-Aufstand, übersetzt und Herausgegeben von A. Lorenz." *Mitteilungen des Seminars für Orientalische Sprachen zu Berlin* (1933): 227–59.

Abrahams, Ray. "Sungusungu: Village Vigilante Groups in Tanzania." *AA* 343 (April 1987): 179–96.

Akinola, G. A. "East African Coastal Rising, 1888–1890." *Journal of the Historical Society of Nigeria* 4 (1975): 609–30.

Avirgan, Tony, and Martha Honey. *War in Uganda: The Legacy of Idi Amin*. Westport, CT: Lawrence Hill, 1982.

Bald, Detlef. "Afrikanischer Kampf Gegen Koloniale Herrschaft: Der Maji-Maji Aufstand in Ost-Afrika." *Militargeschichtliche Mitteilungen* 1 (1976): 23–50.

———. "Der Einsatz der Marine im Ostafrikanischen Austand 1905/06." *Marine Rundschau* 1 (1977): 21–24.

Banks, M. E. B. "Marines in Tanganyika." *Marine Corps Gazette* 10 (1964): 38–40.

Beachey, R. W. "Arms Trade in East Africa in the Late Nineteenth Century." *JAH* 3 (1962): 451–67.

Becker, A. "Subjugation of Chief Meli of Moshi, 1893." *TNR* 57 (September 1961): 199–210.

Bell, R. M. "Maji-Maji Rebellion in the Liwale District." *TNR* 28 (January, 1950): 38–57.

Bienen, Henry. "Army Mutiny in Perspective." In *Tanzania: Party Transformation and Economic Development*, 363–81. Princeton: Princeton University Press, 1967.

———. "Military and Society in East Africa: Thinking Again about Praetorianism." *Comparative Politics* 4 (July 1974): 489–517.

———. "National Security in Tanganyika After the Mutiny." *Transition* 21 (August/ September, 1965): 39–46.

———. "Public Order and the Military in Africa: Mutinies in Kenya, Uganda, and Tanganyika." In *Armies and Parties in Africa*, 138–64, New York and London: Africana Publishing Company, 1978.

Biermann, Werner. "Regionalpolitische Auswirkungen des Tanzanisch-Ugandischen Krieges (1978/79)." *Internat Afrikaforum* 1 (1983): 77–81.

Boell, Ludwig. *Die Operationen in Ostafrika*. Hamburg: Walter Dachert, 1951.

Bomani, Paul. "Behind the Mutinies." *AT* 1 (January 1964): 4–5.

"Brushfire in East Africa: A Chronology of Major Events in Tanganyika, Uganda, and Kenya, from January 1 to February 13, 1964." *AR* 2 (February 1964): 21–24.

Buchanan, Angus. *Three Years of War in East Africa*. London: John Murray, 1919.

Buhler, Karlheinz. "Deutsche Polizei in Deutsch-Ostafrika." *Zeitschrift für Heereskunde* 302/303 (1982): 104–6.

Burrows, Noreen. "Tanzania's Intervention in Uganda: Some Legal Aspects." *The World Today* 7 (July 1979): 306–10.

Campbell, Horace. "Popular Resistance in Tanzania: Lessons from the Sungu Sungu." *Africa Development* 4 (1989): 5–44.

Chatterjee, S. K. "Some Legal Problems of Support Role in International Law: Tanzania and Uganda." *International and Comparative Law Quarterly* (October 1981): 755–68.

Chatterton, E. Keble. *"Konigsberg" Adventure*. London: Hurst and Blackett, 1932.

Chretien, Jean-Pierre. "La révolte de Ndungutse (1912): Forces traditionnelles et pression coloniale au Rwanda allemand." *Revue Française d'Histoire d'Outre-Mer* 4 (1972): 645–80.

Clifford, Hugh. *Gold Coast Regiment in the East African Campaign*. London: John Murray, 1920.

Collyer, J. *South Africans with General Smuts in German East Africa, 1916*. Pretoria: Government Printer, 1939.

Crowe, J.H.V. *General Smuts' Campaign in East Africa*. London: John Murray, 1918.

Deppe, Ludwig. *Mit Lettow-Vorbeck Durch Afrika*. Berlin: Verlag August Scherl, 1919.

Dickson, A. G. "Mobile Propaganda Unit, East Africa Command." *JRAS* 174 (January 1945): 9–18.

Dolbey, R. V. *Sketches of the East African Campaign*. London: John Murray, 1918.

Downes, W. D. *With the Nigerians in German East Africa*. London: Methuen, 1919.

Ejalu, Ateker. "Amin's Doomsday Plans." *New African* 139 (March 1979): 47–50.

Fendall, C. P. *East African Force, 1915–1919*. London: Witherby, 1921.

Fosbrooke, Henry A. "Chagga Forst and Bolt Holes." *TNR* 37 (July 1954): 115–29.

———. "Defensive Measures of Certain Tribes in North-Eastern Tanganyika." *TNR* 35 (July 1953): 1–6; 36 (February 1954): 50–57; 39 (June 1955): 1–11.

Fouquer, Roger P. *Mirambo: Un chef de guerre dans l'Est-Afrique vers 1830–1884*. Paris: Nouvelles Editions Latines, 1967.

Ginwala, Frere. "Tanganyika Mutiny." *The World Today* 3 (March 1964): 93–7.

Glassman, Jonathon Philip. "Social Rebellion and Swahili Culture: The Response to German Conquest of the Northern Mrima, 1888–1890." Ph.D. diss., University of Wisconsin, 1988.

Glickman, Harvey. *Impressions of Military Policy in Tanganyika (East Africa)*. Santa Monica: The Rand Corporation, 1963.

———. *Some Observations on the Army and Political Unrest in Tanganyika*. Pittsburgh: Duquesne University Press, 1964.

Gray, John Milner. "Fort Santiago at Kilwa." *TNR* 35 (July 1953): 45–52.

Great Britain, Naval Intelligence Division. *Handbook of German East Africa*. London: HMSO, 1916.

———. *Handbook of German East Africa*. London: HMSO, 1920.

Great Britain, War Office, General Staff. *Military Report on German East Africa*. London: HMSO, 1902.

Gregorian, Hrach. "Plowshares into Swords: The Former Member States and the 1978–1979 War." In *Integration and Disintegration in East Africa*, ed. Christian P. Potholm and Richard A. Friedland, 167–91. Lanham: University Press of America, 1980.

Gross-Upcott, A.R.W. "Origin of Maji Maji Revolt." *Man* (May 1960): 71–73.

Gupta, Anirudha. "Amin's Fall: Would There be Other Dominoes?" *AQ* 1 (April/June 1979): 4–13.

Gwassa, Gilbert C. K. "African Methods of Warfare During the Maji Maji War, 1905–1907." In *War and Society in Africa*, ed. Bethwell A. Ogot, 123–48. London: Frank Cass and Company Ltd., 1974.

———. "German Intervention and African Resistance in Tanzania." In *A History of Tanzania*, ed. I. N. Kimambo and A. J. Temu, 85–122. Nairobi: EAPH, 1969.

———. "Kinjikitile and the Ideology of Maji Maji." In *The Historical Study of African Religion*, ed. Terence O. Ranger and I. M. Kimambo, 202–17. Berkeley: University of California Press, 1972.

————. "Outbreak and Development of the Maji Maji War, 1905–1907." Ph.D. diss., University of Dar es Salaam, 1973.

Gwassa, Gilbert C. K. and John Iliffe, eds. *Records of the Maji Maji Rising: Part One.* Nairobi: EAPH, 1968

Hassing, Per. "German Missionaries and the Maji Maji Rising." *AHS* 2 (1970): 373–89.

Harvey, Ronald J. "Mirambo, the Napoleon of Central Africa." *TNR* 28 (January 1950): 10–28.

Hatchell, G. W. "British Occupation of the South-Western Area of Tanganyika Territory 1914–1918." *TNR* 51 (December 1958): 131–55.

Hodges, Geoffrey. *Carrier Corps: Military Labor in the East African Campaign, 1914–1918.* Westport, CT: Greenwood Press, 1986.

Holtom, E. C. *Two Years' Captivity in German East Africa.* London: Hutchinson, 1919.

Hordern, Charles. *Military Operations: East Africa.* London: HMSO, 1941.

Hoyt, Edwin P. *Germans Who Never Lost.* New York: Funk and Wagnalls, 1968.

Hozza, J. J. "Hoza Rebellion and After." B.A. thesis, Dar es Salaam, University College, 1969.

Iliffe, John. "Effects of the Maji Maji Rebellion of 1905–06 on German Occupation Policy in East Africa." In *Britain and Germany in Africa*, ed. Prosser Gifford and William Roger Louis, 557–75. New Haven: YUP: *Imperial Rivalry and Colonial Rule,* 1967.

————. "Organization of the Maji Maji Rebellion." *JAH* 3 (1967): 495–512.

Jackson, Robert D. "Resistance to the German Invasion of the Tanganyikan Coast, 1888–1891." In *Protest and Power in Black Africa*, ed. Robert I. Rosberg and Ali A. Mazrui, 37–79. New York: OUP, 1970.

Jackson, Sir Wilfrid. "Tanganyika Had Many German Residents." *EAR* (17 May 1945): 869–71.

————. "War Effort of Tanganyika Territory." *EAR* (29 March 1945): 693–94.

Jellicoe, Marguerite. "Turu Resistance Movement." *TNR* 70 (July 1969): 1–12.

Joly, Wolfgang. "Fahnen, Flaggen, und Standarten Deutscher Einheiten in Ubersee 1885 bis 1918." *Zeitschrift für Heereskunde* 337 (1988): 61–67.

Kabeya, J. B. *King Mirambo: One of the Heroes of Tanzania.* Nairobi: EALB, 1976.

Kato, L. L. "Penological Goals in Socialist Tanzania." *EAJ* 10 (October 1971): 5–14.

Kieran, J. A. "Abushiri and the Germans." In *Hadith 2*, ed. Bethwell Ogot, 157–201. Nairobi: EAPH, 1970.

Killingray, Anthony, and David Killingray. *Khaki and Blue: Military and Police in British Colonial Africa.* Athens: Ohio University Center for International Studies, 1989.

Kock, Nis. *Blockade and Jungle.* London: Robert Hale, 1941.

Komba, Marcelino. "Amin's Pillage in the Kagera." *Africa* 89 (January, 1979): 12–17.

Koponen, Juhani. "War, Famine, and Pestilence in Late Precolonial Tanzania: A Case for a Heightened Mortality." *IJAHS* 4 (1988): 637–76.

Lamburn, R.G.P. "The Angoni Raid on Masasi in 1882." *TNR* 66 (December 1966): 207–13.

Legum, Colin. "Why Tanganyika Accepted a Chinese Military Mission." *AR* 9 (October 1964): 16.

Lettow-Vorbeck, Paul von. *Mein Leben*. Biberach an der Riss: Koehlers, 1957.
————. *My Reminiscences of East Africa*. London: Hurst and Blackett, 1920.
Mabando, Samuel Ismail. *Tanzania-Uganda War in Pictures*. Dar es Salaam: Longman Tanzania, 1980.
Mapunda, O. B., and G. M. Mpangara. *Maji Maji War in Ungoni*. Dar es Salaam and Nairobi: EAPH, 1969.
Mathews, Lloyd. "Tanzania." In *World Armies* 2d edition, ed. John Keegan, 574–76. Detroit: Gale Research Company, 1983.
Mazrui, Ali A. "Anti-militarism and Political Militancy in Tanzania." *Journal of Conflict Resolution* 3 (September 1968): 269–84.
————. "Language in Military History: Command and Communication in East Africa." *Mawazo* 2 (1974): 19–36.
Mazrui, Ali A., and Donald Rothchild. "Soldier and the State in East Africa: Some Theoretical Conclusions on the Army Mutinies of 1964," *Western Political Quarterly* 1 (March 1967): 82–96.
Mbonde, John Pantaleon. *Kuanguka kwa Fashisti Idi Amin*. Dar es Salaam: Swala Publications, 1979.
McDonald, D. R. *Enemy Property in Tanganyika*. Cape Town: Hortors, 1946.
Millar-Craig, H. "East African Staff College." *JMAS* 4 (December 1967): 559–61.
Miller, Charles. *Battle for the Bundu: The First World War in East Africa*. New York: Macmillan, 1974.
Mosley, Leonard. *Duel for Kilimanjaro*. New York: Ballantine Books, 1964.
Moyse-Bartlett, Hubert. *King's African Rifles: A Study in the Military History of East and Central Africa, 1890–1945*. Aldershot: Gale and Polden, 1956.
Msabaha, I.S.R. "War on Idi Amin: Toward a Synthetic Theory of Intervention." *TAR* 1 (1985): 24–43.
"Much Bloodshed Averted in Tanganyika's Fearful State." *EAR* (30 January 1964): 444–45, 47.
Muhanika, Henry R. *Utenzi wa Vita vya Kagera na Anguko la Idi Amin Dada*. Dar es Salaam: DUP, 1981.
Mzirai, Baldwin. *Kuzama kwa Idi Amin*. Dar es Salaam: Publicity International, 1980.
Okoth, P. Godfrey. "OAU and the Uganda-Tanzania War, 1978–79." *JAS* 3 (Fall 1987): 152–62.
Omari, Abillah H. *Beyond the Civil-Military Dichotomy in Africa: The Case of Tanzania*. Halifax: Centre for African Studies, Dalhousie University, 1989.
Pachter, Elise Forbes. "Contra-coup: Civilian Control of the Military in Guinea, Tanzania, and Mozambique." *JMAS* 4 (December 1982): 595–612.
Pennington, A. L. "Refugees in Tanganyika During the Second World War." *TNR* 32 (January 1952): 52–56.
Platt, Sir William. "Studies in War-Time Organisation: (G) East Africa Command." *JRAS* 178 (June 1946): 27–35.
"Prison Service Since Independence." *TNR* 76 (1975): 197–200.
Prunier, Gérard A. "Kuanguka kwa Fashisti Idi Amin: Tanzania's Ambiguous Ugandan Victory." *Cultures et Développement* 3/4 (1984): 735–56.
Redmayne, Alison. "Mkwawa and the Hehe Wars." *JAH* 3 (1968): 409–36.
Redmond, Patrick M. "Maji-Maji in Ungoni: A Reappraisal of Existing Historiography." *IJAHS* 3 (1975): 407–25.

————. "Some Results of Military Contacts Between the Ngoni and Their Neighbours." *TJH* 1 (1976): 75–97.

"The Revolt in German East Africa." *African World* (2 December 1905): 195.

Rodney, Walter. *World War II and the Tanzanian Economy.* Ithaca: Cornell African Studies Center, 1976.

Rotberg, Robert I. "Resistance and Rebellion in British Nyasaland and German East Africa, 1888–1915: A Tentative Comparison." In *Britain and Germany in Africa: Imperial Rivalry and Colonial Rule,* ed. Prosser Gifford and William Roger Louis, 667–90. New Haven: YUP, 1967.

Seeburg, Karl-Martin. *Der Maji-Maji-Krieg Gegen die Deutsche Kolonialherrschaft.* Berlin: DM, 1989.

Sibley, J. R. *Tanganyikan Guerrilla: East African Campaign, 1914–18.* New York: Ballantine Books, 1971.

Singleton, Seth. "Supplementary Military Forces in Sub-Saharan Africa: The Congo, Kenya, Tanzania, Uganda, and Zaire." In *Supplementary Military Forces,* ed. Louis A. Zucker and Gwyn Harries Jenkens, 200–37. Beverly Hills, CA: Sage, 1978.

Slattery, Brian. *A Handbook on Sentencing: With Particular Reference to Tanzania.* Nairobi: EALB, 1972.

Stollowsky, Otto. "On the Background to the Rebellion in German East Africa in 1905–1906," trans. John East. *IJAHS* 4 (1988): 677–96.

Taban, Alfred Logune. "Ugandan Exodus." *Sudanow* 7 (July 1979): 9–11, 13–17.

"Tanzania." In *World Encyclopedia of Police Forces and Penal Systems,* ed. George Thomas Kurian, 109–12. New York and Oxford: Facts on File, 1989.

"Tanzania: Mutiny in the Army." *Indian Ocean Newsletter* (3 June 1989): 1, 4.

"Tanzania People's Defence Forces: Development 1961–1971." *TNR* 76 (1975): 201–2.

"Tanzania Police Force: Law and Order Since Uhuru." *TNR* 76 (1975): 193–96.

Taute, M. "A German Account of the Medical Side of the War in East Africa, 1914–1918." *TNR* 8 (December 1939): 1–20.

Thornhill, Christopher J. *Taking Tanganyika.* London: Stanley Paul, 1937.

Twaddle, Michael. "Ousting of Idi Amin: Regime's Swift Collapse Took Tanzania by Surprise." *The Round Table* 275 (July 1979): 216–21.

"Two Mutinies by Tanganyika Army: British Officers Expelled." *EAR* (23 January 1964): 425, 434.

"Two Mutinies: Statements by Political Leader." *EAR* (6 February 1964): 463, 472.

"Uganda-Tanzania Conflict." *Africa Currents* 12/13 (Autumn/Winter 1978/1979): 25–32.

"Uganda's Historical Moshi Conference." *New African* 141 (May 1979): 14–17.

Umozurike, U. O. "Tanzania's Intervention in Uganda." *Archiv des Volkerrechts* 3 (1982): 301–13.

Ungar, Sanford J. "Tanzania Goes to War." *New Republic* 180 (10 March 1979): 16–18.

United Republic of Tanzania. *Tanzania and the War Against Amin's Uganda.* Dar es Salaam: GP, 1979.

Unomah, A. C. "Maji-Maji in Tanzania (1905–07): African Reaction to German Conquest." *Tarikh* 3 (1973): 35–45.

Venter, A. J. "Amin's Chamber of Horrors." *South African Journal of African Affairs* 2 (1979): 104–10.

Wani, Ibrahim J. "Humanitarian Intervention and the Tanzania-Uganda War." *Horn of Africa* 2 (1980): 18–27.
"Wars and Rumours of War." *Taveta Chronicle* 18 (January 1900): 187–88.
Westcott, Nicholas J. "Impact of the Second World War on Tanganyika, 1939–49." In *Africa and the Second World War*, ed. David Killingray and Richard Rathbone, 143–59. New York: St. Martin's Press, 1986.
————. "The Impact of the Second World War on Tanganyika, 1939–1949. Ph.D. diss., Cambridge University, 1982.
Williams, David. "Minimum Sentences Act, 1972, of Tanzania." *Journal of African Law* 1 (Spring 1974): 79–91.
Young, Francis Brett. *Marching on Tanga.* London: Collins, 1917.

G. Economic Affairs

Addison, Tony. *"Tanzania: Adjusting to the IMF?" AR* 3 (May/June 1986): 81–83.
Aeroe, A. "New Pathways to Industrialisation in Tanzania: Theoretical and Strategic Considerations." *I.D.S. Bulletin* 3 (July 1992): 15–20.
Barongo, S. "Petroleum Development in Tanzania." *TNR* 79/80 (December 1976): 115–21.
Bhuyan, M. Sayefullah. "Can Tanzania Make Transition toward Socialism?" *Dacca University Studies* 33 (1980): 112–24.
Bienefeld, Manfred A. "Trade Unions, the Labour Process, and the Tanzanian State." *JMAS* 4 (December 1979): 553–93.
Bienen, Henry. *Tanzania: Party Transformation and Economic Development.* Princeton: Princeton University Press, 1967.
Biermann, Werner. "Problems of Industrialization in Tanzania." *JAS* 3 (Fall 1987): 127–40.
Biermann, Werner, and Jumanne H. Wagao. "IMF and Economic Policy in Tanzania: 1980–84." *JAS* 3 (Fall 1987): 118–26.
————. "Quest for Adjustment: Tanzania and the IMF, 1980–1986." *ASR* 4 (December 1986): 89–103.
Biersteker, Thomas J. "Self-reliance in Theory and Practice in Tanzanian Trade Relations." *International Organisation* 2 (Spring 1980): 229–64.
Binhammer, H. H. *Institutional Framework for Mobilizing Savings in Tanzania.* Dar es Salaam: Economic Research Bureau, University of Dar es Salaam, 1969.
Blue, R. N., and J. H. Weaver. *Critical Assessment of the Tanzanian Model of Development.* Washington, D.C.: Agency for International Development, 1977.
Bottomley, Richard. "Vuta Kamba: The Development of Trade Unions in Tanganyika." *African Social Research* 11 (1971): 66–71.
Brown, Beverly. "Muslim Influence on Trade and Politics in the Lake Tanganyika Region." *AHS* 3 (1971): 617–29.
Bryceson, Deborah Fahy. *Liberalizing Tanzania's Food Trade: Public and Private Faces of Urban Marketing Policy.* London: James Curry, 1992.
————. *Second Thoughts on Marketing Co-operatives in Tanzania: Background to Their Reinstatement.* Oxford: Plunkett Foundation for Cooperative Studies, 1983.
————. "Trade Roots in Tanzania: Evolution of Urban Grain Markets under Structural Adjustment." *Sociologia Ruralis* 1 (1994): 13–25.

Bukuku, Enos S. *Tanzanian Economy: Income Distribution and Economic Growth.* Westport, CT: Praeger, 1993.

Campbell, Horace. "IMF Debate and the Politics of Demobilisation in Tanzania." *Eastern Africa Social Science Research Review* 2 (June, 1986): 56–76.

Campbell, Horace, and Howard Stein, eds. *Tanzania and the IMF.* Boulder: WP, 1992.

Campbell, John C. "Unmaking of Tanzania and the March towards Capitalism." *Africa* 2 (1991): 264–77.

Caselli, Clara. *Banking System of Tanzania.* Milan: Cassa di Risparnio Delle, 1975.

Central Statistical Bureau. *Employment and Earnings in Tanzania.* Dar es Salaam: GP, 1966.

Chambua, Samuel E. "Choice of Technique and Underdevelopment in Tanzania: The Case of Sugar Development Corporation." *CJAS* 1 (1990): 17–35.

Cliffe, Lionel, and John S. Saul, eds. *Socialism in Tanzania.* 2 vols. Nairobi: EAPH, 1972.

Conyers, Diana. "Organisation for Development: The Tanzanian Experience." *Journal of Administration Overseas* (July 1974): 438–49.

Dahl, H. E., and J. Faaland. *Economy of Tanzania.* Bergen: Christian Michelson Institute, 1967.

Darkoh, M.B.K. "Tanzania's Industrial Development and Planning Experience." *JEARD* (1984): 47–80.

Doherty, Joe. "Tanzania: Twenty Years of African Socialism 1967–87." *Geography* 4 (1987): 344–48.

Elkan, Walter, and Leslie Nulty. *Economic Links between Kenya, Uganda, and Tanzania.* Nairobi: Institute for Development Studies, University of Nairobi, 1972.

Ergas, Zaki. "State and Economic Deterioration: The Tanzanian Case." *Journal of Commonwealth and Comparative Politics* 3 (November 1982): 286–308.

Forss, Kim. *Review of Industrialization and Development Policies in Tanzania.* Stockholm: Institute of International Business, Stockholm School of Economics, 1983.

Freund, W. M. "Class Conflict, Political Economy, and the Struggle for Socialism in Tanzania." *AA* 321 (October 1981): 483–99.

Giblin, James L. "Proletarianization and Labour History: Recent Work from Tanzania." *CJAS* 3 (Summer 1987): 415–19.

Gran, Thorvald. *AID and Entrepreneurship in Tanzania: The Norwegian Development Agency's Contribution to Entrepreneurial Mobilization in the Public Sector.* Dar es Salaam: DUP, 1993.

Green, R. H. "Political Economic Adjustment and IMF Conditionality: The Case of Tanzania 1974–1981." In *IMF Conditionality*, ed. J. Williamson, 347–80. Washington, D.C.: Institute of International Economics and MIT Press, 1983.

Green, R.H., D.G. Rwegasira, and B. Van Arkadie. *Economic Shocks and National Policy Making: Tanzania in the 1970s.* The Hague: Institute for Social Studies, 1980.

Havnevik, Kjell. *Tanzania: The Limits of Development from Above.* Uppsala: Nordiska Afrikainstitutet, 1993.

Hawkins, H.C.G. *Wholesale and Retail Trade in Tanganyika.* New York: Praeger, 1965.

Helleiner, Gerald K. "Socialism and Economic Development in Tanzania." *Journal of Development Studies* (January 1972): 183–204.

————. "Tanzania's Second Plan: Socialism and Self-Reliance." *EAJ* (December 1968): 41–50.

Hundt, Walter. "Ökonomische Aspekte der Entwicklung in Tansania." *Zeitschrift für Geschichtswissenschaft* 12 (1970): 1578–96.

International Bank for Reconstruction and Development. *Economic Development of Tanganyika*. Baltimore: Johns Hopkins University Press, 1961.

International Labor Office. *Report to the Government of the United Republic of Tanzania on Wages, Incomes and Price Policy*. Dar es Salaam: GP, 1967.

Jackson, Dudley. "Disappearance of Strikes in Tanzania: Incomes Policy and Industrial Democracy." *JMAS* 2 (June 1979): 219–51.

Jones, J.V.S. *Resources and Industry in Tanzania: Use, Misuse, and Abuse*. Dar es Salaam: TPH, 1983.

Kahama, C. G., T. Luta Maliyamkono, and S. Wells. *The Challenge for Tanzania's Economy*. Dar es Salaam: TPH, 1986.

Khakee, Abdul. *Development and Planning in Tanzania*. Lund: Studentlitteratur, 1970.

Kim, Kwan S. "Enterprise Performance in the Public and Private Sectors: Tanzanian Experience, 1970–75." *JDA* 15 (April 1981): 471–84.

————. *Issues and Perspectives in Tanzanian Industrial Development, with Special Reference to the Role of SADCC*. Notre Dame, IN: University of Notre Dame Press, 1986.

Kim, Kwan S., Robert Mabele, and Michael J. Schultheis, eds. *Papers on the Political Economy of Tanzania*. Nairobi: Heinemann Educational Books, 1979.

Kimambo, Isaria N. *Penetration and Protest in Tanzania: The Impact of the World Economy on the Pare*. London: James Curry, 1991.

Kimble, Helen. *Price Control in Tanzania*. Dar es Salaam: Economic Research Bureau, 1970.

Kimble, Helen, and O. M. Anderson. *Control of Retail Prices in Tanzania*. Dar es Salaam: National Price Control Advisory Board, 1967.

Kiondo, Andrew Salehe. "Politics of Economic Reforms in Tanzania." Ph.D. diss., University of Toronto, 1990.

Kmietowicz, Zbigniew W., and Mick S. Silver. "Some Problems in the Construction of Indexes of Industrial Production for Developing Countries: The Case of Tanzania, 1965–1972." *JDA* 18 (July 1984): 481–99.

Lipumba, Nguyuru H.I. *Policy Reforms for Economic Development in Tanzania*. Dar es Salaam: Department of Economics, University of Dar es Salaam, 1986.

Little, A. D. *Tanganyika Industrial Development*. Dar es Salaam: GP, 1961.

Livingstone, Ian. "Economic Development of Tanganyika: The World Bank View." *EAER* 1 (June 1961): 1–13.

————. *Socialist Planning in Tanzania: The Second Five Years*. Dar es Salaam: Economic Research Bureau, University of Dar es Salaam, 1969.

Lofchie, Michael F. "Roots of Economic Crisis in Tanzania." *CH* 501 (April 1985): 159–63, 184.

————. "Tanzania's Economic Recovery." *CH* (May 1988): 209–12, 227–29.

Loxley, John. "Financial Planning and Control in Tanzania." *Development and Change* 3 (1971/1972): 43–61.

Loxley, John, and John Saul. "Multinationals, Workers and Parastatals in Tanzania." *ROAPE* 2 (January/April 1975): 54–88.

Makusi, George John. "Perspectives on the Tanzania Experience of Labour Organisation Since the Arusha Declaration." *Taamuli* (1983): 25–38.

Malima, Kighoma A. "IMF and World Bank Conditionality: The Tanzanian Case." In *World Recession and Food Crisis in Africa*, ed. Peter Lawrence, 129–39. London: ROAPE and James Currey, 1986.

———. "International Trade and Economic Transformation of Tanzania." *TAR* (September 1971): 76–90.

Maliyamkono, T. Luta, and Mboya S.D. Bagachwa. *Second Economy in Tanzania*. London: James Currey, 1990.

Mapolu, Henry, ed. *Workers and Management*. Dar es Salaam: TPH, 1976.

Mbelle, A., and T. Sterner. "Foreign Exchange and Industrial Development: A Frontier Production Function Analysis of Two Tanzania Industries." *WD* 4 (April 1991): 341–47.

Mehra, K. S. "Tanzania: Unique Experiment in Economic and Human Development." *AQ* 2 (1983): 65–70.

Mihyo, Paschal. *Industrial Conflict and Change in Tanzania*. Dar es Salaam: TPH, 1983.

Miti, Katabaro. "Nationalist Solution to the Crisis of Accumulation in Tanzania." *TAR* 1 (1983): 74–91.

Modi, J., and I. Kaduma. *Report of the Export Group on Tax Reform Planning: Tanzania*. Dar es Salaam: GP, 1970.

Mramba, Basil P., and Bismark U. Mwansasu. "Management for Socialist Development in Tanzania: The Case of the National Development Corporation." *TAR* 3 (1972): 29–47.

Msambichaka, L. A., and S. Chandrasekhar, eds. *Readings of Economic Policy of Tanzania*. Dar es Salaam: Economic Research Bureau, University of Dar es Salaam, 1984.

Mtatifikolo, Fidelis P. "Tanzania's Incomes Policy: An Analysis of Trends with Proposals for the Future." *ASR* 1 (April 1988): 33–45.

Mushi, Samuel S. "Popular Participation and Regional Development Planning: The Politics of Decentralized Administration." *TNR* 83 (1978): 63–97.

Mushi, Samuel S., and Helge Kjekshus, eds. *Aid and Development: Some Tanzanian Experiences*. Oslo: Norwegian Institute of International Affairs, 1982.

Mutua, Makau wa. "Tanzania's Recent Economic Reform: An Analysis." *TransAfrica Forum* (Winter 1988): 69–85.

Mwanza, Allast. "Structural Adjustment Programmes in Tanzania and Zambia: Some Lessons for Late-Starters in SADCC." *Southern Africa* 7 (April 1991): 4–11.

Mwapachu, Juma Volter. *Management of Public Enterprises in Developing Countries: The Tanzania Experience*. New Delhi: IBH, 1983.

Mwene-Milao, Jalibu M.J. *Industrial Development in Tanzania: The Case of Crafts and Small-Scale Industries*. Bergen: Michelsen Institute, 1985.

Namaki, M.S.S. ed. "Future Organization, Planning and Control over Domestic Trade in Tanzania." *JEARD* 1 (1976): 61–68.

Ndulu, Benno. *Current Economic Stagnation in Tanzania: Causes and Effects*. Boston: African-American Issues Center, 1984.

Neerso, Peter. "Tanzania's Policies on Private Foreign Investment." *TAR* 1 (1974): 61–78.

Nnoli, Okwudiba. "External Stimuli and National Planning in Tanzania." *TAR* 1 (January 1972): 8–28.

Nsekela, A. J. "Role of Commercial Banking in Building a Socialist Tanzania." *TAR* 1 (1974): 25–42.

Nursey-Bray, P. F. "Tanzania: The Development Debate." *AA* 314 (January 1968): 55–78.

Nyang'oro, Julius E. "Nyerere and the Future of Tanzanian Public Policy." *TransAfrica Forum* 4 (1988): 3–17.

Okoko, Kimse. *Socialism and Self-reliance in Tanzania.* London: KPI Press, 1987.

O'Neill, Norman, and Kemal Mustafa, eds. *Capitalism, Socialism and the Development Crisis in Tanzania.* Brookfield, VT: Ashgate Publishing Company, 1990.

Orde-Browne, Granville St. John. *Labour Conditions in East Africa.* London: HMSO, 1946.

Parker, Ian C. "Ideological and Economic Development in Tanzania." *ASR* 1 (April 1972): 43–78.

Payer, Cheryl. *Tanzania and the World Bank.* Trenton: Africa Research and Publications Project, 1982.

———. "Tanzania and the World Bank." *Third World Quarterly* 4 (October 1983): 791–813.

Pratt, R. Cranford. "Administration of Economic Planning in a Newly Independent State: The Tanzanian Experience, 1963–1964." *Journal of Commonwealth Political Studies* 1 (March 1967): 38–59.

Putterman, Louis. "Economic Motivation and the Transition to Collective Socialism: Its Application to Tanzania." *JMAS* 2 (June 1982): 263–85.

Resnick, Idrian N. "Manpower Development in Tanzania." *JMAS* 1 (March 1967): 107–23.

Rutman, Gilbert L. *Economy of Tanganyika.* New York: Praeger, 1968.

Rwegasira, Kami S.P. "Financial Impact of Inflation on the Business Parastatal Sector in an I.D.C., Tanzania." *JEARD* (1981): 9–31.

———. "Financial Institutions in Tanzania: A Review of Performance and Problems." *JEARD* (1984): 112–46.

Rweyemamu, Anthony H. "Managing Planned Development: Tanzania's Experience." *JMAS* 1 (March 1966): 1–16.

Rweyemamu, Anthony H., and B. U. Mwansasu, eds. *Planning in Tanzania: Background to Decentralization.* Nairobi: EALB, 1974.

Rweyemamu, Justinian. *Underdevelopment and Industrialization in Tanzania.* Nairobi: OUP, 1973.

Rweyemamu, P. "From 'Fear Discipline' to Socialist Self-discipline: Problems of Organization and Democracy in Tanzania." *Taamuli* 2 (1973): 14–21.

Schnittger, L. *Development and Development Policy in East Africa: Tanzania.* Munich: IFO, 1965.

Sepheri, A. "Balance of Payments, Output, and Prices in Tanzania." *WD* 2 (February 1992): 289–302.

Shivji, Issa G. *Law, State and the Working Class in Tanzania, c. 1920–1964.* London: James Currey, 1986.

———. "Working Class Struggles and Organisation in Tanzania, 1939–1975." *Mawazo* 2 (1983): 3–24.

Shivji, Issa G., ed. *State and the Working People in Tanzania.* Dakar: CODESRIA, 1985.

Silver, M. S. *Growth of Manufacturing Industry in Tanzania: An Economic History.* Boulder: WP, 1984.

Singh, A. "Present Crisis of the Tanzanian Economy: Notes on the Economics and Politics of Devaluation." *Africa Development* 9 (1984): 36–49.

Smith, Hadley E. *Industrial Development in Tanzania.* Dar es Salaam: Institute of Public Administration, 1966.

Smith, Hadley E., ed. *Readings on Economic Development and Administration in Tanzania.* London: OUP, 1966.

Sogga, Gideon Ephraim. "Developmental Consequences of the Arusha Declaration on the Tanzanian Economy." Ph.D. diss., University of Pittsburgh, 1979.

Sundet, Geir. "Beyond Developmentalism in Tanzania." *ROAPE* 59 (1994): 39–49.

Svendsen, Knud Erik. *Tanzania's Recent Macroeconomic Policies: Report to the Swedish International Development Agency.* Copenhagen: Centre for Development Research, 1984.

Taguaba, Lugon. "Arusha Agreement: Origins, Meaning, and Future Association with the E.E.C." *TAR* 1/2 (1978): 156–84.

Tandau, A. C. *Historia ya Kuundwa kwa TFL (1955–1962) na Kuanzishwa kwa NUTA (1964).* Dar es Salaam: Mwananchi Publishing House, 1965).

Tanzania, Ministry of Economic Affairs and Development Planning. *Economic Recovery Programme II: Economic and Social Programme, 1989/90–1991/92.* Dar es Salaam: GP, 1990.

———. *Five Year Progress Report on the Implementation of the Five-Year Development Plan; Public Sector; July 1964 to June 1965.* Dar es Salaam: GP, 1965.

U.N. Trusteeship Council. *Outline of Working Conditions in the Trust-Territory of Tanganyika.* New York: United Nations, 1952.

United Republic of Tanzania. *Programme for Economic Recovery.* Dar es Salaam: GP, 1986.

———. *Second Five-Year Plan for Economic and Social Development, July 1969 to June 1974.* 4 vols. Dar es Salaam: GP, 1969.

———. *Structural Adjustment Programme for Tanzania.* Dar es Salaam: GP, 1982.

———. *Survey of Industries.* Dar es Salaam: Central Statistical Bureau, 1967.

———. *Tanganyika Five-Year Plan for Economic and Social Development, July, 1964 to June, 1969.* 2 vols. Dar es Salaam: GP, 1964.

Valentine, Theodore R. "Wage Adjustments, Progressive Tax Rates, and Accelerated Inflation: Issues of Equity in the Wage Sector of Tanzania." *ASR* 1 (March 1983): 51–71.

Van der Hoeven, R. *Meeting Basic Needs in a Socialist Framework: The Example of Tanzania.* Geneva: International Labour Organization, 1979.

Wagao, J. "Income Distribution in a Developing Country: The Case of Tanzania." Ph.D. diss., University of Sussex, 1981.

Wangwe, Samuel M. "Factors Influencing Capacity Utilisation in Tanzanian Manufacturing." *International Labour Review* 1 (January/February 1977): 65–77.

———. "Industrialization and Resource Allocation in a Developing Country: The Case of Recent Experiences in Tanzania." *WD* 6 (1983): 483–92.

Weaver, James H., and Alexander Kronemer. "Tanzanian and African Socialism." *WD* 9/10 (September/October 1981): 839–49.

Whitworth, Alan. "Price Control Techniques in Poor Countries: The Tanzanian Case." *WD* 6 (June 1982): 475–88.

World Bank. *Country Economic Memorandum: Tanzania.* Washington, D.C.: World Bank, 1981.

————. *Country Economic Memorandum: Tanzania*. Washington, D.C.: World Bank, 1984.

————. *Tanzania: Economic Report: Towards Sustainable Development in the 1990s*. Washington, D.C.: World Bank, 1991.

Yeager, Rodger. "Demography and Development Policy in Tanzania." *JDA* 4 (July 1982): 489–510.

H. General Studies

Austen, Ralph. *Northwest Tanzania under German and British Rule*. New Haven: YUP, 1968.

Barkan, Joel D., and John J. Okumu, ed. *Politics and Public Policy in Kenya and Tanzania*. New York: Praeger, 1978.

Brode, Heinrich. *British and German East Africa: Their Economic and Commercial Relations*. London: Edward Arnold, 1911.

Clarke, P.H.C. *A Short History of Tanganyika*. London: Longmans, Green, 1960.

Coulson, Andrew. *Tanzania: A Political Economy*. New York: OUP, 1982.

Hatch, John. *Tanzania: A Profile*. New York: Praeger, 1972.

Iliffe, John. *A Modern History of Tanganyika*. Cambridge: CUP, 1979.

————. *Modern Tanzanians*. Nairobi: EAPH for Historical Association of Tanzania, 1973.

Kaplan, Irving, ed. *Tanzania: A Country Study*, 2d edition. Washington, D.C.: USGPO, 1978.

Yeager, Rodger. *Tanzania: An African Experiment*, 2d, rev. ed. Boulder: WP, 1989.

I. Regional Studies

Acland, J. D. *East African Crops: An Introduction to the Production of Field and Plantation Crops in Kenya, Tanzania, and Uganda*. London: Longman for FAO, 1971.

Alpers, Edward A. *East African Slave Trade*. Nairobi: EAPH, 1967.

————. "French Slave Trade in East Africa (1721–1810)." *Cahiers d'Études Africaines* 37 (1970): 80–124.

————. *Ivory and Slaves: Changing Pattern of International Trade in East Central Africa to the Later Nineteenth Century*. Berkeley and Los Angeles: University of California Press, 1975.

Alpers, Edward A., and Christopher Ehret. "Eastern Africa." In *Cambridge History of Africa*, vol. 4, ed. Richard Gray, 469–576. Cambridge: CUP, 1975.

Anderson, David. "Depression, Dust Bowl, Demography, and Drought: The Colonial State and Soil Conservation in East Africa During the 1930s." *AA* 332 (July 1984): 321–41.

Apthorpe, Raymond, ed. *Land Settlement and Rural Development in East Africa*. Kampala: Transition Books, 1968.

Austen, Ralph A. "Nineteenth Century Islamic Slave Trade from East Africa (Swahili and Red Sea Coasts): A Tentative Census." *Slavery and Abolition* (December 1988): 21–44.

————. "Patterns of Development in Nineteenth Century East Africa" *AHS* 3 (1971): 645–57.

Baker, S.J.K. "Population Geography of East Africa." *East African Geographical Review* (April 1963): 1–6.

Balachandran, P. K. "Embattled Community: Asians in East Africa Today." *AA* 320 (July, 1981): 317–25.

Barkan, Joel D., ed. *Beyond Capitalism vs. Socialism in Kenya and Tanzania*. Boulder: Lynne Rienner Publishers, 1994.

Beachey, R. W. "East African Ivory Trade in the Nineteenth Century." *JAH* 2 (1967): 269–90.

————. *Slave Trade of Eastern Africa*. London: Rex Collings, 1976.

Bennet, Norman R. *Studies in East African History*. Boston: Boston University Press, 1963.

Berg-Schlosser, Dirk, and Rainer Siegler. *Political Stability and Development: A Comparative Analysis of Kenya, Tanzania, and Uganda*. Boulder: Lynne Rienner, 1990.

Bohnet, M., and H. Reichelt. *Applied Research and Its Impact on Economic Development: The East African Case*. Munich: IFO, 1972.

Brett, E. A. *Colonialism and Underdevelopment in East Africa: The Politics of Economic Change 1919–39*. London: Heinemann, 1973.

Brode, H. *British and German East Africa*. London: Edward Arnold, 1911.

————. *Tippo Tib*. London: Edward Arnold, 1907.

Brown, B. B. *Women and the Law in East Africa*. New York: Council for Inter-Cultural Studies and Programs, 1982.

Brown, Leslie. *East African Coasts and Reefs*. Nairobi: EAPH, 1975.

"Brushfire in East Africa." *AR* 2 (February 1964): 21–24.

Castle, E. B. *Growing Up in East Africa*. Oxford: OUP, 1966.

Chambers, Robert. *Managing Rural Development: Ideas and Experience from East Africa*. Uppsala: Scandinavian Institute of African Studies, 1974.

Chittick, H. Neville. "East Coast, Madagascar and the Indian Ocean." In *Cambridge History of Africa*, vol. 3, ed. Roland Oliver, 183–231. Cambridge: CUP, 1977.

————. " 'Shirazi' Colonization of East Africa." *JAH* 3 (1965): 275–94.

Chittick, H. Neville and Robert I. Rotberg, eds. *East Africa and the Orient: Cultural Synthesis in Pre-colonial Times*. New York: Africana Publishing Company, 1975.

Church, Archibald. *East Africa: A New Dominion*. London: H. F. and G. Witherby, 1927.

Clark, Paul G. *Development Planning in East Africa*. Nairobi: EAPH, 1966.

————. "Towards a More Comprehensive Planning in East Africa." *East Africa Economic Review* 2 (December 1963): 65–74.

Cliffe, Lionel. "Reflections on Agricultural Development in East Africa." *EAJ* 7 (November 1965): 26–35.

Cohen, Sir Andrew. *British Policy in Changing Africa*. London: Routledge and Kegan Paul, 1959.

Columbia University School of Law. *Public International Development Financing in East Africa*. New York: Columbia University Press, 1962.

Cotran, Eugene. "Unification of Laws in East Africa." *JMAS* 2 (June 1963): 209–20.

Coupland, Sir Reginald. *East Africa and Its Invaders, from the Earliest Times to the Death of Seyyid Said in 1856*. Oxford: Clarendon Press, 1938.

————. *Exploitation of East Africa, 1856–1890: The Slave Trade and the Scramble*. London: Faber and Faber, 1939.

Davidson, Basil. *East and Central Africa to the Late Nineteenth Century*. Nairobi: Longmans, 1967.

Davey, K. J. *Programme Budgeting for East Africa*. Nairobi: East African Staff College, 1972.

————. *Taxing a Peasant Society: The Example of Graduated Taxes in East Africa*. London: Charles Knight, 1974.

Delf, George. *Asians in East Africa*. London: OUP, 1963.

Diamond, Stanley, and Fred G. Burke. *Transformation of East Africa*. New York: Basic Books, 1966.

Due, J. F. "Reform of East African Taxation (Tanganyika, Kenya and Uganda)." *EAER* (December 1964): 57–68.

Durand, P. P. *Index to East African Cases Referred to, 1868–1968*. Nairobi: Legal Publications, 1969.

East African Institute of Social and Cultural Affairs. *Problems of Economic Development in East Africa*. Nairobi: EAPH, 1965.

East African Poll on Federation. Nairobi: Marco Publishers, 1962.

Ehret, C. "The East African Interior." In *Africa from the Seventh to the Eleventh Century*, ed. M. El Fasi, 616–42. London: Heinemann, 1988.

Elkan, Walter. "Some Social and Political Implications on Industrial Development in East Africa." *International Social Science Journal* 3 (September 1964): 390–400.

Engberg, H. L. "Commercial Banking in East Africa, 1950–1963." *JMAS* 2 (August, 1965): 175–200.

Franck, Thomas M. *East African Unity through Law*. New Haven: YUP, 1964.

Frank, C. S. *The Sugar Industry of East Africa*. Nairobi: EAPH, 1965.

Freeman Greenville, G.S.P. *The East African Coast: Select Documents*. Oxford: Clarendon Press, 1962.

Friedland, William H. "Some Urban Myths in East Africa." *Rhodes-Livingston Conference Proceedings* 14 (1960): 83–97.

Friedland, William H., et al. *Public International Development Financing in East Africa: Kenya, Tanganyika, Uganda*. New York: Columbia University Press, 1962.

Furley, O. W., and T. Watson. *History of Education in East Africa*. New York: NOK Publishers, 1977.

Galbraith, John S. *Mackinnon and East Africa, 1878–1895: A Study in the "New Imperialism."* Cambridge: CUP, 1972.

Garver, R. A., ed. *Research Priorities for East Africa*. Nairobi: EAPH, 1966.

Georgulas, Nikos. "Approach to Urban Analysis for East African Towns." *Ekistics* 109 (December 1964): 436–40.

Ghai, Dharam P., ed. *Portrait of a Minority: Asians in East Africa*. Nairobi: OUP, 1965.

————. *Taxation for Development in East Africa*. Nairobi: EAPH, 1967.

Githige, R. M. "Issue of Slavery: Relations Between the CMS and the State on the East African Coast Prior to 1895." *Journal of Religion in Africa* 3 (1986): 209–25.

Goldthorpe, J. E. *Outlines of East African Society*. Kampala: Makerere University College, 1959.

Goldthorpe, J. E., and F. B. Wilson. *Tribal Maps of East Africa and Zanzibar*. Kampala: East African Institute of Social Research, 1960.

Goodman, Stephen H. "Eastern and Western Markets for the Primary Products of East Africa." *EAER* (June 1967): 77–83.

Gray, C. S. "Development Planning in East Africa: A Review Article." *EAER* 2 (December 1966): 1–18.

Gregory, Robert G. *India and East Africa: A History of Race Relations within the British Empire, 1890–1939*. Oxford: OUP, 1971.

Gulliver, Philip Hugh, ed. *Tradition and Transition in East Africa*. Berkeley: University of California Press, 1969.

Hailey, Lord. *An African Survey*. London: OUP, 1957.

———. *Native Administration and Political Development in British Tropical Africa*. London: HMSO, 1940.

———. *Native Administration in British African Territories*, part 1. London: HMSO, 1950.

Hall, Susan. *Preferential Trade Area (PTA) for Eastern and Southern African States: Strategy, Progress, and Problems*. Nairobi: Institute for Development Studies, University of Nairobi, 1987.

Hamilton, A. C. *Environmental History of East Africa: A Study of the Quaternary*. London and New York: Academic Press, 1982.

Harlow, Vincent, and E. M. Chilver, eds. *History of East Africa*, vol. 2, Oxford: Clarendon Press, 1965

Hazlewood, Arthur. *Economic Integration: The East African Experience*. London: Heinemann, 1975.

———. *Rail and Road in East Africa: Transport Coordination in Underdeveloped Countries*. Oxford: Basil Blackwell, 1964.

Hazlewood, Arthur, Jane Armitage, Albert Berry, and Jon Knight. *Education, Work and Pay in East Africa*. Oxford: Clarendon, 1989.

Helleiner, G. K. "The Measurement of Aggregative Economic Performance in East Africa." *EAER* 1 (July 1968): 87–93.

Hollingsworth, Lawrence William. *Asians of East Africa*. London: St. Martins, 1960.

———. *Short History of the East Coast of Africa*. London: Macmillan, 1960.

Hughes, A. J. *East Africa: The Search for Unity*. Baltimore: Penguin Books, 1963.

Hutchinson, E. *Slave Trade of East Africa*. London: Low, Marston, Low, and Searle, 1874.

Hutton, John, ed. *Urban Challenge in East Africa*. Nairobi: EAPH, 1972.

Ingham, Kenneth. *History of East Africa*. London: Longmans, 1962.

Ireri, D. "Proposed Model to Analyse Economic Interdependence among the Member Countries of the East African Community." *East Africa Economic Review* (December 1969): 75–87.

Joelson, Ferdinand Stephen. *Eastern Africa Today*. London: East Africa, 1928.

Kanyinga, Karuti, Andrew S.Z. Kiondo, and Per Tidemand. *New Local Level Politics in East Africa: Studies on Uganda, Tanzania, and Kenya*. Uppsala: SIAS, 1994.

Khapoya, Vincent B., and Baffour Agyeman-Duah. "Cold War and Regional Politics in East Africa." *Conflict Quarterly* (Spring 1985): 18–32.

Kieran, J. "Origins of Commercial Arabica Coffee Production in East Africa." *AHS* 1 (1969): 51–67.

Leys, Colin, and Peter Robson, eds. *Federation in East Africa: Opportunities and Problems*. Nairobi: OUP, 1965.

Leys, Norman. *Colour Bar in East Africa*. London: Hogarth Press, 1941.

Low, D. A., and Alison Smith, eds. *History of East Africa*, vol. 3. Oxford: Clarendon Press, 1976.

Lugard, Sir Frederick D. *Rise of Our East African Empire*. 2 vols. London: Blackwood, 1893.

McEwen, A. C. *International Boundaries of East Africa*. London: OUP, 1971.

McLoughlin, Peter F.M. *Research on Agricultural Development in East Africa*. New York: Agricultural Development Council, 1967.

Malecela, John S. "What Next for the East African Community? The Case for Integration." *TAR* 1 (June 1972): 211–17.

Mangat, J. S. *History of Asians in East Africa c. 1886 to 1945*. Oxford: Clarendon Press, 1969.

Marlin, Peter, ed. *Financial Aspects of Development in East Africa*. Munich: Weltforum Verlag, 1970.

Marsh, Zoe. *East Africa through Contemporary Records*. London: CUP, 1961.

Marsh, Zoe, and G. W. Kingsnorth. *Introduction to the History of East Africa*. Cambridge: CUP, 1957.

Masao, F. T., and H. W. Mutoro. "East African Coast and the Comoros Islands." In *Africa from the Seventh to the Eleventh Century*, ed. M. El Fasi, 586–615. London: Heinemann, 1988.

Massell, Benton F. *Distribution of Economic Gains within the Common Market Formed by Kenya, Uganda and Tanganyika*. Santa Monica, CA: The Rand Corporation, 1964.

———. *East African Economic Union: An Evaluation and Some Implications for Policy*. Santa Monica, CA: The Rand Corporation, 1963.

———. *Economic Union in East Africa: An Evaluation of Gains*. Santa Monica, CA: The Rand Corporation, 1964.

———. "Industrialization and Economic Union in Greater East Africa." *EAER* 2 (December 1962): 108–23.

Mazrui, Ali. "Language and Politics in East Africa." *AR* (June 1967): 59–61.

———. "Socialized Capitalism in East Africa." *AQ* 3 (October/December 1966): 222–27.

———. "Tanzania versus East Africa: A Case of Unwitting Federal Sabotage." *Journal of Commonwealth Political Studies* 3 (November 1965): 209–25.

Mbilinyi, S. M. "East African Export Commodities and the Enlarged European Economic Community." *TAR* 1 (1973): 85–110.

Meeker, Michael E. *Pastoral Son and the Spirit of Patriarchy: Religion, Society and Person among East African Stock Keepers*. Madison: University of Wisconsin Press, 1989.

Meister, Albert. *East Africa: The Past in Chains, the Future in Pawn*. New York: Walker and Company, 1966.

Merritt, Herbert Paul. "Bismarck and the First Partition of East Africa." *English Historical Review* 360 (July 1976): 585–97.

Middleton, John. *World of the Swahili: An African Mercantile Civilization*. New Haven: YUP, 1992.

Morgan, D. J. *British Private Investment in East Africa: Report of a Survey and a Conference*. London: Overseas Development Institute, 1965.

Morgan, W. T. W. *East Africa*. London: Longman, 1973.

Morgan, W. T. W., ed. *East Africa: Its Peoples and Resources*. Nairobi: OUP, 1969.

Morris, Stephen. "Indians in East Africa: A Study in a Plural Society." *British Journal of Sociology* 3 (September 1956): 194–211.

Müller, Fritz Ferdinand. *Deutschland-Zanzibar-Ostafrika*. Berlin: Rütten u. Loening, 1959.

Nanjira, Daniel. *Status of Aliens in East Africa: Asians and Europeans in Tanzania, Uganda, and Kenya*. New York: Praeger, 1976.

Ndegwa, Philip. *Common Market and Development in East Africa*. Nairobi: EAPH for the East African Institute of Social Research, 1965.

Newlyn, W. T. "Gains and Losses in the East African Common Market." *Yorkshire Bulletin of Economic and Social Research* 2 (November 1965): 130–38.

Nye, Joseph S. "East African Economic Integration." *JMAS* 4 (December 1963): 475–502.

———. *Functionalism and Federalism in East Africa*. Geneva: International Political Science Association, 1964.

———. *Pan-Africanism and East African Integration*. Cambridge, MA: Harvard University Press, 1965.

Nyerere Doctrine of State Secession and the New States of East Africa. Arusha: EAPH, 1984.

O'Connor, Anthony M. *Economic Geography of East Africa*. London: Bell, 1966.

Odingo, R. S. "Geopolitical Problems of East Africa." *EAJ* 9 (February 1966): 17–24.

Ogot, Bethwell A., and J. A. Kieran, eds. *Zamani: A Survey of East African History*. Nairobi: EAPH, 1968.

Okoth, P. Godfrey. "Preferential Trade Area for Eastern and Southern African States and Its East African Community Heritage." *JEARD* (1990): 162–85.

Oliver, Roland. "East African Interior." In *Cambridge History of Africa*, vol. 3, ed. Roland Olover, 621–69. Cambridge: CUP, 1977.

Oliver, Roland, and Gervase Mathew, eds. *History of East Africa*, vol. 1. Oxford: Clarendon Press, 1976.

Oloya, J. J. *Some Aspects of Economic Development, With Special Reference to East Africa*. Nairobi: EALB, 1968.

Owen, D. F., ed. *Research and Development in East Africa*. Nairobi: EAPH, 1966.

Pandit, Shanti, ed. *Asians in East and Central Africa*. Nairobi: Panco Publications, 1963.

Pauw, E. J. *Banking in East Africa*. Munich: IFO, 1969.

Pocock, D. F. "Indians in East Africa, with Special Reference to their Social and Economic Situation and Relationship." D.Phil. thesis, Oxford University, 1955.

Problems of Economic Development in East Africa. Nairobi: East African Institute of Social and Cultural Affairs, 1965.

Proctor, J. C. "Efforts to Federate East Africa: A Post Mortem." *Political Quarterly* 1 (January/March 1966): 46–69.

Pruen, C. M. "Slavery in East Africa." *CMIR*, new series (1888): 661–65.

Ramchandani, R. R. "Indian Emigration to East African Countries during XIX and Early XX Centuries." *Journal of the University of Bombay* 77 (1972): 166–88.

Richards, Audrey I., ed. *East African Chiefs*. New York: Praeger, 1960.

Ricks, Thomas M. "Persian Gulf Seafaring and East Africa: Ninth-Twelfth Centuries." *AHS* 2 (1970): 339–57.

Roberts, A. D. "East Africa." In *Cambridge History of Africa*, vol. 7, ed. A. D. Roberts, 649–701. Cambridge: CUP, 1986.

Rotberg, Robert I. "Federation Movement in British East and Central Africa." *Journal of Commonwealth Political Studies* (May 1964): 141–60.
Rothchild, Donald, ed. *Politics of Integration: An East African Documentary*. Nairobi: EAPH, 1968.
Reusch, Richard. *History of East Africa*. Stuttgart: Evangelischer Missionsverlag, 1954.
Russell, E. W., ed. *Natural Resources of East Africa*. Nairobi: EALB, 1962.
Salim, A. I. "East African Coast and Hinterland, 1800–45." In *Africa in the Nineteenth Century Until the 1880s*, ed. J. F. Ade Ajayi, 211–33. Berkeley: University of California Press, 1989.
Saul, John S. *State and Revolution in Eastern Africa*. London and Nairobi: Heinemann, 1979.
Seavoy, Ronald E. *Famine in East Africa: Food Production and Food Policies*. New York: Greenwood Press, 1989.
Segal, Aaron. *East Africa: Strategy for Economic Co-operation*. Nairobi: East African Institute of Social and Cultural Affairs, 1965.
———. "Politics of Land in East Africa." *AR* 4 (April, 1967): 46–50.
———. "Postscript to East African Federation." *AR* 10 (October 1963): 12–13.
Seidman, Ann. *Comparative Development Strategies in East Africa*. Nairobi: EAPH, 1972.
Strandes, Justus. *Portuguese Period in East Africa*. Nairobi: EALB, 1968.
Sutton, John E.G. *Early Trade in Eastern Africa*. Nairobi: EAPH, 1973.
———. *East African Coast: An Historical and Archaeological Review*. Nairobi: EAPH, 1966.
———. *Thousand Years of East Africa*. Nairobi: British Institute in Eastern Africa, 1990.
Tandon, Yashpal, ed. *Technical Assistance Administration in East Africa*. Uppsala: Almqvist and Wiksell, 1973.
Thomas, P. A. *Private Enterprise and the Corporate Form in East Africa*. Nairobi: EAPH, 1968.
Twining, William. *Place of Customary Law in the National Legal Systems of East Africa*. Chicago: University of Chicago Law School, 1964.
Undmah A. C., and J. B. Webster. "East Africa: The Expansion of Commerce." In *Cambridge History of Africa*, vol. 5, ed. John E. Flint, 270–318. Cambridge: CUP, 1976.
Vente, Rolf E. *Planning Processes: The East African Case*. Munich: Weltforum Verlag, 1970.
Waller, Richard. "Ecology, Migration and Expansion in East Africa." *AA* 336 (July 1985): 347–70.
Ward, W. E. F., and L. W. White. *East Africa: A Century of Change 1870–1970*. New York: Africana Publishing Corporation, 1971.
Whitaker, Philip. *Political Theory and East African Problems*. London: OUP, 1964.
Who Wants an East African Federation. Nairobi: Marco Publishers, 1965.
Wright, Marcia. "East Africa, 1870–1905." In *Cambridge History of Africa*, vol. 6, ed. J. D. Fage and Roland Oliver, 539–91. Cambridge: CUP, 1985.
Zajadacs, Paul, ed. *Studies in Production and Trade in East Africa*. Munich: Weltforum Verlag, 1970.

J. Religion, Missions, and Missionaries

Allen, J.W.T. "Muslims in East Africa." *African Ecclesiastical Review* 3 (July 1965): 253–62.

Amiji, H. M. "Islam and Socio-economic Development: A Case Study of a Muslim Minority in Tanzania." *Journal of the Institute of Muslim Minority Affairs* (1982): 175–87.

Anderson, W. *Church in East Africa*. Dodoma: Central Tanganyika Press, 1977.

Anderson-Morshead, A.E.M. *History of the Universities' Mission to Central Africa 1859–1909*. London: Universities' Mission, 1909.

Bax, S. Napier. "Early Church Missionary Society Missions at Buzilima and Usambiro in the Mwanza District." *TNR* 7 (June 1939): 39–55.

Becker, Carl H. "Materials for the Understanding of Islam in German East Africa." *TNR* 68 (1968): 31–61.

Beidelman, T. O. *Colonial Evangelism: A Socio-Historical Study of an East African Mission at the Grassroots*. Bloomington: Indiana University Press, 1982.

———. "Organization and Maintenance of Caravans by the Church Missionary Society in Tanzania in the Nineteenth Century." *IJAHS* 4 (1982): 601–23.

———. "Witchcraft in Ukaguru." In *Witchcraft and Sorcery in East Africa*, ed. John Middleton and E. H. Winter, 57–98. London: Routledge and Kegan Paul, 1963.

Bernander, Gustav Addik. *Lutheran Wartime Assistance to Tanzanian Churches, 1940–1945*. Lund: Gleerup, 1968.

———. *Rising Tide: Christianity Challenged in East Africa*. Rock Island, IL: Augustana Press, 1957.

Catholic Church in Tanzania. Dar es Salaam: Publicity Department, Tanzania Episcopal Council, 1967.

Chambers, G. A. "Church in Central Tanganyika." *East and West Review* (1946): 75–78.

———. *Tanganyika's New Day*. London: CMS, 1931.

Cory, Hans. "Religious Beliefs and Practices of the Sukuma/Nyamwezi Tribal Group." *TNR* 54 (March 1960): 14–26.

Dale, Godfrey. "Some Curiosities of Mohammedan Belief in Zanzibar." *Central Africa* 492 (December 1923): 257–58.

———. "A Swahili Translation of the Koran." *MW* 1 (January 1924): 5–9.

Das, Narain. "Christianity and Islam in East Africa." *Indian Review* 9 (September 1929): 605–9.

Finch, F. G. "Hambageu: Some Additional Notes on the God of the Wasonjo." *TNR* 47/48 (June/September 1957): 203–8.

Fosbrooke, Henry A. "Hambageu, the God of the Wasonjo." *TNR* 35 (July 1953): 38–42.

Frankl, P. J. L. "Anglicanism in South-Eastern Tanganyika: 1876–1926." *TNR* 74 (July 1974): 1–10.

Freeman-Grenville, G.S.P. "Augustinian Missions in East Africa, 1596–1730." *Research Review* 1 (1965): 36–37.

G. F. S. "Closing of the Chagga Mission." *CMIR*, new series (1893): 246–55.

Gayet, Georges. "Zanzibar, Centre de l'Islam de l'Afrique orientale." *Politique Étrangère* 4 (1958): 376–88.

"German East Africa." *MW* (April 1912): 221–22.

"Germany and Islam in East Africa." *MW* (October 1918): 424–25.

Gottneid, Allan J., ed. *Church and Education in Tanzania*. Nairobi: EAPH, 1976.

Govig, Stewart D. "Religion and the Search for Socialism in Tanzania." *JAS* 3 (Fall 1987): 110–17.

Gray, Sir John Milner. *Early Portuguese Missionaries in East Africa*. London: Macmillan, 1958.

Groeschel, P. *Zehn Jahre Christlicher Kulturarbeit in Deutsch-Ostafrika*. Berlin: Berliner Mission, 1911.

Gutmann, Bruno. *Dichten und Danken des Dschagganeger*. Leipzig: Evangelisch-Lutherischen Mission, 1909.

———. *Das Dschaggaland und Seine Christen*. Leipzig: Evangelisch-Lutherischen Mission, 1925.

Hake, Andrew. "Decolonisation of the Church in East Africa." *EAJ* 11 (February 1967): 7–12.

Harries, Lyndon. *Islam in East Africa*. London: UMCA, 1954.

———. "Missionary on the East African Coast." *International Review of Missions* 138 (April 1946): 183–86.

Hellberg, Carl J. *Missions on a Colonial Frontier West of Lake Victoria: Evangelical Missions in North-West Tanganyika to 1932*. Lund: Berlingska Boktryckeriet, 1965.

———. "German Evangelical Mission and the Northwestern Boundaries of Tanganyika." *TNR* 58/59 (March/September 1967): 207–10.

Hellier, A. B. "Korogwe: Its Hopes and Difficulties." *Central Africa* 335 (November 1910): 291–94.

Hokororo, A. M. "Influence of the Church on Tribal Customs at Lukuledi." *TNR* 54 (March 1960): 1–13.

Holway, James D. "C.M.S. Contact with Islam in East Africa before 1914." *Journal of Religion in Africa* 3 (1972): 200–12.

Ingrams, Harold. "Islam and Africanism in Zanzibar." *New Commonwealth* 7 (July 1962): 427–30.

"Islam in Mikindani." *MW* (January 1944): 69–70.

Johnson, Victor Eugene. *Augustana Lutheran Mission of Tanganyika Territory*. Rock Island, IL: Augustana Book Concern, 1939.

Kaholwe, J. "Waislamu wa Tabora." *Kiongozi: Gazeti Katoliki* 5 (May, 1950): 68–69; 7 (July 1950): 101–3; and 8 (August 1950): 124–26.

Kaniki, M. H. Y. "Politics in the Usambara-Digo Lutheran Church, 1961–63." B.A. thesis, University College, Dar es Salaam, 1968.

Karstedt, F. O. "Zur Beurteilung des Islams in Deutsch-Ostafrika." *Koloniale Rundschau* 12 (1913): 728.

Kieran, John A. P. "Holy Ghost Fathers in East Africa, 1863 to 1914." Ph.D. diss., University of London, 1966.

Kijanga, Peter A. S. *Ujamaa and the Role of the Church in Tanzania*. Arusha: Evangelical Lutheran Church in Tanzania, [c. 1978].

Kiwanuka, K. Mayanja. "Politics of Islam in Bukoba District." B.A. thesis, University of Dar es Salaam, 1973.

Kjellberg, Eva. *Ismailis in Tanzania*. Dar es Salaam: Institute of Public Administration, University College of Dar es Salaam, 1967.

Klamroth, Martin. "Beitrage zum Verstandnis der Religiosen Vorstellungen der Saramo im Bezirk Daressalam Deutsch-Ostafrika." *Afrika und Übersee* (1910/1912): 189–223.

————. "Die Erste Deutsch-Ostafrikanische Missionskonferenz in Daressalam." *Allgemeine Missions-Zeitschrift* (1911): 519–29.

————. *Der Islam in Deutschostafrika.* Berlin: Buchhandlung der Berliner Evangelischen Missionsgesellschaft, 1912.

————. *Heidnische Religion und Islam in Ostafrika.* Berlin: Buchhandlung der Berliner Evangelischen Missionsgesellschaft, 1912.

————. "Religionsgespräche mit Einem Führer der Daressalamer Mohammedaner." *Beiblatt No. 5 zur Allgemeine Missions-Fieitschrift* (1913): 65–80.

Komba, James J. *God and Man: Religious Elements of the Ngoni of Southwestern Tanganyika Viewed in Light of Christian Faith.* Rome: Pontifica Universitas Urbanina de Propaganda Fide, 1961.

Knappert, Jan. "Divine Names." *Swahili,* new series, 31 (September 1966): 180–96.

————. "Swahili Islamic Terms." *Dini na Mila* 4 (November 1966): 6–22.

————. "Swahili Religious Terms." *Journal of Religion in Africa* 1 (1970): 67–80.

————. *Traditional Swahili Poetry: An Investigation into the Concepts of East African Islam As Reflected in the Utenzi Literature.* Leiden: Brill, 1967.

Krelle, H. "Beitrage zur Kenntnis der Saramoreligion." *Archiv für Anthropologie* (1935): 223–35.

Lamburn, R.G.P. "Some Notes on the Yao." *TNR* 29 (July 1950): 73–84.

Langford, Smith N. "Revival in East Africa." *International Review of Missions* 169 (January 1954): 77–81.

Last, J. T. "Ussagara Mission: Mamboia." *CMIR* (1891): 554–61.

Lema, Anza Amen. "Lutheran Church's Contribution to Education in Kilimanjaro." *TNR* 68 (February, 1968): 87–94.

McHugh, James F. "Islam in Tanganyika." *Worldmission* (Summer 1961): 18–21.

McLeish, Alexander. *Light and Darkness in East Africa.* London: World Dominion, 1927.

Magesa, Laurenti C. "Some Critical Theological and Pastoral Issues Facing the Church in East Africa." *African Christian Studies* (November/December 1988): 43–60.

Malishi, Lukas. *A History of the Catholic Church in Tanzania.* Dar es Salaam: Tanzania Episcopal Conference, 1990.

Middleton, John, and E. H. Winter, eds. *Witchcraft and Sorcery in East Africa.* London: Routledge and Kegan Paul, 1963.

Milhalyi, Louis J. "German Missionary Activity in the Usambara Highlands, 1885–1914." *EAJ* 2 (February 1971): 26–32.

"Missionary Problem in German East Africa." *MW* (April 1913): 220–21.

Nimtz, August H. *Islam and Politics in East Africa: The Sufi Order in Tanzania.* Minneapolis: University of Minnesota Press, 1980.

————. "Role of the Muslim Sufi Order in Political Change: An Overview and Micro-analysis from Tanzania." Ph.D. Diss., Indiana University, 1973.

Nolan, F. P. "Changing Role of Catechist in Tabora 1879–1967." In *African Initiatives in Religion,* ed. D. B. Barnett, 50–60. Nairobi: EAPH, 1971.

Ojiambo, Hilary H. "Psychology of Witchcraft." *EAJ* 4 (July 1956): 23–25.

Oliver, Roland. *Missionary Factor in East Africa.* London: Longmans, Green and Company, 1952.

Omari, C. K. "Episcopacy: A Sociological Trend in the Lutheran Church in Tanzania." *Africa Theological Journal* 1 (1987): 4–12.

––––––. *Essays on Church and Society in Tanzania.* Arusha: Evangelical Lutheran Church in Tanzania, 1976.

Peel, William George. "Troubles in German East Africa." *CMIR* (1906): 108–12.

––––––. "Usagara and Ugogo Revisited, 1902–1903." *CMIR* (1904): 109–19.

Pruen, C. M. "Some Features of Mpwapwa." *CMIR* (1887): 752–54.

––––––. "Through German East Africa." *CMIR* (1889): 97–107.

Pruen, S. T. "From London to Mpwapwa." *Church Missionary Gleaner* (1887): 40–41.

––––––. "A Visit to Mamboia." *Church Missionary Gleaner* (1888): 70–71.

Ranger, T. O. *African Churches of Tanzania.* Nairobi: EAPH, 1972.

Raum, O. "Dr. Gutmann's Work on Kilimanjaro: Critical Studies of His Theories of Missionary Methods." *International Review of Missions* (1937): 500–13.

Rees, D. J. "In the Berega Country." *Church Missionary Gleaner* (1913): 154–55.

Rees, D. J., and E. Baxter. "German East Africa." *Church Missionary Review* (1912): 156–61.

Richter, Julius. *Tanganyika and its Future.* London: World Dominion Press, 1934.

Robinson, D. W. "Church in Tanganyika." *African Ecclesiastical Review* (July 1963): 256–64.

Schacht, Joseph. "Notes on Islam in East Africa." *Studia Islamica* (1965): 91–136.

Scholten, Heinz. "Growth and Expansion of an East African Church." *International Review of Missions* 155 (July 1950): 270–76.

Shorter, Aylward. "Spirit Possession and Christian Healing in Tanzania." *AA* 314 (January 1980): 45–53.

Sicard, Sigvard von. "First Ecumenical Conference in Tanzania, 1911." *Bulletin of the Society for African Church History* (1968): 323–33.

––––––. *Lutheran Church on the Coast of Tanzania 1887–1914.* Lund: Gleerup, 1970.

––––––. "Lutheran Church on the Coast of Tanzania: The War Years, 1914–1920." *Africa Theological Journal* 2 (1986): 91–102.

Simenauer, E. "Miraculous Birth of Hambageu, Hero-God of the Sonjo: A Tanganyikan Theogony." *TNR* 38 (March 1955): 23–30.

Smedjebacka, Henrik. *Lutheran Church Autonomy in Northern Tanzania 1940–1963.* Abo: Abo Akademi, 1973.

Smith, Anthony. "Missionary Contribution to Education (Tanganyika) to 1914." *TNR* 60 (March 1963): 91–109.

Smith, Peter D. "An Experience of Christian-Muslim Relations in Tanzania." *African Ecclesiastical Review* (April 1988): 106–11.

Stirnimann, Hans. "Zur Gesellschaftsordnung und Religion der Pangwa." *Anthropos* (1967): 394–418.

Sundkler, B.G.M. "Marriage Problems in the Church in Tanganyika." *International Review of Missions* 135 (1945): 253–66.

Swantz, Lloyd W. *Church, Mission and State Relations in Pre and Post-independent Tanzania 1955–1964.* Syracuse: Syracuse University, 1965.

Tanner, Ralph E.S. "Sukuma Ancestor Worship and Its Relationship to Social Structure." *TNR* 50 (June 1958): 52–62.

––––––. *Transition in African Beliefs: Traditional Religion and Christian Change:*

A Study in Sukumaland, Tanzania, East Africa. Maryknoll, NY: Maryknoll Publications, 1967.

Trimingham, J. Spencer. *Islam in East Africa.* London: Edinburgh House Press, 1962.

Versteijnen, Frits. *Catholic Mission at Bagamoyo.* Bagamoyo: n.p., 1968.

Watt, W. Montgomery. "Political Relevance of Islam in East Africa." *International Affairs* 1 (January 1966): 35–44.

Welbourn, Frederick Burkewood. *East African Rebels: A Study of Some Independent Churches.* London: Society of Christian Missions Press, 1961.

Westerlund, David. "Christianity and Socialism in Tanzania: 1967–1977." *Journal of Religion in Africa* 1 (1980): 30–55.

———. "Freedom of Religion under Socialist Rule in Tanzania, 1961–1977." *Journal of Church and State*, (Winter 1982): 87–103.

Willis, Roy G. "Changes in Mystical Concepts and Practices among the Fipa." *Ethnology* (1968): 139–57.

———. "Kamcape: An Anti-sorcery Movement in South-West Tanzania." *Africa* (1968): 1–15.

———. "Kaswa: Oral Tradition of a Fipa Prophet." *Africa* (1970): 248–56.

Wilson, George Herbert. *History of the UMCA.* London: Universities' Mission, 1936.

Wilson, Monica. *Communal Rituals of the Nyakyusa.* London: OUP, 1959.

Wolf, James B., ed. *Missionary to Tanganyika, 1877–1888: The Writings of Edward Coode Hore, Master Mariner.* London: Frank Cass, 1971.

Wright, Marcia. "German Evangelical Missions in Tanganyika, 1891–1939, with Special Reference to the Southern Highlands." Ph.D. diss., University of London, 1966.

———. *German Missions in Tanganyika, 1891–1941: Lutherans and Moravians in the Southern Highlands.* Oxford: Clarendon Press, 1971.

K. Ethnography, Sociology, and Folklore

Abrahams, Ray. *Nyamwezi Today: A Tanzanian People in the 1970s.* Cambridge: CUP, 1981.

———. *Peoples of Greater Unyamwezi.* London: International African Institute, 1967.

———. *Political Organisation of Unyamwezi.* Cambridge: CUP, 1967.

———. *Villagers, Villages, and the State in Modern Tanzania.* Cambridge: African Studies Centre, 1985.

———. *Witchcraft in Contemporary Tanzania.* Cambridge: African Studies Centre, 1994.

Beidelman, T. O. *Matrilineal Peoples of Eastern Tanzania.* London: International African Institute, 1967.

Cory, Hans. *African Figurines: Their Ceremonial Use in Puberty Rites in Tanganyika.* London: Faber and Faber, 1956.

———. "The Buyeye: A Secret Society of Snake-Charmers in Sukumaland, Tanganyika Territory." *Africa* 3 (July 1946): 160–78.

————. *Ntemi: The Traditional Rule of a Sukuma Chief in Tanganyika*. London: Macmillan, 1951.

————. *Indigenous Political System of the Sukuma*. Nairobi: Eagle Press, 1954.

————. "Religious Beliefs and Practices of the Sukuma/Nyamwezi Tribal Group." *TNR* 54 (March 1960): 14–26.

————. *Wall-Painting by Snake Charmers in Tanganyika*. New York: Grove Press, 1953.

Culwick, A. T., and G. M. Culwick. *Ubena of the Rivers*. London: George Allen and Unwin, 1935).

Feierman, Steven. "Concepts of Sovereignty among the Shambaa and Their Relation to Political Action." D.Phil. thesis, Oxford University, 1972.

————. *Peasant Intellectuals: Anthropology and History in Tanzania*. Madison: University of Wisconsin Press, 1990.

————. *Shambaa Kingdom: A History*. Madison: University of Wisconsin Press, 1974.

Gray, Robert F. *Sonjo of Tanganyika: An Anthropological Study of an Irrigation-Based Society*. London: OUP, 1963.

Gulliver, Philip Hugh. *Neighbours and Networks*. Berkeley: University of California Press, 1971.

Harwood, Alan. "Witchcraft, Sorcery, and Social Classification in a Bantu-Speaking Tribe of South-Western Tanzania." Ph.D. diss., Columbia University, 1967.

————. *Witchcraft, Sorcery, and Social Categories Among the Safwa*. London: OUP, 1970.

Mackenzie, Duncan R. *Spirit-Ridden Konde*. London: Seeley, Service and Company, 1925.

Maguire, Gene Andrew. *Toward "Uhuru" in Tanzania: A Study in Micro Politics in Sukumaland, 1945–1959*. Cambridge: CUP, 1969.

Malcolm, Donald W. *Sukumaland: An African People and Their Country: A Study of Land Use in Tanganyika*. London: OUP, 1953.

Mdee, Abdullah A. "Kinloss Prize, 1961: Some Experiences of Witchcraft." *TNR* 57 (September 1961): 149–52.

Moore, Sally Falk, and Paul Puritt. *Chagga and Meru of Tanzania*. London: International Affairs Institute, 1977.

Moreau, R. E. "The Joking Relationship (Utani) in Tanganyika." *TNR* 12 (December, 1941): 1–10.

Mtoro bin Mwinyi Bakari. *Customs of the Swahili People: The Desturi za Waswahili*, ed. J. W. T. Allen. Berkeley: University of California Press, 1981.

Puritt, Paul. "Meru of Tanzania: A Study of Their Social and Political Organization." Ph.D. diss., University of Illinois, 1970.

Raum, Otto Friedrich. *Chaga Childhood*. Oxford: OUP, 1940.

Redmayne, Alison H. "Wahehe People of Tanganyika." Ph.D. diss., Oxford University, 1964.

Redmond, Patrick M. *Politics of Power in Songea Ngoni Society, 1860–1962*. Chicago: Adams, 1985.

Scherer, J. H. "Ha of Taanganyika." *Anthropos* 5/6 (1959): 841–904.

Shorter, Aylward. *Chiefship in Western Tanzania*. Oxford: Clarendon Press, 1972.

Snyder, Katherine Ann. " 'Like Water and Honey': Moral Ideology and the Construction of Community among the Iraqw of Northern Tanzania." Ph.D. diss., Yale University, 1993.

Stahl, Kathleen. *History of the Chagga People of Kilimanjaro.* The Hague: Mouton, 1964.
———. "Outline of Chagga History." *TNR* 64 (March 1965): 35–49.
Swantz, Marja-Liisa. *Ritual and Symbol in Transitional Zaramo Society.* Uppsala: SIAS, 1986.
Tanner, Ralph E.S. "Magician in Northern Sukumaland, Tanganyika." *Southwestern Journal of Anthropology* 4 (1957): 344–51.
———. "Sorcerer in Northern Sukumaland, Tanganyika." *Southwestern Journal of Anthropology* (1956): 437–43.
———. *Witch Murders in Sukumaland: A Sociological Commentary.* Uppsala: SIAS, 1970.
Van Pelt, P. *Bantu Customs in Mainland Tanzania.* Tabora: T. P. M. Book Department, 1982.
Wilson, Monica Hunter. *Communal Rituals of the Nyakyusa.* London: OUP, 1959.
———. *Peoples of the Nyasa-Tanganyika Corridor.* Cape Town: University of Cape Town, 1958.
Winans, Edgar V. *Shambala: The Constitution of a Traditional State.* Berkeley and Los Angeles: University of California Press, 1962.
Young, Roland, and Henry Fosbrooke. *Smoke in the Hills: Political Tension in the Morogoro District of Tanganyika.* Evanston, IL: Northwestern University Press, 1960.

L. Agriculture, Land, Tenure, and Local Administration

"Agricultural Credit in Tanzania: A Peasant Perspective." *Savings Development* 4 (1987): 379–402.
Asmerom, H. K. "Tanzanian Village Council: Agent of Rural Development or Merely Device of State Penetration into the Periphery?" *Cahiers du CEDAF* 4 (1986): 177–97.
Awiti, Adhu. "Economic Differentiation in Ismani, Iringi Region: A Critical Assessment of Peasants' Response to the Ujamaa Vijinini Programme." *TAR* 2 (1973): 209–39.
Barker, Jonathan S. "Ujamaa in Cash-Crop Areas of Tanzania: Some Problems and Reflections." *JAS* 4 (Winter 1974): 441–63.
Bellamy, J. *Cotton Industry of Tanganyika.* Dar es Salaam: Lint and Seed Marketing Board, 1963.
Bernstein, Henry. "Notes on State and Peasantry: The Tanzanian Case." *ROAPE* 21 (May/September 1981): 44–62.
Binhammer, H. H. *Institutional Arrangements for Supplying Credit and Finance to the Rural Sector of the Economy in Tanzania.* Dar es Salaam: Economic Research Bureau, University of Dar es Salaam, 1968.
Blue, R. N., and J. H. Weaver. *Critical Assessment of the Tanzanian Model of Development.* Washington, D.C.: U. S. Agency for International Development, 1977.
Boesen, Jannik, B. S. Madsen, and T. Moody. *Ujamaa: Socialism from Above.* Uppsala: SIAS, 1977.
Boesen, Jannik, and A. T. Mohele. *"Success Story" of Peasant Tobacco Production*

in Tanzania: The Political Economy of a Commodity Producing Peasantry. Uppsala: SIAS, 1980.

Booth, D. "Economic Liberalization, Real Markets, and the (Un) Reality of Structural Adjustment in Rural Tanzania." *Sociologia Ruralis* 1 (1994): 45–62.

Brain, James L. "Is Transformation Possible? Styles of Settlement in Post-independence Tanzania." *AA* 303 (1977): 231–45.

———. "The Uluguru Land Usage Scheme: Success and Failure." *JDA* 14 (January 1980): 175–90.

Bridger, G. A. *Peasant Tea Production in Tanganyika.* Addis Ababa: Economic Commission for Africa, 1961.

Bryceson, Deborah Fahy. "Changes in Peasant Food Production and Food Supply in Relation to the Historical Development of Commodity Production in Pre-colonial and Colonial Tanganyika." *Journal of Peasant Studies* 3 (1980): 281–311.

———. *Food Insecurity and the Social Division of Labour in Tanzania, 1919–1985.* London: St. Martin's Press, 1990.

———. "Peasant Cash Cropping versus Self-sufficiency in Tanzania: A Historical Perspective." *Institute of Development Studies Bulletin* 2 (April 1988): 37–46.

———. "Peasant Commodity Production in Post-Colonial Tanzania." *AA* 325 (October 1982): 547–67.

———. *Second Thoughts on Marketing Co-operatives in Tanzania: Background to Their Re-instatement.* Oxford: Plunkett Foundation for Co-operative Studies, 1983.

Chant, J. *Some Problems of Agricultural Credit in Tanzania.* Kampala: Makerere Institute of Social Research, 1968.

Chipungu, Samuel N. "Social Stratification in Relation to Cattle-Marketing in Rural Sukumaland, 1951–1961." *JEARD* (1982): 57–72.

Clemm, Michael von. "Agricultural Productivity and Sentiment on Kilimanjaro." *Economic Botany* (1964): 99–121.

———. "People of the White Mountain: The Interdependence of Political and Economic Activity amongst the Chagga in Tanganyika with Special Reference to Recent Changes." Ph.D. diss., Oxford University, 1962.

Cliffe, Lionel. "Policy of Ujamaa Vijijini and the Class Struggle in Tanzania." *Rural Africana* 13 (Winter 1971): 5–27.

Cliffe, Lionel, et al., eds. *Rural Cooperation in Tanzania.* Dar es Salaam: TPH, 1975.

Collette, Suda. "Agricultural Development Policies and Institutional Support Systems in Post Colonial Kenya and Tanzania." *JEARD* (1990): 104–26.

Collier, Paul, Samir Radwan, and Samuel Wangwe with Albert Wagner. *Labour and Poverty in Rural Tanzania: Ujamaa and Rural Development in the United Republic of Tanzania.* Oxford: Clarendon, 1986.

Collins, P. "Working of Tanzania's Rural Development Fund: A Problem in Decentralisation." *East African Journal of Rural Development* 1/2 (1972): 141–62.

Coulson, Andrew. "Agricultural Policies in Mainland Tanzania 1946–1976." *Review of African Political Economy* 10 (1978): 74–100.

———. "Crop Priorities for the Lowlands of Tanga Region." *TNR* 81/82 (1977): 43–54.

———. "Tanzania's Fertilizer Factory." *JMAS* 1 (March 1977): 119–125.

Cunningham, Griffiths. "Ujamaa Village Movement in Tanzania." *Rural Africana* 13 (Winter 1971): 28–35.

――――. "Peasants and Rural Development in Tanzania." *AT* 4 (Fall 1973): 3–18.

Dobson, E.B. "Land Tenure of the Wasambaa." *TNR* 10 (December 1940): 1–27.

Dryden, Stanley. *Local Administration in Tanzania*. Nairobi: EAPH, 1968.

Due, Jean M. "Allocation of Credit to Ujamaa Villages in Tanzania and Small Farms in Zambia." *ASR* 3 (December 1980): 33–48.

Eden, T. *Report on the Possible Extension of Tea Cultivation in Tanganyika*. Dar es Salaam: GP, 1956.

Edie, Carlene J. "Socialism, the State, and Rural Development in Tanzania and Jamaica." *JAS* 3 (Fall 1987): 141–51.

Ellis, Frank. "Agricultural Marketing and Peasant-State Transfers in Tanzania." *Journal of Peasant Studies* 4 (July 1983): 214–42.

――――. "Agricultural Price Policy in Tanzania." *WD* 4 (April 1982): 263–83.

――――. "Prices and the Transformation of Peasant Agriculture: The Tanzanian Case." *Institute of Development Studies Bulletin* 4 (1982): 66–72.

Ergas, Zaki. "Why Did the Ujamaa Village Policy Fail? Towards a Global Analysis." *JMAS* 3 (September 1980): 387–410.

Eriksson, Gun. *Peasant Response to Price Incentives in Tanzania: A Theoretical and Empirical Investigation*. Uppsala: SIAS, 1993.

Fair, T.D.J. "Rural Development in Tanzania. *Africa Insight* 2 (1984): 78–82.

Feierman, Steven. *Peasant Intellectuals: Anthropology and History in Tanzania*. Madison: University of Wisconsin Press, 1990.

Feldman, Rayah. "Custom and Capitalism: Changes in the Basis of Land Tenure in Ismani, Tanzania. *Journal of Development Studies* 3/4 (1974): 305–20.

――――. *Ismani: Agricultural Change and the Politics of Ujamaa*. Norwich: School of Development Studies, University of East Anglia, 1983.

Finucane, James R. *Rural Development and Bureaucracy in Tanzania: The Case of Mwanza Region*. Uppsala: SIAS, 1974.

Fleuret, Patrick. "Sources of Material Inequality in Lushoto District, Tanzania. *ASR* 3 (December 1980): 69–88.

Forster, Peter, and Sam Maghimbi, eds. *Tanzanian Peasantry: Economy in Crisis*. Brookfield, VT: Avebury, 1992.

Fortmann, Louise. *Peasants, Officials and Participation in Rural Tanzania: Experience with Villagization and Decentralization*. Ithaca: Rural Development Committee, Cornell University, 1980.

Fuggles-Couchman, N. R. *Agricultural Change in Tanganyika, 1945–1960*. Stanford: Food Research Institute, 1964.

Gasarasi, Charles P. *Tripartite Approach to the Resettlement and Integration of Rural Refugees in Tanzania*. Uppsala: SIAS, 1984.

Geiger, Susan. "Umoja wa Wanawake wa Tanzania and the Needs of the Rural Poor." *ASR* 2/3 (June/September 1982): 45–65.

Georgulas, Nikos. *Approach to the Economic Development of Rural Areas in Tanganyika, with Special Reference to the Village Settlement Program*. Syracuse: Program for Eastern African Studies, Syracuse University, 1964.

――――. *Settlement Patterns and Rural Development in Tanganyika*. Syracuse: Program for Eastern African Studies, Syracuse University, 1967.

Giblin, James L. "Peasant Self-Sufficiency in Tanzania: Precolonial Legacy or Colonial Imposition?" In *Sustainable Agriculture in Africa*, ed. E. Ann McDougall, 257–72. Trenton, NJ: Africa World Press, 1990.

Gibogwe, V. "A Critical Assessment of Capital Supply to Rural Small-Scale Industries in Tanzania." *Small Enterprise Development* 3 (September 1991): 49–53.

Gottleib, Manuel. "The Extent and Characterisation of Differentiation in Tanzanian Agricultural and Rural Society." *TAR* 2 (1973): 241–62.

Graham, James D. "Case Study of Migrant Labor in Tanzania." *ASR* 1 (April 1970): 23–33.

————. "Changing Patterns of Wage Labor and European Capitalism in Njombe District, 1913–1961." Ph.D. diss., Northwestern University, 1968.

Green, R. H., D. G. Rwegasira, and B. Van Arkadie. *Economic Shocks and National Policy Making: Tanzania in the 1970s*. The Hague: Institute for Social Studies, 1980.

Guillebaud, Claude Williams. *Economic Survey of the Sisal Industry of Tanganyika*. London: Nisbet, 1966.

Gulliver, Philip Hugh. *Labour Migration in a Rural Economy*. Nairobi: EALB, 1955.

————. *Land Tenure and Social Change among the Nyakyusa*. Kampala: East African Institute of Social Research, 1958.

————. *Social Control in an African Society*. London: Routledge and Kegan Paul, 1963.

Hadjivayanis, Georgios G. "Perverse Capitalism in Agriculture: A Study of Nyandira Village." *Eastern Africa Social Science Research Review* 1 (January 1987): 75–110.

Havnevik, Kjell J. *Tanzania: The Limits to Development from Above*. Uppsala: SIAS, 1993.

Havnevik, Kjell J., and Rune Skarstein. *Agricultural Decline and Foreign Aid in Tanzania*. Bergen: Michelsen Institute, 1985.

Hedlund, Stefan, and M. Lundahl. *Ideology As a System Determinant: Nyerere and Ujamaa in Tanzania*. Uppsala: SIAS, 1989.

Hitchcock, Sir E. "Sisal Industry of East Africa." *TNR* 52 (1959): 4–17.

Hydén, Göran. *Beyond Ujamaa in Tanzania: Underdevelopment and an Uncaptured Peasantry*. London: Heinemann Educational Books, 1980.

————. *Political Development in Rural Tanzania: TANU Yajenga Nchi*. Nairobi: EAPH, 1969.

————. "Ujamaa, Villagisation, and Rural Development in Tanzania." *ODI Review* 1 (1975): 53–72.

Hydén Göran, ed. *Cooperatives in Tanzania*. Dar es Salaam: TPH, 1976.

Iliffe, John. *Agricultural Change in Modern Tanganyika*. Nairobi: EAPH, 1971.

Ingle, Clyde R. "Compulsion and Rural Development in Tanzania." *CJAS* 1 (Winter 1970): 77–100.

————. *From Village to State in Tanzania: The Politics of Rural Development*. Ithaca: Cornell University Press, 1972.

Jack, D. T. *Report on the State of Industrial Relations in the Sisal Industry*. Dar es Salaam: GP, 1959.

Jervis, T. "History of Robusta Coffee in Bukoba." *TNR* 8 (December 1939): 47–58.

Kaitilla, Sababu. "Upgrading of Squatter Settlements in Tanzania: The Role of Security of Land Tenure and the Provision of Amenities in Housing Improvement." *Journal of Asian and African Studies* 3/4 (1991): 220–36.

Kent, A. W. *Report of the Services to be Administered by Local Authorities in Tanganyika and the Consequential Financial Arrangements*. Dar es Salaam: GP, 1963.

Kirilo, Japhet, and E. Seaton. *Meru Land Case*. Nairobi: EAPH, 1967.

Kjaerby, Finn. *Problems and Contradictions in the Development of Ox-Cultivation in Tanzania*. Uppsala: SIAS, 1983.

Kjekshus, Helge. "Tanzanian Villagization Policy: Implementational Lessons and Ecological Dimensions." *CJAS* 2 (1977): 269–82.

Kleemeier, Lizz. "Domestic Policies versus Poverty-Oriented Foreign Assistance in Tanzania." *Journal of Development Studies* 2 (1984): 171–201.

———. "Integrated Rural Development in Tanzania." *Public Administration and Development* (January/March 1988): 61–74.

———. "Tanzanian Policy towards Foreign Assistance in Rural Development: Insights Drawn from a Study of Regional Integrated Development Programs." *Taamuli* 1/2 (1982): 62–85.

Kocher, James E. *Rural Development and Fertility Change in Tropical Africa: Evidence from Tanzania*. East Lansing: Michigan State University, 1979.

Lee, Eugene C. *Local Taxation in Tanzania*. London: OUP, 1965.

Lemarchand, René. "Village-by-Village Nation Building in Tanzania." *AR* 2 (February 1965): 11–13.

Liviga, A. J. "Local Government in Tanzania: Partners in Development or Administrative Agent for Central Government?" *Local Government Studies* 3 (1992): 208–25.

Lofchie, Michael F. "Agrarian Crisis and Economic Liberalisation in Tanzania." *JMAS* 3 (September 1978): 451–475.

———. "Agrarian Socialism in the Third World: The Tanzania Case." *Comparative Politics* 3 (April 1976): 479–99.

———. *Policy Factor: Agriculture Performance in Kenya and Tanzania*. Boulder: Lynne Rienner Publishers, 1988.

Lomoy, Jon. *Planning Spatial Change: The Use of Settlement Pattern as a Planning Variable in Kigoma, Tanzania*. Trondheim, Norway: Department of Geography, University of Trondheim, 1982.

Lwoga, C.M.F. "Development Plans and Rural Development Strategies in Tanzania, 1961–1981: A Critical Review." *JEARD* (1989): 102–18.

———. "Historical Roots of the Labour Shortage Problem in the Sisal Industry in Tanzania: Contradictions of the Cheap Labour System." *JEARD* (1987): 18–33.

McHenry, Dean E. "Communal Farming in Tanzania: A Comparison of Male and Female Participants." *ASR* 4 (December 1982): 49–64.

———. *Tanzania's Ujamaa Villages: The Implementation of a Rural Development Strategy*. Berkeley: University of California, Institute of International Studies, 1979.

———. "The Utility of Compulsion in the Implementation of Agricultural Policies: A Case Study from Tanzania." *CJAS* 2 (1973): 305–16.

Maeda, Justin H. J. "Peasant Organisation and Participation in Tanzania." In *Studies in Rural Participation*, ed. Amit Bhaduri and M. D. Anisur Rahman, 15–33. New Delhi: OUP, 1982.

Magoti, Charles K. *Peasant Participation and Rural Productivity in Tanzania: The Case of Mara Cotton Producers, 1955–1977*. Hamburg: Institut für Afrika-Kunde, 1984.

Makere, E.N. "Ujamaa Villages in Practice." *Taamuli* 2 (1972): 17–26.

Manning, Diana Louise. "Spatial Structure of Development in the United Republic of Tanzania: With an Analytical Framework for Small Scale Agro-Related Activities in the Mbeya Region." Ph.D. diss., Cornell University, 1991.

Maro, Paul S. "Impact of Decentralization on Spatial Equity and Rural Development in Tanzania." *WD* 5 (May 1990): 673–93.

Mbilinyi, Marjorie. "Agribusiness and Casual Labor in Tanzania." *African Economic History* (1986): 107–41.

Miller, Norman N. "Village Leadership and Modernization in Tanzania: Rural Politics Among the Nyamwezi People of the Tabora Region." Ph.D. diss., Indiana University, 1966.

Mlambiti, M. E. "Rural Development: The Tanzania Type." *TNR* 79/80 (1976): 1–12.

Mlawa, Hasa Mfaume. "Technology Policy and Planning in the Informal Sector: The Case of Food, Agriculture, and Energy in Tanzania." *Afrique Développement* 1 (1986): 47–60.

Monson, Jamie. "Agricultural Transformation in the Inner Kilombero Valley of Tanzania, 1840–1940." Ph.D. diss., University of California, 1991.

Moris, Jon R. "Administrative Authority and the Problem of Effective Agricultural Administration in East Africa." *Africa Review* (June 1972): 105–46.

Moshiro, Gervas. "Impact of Information on Rural Development: A Case Study of the Community Media for Rural Development Project (Tanzania)." In *Communication Processes: Alternative Channels and Strategies for Development Support*, 21–30. Ottawa: International Development Research Centre, 1991.

Mothander, Björn, Finn Kjaerby, and Kjell Havnevik. *Farm Implements for Small-Scale Farmers in Tanzania*. Uppsala: SIAS, 1989.

Nindi, B. C. "Agriculture Change in Tanzania: With Examples from Iringa Region." *TJH* (1985): 101–11.

———. "Evolution of Agricultural Marketing Institutions and the Public versus Private Debate in Tanzania." *TJH* (1990): 117–38.

———. "Institutional Forms of Government Agricultural Marketing in Tanzania." *JEARD* (1989): 95–101.

———. "State Intervention, Contradictions, and Agricultural Stagnation in Tanzania: Cashew Nuts vs. Charcoal Production." *Public Administration and Development* 4 (July/August 1991): 307–24.

———. "Traditional Agricultural Extension System in Tanzania: A Critical Analysis." *JEARD* (1986): 122–33.

Nyerere, Julius K. *Socialism and Rural Development*. Dar es Salaam: GP, 1967.

Oldaker, A. A. *Interim Report on Tribal Customary Land Tenure in Tanganyika*. Dar es Salaam: GP, 1957.

———. "Tribal Customary Land Tenure in Tanganyika." *TNR* 47/48 (June/September 1957): 117–44.

Omari, C. K. "Tanzania's Emerging Rural Development Policy." *AT* 3 (1974): 9–14.

Omari, C. K., ed. *Towards Rural Development in Tanzania: Some Issues on Policy Implications in the 1970s*. Arusha: Eastern Africa Publications, 1984.

Parker, Ian C. "Ideological and Economic Development in Tanzania." *ASR* 1 (April 1972): 43–78.

Penner, R. G. *Financing Local Government in Tanzania*. Nairobi: EAPH, 1970.

Putterman, Louis. *Peasants, Collectives, and Choice: Economic Theory and Tanzania's Villages*. Greenwich, CT: Jai (Johnson Associates, Inc.), 1986.

————. "Village Communities, Cooperation, and Inequality in Tanzania: Comments on Collier et al." *WD* 1 (January 1990): 147–53.

Raikes, Philip. "State and Peasantry in Tanzania." In *Rural Development: Theories of Peasant Economy and Agrarian Change*, ed. John Hariss, 350–80. London: Hutchinson University Library for Africa, 1982.

Rald, Jorgen, and Karen Rald. *Rural Organization in Bukoba District, Tanzania.* New York: Holmes and Meier, 1976.

Redmond, P. "The NMCMU and Tobacco Production in Songea." *TNR* 79/80 (1976): 65–98.

Republic of Tanzania, Ministry of Agriculture. *Agricultural Policy of Tanzania.* Dar es Salaam: GP, 1983.

————. *Tanzania National Agricultural Policy (Final Report).* Dar es Salaam: GP, 1982.

Rimmer, Martin. "From Bad to . . . Not Quite So Bad." *Africa Events* (December, 1990): 22–24.

Rodney, W. "Tanzanian Ujamaa and Scientific Socialism." *AR* 4 (1972): 61–76.

Rubin, Deborah S. "People of Good Heart: Rural Response to Economic Crisis in Tanzania." Ph.D. diss., Johns Hopkins University, 1986.

Rudengren, Jan. *Peasants by Preference? Socio-economic and Environmental Aspects of Rural Development in Tanzania.* Uppsala: SIAS, 1981.

Ruthenberg, Hans. *Agricultural Development in Tanzania.* Berlin: Springer-Verlag, 1964.

————. *Smallholder Farming and Smallholder Development in Tanzania: Ten Case Studies.* Munich: Springer-Weltforum, 1968.

Samoff, Joel. "Pluralism and Conflict in Africa: Ethnicity, Institutions, and Class in Tanzania." *Civilisations* 2/1 (1982/83): 97–134.

————. "Popular Initiatives and Local Government in Tanzania." *JDA* 24 (October, 1989): 1–18.

————. "Populist Initiatives and Local Government in Tanzania." *African Studies Association Papers* 83 (October/November 1986): 1–16.

————. *Tanzania: Local Politics and the Structure of Power.* Madison: University of Wisconsin Press, 1972.

Segal, Aaron. "Cooperative Farms for Tanzania." *Atlas* 4 (October 1965): 204–06.

Semboja, Joseph, and S.M.H. Rugumisa. "Price Control in the Management of an Economic Crisis: The National Price Commission in Tanzania." *ASR* 1 (April 1988): 47–65.

Sender, John, and Sheila Smith. *Poverty, Class, and Gender in Rural Africa: A Tanzanian Case Study.* London and New York: Routledge, 1990.

Seth, G. R. *Report to the Government of Tanzania on Development of Agricultural Statistics.* Rome: FAO, 1965.

Shao, Ibrahim F. "Neo-colony and Its Problems during the Process of Attempting to Bring About Socialist Rural Transformation: The Case of Tanzania." *Taamuli* 1/2 (1982): 29–46.

Shao, John. "Politics and the Food Production Crisis in Tanzania." *Issue: A Journal of Africanist Opinion* (1985): 10–24.

Simmons, Reggie Leigh. "Tanzanian Agricultural Policy: A Regional Assessment." *JAS* 3 (Fall 1987): 95–109.

Singleton, Carey B. *Agricultural Economy of Tanganyika.* Washington, D.C.: USGPO, 1964.

Smith, Charles. *Did Colonialism Capture the Peasantry? A Case Study of the Kagera District, Tanzania.* Uppsala: SIAS, 1989.

Smith, Hadley E., ed. *Agricultural Development in Tanganyika.* Dar es Salaam: OUP, 1965.

Spear, Thomas. "Return to the Land." *AR* 2 (March/April 1989): 45–47.

Spencer, Paul. "Pastoralists and the Ghost of Capitalism." *Production Pastorale Society* (1984): 61–76.

Swanberg, Kenneth G., and Ed Hogan. *Implications of the Drought Syndrome for Agricultural Planning in East Africa: The Case of Tanzania.* Cambridge, MA: Harvard Institute for Development, 1981.

Tanganyika Territory. *Report of the Arusha-Moshi Land Commission.* Dar es Salaam: GP, 1947.

Tanzania, Ministry of Agriculture. *Agricultural Policy of Tanzania.* Dar es Salaam: The United Republic of Tanzania, Ministry of Agriculture, 1983.

Tenraa, Eric. "Bush Foraging and Agricultural Development: A History of Sandawe Families." *TNR* 69 (1968): 33–40.

Therkildsen, Ole. *Watering White Elephants? Lessons from Donor Funded Planning and Implementation of Rural Water Supplies in Tanzania.* Uppsala: SIAS, 1988.

Therkildsen, Ole, and J. Semboja. "Short-Term Resource Mobilization for Recurrent Financing of Rural Local Governments in Tanzania." *WD* 8 (August 1992): 1101–113.

Thomas, Garry. "Agricultural Capitalism and Rural Development in Tanzania." *EAJ* 7 (November 1967): 29–31.

Tordoff, William. "Regional Administration in Tanzania." *JMAS* 2 (May 1965): 63–89.

Townsend, Meta Karlise. "Central-Local Government Relations in Agricultural Management of Tanzania: Case Study of the Coffee and Sisal Sectors." Ph.D. diss., George Washington University, 1991.

"Trespassers on Their Own Land." *Africa Events* (November 1990): 31–35.

Vail, David J. *Technology for Ujamaa Village Development in Tanzania.* Syracuse: Syracuse University, 1975.

Van Cranenberg, O. *Widening Gyre: The Tanzanian One-Party State and Policy towards Rural Co-operation.* Delft: Eburon, 1990.

Van der Meulen, J. Q. *Report to the Government of Tanganyika on Rice Production.* Rome: FAO, 1958.

Van Donge, Jan Kees. "Agriculture Decline in Tanzania: The Case of the Uluguru Mountains." *AA* 362 (1992): 73–94.

———. "The Arbitrary State in the Uluguru Mountains: Legal Arenas and Land Disputes in Tanzania." *JMAS* 3 (September 1993): 431–48.

———. "Legal Insecurity and Land Conflicts in Mgeta, Uluguru Mountains, Tanzania." *Africa* 2 (1993): 197–218.

Van Hekken, P. M., and H. U. E. Thoden Van Velsen. *Land Scarcity and Rural Inequality in Tanzania: Some Case Studies from Rungwe District.* The Hague: Mouton, 1972.

von Freyhold, Michaela. *Ujamaa Villages in Tanzania: Analysis of a Social Experiment.* London: Heinemann Educational Books, 1979.

Waters, Tony. "Cultural Analysis of the Economy of Affection and the Uncaptured Peasantry in Tanzania." *JMAS* 1 (March 1992): 163–75.

————. "Lifeworld and System: Of Water Systems and Grain Mill Development in Rural Tanzania." *ASR* 2 (September 1992): 35–54.

————. "Of Water Systems and Grain Mills: Observations of Felt Needs in Western Tanzania." *Issue: A Journal of Opinion* (1989): 47–50.

————. "Practical Problems Associated with Refugee Protection in Western Tanzania." *Disasters* 3 (1988): 189–95.

————. "Some Practical Notes on a Names Taboo in Western Tanzania." *Disasters* 2 (1989): 186–87.

Wijeyewardene, G. E. T. "Some Aspects of Village Solidarity in Ki-Swahili Speaking Coastal Communities of Kenya and Tanganyika." Ph.D. diss., Cambridge University, 1961.

Winans, Edgar V. "Political Context of Economic Adaption in the Southern Highlands of Tanganyika." *American Anthropologist* 2 (April 1965): 435–551.

Wright, Ian Michael. "Meru Land Case." *TNR* 66 (December 1966): 136–46.

Wuyts, M. "Accumulation, Industrialization, and the Peasantry: A Reinterpretation of the Tanzanian Experience." *Journal of Peasant Studies* 2 (January 1994): 159–93.

Yeager, Rodger, "Micropolitics and Transformation in Tanzania: A Study in the Process of Political Institutionalization." Ph.D. diss., Syracuse University, 1968.

————. "Demography and Development Policy in Tanzania." *JDA* 16 (July 1982): 489–509.

M. Foreign Affairs

Alier, Abel. *Visit of President Nyerere to the Southern Region, 1974.* Juba: Regional Ministry of Culture, Information, Youth, and Sports, [c. 1975].

Bailey, Martin. "Chinese Aid in Action: Building the Tanzania-Zambia Railway." *WD* 7/8 (July/September 1975): 587–94.

————. "Freedom Railroad." *Monthly Review* 11 (November 1976): 34–44.

————. *Freedom Railway: China and the Tanzania-Zambia Link.* London: Rex Collings, 1976.

————. "Tanzania and China." *AA* 294 (January 1975): 39–50.

————. "Tanzania-Zambia: Iron Links." *Africa: An International Business, Economic, and Political Monthly* 61 (September 1976): 46–52.

Bennett, George. "Kenya and Tanzania." *AA* 265 (October 1967): 329–35.

Carter, Rudolf. "Domestic and Foreign Policy of Tanzania." *Pan-African Journal* 4 (Fall 1969): 339–61.

Chhabra, Hari Sharan. "Southern Africa: The External Environment." *ISDA Journal* 4 (April/June 1977): 349–57.

Crouch, Susan. *Western Responses to Tanzanian Socialism, 1967–1983.* Aldershot: Avebury, 1987.

Dash, Michael E. "Inroads into East Africa: The People's Republic of China and Tanzania." *Military Review* 4 (April 1976): 58–64.

Decherf, D. "Du non-alignment au pan-socialisme: L'évolution de la politique étrangère de la Tanzanie, expliquée par son contexte régional." *Politique Etrangère* 5 (1975): 493–523.

———. "Socialisme Ujamaa et relations extérieures de la Tanzanie." *Revue Juridique et Politique Indépendance et Coopération* 1 (January/March 1976): 44–57.

———. "La Tanzanie entre l'Océan Indien et la Continent Sud-Africain." *Défense Nationale* (February 1976): 115–24.

Elgström, Ole. *Foreign Aid Negotiations: Interpreting Swedish-Tanzanian Aid Dialogue*. Brookfield, VT: Avebury, 1992.

Frangonikolopoulos, Christos A. "Tanzanian Foreign Policy." *Round Table* 307 (July 1988): 276–292.

Freemann, Linda. "CIDA, Wheat, and Rural Development in Tanzania." *CJAS* 3 (1982): 479–504.

Gordenker, Leon. *International Aid and National Decisions: Development Programs in Malawi, Tanzania, and Zambia*. Princeton: Princeton University Press, 1976.

Hartmann, Jeanette. "Tanzania and the Indian Ocean." *JEARD* 2 (1981): 62–79.

Hassan, A. D. "Big Power Rivalry in the Indian Ocean: A Tanzanian View." *AQ* 3 (1976): 80–86.

Hoskins, Catherine. "Africa's Foreign Relations: The Case of Tanzania." *International Affairs* 3 (July 1968): 446–62.

Huddleston, Trevor. *State of Anglo-Tanzanian Relations*. London: Africa Bureau, 1968.

Jacob, Abel. "Foreign Aid in Agriculture: Introducing Israel's Land Settlement Scheme in Tanzania." *AA* 283 (April 1972): 186–94.

Johns, David H. "The Foreign Policy of Tanzania." In *The Foreign Policies of African States*, ed. Olajide Aluko, 196–219. London: Hodder and Stoughton, 1977.

"Kenya-Tanzania Crisis." *Africa: An International Business, Economic and Political Monthly* 67 (March 1977): 25–26.

"Kenya-Tanzania: Nyerere Tightens the Screws." *Africa: An International Business, Economic and Political Monthly* 69 (May 1977): 32–33.

Kibwana, J. R. "The Military Balance in East Africa: A Kenyan View." *Naval War College Review* 2 (Fall 1977): 97–101.

Leys, Colin. "Recent Relations between the States of East Africa." *International Journal* (Autumn 1965): 510–23.

Marinas Otero, Luis. "Gran Bretana y Tanzania: Evolution de unas relaciones en la era postcolonial." *Revista de Estudios Internacionales* 2 (1981): 333–58.

Mathews, K. "Tanzania's Foreign Policy as a Frontline State in the Liberation of Southern Africa." *AQ* 2/4 (1982): 41–61.

Mathews, K., and S. S. Mushi, eds. *Foreign Policy of Tanzania, 1961–1981: A Reader*. Dar es Salaam: TPH, n.d.

Mayall, James. "Malawi-Tanzania Boundary Dispute." *JMAS* 4 (December 1973): 611–28.

Mazrui, Ali A. "Tanzania versus East Africa: A Case of Unwitting Federal Sabotage." *Journal of Commonwealth Political Studies* 3 (November 1965): 209–25.

Mfinanga, Kassim. *Origin of Tanzania's Support for Liberation in Southern Africa*. Dar es Salaam: Mozambique/Tanzania Center for Foreign Relations, 1983.

Mgonja, C. Y. "Tanzania's Recognition of Biafra." *African Scholar* (August/November 1968): 14–17.

Msabaha, Ibrahim S.R., and Jeannette Hartman. "Tanzania After the Nkomati Accord: Foreign Policy Restructuring in the Changing Strategic Balance in Southern Africa." *Mawazo* (June 1985): 72–86.

Mushi, Samwell S. "Tanzania Foreign Relations and the Policies of Non-alignment, Socialism, and Self-reliance." *Taamuli* 1/2 (1979): 3–40.

Mwango, G. C. *Foreign Aid and Tanzania Development Strategy.* Dar es Salaam: University of Dar es Salaam, 1972.

Mwinyi, Aboud Jumbe. "India and Tanzania." *India Quarterly* 1 (January/March 1973): 1–8.

Niblock, Timothy C. "Aid and Foreign Policy in Tanzania, 1961–1968." Ph.D. diss., University of Sussex, 1971.

———. "Tanzanian Foreign Policy: An Analysis." *TAR* 2 (September 1971): 91–101.

Nnoli, Okwudiba. "Political Will and the Margin of Autonomy in Tanzanian Foreign Policy." *AQ* 1 (1977): 5–36.

———. *Self Reliance and Foreign Policy in Tanzania: The Dynamics of the Diplomacy of a New State, 1961 to 1971.* New York: NOK Publishers, 1978.

Nyerere, Julius K. "The Costs of Nonalignment." *AR* 7 (October 1966): 61–67.

———. *Nigeria-Biafra Crisis.* Dar es Salaam: GP, 1969.

———. "Rhodesia in the Context of Southern Africa." *Foreign Affairs* 3 (April 1966): 373–86.

———. *South Africa and the Commonwealth.* Dar es Salaam: GP, 1971.

———. *Tanzania Policy on Foreign Affairs.* Dar es Salaam: Ministry of Information and Tourism, 1967.

———. *Tanzania Rejects Western Domination of Africa.* Dar es Salaam: Information Service Division, Ministry of Information and Broadcasting, 1978.

———. *We Are Brothers in a Common Struggle.* Maputo: Empresa Moderna, 1975.

Othman, H. M. "Arusha Declaration and 'The Triangle Principles' of Tanzania Foreign Policy." *EAJ* 5 (May 1970): 35–42.

Pratt, R. Cranford. "African Reactions to the Rhodesian Crisis." *International Journal* 2 (Spring 1966): 186–98.

———. "Foreign-Policy Issues and the Emergence of Socialism in Tanzania, 1961–1968." *International Journal* 3 (Summer 1975): 445–60.

Rettman, Rosalyn J. "Tanzam Rail Link: China's 'Loss-Leader' in Africa." *World Affairs* 3 (Winter 1973/1974): 232–58.

Samoff, Joel, J. M. Wuyts, B. Mothander, and K. Flodman. *Swedish Public Administration Assistance to Tanzania.* Uppsala: SIAS, 1988/89.

Sathyamurthy, T. V. "Tanzania's Non-Aligned Role in International Relations." *India Quarterly* 1 (1981): 1–23.

Seaton, Earle E., and Sosthenes T. Maliti. *Tanzania Treaty Practice.* Nairobi: OUP, 1973.

Shaw, Timothy M. "African States and International Stratification: The Adaptive Foreign Policy of Tanzania." In *Foreign Relations of African States,* ed. Kenneth Ingham, 213–33. London: Butterworths, 1974.

———. "The Foreign Policy of Tanzania 1961–1968." M.A. thesis, University of East Africa, Makerere, 1969.

———. *Foreign Policy of Tanzania, 1961–69.* Nairobi: EAPH, 1975.

Shinn, David Hamilton. "Tanzania's Relations with Independent Africa: An Events and Transaction Analysis." Ph.D. diss., George Washington University, 1980.

Sinclair, M. R. *Strategic Significance of Tanzania.* Pretoria: Institute for Strategic Studies, University of Pretoria, [1979?].

Sircar, Pirbatt K. "Great Uhuru (Freedom) Railway: China's Link to Africa." *China Report* 2 (March/April 1978): 15–23.

Tandon, Yashpal. "Organization of African Unity and the Principles of Universality of Membership." *TAR* 4 (April 1972): 52–60.

Tansania in der Sicht der Sowjetunion: Eine Studie zur Sowjetischen Schwarzafrika-Politik. Hamburg: Institut für Afrika-Kunde, 1978.

"Tanzam-Railway: Breakthrough for Red China." *Bulletin of the Africa Institute of South Africa* (July 1972): 237–41.

Tanzania. *The Lusaka Manifesto on Southern Africa.* Dar es Salaam: GP, 1969.

Tanzanian Government Statement on the Recognition of Biafra. Dar es Salaam: GP, 1968.

Temu, Peter. "Employment of Foreign Consultants in Tanzania: Its Values and Limitations." *TAR* 1 (1973): 69–84.

U.S. Department of State, Office of the Geographer. *Burundi-Tanzania Boundary.* Washington, D.C.: U.S. Department of State, Office of the Geographer, 1966.

———. *Congo (Leopoldville)–Tanzania Boundary.* Washington, D.C.: U.S. Department of State, Office of the Geographer, 1965.

———. *Kenya–Tanzania Boundary.* Washington, D.C.: U.S. Department of State, Office of the Geographer, 1966.

———. *Malawi–Tanganyika and Zanzibar Boundary.* Washington, D.C.: U.S. Department of State, Office of the Geographer, 1964.

———. *Maritime Boundary: Kenya–Tanzania.* Washington, D.C.: U.S. Department of State, Office of the Geographer, 1981.

———. *Mozambique–Tanzania Boundary.* Washington, D.C.: U.S. Department of State, Office of the Geographer, 1964.

———. *Rwanda–Tanzania Boundary.* Washington, D.C.: U.S. Department of State, Office of the Geographer, 1966.

———. *Tanzania–Uganda Boundary.* Washington, D.C.: U.S. Department of State, Office of the Geographer, 1965.

———. *Tanzania–Zambia Boundary.* Washington, D.C.: U.S. Department of State, Office of the Geographer, 1965.

United Republic of Tanzania News Service. *Case for Recognition of Biafra: Statement by Government of the United Republic of Tanzania.* New York: Tanzanian Mission to the United Nations, 1968.

Urfer, Sylvain. "Coopération sino-tanzanienne." *Afrique Contemporaine* 83 (January/February): 12–16.

Wilson, Amrit. *U.S. Foreign Policy and Revolution: The Creation of Tanzania.* London: Pluto Press, 1989.

Young, Roger. *Canadian Development Assistance to Tanzania: An Independent Study.* Ottawa: North–South Institute, 1983.

Yu, George T. *China's Africa Policy: A Study of Tanzania.* New York: Praeger, 1975.

———. "Chinese Aid to Africa: The Tanzania–Zambia Railway." In *Chinese and Soviet Aid to Africa,* ed. Warren Weinstein, 29–55. New York: Praeger Publishers, 1976.

———. *China and Tanzania: A Study in Cooperative Interaction.* Berkeley: Center for Chinese Studies, University of California, 1970.

———. "Peking's African Diplomacy." *Problems of Communism* 2 (March/April 1972): 16–24, 111.

———. "Working on the Railroad: China and the Tanzania-Zambia Railway." *Asian Survey* 11 (November 1971): 1101–17.

N. Women's Affairs

Brain, James L. "Witchcraft and Development." *AA* 324 (July 1982): 371–84.

———. *Witchcraft and Development.* Dar es Salaam: DUP, 1981.

Bryceson, D. F. "Women's Proletarianization and the Family Wage in Tanzania." In *Women, Work and Ideology in the Third World*, ed. H. Afshar, 128–52. London: Tavistock, 1985.

Bujra, Janet. "Gender, Class and Empowerment: A Tale of Two Tanzanian Servants." *ROAPE* 56 (March 1993): 68–78.

———. "Taxing Development in Tanzania: Why Must Women Pay?" *ROAPE* 47 (Spring 1990): 44–63.

Caplan, Pat. "Development Policies in Tanzania: Some Implications for Women." In *African Women in the Development Process*, ed. Nici Nelson, 98–108. London: Frank Cass, 1981.

Cook, Kristy, and Donna O. Kerner. "Gender and Food Shortage in Tanzania." *Feminist Issues* (Spring 1989): 57–72.

Croll, Elizabeth J. "Women in Rural Production and Reproduction in the Soviet Union, China, Cuba, and Tanzania: Socialist Development Experiences." *Signs* 2 (1981): 361–74.

Geiger, Susan. "Women in Nationalist Struggle: TANU Activists in Dar es Salaam." *IJAHS* 1 (1987): 1–26.

Greuter, Susy. "Changes of Women's Position and Women's Organisation during UN Decade of Women, 1975–1985: The Case of Tanzania." *Vierteljahresber* (1985): 281–95.

Hannan-Andersson, Carolyn. *Women, Water, and Development in a Pare Settlement, Tanzania.* Dar es Salaam: University of Dar es Salaam, 1982.

Hollander, Roberta Beth. "Out of Tradition: The Position of Women in Kenya and Tanzania During the Pre-Colonial, Colonial and Post-independence Eras." Ph.D. diss., American University, 1979.

Hollis, A. Claude. "Dance of Sagara Women, Tanganyika Territory." *Man* 4 (January 1924): 5–6.

Jackson, Sandra Carter. "Women in Development: A Study of Access to Education and Work in Tanzania and Cuba, 1960–1980." Ph.D. diss., University of California, 1987.

Kikopa, Jane Rose K. *Law and the Status of Women in Tanzania.* Addis Ababa: African Training and Research Center for Women, 1981.

Kilbride, Philip, and Janet Kilbride. *Changing Family Life in East Africa: Women and Children at Risk.* University Park: Pennsylvania State University Press, 1990.

Koda, Bertha. "Liberation of Women in Tanzania." *Maji Maji* 35 (1978): 54–61.

Kurwijila, Rosebud, and Dawn M. Due. "Credit for Women's Income Generation: A Tanzanian Case Study." *CJAS* 1 (1991): 90–103.

Ladner, Joyce. "Tanzanian Women and Nation Building." *Black Scholar* 4 (1971): 22–28.

————. "Tanzanian Women in Nation Building." In *Black Woman Cross-Culturally*, ed. Filomina Chioma Steady, 107–18. Cambridge, MA: Schenkman, 1981.

Larsson, Birgitta. *Conversion to Greater Freedom? Women, Church and Social Change in North-Western Tanzania under Colonial Rule*. Uppsala: Almqvist and Wiksell International, 1991.

Lovett, Margot. "On Power and Powerlessness: Marriage and Political Metaphor in Colonial Western Tanzania." *IJAHS* 2 (1994): 273–301.

Madsen, Birgit. *Women's Mobilization and Integration in Development: A Village Case Study from Tanzania*. Copenhagen: Centre for Development Research, 1984.

Mascarenhas, Ophelia. *Rural Women under Rapid Industrialization in Tanzania*. Dar es Salaam: University of Dar es Salaam, 1983.

Mbilinyi, Marjorie J. "Agribusiness and Casual Labor in Tanzania." *African Economic History* (1986): 107–41.

————. "Agribusiness and Women Peasants in Tanzania." *Development and Change* 4 (1988): 549–83.

————. *Big Slavery: Agribusiness and the Crisis in Women's Employment in Tanzania*. Dar es Salaam: DUP, 1991.

————. "The 'New Woman' and Traditional Norms in Tanzania." *JMAS* 1 (March 1972): 57–72.

————. "Runaway Wives in Colonial Tanganyika: Forced Labour and Forced Marriage in Rungwe District, 1919–1961." *International Journal of the Sociology of Law* 1 (1988): 1–29.

————. "The Status of Women in Tanzania." *CJAS* 2 (1972): 371–77.

————. "Wife, Slave, and Subject of the King: The Oppression of Women in the Shambala Kingdom." *TNR* 88/89 (1982): 1–13.

————." 'Women in Development' Ideology: The Promotion of Competition and Exploitation." *TAR* 1 (1984): 14–33.

Meena, Ruth. "Crisis and Structural Adjustment: Tanzanian Women's Politics." *Issue: A Journal of Opinion* 2 (1989): 29–31.

Meghji, Z. "Women and Cooperatives: Some Realities Affecting Development in Tanzania." *Community Development Journal* 3 (1985): 185–88.

Mekacha, R.D.K. "Are Women Devils? The Portrayal of Women in Tanzanian Popular Music." *Matatu* 9 (1992): 99–113.

Mesaki, Simeon. "Witchcraft and Witch-Killings in Tanzania: Paradox and Dilemma." Ph.D. diss., University of Minnesota, 1993.

Moreau, R. E. "Suicide by 'Breaking the Cooking Pot.' " *TNR* 12 (December 1941): 49–50.

Msangi, Josephine P. "Access of Young Women to General Occupational and Vocational Training in Tanzania." *JEARD* (1988): 119–27.

Mtengeti-Migiro, Rose. "The Division of Matrimonial Property in Tanzania." *JMAS* 3 (September 1990): 521–26.

Mukurasi, Laeticia. *Post Abolished: One Women's Struggle for Employment Rights in Tanzania*. Ithaca: ILR Press, 1991.

Puja, Grace Khwaya. *School Girls' Knowledge about and Attitudes Towards Modern Contraceptive Usage in Tanzania: The Case of Ihanja, Mwenge, and Shaaban Robert Secondary Schools*. Dar es Salaam: Women and Research Documentation Project, 1990.

Raum, Otto Friedrich. "Female Initiation among the Chagga." *American Anthropologist* (1939): 554–65.

Rogers, Susan G. "Efforts toward Women's Development in Tanzania: Gender Rhetoric v. Gender Realities." *Women and Politics* (Winter 1982): 23–41.

Sender, John, and Sheila Smith. *Poverty, Class, and Gender in Rural Africa: A Tanzanian Case Study.* London and New York: Routledge, 1990.

Siti, Sauti ya. "Violence against Women in Tanzania." *ROAPE* 56 (March 1993): 111–16.

Swantz, Marja-Liisa. *Ritual and Symbol in Transitional Zaramo Society, with Special Reference to Women.* Uppsala: SIAS, 1986.

———. *Women in Development: A Creative Role Denied? The Case of Tanzania.* New York: St. Martin's Press, 1985.

Tanner, Ralph E.S. "The Relationship between the Sexes in a Coastal Islamic Society: Pangani District, Tanganyika." *AS* 2 (1962): 70–82.

Tripp, Aili Mari. "Gender, Political Participation, and the Transformation of Associational Life in Uganda and Tanzania." *ASR* 1 (April 1994): 107–31.

———. "Women and the Changing Urban Household Economy in Tanzania." *JMAS* 4 (December 1989): 601–23.

Tumbo-Masabo, Zubeida, and Rita Liljeström, eds. *Chelewa, Chelewa: The Dilemma of Teenage Girls.* Uppsala: SIAS, 1994.

Vuorela, Ulla. *Women's Question and the Modes of Human Reproduction: An Analysis of a Tanzanian Village.* Uppsala: SIAS, 1987.

Wandel, M., and G. Holmboe-Ottesen. "Women's Work in Agriculture and Child Nutrition in Tanzania." *Journal of Tropical Pediatrics* 5 (1992): 252–55.

Wilson, Monica. "Zig-Zag Change." *Africa* 4 (1976): 399–409.

World Bank. *Tanzania: Women and Development.* Washington: D.C.: World Bank, 1991.

O. Arts, Architecture, and Music

Berrini, Andrea. "La politica culturale in Tanzania dall'indipendenza ad oggi." *Africa* 3 (1986): 448–71.

Duckworth, Aidron. *Modern Makonde Sculpture.* Syracuse: Syracuse University, [1968?].

Freyvogel, T. A. "Collection of Plaited Mats from the Ulanga District of Tanganyika." *TNR* 57 (September 1961): 139–48.

Garlake, Peter S. *Early Islamic Architecture of the East African Coast.* Nairobi: OUP, 1966.

Jengo, E. "Towards a National Cultural Policy for the Promotion of Art in Tanzania." *Utafiti* 1 (1985): 1–8.

Koritschoner, Hans. "Some East African Native Songs." *TNR* 4 (October 1937): 51–64.

Miller, Judith von d. *Art in East Africa: A Contemporary Guide to East African Art.* London: Muller, 1975.

Obatala, J. K. "Soul Music in Africa: Has Charlie Got a Brand New Bag?" *Black Scholar* 6 (1971): 8–12.

Ranger, Terence O. *Dance and Society in Eastern Africa, 1890–1970: The Beni Ngoma.* London: Heinemann, 1975.

Stout, J. Anthony. *Modern Makonde Sculpture.* London: Kegan Paul, 1966.

Suleiman, A. A. "Swahili Singing Star Siti Binti Saad and the Taarab Tradition in Zanzibar." *Swahili* 1/2 (1969): 87–90.

Tenraa, Eric. "Sandawe Musical and Other Sound-Producing Instruments." *TNR* 60 (March 1963): 23–48; and 62 (March 1964): 91–95.

Tracey, Hugh. "Development of Music in East Africa." *TNR* 63 (September 1964): 213–21.

———. "Recording Tour in Tanganyika by a Team of the African Music Society." *TNR* 32 (January 1952): 43–49.

P. Education

Ahmed, Mauzoor. "The Education Revolution in Tanzania." *Assignment Children* 65/68 (1984): 225–45.

Almasi, Oswald. "Factors Associated with Accessibility to University Education: A Tanzanian Experience." Ph.D. diss., University of Toronto, 1993.

Blaxland, R. W. "Mass Education in Tanganyika." *Overseas Education* 2 (January 1951): 52–59.

Block, Leslie S. "National Development Policy and Outcome at the University of Dar es Salaam." *ASR* 1 (March 1984): 97–115.

Buchert, Lene. *Education in the Development of Tanzania 1919–1990*. London: James Currey, 1994.

Cameron, John. "Wastage in Tanganyika, with Special Reference to Primary Schools." *Teacher Education* 2 (1965): 103–14.

Cameron, John, and W. A. Dodd. *Society, Schools, and Progress in Tanzania*. London: Pergamon Press, 1970.

Carr-Hill, Roy A. *Primary Education in Tanzania*. Stockholm: Swedish International Development Authority, 1984.

Carthew, John. "Life Imitates Art: The Student Expulsion in Dar es Salaam, October 1966, as Dramatic Ritual." *JMAS* 3 (September 1980): 541–49.

Cooksey, B. "Policy and Practice in Tanzanian Secondary Education Since 1967." *International Journal of Education Development* 3 (1986): 183–202.

Court, David. "The Social Function of Formal Schooling in Tanzania." *TAR* 4 (1973): 577–93.

Dodd, William. "Centralization in Education in Mainland Tanzania." *Comparative Education Review* 3 (October 1968): 268–80.

Eliufoo, S. N. "Tanzania's Higher Education Policy." *EAJ* 8 (December 1967): 23–24.

Ergas, Zaki R. "Can Education Be Used as a Tool to Build a Socialist Society in Africa? The Tanzanian Case." *JMAS* 4 (December 1982): 571–94.

Galabawa, C. J. *Implementing Educational Policies in Tanzania*. Washington, D.C.: World Bank, 1990.

George, Betty. *Education for Africans in Tanganyika*. Washington, D.C.: U.S. Office of Education, 1960.

———. *Recent Educational Developments in Tanganyika*. Washington, D.C.: Office of Education, 1961.

Göranson, Ulf. *Education in Zanzibar*. Uppsala: SIAS, 1986.

"Higher Education in Tanzania." *Educafrica* (1986): 297–320.

Hall, Budd L. *Adult Education and the Development of Socialism in Tanzania*. Nairobi: EALB, 1975.

Hinzen, H., and V. H. Hundsdorfer, eds. *Education for Liberation and Development: The Tanzanian Experience*. Hamburg: UNESCO, 1979.

Hornsby, George. "A Brief History of Tanga School up to 1914." *TNR* 58/59 (March/September 1962): 148–50.

———. "German Educational Achievement in East Africa." *TNR* 62 (March 1964): 83–90.

Johnsson, Anders I., Kjell Nystrom, and Rolf Sunden. *Adult Education in Tanzania*. Stockholm: Swedish International Development Authority, 1983.

Khamisi, L. *Imperialism Today: A Contribution to the University of Dar es Salaam Debate*. Dar es Salaam: TPH, 1993.

King, Kenneth. *End of Educational Self-reliance in Tanzania?* Edinburgh: Centre of African Studies, Edinburgh University, 1984.

Kweka, Aikael N. *Adult Education in a Village in Tanzania*. Uppsala: SIAS, 1987.

Mbilinyi, Marjorie. "Decision to Educate in Rural Tanzania." Ph.D. diss., University of Dar es Salaam, 1972.

———. "Education, Stratification and Sexism in Tanzania: Policy Implications." *TAR* 2 (1973): 327–40.

Mbilinyi, Marjorie, and Patricia Mbughuni, eds. *Education in Tanzania, with a Gender Perspective*. Stockholm: Swedish International Development Authority, Education Division, 1991.

Mbunda, Daniel. "Education and Ujamaa: An Examination of Their Relationship in Traditional and Contemporary Society in Tanzania." Ph.D. diss., University of Southhamptom, 1982.

Meena, E.A.K. *Some Aspects of Education in Tanzania*. Dar es Salaam: Longman Tanzania, 1983.

Morrison, David. *Education and Politics in Africa: The Tanzanian Case*. Nairobi: Heinemann, 1976.

Mpogolo, Zakayo. "Post-literacy and Continuing Education in Tanzania." *International Review of Education* 3 (1984): 351–58.

Msekwa, Pius, and T. L. Maliyamkono. *Experiments: Education Policy Formation before and after the Arusha Declaration*. Dar es Salaam: Black Star Agencies, 1979.

Mvungi, M. "Interactions between Education, Culture, and Communication in Tanzania's Socio-economic Development: A Historical Presentation." *Educafrica* 11 (1984): 147–62.

Nwa-chil, Chudi C. "Socio-economic Factors and Schooling in Tanzania." *African Social Research* 32 (December 1981): 83–95.

Nyerere, Julius K. *Education for Self Reliance*. Dar es Salaam: GP, 1967.

———. "Education in Tanzania." *Harvard Educational Review* 1 (1985): 45–52.

Omari, I.M. "Innovation and Change in Higher Education in Developing Countries: Experiences from Tanzania." *Comparative Education* 2 (June 1991): 181–205.

Pratt, R. Cranford. "Foreign Scholarship in Tanzania." *CJAS* 1 (1974): 166–69.

Rubagumya, Casmir M., ed. *Language in Education in Africa: A Tanzanian Perspective*. Clevedon, UK: Multilingual Matters, 1990.

Samoff, Joel. "Education in Tanzania: Class Formation and the Structure of Power." *JMAS* 1 (March 1979): 47–69.

————. *Educational Reform in Tanzania: Schools, Skills, and Social Transformation*. Rodenbosch: University of Cape Town, 1984.

————. "The Façade of Precision in Education Data and Statistics: A Troubling Example from Tanzania." *JMAS* 4 (December 1991): 669–89.

————. "School Expansion in Tanzania: Private Initiatives and Public Policy." *Comparative Education Review* 3 (August 1987): 333–60.

————. "Schooling and Socialism: Educational Reform in Tanzania." *Genève-Afrique* 1 (1983): 55–72.

Sheffield, James R. "Basic Education for the Rural Poor: The Tanzanian Case." *JDA* 14 (October 1979): 99–110.

Shengena, Joe J. "The Teaching of Political Education in Tanzanian Schools." *Taamuli* 2 (1973): 27–35.

Spitzberg, Irving J. "Educational Planning: Politics, Ideology, and Development." *ASR* 3 (December 1978): 101–10.

Stabler, Ernest. "Kenya and Tanzania: Strategies and Realities in Education and Development." *AA* 310 (January 1979): 33–56.

Sumra, Suleman Alarakhia. "Primary Education and Transition to Socialism in Rural Tanzania: A Case Study of an Ujamaa Village in Mswaki, Handeni District." Ph.D. diss., Stanford University, 1986.

Swai, Bonaventure. "Political Economy of Tanzanian Primary School Leavers: A Theoretical Consideration." *Taamuli* 1 (1978): 38–49.

Swatman, J. E. D. "Access to Education: The Changing Pattern in the Location of Schools." *TNR* 79/80 (December 1976): 107–14.

Thompson, A. R. "Partnership in Education in Tanganyika 1919–1961." M.A. thesis, University of London, 1965.

United Republic of Tanzania. *Basic Facts About Education in Tanzania*, rev. ed. Dar es Salaam: GP, 1984.

————. *Educational System in Tanzania toward the Year 2000*. Dar es Salaam: GP, 1984.

Unsicker, Jeff. "Political Economy of the Folk Development Colleges: A Preliminary Analysis of Adult Education, International Aid, and Socialism in Tanzania." *African Studies Association Papers* 107 (October 1984): 1–30.

Urch, George E. "Education in Tanzania: A New Direction?" *Africana Journal* (1994): 215–30.

Vitta, Paul B. "Progress and Problems in Tanzania's Science Education." *Taamuli* 2 (1973): 22–26.

World Bank. *Tanzania: Teachers and the Financing of Education*. Washington, D.C.: World Bank, 1991.

Q. Environment and Geography

Alexander, Shana. "Serengeti: The Glory of Life." *NGM* 5 (May 1986): 585–601.

Århem, Kaj. *Pastoral Man in the Garden of Eden: The Maasai of the Ngorongoro Conservation Area, Tanzania*. Uppsala: SIAS, 1985.

Berry, L., ed. *Tanzania in Maps*. London: University of London Press, 1971.

Blunt, David Enderby. *Elephant*. Boston and New York: Houghton Mifflin, 1933.

Bulpin, Thomas Victor. *Hunter in Death*. Cape Town: Books of Africa, 1968.

Christiansson, Carl. *Soil-Erosion and Sedimentation in Semi-arid Tanzania*. Uppsala: SIAS, 1981.

Coulter, G. W., ed. *Lake Tanganyika and Its Life*. London: OUP, 1991.

DANIDA. *Country Strategy for Strengthening Environmental Considerations in Danish Development Assistance to Tanzania*. Copenhagen: DANIDA, 1989.

Douglas-Hamilton, Iain, and Oria Douglas-Hamilton. *Among the Elephants*. New York: Viking Press, 1975.

———. *Battle for the Elephants*. New York: Viking, 1992.

Fosbrooke, Henry A. "Ngorongoro Conservation Area, 1961 to 1971." *TNR* 76 (1975): 85–88.

Giblin, James L. *Politics of Environmental Control in Northeastern Tanzania, 1840–1940*. Philadelphia: University of Pennsylvania Press, 1992.

Gillman, Clement. "Synopsis of the Geography of Tanganyika Territory." *TNR* 1 (March 1936): 5–13.

Goodall, Jane. *Chimpanzees of Gombe: Patterns of Behavior*. Cambridge, MA: Belknap Press of Harvard University Press, 1986.

———. *In the Shadow of Man*. London: Collins, 1971.

———. "Life and Death at Gombe." *NGM* 5 (May 1979): 592–621.

———. *My Friends the Wild Chimpanzees*. Washington, D.C.: The National Geographic Society, 1967.

———. "My Life among the Wild Chimpanzees." *NGM* 8 (August 1963): 272–308.

———. "New Discoveries among Africa's Chimpanzees." *NGM* 12 (December 1965): 802–31.

———. *Through a Window: My Thirty Years with the Chimpanzees of Gombe*. Boston: Houghton Mifflin, 1990.

Goodall, Jane, and Hugo van Lawick. *Innocent Killers*. Boston: Houghton Mifflin, 1970.

Gray, B. A. *Beyond the Serengeti Plains: Adventures of an Anthropologist's Wife in the East African Hinterland*. New York: Vantage Press, 1971.

Grzimek, Bernard, and Michael Grzimek. *Serengeti Shall Not Die*. London: Hamish Hamilton, 1960.

Hanby, Jeannette. *Lions Share: The Story of a Serengeti Pride*. Boston: Houghton Mifflin, 1982.

Hayes, Harold T. P. *Last Place on Earth*. New York: Stein and Day, 1977.

Herne, Brian. *Tanzania Safaris*. Clinton, NJ: Amwell Press, 1982.

Ionides, Constantine J.P. *Mambas and Man Eaters: A Hunter's Story*. New York: Holt, Rhinehart and Winston, 1966.

Kjekshus, Helge. *Ecology Control and Economic Development in East African History: The Case of Tanganyika, 1850–1950*. London: Heinemann, 1977.

———. "Tanzanian Villagization Policy: Implementational Lessons and Ecological Dimensions." *CJAS* (1977): 269–82.

Lamprey, Hugh F. "Elephant Control in Tanganyika: A Discussion." *TNR* 47/48 (January 1957): 145–48.

———. "Study of the Ecology of the Mammal Population of a Game Reserve in the Acacia Savanna of Tanganyika, with Particular Reference to Animal Numbers and Biomass." Ph.D. diss., Oxford University, 1962.

Lane, Margaret. *Life with Ionides*. London: Hamish Hamilton, 1963.

Maberley, C.T.A. *Animals of East Africa*. Cape Town: Howard Timmins, 1962.

Matthiessen, Peter. *Sand Rivers*. New York: Viking Press, 1981.

Matzke, Gordon. "Development of the Selous Game Reserve." *TNR* 79/80 (December 1976): 37–48.

———. "Large Mammals, Small Settlements, and Big Problems: A Study of Overlapping Space Preferences in Southern Tanzania." Ph.D. diss., Syracuse University, 1975.

———. *Wildlife in Tanzanian Settlement Policy: The Case of the Selous*. Syracuse: Maxwell School of Citizenship and Public Affairs, Syracuse University, 1977.

Mence, A. J. "College of African Wildlife Management: Ten Years After." *TNR* 76 (1975): 89–92.

Millais, J. G. *Life of Frederick Courtenay Selous, D.S.O.* London: Longmans, Green, 1919.

Misana, Salome B. "Shrinking Forests and the Problem of Deforestation in Tanzania." *JEARD* (1988): 108–18.

Moore, Audrey. *Serengeti*. London: Country Life, 1938.

Moore, Ernest D. *Ivory, Scourge of Africa*. New York and London: Harper Brothers, 1931.

Moorehead, Alan. "Survival in Serengeti." *Sunday Times Magazine* (27 August 1967): 4–15.

Msangi, J. P. "Water Resources Conservation in the Semi-arid Parts of Tanzania." *JEARD* (1987): 63–73.

Mturi, A. A. "Protection, Preservation, and Development of Tanzania's Heritage." *TNR* 76 (1975): 93–101.

Newmark, William D., ed. *The Conservation of Mount Kilimanjaro*. Gland, Switzerland: International Union for Conservation of Nature and Natural Resources, 1991.

Parker, Craig. *Into Africa*. Chicago: University of Chicago Press, 1994.

Pearsall, W. *Report on an Ecological Survey of the Serengeti National Park*. London: Fauna Preservation Society, 1957.

Pike, A. H. "Soil Conservation amongst the Matengo Tribe." *TNR* 6 (December 1938): 79–81.

Rodgers, W. A. "Past Wangindo Settlement in the Eastern Selous Game Reserve." *TNR* 77/78 (June 1976): 21–26.

Rodgers, W. A., and J. D. Lobo. "Elephant Control and Legal Ivory Exploitation: 1920 to 1976." *TNR* 84/85 (1980): 25–54.

Ruess, R. W., and S. W. Seagle. "Landscape Patterns in Soil Microbial Processes in the Serengeti National Park, Tanzania." *Ecology* 4 (June 1994): 892–904.

Rushby, George C. *No More the Tusker*. London: W. H. Allen and Sons, 1965.

Schaller, George B. *Golden Shadows, Flying Hooves*. Chicago: University of Chicago Press, 1983.

———. "Endless Race of Life." *Natural History* 4 (April 1972): 38–43.

———. *Serengeti: A Kingdom of Predators*. London: Collins, 1973.

———. *Serengeti Lion*. Chicago: University of Chicago Press, 1974.

Shao, John. "Villagization Program and the Disruption of the Ecological Balance in Tanzania." *CJAS* 2 (1986): 219–39.

Siedentopf, Andreas Robert. *Last Stronghold of Big Game*. London: Hodder and Stoughton, 1947.

Sillery, Anthony. "Indian Elephant in Tanganyika." *TNR* 11 (April 1941): 64–65.

Singh, S. B. "Fisheries and Marine Resources: An Outline of Progress." *TNR* 76 (1975): 71–74.

Thomas, D. K. "Illegal Hunting in Tanganyika." *TNR* 61 (1963): 190–94.

Turner, Kay. *Serengeti Home.* London: George Allen and Unwin, 1978.

White, Stewart Edward. *Rediscovered Country.* New York: Doubleday, Page, and Company, 1915.

Wykes, Alan. *Snake Man: The Story of C.J.P. Ionides.* New York: Simon and Schuster, 1961.

Yeager, Rodger, and Norman N. Miller. *Wildlife, Wild Death: Land Use and Survival in Eastern Africa.* Albany: State University of New York Press, 1986.

R. Legal Affairs

Abrahams, Ray. "Law and Order and the State in the Nyamwezi and Sukumu Area of Tanzania." *Africa: Journal of the International African Institute* 3 (1989): 356–70.

Cole, J. S. R., and W. N. Dennison. *Tanganyika: The Development of Its Laws and Constitutions.* London: Stevens and Sons, 1964.

"Constitution of Tanganyika." *Journal of the Parliaments of the Commonwealth* 2 (April 1963): 135–42.

Cory, Hans. *Sukuma Law and Custom.* London: OUP, 1953.

Cory, Hans, and M. M. Hartnoll. *Customary Law of the Haya Tribe.* London: Frank Cass, 1971.

Fundikera, Chief. "Reorganization of the Courts in Tanganyika." *Journal of Local Administration Overseas* 4 (October 1962): 257–58.

Harries, L. "Language and Law in Tanzania." *Journal of African Law* 3 (1966): 164–67.

Itemba, J. M. *Law Relating to Bail in Tanzania.* Dar es Salaam: DUP, 1991.

James, R. W. "Implementing the Arusha Declaration: The Role of the Legal System." *TAR* 2 (1973): 179–208.

Kalunga, L. T. "Human Rights and the Preventive Detention Act of 1962 of the United Republic of Tanzania: Some Operative Aspects." *EALR* (1978/1981): 281–325.

Kambona, Oscar S. *Tanzania and the Rule of Law.* London: Africa News Services, n.d.

Kumar, Umesh. "Justice in a One-Party African State: The Tanzanian Experience." *Verfassung und Recht in Übersee* 3 (1986): 255–74.

———. "Some Preliminary Observations on the Administration of Justice in a One Party African State: The Tanzanian Experience." *Lesotho Law Journal* 1 (1986): 119–54.

Lee, Eugene C. *Local Taxation in Tanzania.* London: OUP, 1966.

Lewis-Barned, J. F. "Integration of Judicial Systems: The Recent Reform of the Local Courts Appeal System of Tanganyika." *Journal of African Law* 2 (Summer 1963): 84–94.

Lugakingira, K. "Travail of Law Reform." *Commonwealth Judicial Journal* (June 1986): 3–9.

Maini, Krishnan. *Land Law in East Africa.* Nairobi: OUP, 1967.

Martin, Robert. *Personal Freedom and the Law in Tanzania: A Study of Socialist State Administration.* Nairobi: OUP, 1974.

Mbunda, L. X. "Limitation Clauses and the Bill of Rights in Tanzania." *Lesotho Law Journal* 2 (1988): 153–67.

Modi, J. R. "Income Tax Policy Problems in Less Developed Economies of Tropical Africa: With Special Reference to Tanganyika." Ph.D. diss., University of Edinburgh, 1964.

Moffett, J. P. "Native Courts in Tanganyika." *JAA* 1 (January 1952): 17–25.

Moore, Sally Falk. "Politics, Procedures and Norms in Changing Chagga Law." *Africa* 4 (1970): 321–43.

———. *Social Facts and Fabrications: 'Customary' Law on Kilimanjaro, 1880–1980*. Cambridge: CUP, 1986.

Nicholson, M.E.R. "Change without Conflict: A Case Study of Legal Change in Tanzania." *Law and Society Review* 4 (1973): 747–66.

Oldaker, A. A. *Interim Report on Tribal Customary Law in Tanganyika*. Dar es Salaam: GP, 1957.

Ong'wamuhana, Kibuta. "Human Rights in Tanzania: A Constitutional Overview." *EALR* (1978/1981): 240–80.

Pfeiffer, Steven B. "Judiciary Constitutional Systems of Kenya, Tanzania, Uganda." *Legal History* 2 (1976): 27–72.

———. "Role of the Judiciary in the Constitutional Systems of East Africa." *JMAS* 1 (March 1978): 33–66.

Ramadhani, Augustino. "Judicial System of Tanzania, Zanzibar." *EALR* (1978/1981): 225–39.

Redmayne, A. "Research on Customary Law in German East Africa." *Journal of African Law* 1 (1983): 22–41.

"Reflections on Tanzania's Bill of Rights." *Commonwealth Law Bulletin* (April 1988): 853–57.

Rwezaura, Barthazar A. *Sheria juu ya Hali na Haki za Watoto Tanzania*. Dar es Salaam: TPH, 1992.

———. "Tanzania: Family Law and the New Bill of Rights." *Journal of Family Law* 2 (1991): 453–63.

Seaton, E. E., and J. S. Warioba. "Constitution of Tanzania: An Overview." *EALR* (1978/1981): 35–72.

Shivji, Issa G. *Law, State, and the Working Class in Tanzania, c. 1920–1964*. London: James Currey, 1986.

———. "State of the Constitution and the Constitution of the State in Tanzania." *EALR* (1978/1981): 1–34.

Tanner, Ralph E. S. "Codification of Customary Law in Tanzania." *East Africa Law Journal* 2 (June 1966): 105–16.

———. "Crime and Punishment in East Africa." *Transition* 21 (October/November 1965): 39–46.

———. "Law Enforcement by Communal Action in Sukumaland, Tanganyika Territory." *JAA* (October 1955): 159–65.

S. Medicine, Health, and Social Services

African Medical and Research Foundation. Health Services of Tanganyika: A Report to the Government. London: Pitman Medical Publishing Company, 1964.

Apted, F.I.C. "Sleeping Sickness in Tanganyika, Past, Present, and Future." *Transactions of the Royal Society of Tropical Medicine and Hygiene* (1962): 15–29.

Balslev, Knud. *History of Leprosy in Tanzania*. Nairobi: African Medical and Research Foundation, 1989.

Bax, S. Napier. "Notes on the Presence of Tsetse Fly, between 1857 and 1915, in the Dar es Salaam Area." *TNR* 16 (December 1943): 33–48.

Beck, Ann. *History of the British Medical Administration of East Africa, 1900–1950*. Cambridge, MA: Harvard University Press, 1970.

———. *Medicine and Society in Tanganyika, 1890–1930: A Historical Inquiry*. Philadelphia: American Philosophical Society, 1977.

———. *Medicine, Tradition, and Development in Kenya and Tanzania, 1920–1970*. Waltham, MA: Crossroads Press, 1981.

———. "Priorities in Biological Research at Amani, 1902–14." *TNR* 86/87 (1981): 13–16.

———. "Role of Medicine in German East Africa." *Bulletin of the History of Medicine* 2 (1971): 170–78.

Bennet, F. J., S. A. Hall, J. S. Lutwama, and E. R. Rado. "Medical Manpower in East Africa: Prospects and Problems." *EAMJ* 4 (April 1965): 149–61.

Blacker, J. G. C. "Fertility Trends of the Asian Population of Tanganyika." *Population Studies* 1 (July 1959): 41–60.

Blacker, J. G. C., D. F. Roberts, and Ralph E. S. Tanner. "Population Growth and Differential Fertility in Zanzibar Protectorate." *Population Studies* 3 (March 1962): 258–66.

Blackman, V. "Some Observations on the Severe Anaemias of Dar es Salaam." *EAMJ* (1962): 235–49.

Christie, James. *Cholera Epidemics in East Africa*. London: Macmillan, 1876.

Clyde, David F. "Drug Resistance of Malaria Parasites in Tanzania." *EAMJ* 10 (October 1966): 405–08.

———. *History of the Medical Services of Tanganyika*. Dar es Salaam: GP, 1962.

———. *Malaria in Tanzania*. London: OUP, 1966.

Clyde, David F., and S. Mluba. "Malaria Distribution in Tanganyika: Part IV: Central Tanganyika." *EAMJ* 8 (August 1964): 375–85.

Colas, J. L. "Geographical Distribution of Onchocerciasis in the Ulanga Area, Tanzania." *EAMJ* 10 (October 1966): 426–29.

Davey, J. B. "Outbreak of Human Trypanosomiasis (*Trypanosoma rhodesiense* Infection) in Mwanza District, Tanganyika Territory." *Transactions of the Royal Society of Tropical Medicine and Hygiene* (1924): 474–81.

Davies, J.N.P. "James Christie and the Cholera Epidemics of East Africa." *EAMJ* (1959): 1–6.

Diefenbacher, Albert. "Das Irrenasyl Lutindi in der Kolonie Deutsch-Ostafrika." *Historia Hospitalium* (1986/88): 200–8.

———. *Psychiatrie und Kolonialismus: Zur 'Irrenfursorge' in der Kolonie Deutsch-Ostafrika*. New York: Campus, 1985.

Fairbairn, H. "Agricultural Problems Posed by Sleeping Sickness Settlements." *East African Agricultural Journal* (1943): 17–22.

———. "Sleeping Sickness in Tanganyika Territory, 1922–1946." *Tropical Diseases Bulletin* (1948): 1–17.

Gallivan, John. *Review of Zanzibar's Health Sector*. Washington, D.C.: Department of Health, Education, and Welfare, 1979.

Giblin, James. "Trypanosomiasis Control in African Society: An Evaded Issue?" *JAH* 1 (1990): 59–80.

Gish, Oscar. *Planning the Health Sector: The Tanzanian Experience*. London: Croom Helm, 1975.

Goatley, K. D., and P. Jordan. "Schistosomiasis in Zanzibar and Pemba." *EAMJ* 1 (January, 1965): 1–9.

Gottlieb, Manuel. *Health Care Financing in Mainland Tanzania*. Syracuse: Maxwell School of Citizenship and Public Affairs, Syracuse University, 1975.

Grech, P. "Fluorosis in Young Persons: A Further Survey in Northern Tanganyika, Tanzania." *British Journal of Radiology* (1966): 761–64.

Grech, P., and M. C. Latham. "Fluorosis in the Northern Region of Tanganyika." *Transactions of the Royal Society for Tropical Medicine and Hygiene* (1964): 566–74.

Griffiths, J.E.S. "Aba-Ha of the Tanganyika Territory: Some Aspects of Their Tribal Organizations and Sleeping Sickness Concentrations." *TNR* 2 (October 1936): 72–76.

Haddock, D.R.W. "Neurological Disorders in Tanzania." *Journal of Tropical Medicine and Hygiene* (1965): 161–66.

Hamza, M. H., and Malcolm M. Segall. *Care of the Newborn Baby in Tanzania*. Dar es Salaam: TPH, 1975.

Hart, R. "Maternal and Child Health Services in Tanzania." *Tropical Doctor* (1977): 179–85.

Hartwig, Gerald W. "Economic Consequences of Long-Distance Trade in East Africa: The Disease Factor." *ASR* 2 (September 1975): 63–73.

Hatchell, C. W. "Early 'Sleeping Sickness Settlement' in South-Western Tanganyika." *TNR* 27 (June 1949): 60–64.

———. "Resettlement in Areas Reclaimed from Tsetse Fly." *TNR* 53 (October 1959): 243–49.

Heggenhougen, Kris, Eustace P.Y. Muhondwa, Patrick Vaughan, and J. Rutabanzibwa-Ngaiza, eds. *Community Health Workers: The Tanzanian Experience*. Oxford: OUP, 1987.

Henn, Albert E. *Tanzania: Health Sector Strategy*. Dar es Salaam: USAID/Tanzania, 1980.

Hobbs, Violet H. "Medical Work in Kongwa, Tanganyika Territory." *Mission Hospital* (1927): 313–16.

Imperato, P. J. "Witchcraft and Traditional Medicine Among the Luo of Tanzania." *TNR* 66 (December 1966): 193–201.

Innes, James Ross. "Leprosy in Tanganyika." *EAMJ* 8 (August 1949): 212–15.

Jonsson, U. "Ideological Framework and Health Development in Tanzania, 1961–2000." *Social Science and Medicine* 7 (1986): 745–53.

Kilama, Wen. *War against Mosquitoes and Mosquito-Borne Diseases in Tanzania: Some Lost Battles*. Dar es Salaam: DUP, 1994.

Kimati, V. P. *World's Best Medicine and a New Health Prescription*. Dar es Salaam: DUP, 1983.

Koch, Robert. "Report on West Usambara from the Point of View of Health (5/8/1898)." *TNR* 35 (July 1953): 7–13.

Kohi, T. W., and M. J. Kohi. "Knowledge, Attitudes, and Perceived Support of Tanzanian Nurses When Caring for Patients with AIDS." *International Journal of Nursing Studies* 1 (1994): 77–86.

Korn, J. "Intensive Survey for Leprosy in a Tanzania Village." *EAMJ* 3 (March 1966): 96–98.

Latham, M. C. "Clinical Nutrition Survey of Certain Areas of the Dodoma and Kondoa Districts of Tanganyika." *EAMJ* 2 (February 1964): 69–77.

———. "Clinical Nutritional Survey of Certain Areas of the Rufuji District of Tanganyika." *EAMJ* (1963): 87–95.

———. "Goiter Survey in Ukinga, Tanzania (formerly Tanganyika)." *Transactions of the Royal Society for Tropical Medicine* (1965): 342–48.

———. "Nutritional Aetiology of a Neuropathy Found in Tanganyika." *British Journal of Nutrition* (1964): 129–34.

Latham, M. C., and F. J. Stare. "Nutritional Studies in Tanzania (Tanganyika)." *World Review of Nutrition and Dietetics* (1967): 31–71.

Legislative Council of Tanganyika. *Review of the Medical Policy of Tanganyika, 1949.* Dar es Salaam: GP, 1949.

Little, Marilyn. " 'Native Development' and Chronic Malnutrition in Sukumaland, Tanganyika, 1925–1945." Ph.D. diss., University of Minnesota, 1987.

Lwihula, G., L. Dahlgren, J. Killewo, and A. Sandström. "AIDS Epidemic in Kagera Region, Tanzania: The Experiences of Local People." *AIDS Care* 3 (1993): 347–55.

McKenzie, D. A. "Native Authority Dispensary System in Tanganyika Territory." *EAMJ* 7 (July 1948): 273–80.

McMahon, J. E., and S. S. Baalawy. "Search for Animal Reservoirs of *Schistosome mansoni* in the Mwanza Area of Tanzania." *EAMJ* 8 (August 1967): 325–26.

Moffett, J. P. "Strategic Retreat From Tsetse Fly: Uyowa and Bugoma Concentrations, 1937." *TNR* 7 (June 1939): 35–38.

Nhonoli, A. M. "Enquiry into the Infant Mortality Rate in Rural Areas of Unyamwezi." *EAMJ* 1 (January 1954): 1–12.

Nsekela, Amon J., and Aloysius M. Nhonoli. *Development of Health Services and Society in Mainland Tanzania: A Historical Overview: Tumetoka Mbali.* Kampala: EALB, 1976.

Redmayne, Alison. "Hehe Medicine." *TNR* 70 (July 1969): 29–40.

Scott, H. R. "Public Health Services in Dar es Salaam in the 'Twenties." *EAMJ* 7 (1963): 339–56.

Scott, R. R. *Memorandum on the Future Development of the Medical Services of Tanganyika Territory.* Dar es Salaam: GP, 1942.

Setel, Philip Wittman. "Bo'n Town Life: Youth, AIDS, and the Changing Character of Adulthood in Kilimanjaro, Tanzania." Ph.D. diss., Boston University, 1994.

Shija, J. K. *Surgery in Tanzania.* Dar es Salaam: DUP, 1991.

"Sleeping Sickness Investigation in German East Africa." *Society for the Preservation of the Wild Fauna of the Empire* (1913): 87–88.

Stirling, Leader. *Tanzanian Doctor.* London: C. Hurst, 1977.

Sturrock, R. F. "Hookworm Studies in Tanganyika." *EAMJ* 11 (November 1964): 520–29.

———. "Hookworm Studies in Tanganyika (Tanzania)." *EAMJ* 3 (March 1967): 142–49.

Swantz, Lloyd W. *Medicine Man among the Zaramo of Dar es Salaam.* Uppsala: SIAS, 1990.

Swinnerton, C. F. M. "Entomological Aspects of an Outbreak of Sleeping Sickness

Near Mwanza, Tanganyika Territory." *Bulletin of Entomological Research* (1923): 317–70.

———. "Experiment in Control of Tsetse Flies at Shinyanga, Tanganyika Territory." *Bulletin of Entomological Research* (1924/25): 313–37.

Tanganyika Territory. *Plan for the Development of Medical Services in Tanganyika*. Dar es Salaam: GP, 1956.

———. *Revised Development and Welfare Plan for Tanganyika*. Dar es Salaam: GP, 1951.

Tanner, Ralph E. S. "Sukuma Fertility: An Analysis of 148 Marriages in Mwanza District, Tanganyika." *EAMJ* 3 (March 1956): 96–99.

Titmuss, Richard. *Health Services of Tanganyika: A Report to the Government*. London: Pitman's Medical Publishing Company, 1964.

Turshen, Meredith. "Impact of Colonialism on Health and Health Services in Tanzania." *International Journal of Health Services* (1977): 7–35.

———. *Political Ecology of Disease in Tanzania*. New Brunswick: Rutgers University Press, 1984.

United Republic of Tanzania, Ministry of Health. *National AIDS Control Programme AIDS Surveillance*. Dar es Salaam: NACP Epidemiology Unit, 1991.

Van Etten, G. M. *Rural Health Development in Tanzania*. Amsterdam: Gorcum, 1976.

Walter Reed Army Institute of Research. *Tanganyika*. Washington, D.C.: Walter Reed Army Medical Center, 1962.

Weiss, B. " 'Buying Her Grave': Money, Movement, and AIDS in North-West Tanzania." *Africa* 1 (1993): 19–35.

White, Paul. *Alias Jungle Doctor: An Autobiography*. London: Paternoster, 1977.

———. *Doctor of Tanganyika*. London: Paternoster, 1952.

———. *Jungle Doctor Panorama*. London: Paternoster, 1960.

Wilcocks, C. *Tuberculosis in Tanganyika Territory*. Dar es Salaam: GP, 1938.

Willett, K. C. "Trypanosomiasis Research at Tinde." *TNR* 34 (January 1953): 33–34.

Williams, M. C., and J. P. Woodall. "Epidemic of an Illness Resembling Dengue in the Morogoro District of Tanganyika." *EAMJ* 6 (June 1964): 271–75.

Wilson, D.B. *Report of the Malaria Unit, Moshi, 1936*. Dar es Salaam: GP, 1938.

———. *Report of the Malaria Unit, Tanga, 1933–34*. Dar es Salaam: GP, 1936.

Winteler, John C. "Medicine in the Groundnut Scheme." *EAMJ* 11 (November 1949): 332–35.

World Bank. *Tanzania: AIDS Assessment and Planning Study*. Washington, D.C.: World Bank, 1992.

———. *Tanzania Population, Health and Nutrition Sector Review*. Washington, D.C.: World Bank, 1989.

Young, T. Kue. "Socialist Development and Primary Health Care: The Case of Tanzania." *Human Organization* 2 (Summer 1986): 128–34.

Yudkin, John S. "Economics of Pharmaceutical Supply in Tanzania." *International Journal of Health Services* 3 (1980): 455–78.

T. Literature and Language

Abdulaziz, M. H. *Muyaka: Nineteenth-Century Swahili Popular Poetry*. Nairobi: EAPH, 1977.

Arnold, Stephen H. "Popular Literature in Tanzania: Its Background and Relation to 'East African' Literature." *Kiswahili* 1/2 (1984): 60–86.

Harries, Lyndon. "Swahili Literature in the National Context." *Review of National Literatures* 2 (1971): 38–65.

———. *Swahili Poetry.* Oxford: Clarendon Press, 1962.

———. "Syntactic Features of Swahili Sentences." *AS* 3 (1973): 153–62.

Glinga, Werber. "Life Story, Utendi, and Colonial Novel: Literature in 'German East Africa.' " *Afrika Übersee* 2 (1987): 257–77.

Harries, Lyndon. *Swahili Poetry.* Oxford: OUP, 1962.

Hartwig, Gerald W. "Oral Traditions Concerning the Early Iron Age in Northwestern Tanzania." *African Historical Studies* 1 (1971): 93–114.

Jerrard, R. C. "Three Swahili Fables." *TNR* 6 (December 1938): 93–98.

Kiraithe, Jacqueline M., and Nancy T. Baden. "Portuguese Influence in East African Languages." *AS* 1 (1976): 3–31.

Knappert, Jan. *Choice of Flowers: Swahili Songs of Love and Passion.* London: Heinemann, 1972.

———. *Four Centuries of Swahili Verse: A Literary History and Anthology.* London: Heinemann, 1979.

———. *Traditional Swahili Poetry: An Investigation into the Concepts of East African Islam as Reflected in the Utenzi Literature.* Leiden: E. J. Brill, 1967.

———. "Social and Moral Concepts in Swahili Islamic Literature." *Africa* 2 (1970): 125–36.

Mlacha, S.A.K. "Uprooting the Traditional Culture in Kiswahili Prose Fiction." *African Marburgensia* 2 (1986): 95–106.

Nyerere, Julius K. *Tanzania! Tanzania!* Dar es Salaam: TPH, 1993.

Pike, Charles. "History and Imagination: Swahili Literature and Resistance to German Language Imperialism in Tanzania, 1885–1910." *IJAHS* 2 (1986): 201–33.

Polomé, Edgar C. *Swahili Language Handbook.* Washington, D.C.: Center for Applied Linguistics, 1967.

Polomé, Edgar C., and C. P. Hill, eds. *Language in Tanzania.* London: OUP, 1980.

Pouwels, Randall L. "Swahili Literature and History in the Post-structuralist Era." *IJAHS* 2 (1992): 261–83.

Rubagumya, Casmir M. "Language Planning in the Tanzanian Educational System: Problems and Prospects." *Journal of Multilingual and Multicultural Development* 4 (1986): 283–300.

Tucker, A. N. "Foreign Sounds in Swahili." *Bulletin of the School of Oriental and African Studies* (1946): 854–71; and (1947): 214–32.

Westermann, D. "Swahili as the Lingua Franca of East Africa." *Church Overseas* (1933): 20–31.

White, P. F. "Diva: The Swahili Aesop." *TNR* 73 (July 1937): 55–62.

Whiteley, W. H. "Changing Position of Swahili in East Africa." *Afrika* (1956): 343–54.

———. *Swahili: The Rise of a National Language.* London: Methuen, 1969.

Zawawi, Sharifa M. *What's in a Name? Unaitwaje? A Swahili Book of Names.* Lawrenceville, NJ: Africa World Press, 1993.

U. Communications, Media, and Transport

Blöhm, Kurt. *Tanganyika Territorium und Englische Presse.* Berlin: Junker und Dünnhaupt, 1935.

Cliffe, Lionel. "Implications of the Tanzam Railway for the Liberation and Development of Southeastern Africa." In *Land-Locked Countries of Africa*, ed. Z. Cervenka, 293–99. Uppsala: SIAS, 1973.

Condon, John C. "Nation Building and Image Building in the Tanzanian Press." *JMAS* 3 (November 1967): 335–54.

Gillman, Clement. "Short History of the Tanganyika Railways." *TNR* 13 (June 1942): 14–56.

Hall, Richard, and Hugh Peyman. *Great Uhuru Railway: China's Showpiece in Africa*. London: Victor Gollancz, 1976.

Hill, M. F. *Permanent Way*. Vol. 2, *The Story of the Tanganyika Railways*. Nairobi: East African Railways and Harbours, 1957.

Hoyle, B. S. *Seaports and Development: The Experience of Kenya and Tanzania*. London: Gordon and Breach, 1983.

———. *Seaports of East Africa: A Geographical Study*. Nairobi: EAPH, 1967.

Konde, Hafji S. *Press Freedom in Tanzania*. Arusha: Eastern Africa Publications, 1984.

Makoni, Tonderai. "Economic Appraisal of the Tanzania-Zambia Railway." *TAR* 4 (1972): 599–616.

Mcha, Marietta C. *North-South Information Flow and the Role of Foreign Correspondents in Promoting National Development Strategies: A Case Study of Tanzania*. Dar es Salaam: Center for Foreign Relations, 1981.

Ng'wanakilala, Nkwabi. *Mass Communication and Development of Socialism in Tanzania*. Dar es Salaam: TPH, 1981.

Omari, I. M. "Kiswahili Press and Nationalism in Tanganyika 1954–1958." *Taamuli* 2 (1972): 34–46.

Pipping–van Hulten, Ida. *Episode of Colonial History: The German Press in Tanzania*. Uppsala: SIAS, 1974.

Redeker, Dietrich. *Die Geschichte der Tagespresse Deutsch-Ostafrikas (1899–1916)*. Berlin: Triltsch und Huther, 1937.

———. *Journalismus in Deutsch-Ostafrika 1899–1916*. Frankfurt: Diesterweg, 1937.

Scotten, James F. "Tanganyika's African Press, 1937–1960: A Nearly Forgotten Preindependence Forum." *ASR* 1 (April 1978): 1–18.

Seidlitz, Peter. "Along the Tanzam Railway." *Swiss Review of World Affairs* (April 1976): 20–21.

Smyth, Rosaleen. "Feature Film in Tanzania." *AA* 352 (July 1989): 389–96.

Tanzania-Zambia Railway Authority. *TZR: Ten Years of Tazara Operations, Review and Perspective*. [Dar es Salaam?]: The Authority, 1988.

V. Urban Centers and Urbanization Studies

Banyikwa, W. F. "Effects of Insensitivity in Planning Land for Urban Development in Dar es Salaam." *African Review* 2 (1988): 35–43.

———. "Effects of Insensitivity in Planning Land for Urban Development in Tanzania: The Case of Dar es Salaam." *JEARD* (1989): 83–94.

Casson, W. T. "Architectural Notes on Dar es Salaam." *TNR* 71 (1970): 181–83.

De Blij, H. J. *Dar es Salaam: A Study in Urban Geography*. Evanston: Northwestern University Press, 1963.

Ellis, Frank. "Relative Agricultural Prices and the Urban Bias Model: A Comparative Analysis of Tanzania and Fiji." *Journal of Development Studies* 3 (1984): 28–51.

Fair, T. J. D. "Tanzania: Some Aspects of Urban Growth and Policy." *Africa Insight* 1 (1984): 33–40.

Gillman, Clement. "Dar es Salaam, 1860 to 1940: A Story of Growth and Change." *TNR* 20 (December, 1945): 1–23.

Gleave, M. B. "Dar es Salaam Transport Corridor: An Appraisal." *AA* 363 (April 1992): 249–67.

Hayuma, A. M. "Growth of Population and Employment in the Dar es Salaam City Region, Tanzania." *Ekistics* 301 (1983): 255–59.

Hosier, Richard H. "Urban Energy Systems in Tanzania: A Tale of Three Cities." *Energy Policy* (May 1993): 510–23.

Hosier, Richard H., and W. Kipondya. "Urban Household Energy Use in Tanzania: Prices, Substitutes, and Poverty." *Energy Policy* (May 1993): 454–73.

Hosier, Richard H., Mark J. Mwandosya, and Matthew L. Luhanga. "Future Energy Development in Tanzania: The Energy Costs of Urbanization." *Energy Policy* (May 1993): 524–42.

Hoyle, B. S. "African Politics and Port Expansion at Dar es Salaam." *Geographical Review* 1 (1978): 31–50.

Leslie, J. A. K. *Survey of Dar es Salaam*. London: OUP, 1963.

Lugalla, Joe L. P. "Is Dodoma, the New Capital City of Tanzania, a Socialist City?" *African Urban Quarterly* 2 (1987): 134–48.

Lusugga Kironde, J. M. "Will Dodoma Ever Be the New Capital of Tanzania?" *Geoforum* 4 (1993): 435–53.

Mosha, A. C. "Urban Planning in Tanzania at the Crossroads." *Review of Rural and Urban Planning in Southern and Eastern Africa* (1989): 79–91.

Sabot, R. H. *Economic Development and Urban Migration*. Oxford: Clarendon Press, 1979.

Sawers, Larry. "Urban Primacy in Tanzania." *Economic Development and Cultural Change* 4 (July 1989): 841–59.

Sutton, J.E.G. "Dar es Salaam: A Sketch of a Hundred Years." *TNR* 71 (1970): 1–19.

Van Donge, Jan Kees. "Waluguru Traders in Dar es Salaam." *AA* 363 (April 1992): 181–205.

W. Zanzibar and the Islands

Abdurahman, Muhammad. "Anthropological Notes from the Zanzibar Protectorate." *TNR* 8 (December 1939): 59–84.

Akinola, G. A. "Slavery and Slave Revolts in the Sultanate of Zanzibar in the Nineteenth Century." *Journal of the Historical Society of Nigeria* (1972): 215–28.

Albrand, Fortuné. "Extrait d'une mémoire sur Zanzibar et sur Quiloa." *Bulletin de la Société de Géographie*, second series, 10 (August 1838): 65–84.

Alpers, Edward A. " 'Ordinary Household Chores': Ritual and Power in a Nineteenth Century Swahili Women's Spirit Possession Cult." *IJAHS* 4 (1984): 677–702.

Afro-Shirazi Party. *Afro-Shirazi Party: A Liberation Movement.* Zanzibar: Printing Press Corporation, 1973.

———. *Afro-Shirazi Party Revolution, 1964–1974.* Zanzibar: Printing Press Corporation, 1974.

———. *Short History of Zanzibar.* Zanzibar: Printing Press Corporation, 1973.

Ayany, Samuel G. *History of Zanzibar: A Study in Constitutional Development, 1934–1964.* Nairobi: EALB, 1970.

Bailey, Martin. "Les relations extérieures de Zanzibar." *Revue Française d'Etudes Politiques Africaines* (March 1972): 65–84.

———. *Union of Tanganyika and Zanzibar: A Study in Political Integration.* Syracuse: Maxwell School of Citizenship and Public Affairs, Syracuse University, 1973.

———. "Zanzibar's External Relations." *International Journal of Politics* 4 (Winter 1974): 35–57.

Barton, F. R. "Zanzibar Doors." *Man* 63 (June 1924): 81–83.

Bateman, George W. *Zanzibar Tales Told by Natives of the East Coast of Africa.* Chicago: A. C. McClung, 1901.

Baumann, Oscar. *Die Insel Pemba.* Leipzig: Duncker und Humblot, 1899.

———. *Die Insel Sansibar.* Leipzig: Duncker und Humblot, 1897.

———. "Mafia Island." *TNR* 46 (January, 1957): 1–24.

Baxter, H. C. "Pangani: The Trade Centre of Ancient History." *TNR* 17 (June 1944): 15–25.

Beech, Mervyn W. "Slavery on the East Coast of Africa." *Journal of the African Society* (1916): 145–49.

Beecher, W. H. *Cruise of the "Brooklyn."* Philadelphia: Lippincott, 1885.

Belleville, A. "Trip around the South End of Zanzibar Island." *Proceedings of the Royal Geographical Society* (1875/76): 69–74.

Bennett, Norman R. "Americans in Zanzibar: 1825–1845." *TNR* 56 (March 1961): 93–108.

———. "Americans in Zanzibar: 1845–1865." *TNR* (July 1961): 121–38.

———. "Americans in Zanzibar: 1865–1915." *EIHC* 1 (January 1962): 36–61.

———. "France and Zanzibar, 1844 to the 1860s." *IJAHS* 4 (1973): 602–32; and 1 (1974): 27–55.

Bennett, Norman R., ed. *From Zanzibar to Ujiji: The Journal of Arthur W. Dodgshun, 1877–1879.* Boston: African Studies Center, Boston University, 1969.

———. *History of the Arab State of Zanzibar.* London: Methuen, 1978.

———. "Stanley and the American Consuls at Zanzibar." *EIHC* 1 (January 1964): 41–58.

———. "William H. Hathorne: Merchant and Consul in Zanzibar." *EIHC* (1963): 117–46.

———. *Zanzibar Letters of Edward D. Ropes, Jr., 1882–1892.* Boston: African Studies Center, Boston University, 1973.

Berman, Edward H. "Salem and Zanzibar: 1825–1850: Twenty-Five Years of Commercial Relations." *EIHC* 4 (October 1969): 338–62.

Bhacker, M. Reda. "Family Strife and Foreign Intervention: Causes in the Separation of Zanzibar from Oman: A Reappraisal." *Bulletin of the School of Oriental and African Studies* (1991): 269–80.

————. "Roots of Domination and Dependency: British Reaction towards the Development of Omani Commerce at Muscat and Zanzibar in the Nineteenth Century." D.Phil. diss., Oxford University, 1988.

————. *Trade and Empire in Muscat and Zanzibar: Roots of British Dimension.* London and New York: Routledge, 1992.

Blais, J. "Les anciens esclaves à Zanzibar." *Anthropos* (1915/16): 504–11.

Bochkaryov, Yuri. "Background to Zanzibar." *New Times* (5 February 1964): 13–15.

Brady, Cyrus Townsend. *Commerce and Conquest in East Africa, with Particular Reference to the Salem Trade with Zanzibar.* Salem: Essex Institute, 1950.

Brown, Walter T. "Politics of Business: Relations between Zanzibar and Bagamoyo in the Late Nineteenth Century." *AHS* 3 (1971): 631–43.

Browne, J. Ross. *Etchings of a Whaling Cruise with Notes of a Sojourn on the Island of Zanzibar.* Cambridge, MA: Harvard University Press, 1968.

Burton, F. R. "Zanzibar Doors." *Man* 6 (June 1924): 63–65.

Burton, Richard F. *Zanzibar: City, Island, and Coast.* 2 vols. London: Tinsley Brothers, 1872.

————. "Zanzibar: and Two Months in East Africa." *Blackwood's Magazine* (1858): 200–24, 276–90, 572–89.

Calton, W. E., G. E. Tidbury, and G. F. Walker. "Study of the More Important Soils of Zanzibar Protectorate." *East African Agricultural Journal* 1 (July 1955): 53–60.

Campbell, Jane. "Multiracialism and Politics in Zanzibar." *Political Science Quarterly* 1 (March 1962): 72–87.

Caprivi, Leopold von. *Die Ostafrikanische Frage und der Helgoland-Sansibar-Vertrag.* Berlin: Triltsch und Huther, 1934.

Cave, Basil. "End of Slavery in Zanzibar and British East Africa." *Journal of the African Society* (1909): 19–30.

Charmetant, Le P. *D'Alger à Zanzibar.* Paris: Librairie de la Société Bibliographique, 1882.

Chase, Hank. "Zanzibar Treason Trial." *ROAPE* (May/August 1976): 14–33.

Childs, Mrs. Harris R. "Zanzibar." *NGM* 8 (August 1912): 810–24.

Chittick, H. Neville. "Kilwa and the Arab Settlement of the East African Coast." *JAH* 2 (1963): 179–90.

————. "Notes on Kilwa." *TNR* 53 (October 1959): 179–203.

————. "New Look at the History of Pate." *JAH* 4 (1969): 375–91.

Christie, J. "Slavery in Zanzibar As It Is." In *East African Slave Trade*, ed. H. A. Fraser, Bishop Tozer, and J. Christie, 31–64. London: Harrison, 1871.

Clayton, Anthony. *1948 Zanzibar General Strike.* Uppsala: SIAS, 1976.

————. "General Strike in Zanzibar, 1948." *JAH* 3 (1976): 417–34.

————. *Zanzibar Revolution and Its Aftermath.* Hamden: Archon Books, 1981.

Colomb, John C.R. *Slave Catching in the Indian Ocean.* London: Longmans, 1873.

Conner, A. "Aspects of Zanzibar." *Reporter* (28 March 1963): 44–45.

Cooke, James J. "Madagascar and Zanzibar: A Case Study in African Colonial Friction, 1894–1897." *ASR* 3 (December 1970): 435–43.

Cooper Frederick. *From Slaves to Squatters: Plantation Labor and Agriculture in Zanzibar and Coastal Kenya, 1890–1925.* New Haven: YUP, 1980.

————. *Plantation Slavery on the East Coast of Africa.* New Haven: YUP, 1977.

Cornevin, Robert. "Zanzibar et Pemba." *Revue Française d'Etudes Politiques Africaines* 44 (August 1969): 40–54.

Coulbois, François. "Le Sultanat de Zanguebar." *Les Missions Catholiques* 18 (1886): 382–84, 393–95, 404–06, 412–14.

———. Seconde tournée dans le vicariat apostolique du Zanguebar." *Les Missions Catholiques* (1886): 594–97, 604–05, 615–20.

———. "La situation politique et eligieuse au Zanguebar." *Les Missions Catholiques* (1889): 109–12.

———. "Une tournée dans le vicariat apostolique du Zanguebar." *Les Missions Catholiques* (1885): 462–66, 485–89, 497–502, 512–15, 521–25, 536–38, 545–48.

Craster, John Evelyn Edmund. *Pemba: the Spice Island of Zanzibar.* London: T. Fisher Unwin, 1913.

Crofton, Richard Hayes. *Old Consulate at Zanzibar.* London: OUP, 1935.

———. *Pageant of the Spice Islands.* London: John Bale, Sons and Danielsson, 1936.

———. *Statistics of the Zanzibar Protectorate, 1893–1920.* London: Eastern Press, 1921.

———. *Zanzibar Affairs, 1914–33.* London: Francis Edwards, 1953.

Crozon, Ariel. "L'adhésion de Zanzibar à l'Organisation de la Conférence Islamique: Chronique d'une crise." *Politique Africaine* 52 (December 1993): 140–44.

Dale, Godfrey. *Peoples of Zanzibar.* London: UMCA, 1920.

De Groot, Emile. "Great Britain and Germany in Zanzibar: Consul Holmwood's Papers, 1886–1887." *JMAS* 2 (June 1953): 120–38.

Decraene, Philippe. "Zanzibar: La mort d'un tyran." *Revue Française d'Etudes Politiques Africaines* 76 (April 1972): 22–23.

Devereux, W. Cope. *Cruise in the "Gorgon."* London: Dawsons of Pall Mall, 1968.

Dorman, M. H. "Kilwa Civilization and the Kilwa Ruins." *TNR* 6 (December 1938): 61–71.

Duggan, William R. "Sultan and the Baseball Game." *Foreign Service Journal* 6 (1977): 21–23, 36–37.

East African Common Services Organization. *Pattern of Income Expenditure and Consumption of Unskilled Workers in Zanzibar: Report on a Survey Carried Out in April 1962.* Nairobi: East African Statistical Department, 1963.

Elton, Frederic. "On the Coastal Country of East Africa, South of Zanzibar." *Journal of the Royal Geographical Society* (1874): 227–52.

Federation of Progressive Trade Unions. *Memorandum of the Federation of Progressive Trade Unions to Mr. Duncan Sandys, Secretary of State for the Colonies and Commonwealth Relations, 23rd February 1963.* Zanzibar: FPTU, 1963.

———, Political Bureau. *Brief History of International Working Class Struggle.* Zanzibar: FPTU, 1962.

Farsy, Abdulla Saleh. *Sayyid Said bin Sultan.* Zanzibar: Mwongozi Printing Press, 1942.

———. *Tarehe ya Iman Shafi na Wanavyuoni Wakubwa wa Mashariki ya Afrika.* Zanzibar: Federal Department, 1944.

Fawcus, W. P. Jones. "Experience in Zanzibar and East Africa." *Manchester Geographical Journal* (1908): 5–11.

Firminger, W. K. "Protectorate of Zanzibar." *British Empire Series* (1899): 259–78.

Fitzgerald, William Walter Augustine. *Travels in the Coastlands of British East Africa and the Islands of Zanzibar and Pemba: Their Agricultural Resources and General Characteristics.* London: Chapman and Hall, 1898.

Flint, J. E. "Zanzibar 1890–1950." In *History of East Africa*, vol. 2, ed. Vincent Harlow and E. M. Chilver, 641–71. Oxford: Clarendon Press, 1965.

Flury, S. "Kufic Inscriptions of the Kizimkazi Mosque, Zanzibar, A.D. 1107." *Journal of the Royal Asiatic Society* (1922): 257–64.

Freeman-Grenville, G.S.P. "Coinage in East Africa before Portuguese Times." *Numismatic Chronicle*, new series, (1957): 151–75.

———. "East African Coin Finds and Their Historical Significance." *JAH* 1 (1960): 31–43.

———. "A Few Remarks on Zanzibar and the East Coast of Africa." *Proceedings of the Royal Geographical Society* (1875/76): 343–54.

———. *French at Kilwa Island.* Oxford: Clarendon Press, 1965.

———. "The History and Coinage of the Sultans of Kilwa." *TNR* 45 (December 1956): 33–66.

———. "New Hoard and Some Unpublished Variants of the Coinage of the Sultans of Kilwa." *Numismatic Chronicle* (1954): 220–25.

———. "Some Problems of East African Coinage." *TNR* 52 (October 1959): 250–60.

———. "Zanzibar, A Commercial Power." *Macmillans's Magazine* (1875): 275–88.

———. "Zanzibar and Its Sultan." *Macmillan's Magazine* (1875): 183–92.

Galton, Francis. "Zanzibar: A Lecture at the S. P. G." *Mission Field* (1861): 121–30.

Gates-Hunt, Richard H. "Salem and Zanzibar: A Special Relationship." *EIHC* 1 (1981): 1–26.

Gavin, R. J. "Bartle Frere Mission to Zanzibar." *Historical Journal* 2 (1962): 122–48.

———. "Sayyid Sa'id." *Tarikh* 1 (1965): 16–29.

Germain, A. "Notes sur Zanzibar et la côte orientale d'Afrique." *Bulletin de la Société de Géographie de Paris* (1868): 530–59.

Gramly, R. M. "Archaeological Reconnaissance at Pangani Bay." *TNR* 86/87 (1981): 17–28.

Grandidier, Alfred. *Notice sur l'Isle de Zanzibar.* Saint-Denis: Roussin, 1868.

Grant, James A. "Zanzibar: A Review." *Blackwood's Magazine* (1872): 691–708.

Gray, Sir John Milner. "The British Vice-Consulate at Kilwa Kivinji, 1884–1885." *TNR* 51 (December 1958): 174–193.

———. "Commercial Intercourse between Angola and Kilwa in the Sixteenth Century." *TNR* 57 (September 1961): 173–74.

———. "Dar es Salaam under the Sultans of Zanzibar." *TNR* 33 (July 1952): 1–21.

———. "Early Portuguese Visitors to Kilwa: A Further Note." *TNR* 57 (September 1961): 175–76.

———. "Fort Santiago at Kilwa." *TNR* 58/59 (March/September 1962): 175–78.

———. "French Account of Kilwa at the End of the Eighteenth Century." *TNR* 63 (1964): 222–28.

———. "French at Kilwa, 1776–1784." *TNR* 44 (September 1956): 28–49.

———. "French at Kilwa in 1797," *TNR* 58/59 (March/September 1962): 172–73.

———. "The Hadimu and Tumbatu of Zanzibar." *TNR* 81/82 (1977): 135–53.

————. "History of Kilwa." *TNR* 31 (July 1951): 1–25; and 32 (January 1952): 11–38.

————. *History of Zanzibar from the Middle Ages to 1856*. London: OUP, 1962.

————. "Recovery of Kilwa by the Arabs in 1785." *TNR* 62 (March, 1964): 20–24.

————. *Report on the Inquiry into Claims to Certain Lands at or Near Ngezi, Vitongoji, in the Mudiria of Chake Chake, in the District of Pemba*. Zanzibar: GP, 1956.

————. "Sir John Henderson and the Princess of Zanzibar." *TNR* 40 (September 1955): 15–19.

————. "Zanzibar and the Coastal Belt, 1840–1885." In *History of East Africa*, vol. 1, ed. Roland Oliver and Gervase Mathew, 212–51. Oxford: Clarendon Press, 1963.

Grazebrook, W. *Clove of Commerce*. London: Commercial Calculating Company, 1925.

Great Britain, Central Office of Information. *Protectorate of Zanzibar*. London: HMSO, 1959.

————. *Zanzibar*. London: HMSO, 1963.

Great Britain, Colonial Office. *Commission of Inquiry into Disturbances in Zanzibar during June 1961*. London: HMSO, 1961.

————. *Notes on Conditions in Zanzibar*. London: HMSO, 1960.

Greffulhe, H. "Voyage de Lamoo à Zanzibar." *Bulletin de la Société de Géographie et d'Etudes Coloniales de Marseille* (1878): 209–17, 327–60.

Grundy, Kenneth W. "East Africa's Unexpected Marriage: The United Republic of Tanganyika and Zanzibar." *New Leader* (25 May 1964): 15–17.

Guide to Zanzibar. Zanzibar: GP, 1939.

Guillain, Charles. "Côte de Zanguebar et Mascate, 1841." *Revue Coloniale* (1843): 520–63.

Gundara, Jagdish S. "Aspects of Indian Culture in Nineteenth Century Zanzibar." *South Asia* 1 (1980): 14–27.

————. "British Extraterritorial Jurisdiction in Nineteenth Century Zanzibar." *AQ* 3/4 (1983) 10–27.

————. "Fragment of Indian Society in Zanzibar: Conflict and Change in the Nineteenth Century." *AQ* 2/4 (1982): 23–40.

Hailey, Lord. *Native Administration in the British African Territories: Part II. Central Africa: Zanzibar, Nyasaland, Northern Rhodesia*. London: HMSO, 1950.

Hamilton, Genesta. *Princes of Zinj: The Rulers of Zanzibar*. London: Hutchinson and Company, 1957.

Harkema, Roelof Cornelius. *De Stad Zanzibar in de Tweede Helft van de Negentiende Eeuw en Enkele Ondere Osstafrikaanse Kuststeden*. Loenen aan de Vecht, 1967.

Hart, Captain. "Extracts from Brief Notes of a Visit to Zanzibar." *Selections from the Records of the Bombay Government* (1855): 274–83.

Heepe, M. "Suaheli-Chronik von Pate." *Mitteilungen des Seminars für Orientalische Sprachen zu Berlin, Erste Abteilung, Ostasiatische Studien* 3 (1928): 145–92.

Henry, W. "Some Aspects of Education in Zanzibar." *Journal of the African Society* 108 (July 1928): 342–52.

Hichens, W., ed. "Chronicle of Lamu." *Bantu Studies* 1 (1938): 3–33.

Hollingsworth, Lawrence William. *Zanzibar Under the Foreign Office, 1890–1913*. London: Macmillan, 1953.

Hollis, A. C. "Zanzibar: Present Conditions and Interests." *Journal of the African Society* (1929): 217–23.

Holmes, C. F. "Zanzibari Influence at the Southern End of Lake Victoria: The Lake Route." *AHS* 3 (1971): 477–503.

Horton, M. C., and C. M. Clark. "Archaeological Survey of Zanzibar." *Azania* (1985): 167–71.

Hughes, Tony. "Profile on Zanzibar." *Africa South* 3 (April 1961): 85–89.

Hutchison, Alan. "Exorcising the Ghost of Karume." *AR* 2 (March/April 1974): 46–51.

Iannetonne, G. "Zanzibar: Dal Sultanato Arabo alla Republica Popolare." *Rivista di Studi Politici Internazionali* 2 (April/June 1964): 199–209.

Illarionov, N. S. "Etnopoliticheskie Problemy Sovremennogo Zanzibara (Etnos Ostrovnykh Suakhili V 1960–1970 (Gody)." *Sovetskaia Etnografiia* 1 (1982): 46–55.

Imbert, Albert. *Le droit Abadhite chez les musulmans de Zanzibar et de l'Afrique orientale.* Algiers: Adolphe Jourdan, 1903.

Ingrams, William Harold. *Chronology and Genealogies of Zanzibar Rulers.* Zanzibar: GP, 1926.

———. *Zanzibar: Its History and Its People.* London: H. F. and G. Witherby, 1931.

Ingrams, William Harold, and Lawrence William Hollingsworth. *School History of Zanzibar.* London: Macmillan, 1925.

"Investiture of the Sultan of Zanzibar." *Central Africa* (1883): 173–75.

Jablonski, M. "Note sur la géographie de l'Ile de Zanzibar." *Bulletin de la Société de Géographie* (1866): 353–70.

Johnston, Sir Harry Hamilton. "Zanzibar." In *Oxford Survey of the British Empire: Africa,* ed. A. J. Herbertson and O. J. R. Howarth, 251–61. Oxford: Clarendon Press, 1914.

Juma, Aley. *Zanzibar: In the Context.* New Delhi: Lancers International, 1988.

Kabudi, Palamagamba John. "Union of Tanganyika and Zanzibar: Examination of the Treaty of a Political-Legal Union." *Mawazo* 2 (1985): 1–17.

Khamis, I. A. "Zanzibar's Economic Revolution." *EAJ* 2 (February 1972): 19–25.

Kerdudal, Lemauff de. "Quiloa ou Kelous, 1843." *Revue Coloniale* (February 1844): 214–23.

King, Norman. "Mafia." *GJ* 2 (August 1917): 117–25.

Kingdon, H. E. *Conflict of Laws in Zanzibar.* Zanzibar: GP, 1940.

Kirk, John. "Agricultural Resources of Zanzibar." *Kew Bulletin* (1892): 87–91.

Kirkman, James S. "Early History of Oman in East Africa." *Journal of Oman Studies* 6 (1983): 41–58.

———. "Excavations at Ras Mkumbuu on the Island of Pemba." *TNR* 53 (October 1959): 161–78.

———. "Zanzibar Diary of John Studdy Leigh." *IJAHS* 2 (1980): 281–312; and 3 (1980): 492–507.

Kyle, Keith. "Coup in Zanzibar." *AR* 2 (February 1964): 18–20.

———. "Letter from Zanzibar: The Inevitable Coup." *New Leader* (17 February 1964): 11–13.

———. "More Pieces for the East African Puzzle." *AR* 3 (March 1964): 24.

Lanchester, H. V. *Zanzibar: A Study in Tropical Town Planning.* Cheltenham: J. Burrow, 1923.

Last, J.S. *Economic Fisheries of Zanzibar, 1928.* Zanzibar: GP, 1929.

Lemarchand, René. "Revolutionary Phenomena in Stratified Societies: Rwanda and Zanzibar." *Civilisations* 1 (1968): 16–51.

LeRoy, Alexandre. *D'Aden à Zanzibar.* Tours: Alfred Mame et Fils, 1899.

———. Le long des côtes: De Zanzibar à Lamo." *Les Missions Catholiques* (1889): 8–12, 18–20, 30–33, 40–44, 52–56, 65–70, 77–81, 89–92, 101–4, 114–17, 129–32.

———. *Mission du Zanguebar.* Lyon: Imprimerie Pitrat Aine, 1884.

———. "Au Zanguebar Anglais." *Les Missions Catholiques* (1890): 435–37, 448–634.

Liebst, Flo. *Zanzibar: History of the Ruins at Mbweni.* Zanzibar: Out of Africa Ltd., 1992.

Lienhardt, Peter A. "Mosque College of Lamu and Its Social Background." *TNR* 53 (October 1959): 228–42.

Loarer, Captain. "L'Ile de Zanzibar." *Revue de l'Orient* (1851): 240–99.

Lodhi, Abdul Aziz Y. *Institution of Slavery in Zanzibar and Pemba.* Uppsala: SIAS, 1973.

———. "Arabs in Zanzibar: From Sultanate to People's Republic." *Journal of the Institute of Muslim Minority Affairs* (1986): 404–18.

Lofchie, Michael F. "Party Conflict in Zanzibar." *JMAS* 2 (June 1963): 185–207.

———. "Was Okello's Revolution a Conspiracy?" *Transition* 33 (October/November 1967): 39–42.

———. "Zanzibar." In *Political Parties and National Integration in Tropical Africa,* ed. James S. Coleman and Carl Rosberg, 482–509. Berkeley: University of California Press, 1966.

———. *Zanzibar: Background to Revolution.* Princeton: Princeton University Press, 1965.

———. "Zanzibar: Problems and Prospects." *Commonwealth Journal* 6 (December 1963): 247–51.

———. "Zanzibari Revolution: African Protest in a Racially Plural Society." In *Power and Protest in Black Africa,* ed. Robert I. Rotberg and Ali A. Mazrui, 924–67. New York: OUP, 1970.

Luders, Karl. "Sansibar." *Deutsche Rundschau für Geographie und Statistik* (1885): 529–35.

Luwel, M. "Kapitein Ernest Cambier Te Zanzibar, 1882–1885." *Africa-Tervuren* (1962): 85–96; and (1963): 11–31.

Lyne, Robert Nunez. *Apostle of Empire, Being the Life of Sir Lloyd William Mathews.* London: George Allen and Unwin, 1936.

———. "Causes Contributing to the Success of the Zanzibar Clove Industry." *Bulletin of the Imperial Institute* (1910): 143–44.

———. *Zanzibar in Contemporary Times.* London: Hurst and Blackett, 1905.

McClellan, F. C. "Agricultural Resources of the Zanzibar Protectorate." *Bulletin of the Imperial Institute* (1914): 407–29.

Mackay, A. M. "Muscat, Zanzibar and Central Africa." *Church Missionary Intelligencer* (1889): 19–24.

Mackenzie, Donald. "Report on Slavery and the Slave Trade in Zanzibar, Pemba and the Mainland of the British Protectorates of East Africa." *Anti-Slavery Reporter,* 4th series (June/August 1895): 69–96.

Marno, Ernst. "Bericht über eine Excursion von Zanzibar (Saadani) nach Koa-Kiora." *Mittheilungen der kais. und kon. Geographischen Gesellschaft in Wien* (1878): 353–95.

Marras, Etienne. "L'Isle de Zanzibar." *Bulletin de la Société de Géographie de Marseille* (1881): 192–200.

Martin, B. G. "Notes on Some Members of the Learned Classes of Zanzibar and East Africa in the Nineteenth Century." *AHS* 3 (1971): 525–45.

Martin, Esmond Bradley. *Zanzibar: Tradition and Revolution*. London: Hamish Hamilton, 1978.

Martin, Peter J., et al. "Causes of Irregular Clove Production in the Islands of Zanzibar and Pemba." *Experimental Agriculture* 1 (1988): 105–14.

Matola, Y. G., et al. "Malaria in the Islands of Zanzibar and Pemba Eleven Years After the Suspension of a Malaria Eradication Programme." *Central African Journal of Medicine* 5 (1984): 91–96.

Meineke, G. "Sansibar." *Deutsche Kolonialzeitung* (1895): 403–5.

Middleton, John. *Land Tenure in Zanzibar*. London: HMSO, 1961.

———. "Society and Politics in Zanzibar." *Civilisations* 3 (1962): 375–83.

Middleton, John, and Jane Campbell. *Zanzibar: Its Society and Its Politics*. New York and London: OUP, 1965.

Mmuya, Maximilian, and Amon Chaligha. *Anticlimax in Kwahani, Zanzibar: Participation and Multipartism in Tanzania*. Dar es Salaam: DUP, 1993.

Mohammed, Abdul Rahman (Babu). *Utawala wa Kibeheru (Colonial Government)*. Zanzibar: ZNP, 1959.

Mohammed, Ali Mafudh, and Mohammed Ali Foum. *Forge Ahead to Emancipation*. Havana: ZNP, 1963.

Mondevit, Saulnier de. "Observations sur la côte de Zanguebar en 1787." *Nouvelles Annales des Voyages* (1820): 338–59.

Moore, W. Robert. "Clove-Scented Zanzibar." *NGM* 2 (February 1952): 261–78.

Moreau, R. E., and R. H. Pakenham. "Land Vertebrates of Pemba, Zanzibar, and Mafia: A Zoo-Geographical Study." *Proceedings of the Zoological Society of London*, Series A, 3/4 (1940): 97–128.

Morris, H. F. "Some Recent Changes in the Judicial Systems of East Africa: Zanzibar." *Journal of African Law* 1 (Spring 1967): 46–50.

Mosare, Johannes. "Background to the Revolution in Zanzibar." In *A History of Tanzania*, ed. I. N. Kimambo and A. J. Temu, 214–38. Nairobi: EAPH, 1969.

Müller, Fritz Ferdinand. *Deutschland-Zanzibar-Ostafrika: Geschichte einer Deutschen Kolonialeroberung, 1884–1890*. Berlin: Rütten und Loening, 1959.

Mwanjisi, R. K. *Abeid Amani Karume*. [Nairobi]: EAPH, [1976].

Newbury, Catherine M. "Colonialism, Ethnicity, and Rural Political Protest: Rwanda and Zanzibar in Comparative Perspective." *Comparative Politics* 3 (1983): 253–80.

Newmann, Henry Stanley. *Banani: The Transition from Slavery to Freedom in Zanzibar and Pemba*. London: Headley Brothers, 1898.

Ngoile, M.A.K. "Survey of Fishing Units in Zanzibar and Pemba." *TNR* 88/89 (1982): 89–96.

Nicholls, Christine S. *Swahili Coast: Politics, Diplomacy and Trade on the East African Littoral, 1798–1856*. London: George Allen and Unwin, 1971.

Northway, Phillip H. "Salem and the Zanzibar–East African Trade, 1825–1845." *EIHC* (April 1954): 123–53, 261–73, 361–88.

Nwulia, Moses D.E. "Role of Missionaries in the Emancipation of Slaves in Zanzibar." *Journal of Negro History* 2 (1975): 268–87.

"The 'Official' Version of the Zanzibar Revolution." In *Socialism in Tanzania*, vol. 1, ed. Lionel Cliffe, 38–40. Nairobi: EAPH, 1972.

Okello, John. *Revolution in Zanzibar*. Nairobi: EAPH, 1967.

Ommaney, Francis Downes. *Isles of Cloves: A View of Zanzibar*. London: Longmans, Green and Company, 1955.

Othman, Haroub. *Zanzibar's Political History: The Past Haunting the Present?* Copenhagen: CDR, 1993.

Othman, Haroub, and L. P. Shaidi. "Zanzibar's Constitutional Development." *Eastern Africa Law Review* (1978/1981): 181–224.

Pakenham, R.H.W. *Land Tenure among the Wahadimu of Chwaka, Zanzibar Island*. Zanzibar: GP, 1947.

———. "Two Zanzibar Ngomas." *TNR* 52 (March 1959): 111–13.

Parry, Charles R. "The General Post Office's Zanzibar Shipping Contracts, 1860–1914." *Mariner's Mirror* 1 (1982): 57–67.

Pearce, Francis Barrow. *Zanzibar: The Island Metropolis of Eastern Africa*. London: T. Fisher Unwin, 1920.

Penney, J. C. "Notes on the Election in the Protectorate of Zanzibar, 1957." *Journal of African Administration* 3 (July 1958): 144–52.

Picon, Sophie. "Zanzibar, terre d'esclaves." *Histoire* 29 (1980): 52–60.

Pierson, Gerald J. "U.S. Consuls in Zanzibar and the Slave Trade, 1870–1890." *Historian* 1 (Autumn 1992): 53–68.

Piggott, D. W. I. "Description of a Visit to Kilwa in 1859, by Richard Burton." *TNR* 12 (December 1941): 45–48.

Piggott, R. J. *School Geography of Zanzibar*. London: Macmillan, 1961.

Potter, Henry. "Zanzibar Today and Tomorrow." In *Rhodesia and East Africa*, ed. F. S. Joelson, 232–39. London: East Africa and Rhodesia, 1958.

Price, R. *Report of the Rev. R. Price of His Visit to Zanzibar and the Coast of East Africa*. London: London Missionary Society, 1876.

Prins, Adriaan H.J. "On Swahili Historiography." *Swahili* 28 (1958): 26–41.

———. *Sailing from Lamu: A Study of Maritime Culture in Islamic East Africa*. Assen: Van Gorcum, 1965.

———. *Swahili-Speaking Peoples of Zanzibar and the East African Coast*. London: International African Institute, 1961.

Quaas, E. "Die Bewohner Zanzibar's." *Zeitschrift für Allgemeine Erdkunde* (1860): 331–65.

———. "Die Szuri's, die Kuli's, und die Sclaven in Zanzibar." *Zeitschrift für Allegemeine Erdkunde* (1860): 421–60.

Rabaud, A. "Zanzibar." *Bulletin de la Société de Géographie de Marseille* (1879): 158–77.

Raffray, Achille. "Voyage chez les Ouanika sur la côte de Zanguebar." *Tour du Monde* (1878): 284–304.

———. "Voyage en Abyssinie, à Zanguebar, et aux pays des Ouanika." *Bulletin de la Société de Géographie* (1879): 291–313.

Rankine, Richard. "The Sultan of Zanzibar." In *Rhodesia and East Africa*, ed. F. S. Joelson, 240–41. London: East Africa and Rhodesia, 1958.

Revington, T. M. "Some Notes on the Mafia Island Group (Mafia, Chole, Juani and Jibondo)." *TNR* 1 (March 1926): 34–37.

"Revolution in Zanzibar and Union with Tanganyika." *International Bulletin* (June 1964): 180–85.

Rey, Lucien. "Revolution in Zanzibar." *New Left Review* 25 (May/June 1964): 29–32.

Richardson, Katherine W. "Travels and Tribulations of Charles Benson, Steward on the Glide." *EIHC* 2 (1984): 73–109.

Ricklin, L. A. *La mission Catholique du Zanguebar: Travaux et voyages du R. P. Horner.* Paris: Gaume et Ciet, 1880.

Rodd, James Rennel. *Social and Diplomatic Memories, 1884–1893.* London: Edward Arnold, 1922.

Rohlfs, Lonny. "Aus dem Reiche des Sultans von Sansibar." *Daheim* (1866): 216–20, 228–32, 262–66, 279–83.

Rolleston, Ian H.O. "Watumbatu of Zanzibar." *TNR* 8 (December 1939): 85–97.

Rotberg, Robert I. "Political Outlook in Zanzibar." *AR* 9 (October 1961): 5–6, 12.

Roy, A. le. *A travers le Zanguebar.* Tours: Alfred Mame et Fils, 1887.

Ruete, Emily. *Memoirs of an Arabian Princess: An Autobiography.* London: Ward and Downey, 1888.

Russell, Mrs. Charles E. B., ed. *General Rigby, Zanzibar, and the Slave Trade.* London: George Allen and Unwin, 1935.

Said bin Habeeb. "Narrative of an Arab Inhabitant of Zanzibar." *Transactions of the Bombay Geographical Society* (1860): 146–48.

Said-Ruete, Rudolph. *Said bin Sultan (1791–1856), Ruler of Oman and Zanzibar.* London: Alexander Ousley, 1929.

Saleh, Ali. "Les partis politiques de Zanzibar." *Revue Française d'Etudes Politiques Africaines* 89 (May 1973): 50–66.

Saleh, Ibuni. *Short History of the Comorians in Zanzibar.* Dar es Salaam: Tanganyika Standard Press, 1936.

Sanger, Clyde. "Zanzibar Revisited." *AR* 6 (June 1963): 19–22.

Schmidt, Karl Wilhelm. *Sansibar: Ein Ostafrikanischen Kulturbild.* Leipzig: Brockhaus, 1888.

Selwyn, P., and T. Y. Webster. *Report on the Economic Development of Zanzibar Protectorate.* Zanzibar: GP, 1962.

Shelswell-White, G. H. *Guide to Zanzibar,* new edition. Zanzibar: GP, 1949.

Sheriff, Abdul M. H. *Slaves, Spices and Ivory in Zanzibar: Economic Integration of East Africa into the World Economy, 1770–1873.* Athens: Ohio University Press, 1987.

———. "Peasantry in Zanzibar under Colonial Rule." *Maji Maji* (1976): 1–32.

———. "Rise of a Commercial Empire: An Aspect of the Economic History of Zanzibar, 1770–1873." Ph.D. diss., University of London, 1971.

Sheriff, Abdul M. H., and Ed Ferguson, eds. *Zanzibar under Colonial Rule.* Athens: Ohio University Press, 1991.

Shivji, Issa G. *Legal Foundations of the Union in Tanzania's and Zanzibar's Constitutions.* Dar es Salaam: DUP, 1990.

Singleton, C. B. "Tanganyika and Zanzibar Merge into a Single Nation." *Foreign Agriculture* (25 May 1964): 6–8.

Smith, H. "Jubilee Festivities in Zanzibar." *Central Africa* (1887): 162–64.

Smith, H. Maynard. *Frank, Bishop of Zanzibar: Life of Frank Weston, D.D., 1871–1924.* London: Society for Promoting Christian Knowledge, 1926.

Steere, Edward. *East African Slave Trade.* London: Harrison, 1871.

―――. *Some Accounts of the Town of Zanzibar.* London: Bell and Daldy, 1869.

―――. *Swahili Tales as Told by Natives of Zanzibar.* London: Bell and Daldy, 1870.

Stern, J. *Zanzibar.* Pretoria: Van Schaik, 1948.

Strong, S. A., ed. "History of Kilwa." *Journal of the Royal Asiatic Society* (1895): 385–430.

Stubbings, B. J. J. "Notes on Native Methods of Fishing in the Mafia Islands." *TNR* 19 (June 1945): 49–53.

Sulivan, G. L. *Dhow Chasing in Zanzibar Waters.* London: Sampson, Low, Marston, Low and Searle, 1873).

Sundiata, Ibrahim. "Twentieth Century Reflections on Death in Zanzibar." *IJAHS* 1 (1987): 45–60.

Sykes, W. H. "Notes on the Possessions of the Imaum of Muskat, on the Climate and Productions of Zanzibar, and the Prospects of Africa: Discovery from Mombasa." *Journal of the Royal Geographical Society* (1853): 101–19.

Tanner, Ralph E. S. "Some Chinese Pottery Found at Kilwa Kisiwani." *TNR* 32 (January 1952): 83–85.

Thompson, J. L. P. "Denial, Polarisation and Massacre: A Comparative Analysis of Northern Ireland and Zanzibar." *Economic and Social Review* 4 (1986): 293–314.

Thurston, Anne. "The Royal Geographical Society Expedition to Zanzibar." *Africa Research and Documentation* 31 (1983): 28–30.

Tidbury, Grace Elizabeth. *Clove Tree.* London: Crosby Lockwood and Son, 1949.

Tourneux, H. *Le nuits de Zanzibar: Contes Swahili.* Paris: Karthala et A.C.C.T., 1983.

Triplett, George W. "Zanzibar: The Politics of Revolutionary Inequality." *JMAS* 4 (December 1971): 612–17.

Troup, R.S. *Report on Clove Cultivation in the Zanzibar Protectorate.* Zanzibar: GP, 1932.

Van Donge, Jan Kees, and Athumani J. Liviga. "Democratisation of Zanzibar and the 1985 General Elections." *Journal of Commonwealth and Comparative Politics* 2 (July 1990): 201–18.

Vaughan, John Henry. *Dual Jurisdiction in Zanzibar.* Bradford and London: Watmoughs Ltd., 1935.

Vienne, Charles de. "De Zanzibar à l'Oukami: Route des lacs de l'Afrique équatoriale." *Bulletin de la Société de Géographie* (1872): 356–69.

Vizetelly, Edward. *From Cyprus to Zanzibar by the Egyptian Delta.* London: Pearson, 1901.

Walker, John. "History and Coinage of the Sultans of Kilwa." *Numismatic Chronicle* (1936): 43–81.

―――. "Some New Coins from Kilwa." *Numismatic Chronicle* (1939): 223–27.

Waller, Horace. *Case of Our Zanzibar Slaves: Why Not Liberate Them?* London: King, 1896.

―――. *Heligoland for Zanzibar.* London: Edward Stanford, 1893.

Werner, Alice, ed. "Swahili History of Pate." *Journal of the African Society* 54 (1914): 148–66; 55 (1915): 278–97; and 56 (1916): 392–413.

―――. "Wahadimu of Zanzibar." *Journal of the African Society* 60 (July 1916): 356–60.

Wilkinson, J. C. "Oman and East Africa: New Light on Early Kilwan History from the Omani Sources." *IJAHS* 2 (1981): 272–305.

Williams, R. O. *Useful and Ornamental Plants in Zanzibar and Pemba*. Zanzibar: GP, 1949.

Wilson, F. B. "Emergency Food Production in Zanzibar." *East African Agricultural Journal* (1944): 93–100.

Wilson, R. O., and G. E. Tidbury. "Native Paddy Cultivation and Yields in Zanzibar." *East African Agricultural Journal* (1944): 231–35.

Younghusband, Ethel. *Glimpses of East Africa and Zanzibar*. London: John Long, 1910.

Zanzibar: An Account of Its People, Industry and History. Zanzibar: Local Committee of the British Empire Exhibition, 1924.

Zanzibar Government. *Fruits of Revolution in the Islands, 1964–67*. Zanzibar: GP, 1967.

Zanzibar, Legislative Council. *Programme of Social and Economic Development in the Zanzibar Protectorate for the Ten-Year Period, 1946–1955*. Zanzibar: GP, 1946.

Zanzibar Protectorate. *Gazetteer of Zanzibar Islands*. Zanzibar: GP, 1962.

———. *Notes on the Census of the Zanzibar Protectorate, 1948*. Zanzibar: GP, 1953.

———. *Report of the Census of Population Taken on the Night of the 19th and 20th March 1958*. Zanzibar: GP, 1960.

———. *Report of the Supervisor of Elections on the Elections in Zanzibar, 1957*. Zanzibar: GP, 1958.

Zanzibar na Kuundwa kwa Historia ya Waafrika wa Chama cha Afro-Shirazi. Dar es Salaam: Dar es Salaam Printers, 1969.

Zanzibar National Party. *Whither Zanzibar? The Growth of Policy of Zanzibar Nationalism*. Cairo: ZNP, 1960.

About the Authors

Thomas P. Ofcansky received a Ph.D. in East African history from West Virginia University (1981). Since then, he has held several academic posts and is currently with the Department of Defense. He has published numerous books and articles about East Africa, the most recent of which is *Uganda: The Tarnished Pearl of Africa* (Westview Press, 1996). He also has traveled widely throughout East Africa.

Rodger Yeager is professor of political science, adjunct professor of African history, and director of international studies at West Virginia University. He is the author and coauthor of several books on African political economy, including *Tanzania: An African Experiment* (2d rev. ed., Westview Press, 1989) and *Kenya: The Quest for Prosperity* (2d ed., Westview Press, 1994). His current research is focused on public policy problems of natural resource conservation, demographic change, and public health in eastern and southern Africa.

Paula Fox

The Library of Author Biographies™

Paula Fox

Susanna Daniel

rosen
central™

The Rosen Publishing Group, Inc., New York

For John

Published in 2004 by The Rosen Publishing Group, Inc.
29 East 21st Street, New York, NY 10010

First Edition

Library of Congress Cataloging-in-Publication Data

Daniel, Susanna.
Paula Fox / by Susanna Daniel.— 1st ed.
     p. cm. — (The library of author biographies)
Summary: Discusses the life and work of this popular author, including her writing process and methods, inspirations, a critical discussion of her books, biographical timeline, and awards.
Includes bibliographical references and index.
ISBN 0-8239-4525-1 (library binding)
1. Fox, Paula—Juvenile literature. 2. Authors, American—20th century—Biography—Juvenile literature. 3. Children's stories—Authorship—Juvenile literature. [1. Fox, Paula. 2. Authors, American. 3. Women—Biography. 4. Authorship.]
I. Title. II. Series.
PS3556.O94Z73 2004
813'.54—dc21

                                                    2003009176

Manufactured in the United States of America

Excerpts from *Borrowed Finery* by Paula Fox © 2001 by Paula Fox. Reprinted by permission of Henry Holt and Company, LLC.

Text from "Author Pages Through Painful Past," October 4, 2001, reprinted with permission of *New York Daily News*, L.P.

Text from Literature Resource Center reprinted with permission from Gale Group.

Text from "Advancing Through Water," July 2, 2001, originally published online at www.newyorker.com. Reprinted by permission. © 2001.

Table of Contents

Introduction: Room to Grow

At eighty years of age, Paula Fox is considered one of the most out-standing and talented writers for children living today. Critics and reviewers have time and again praised her honest, straightforward development of intense, complex, and often tragic stories, as well as her captivating use of language. Fox's characters are often in crisis, confronting serious challenges such as homelessness, illness in the family, or a parent's death. Rather than shrink in the face of hardship, Fox's characters use their imaginations and courage to triumph, often without the assistance of adults.

To date, Paula Fox has written twenty-three books for children, including *The Slave Dancer* (1973), which won the American Library Association's distinguished Newbery Medal in 1974, and *The Little Swineherd and Other Tales* (1978), which was nominated for the National Book Award in 1979. Fox's body of work for young people was awarded the prestigious Hans Christian Andersen Award in 1978. Fox has also written six novels for adults and a memoir, or autobiography, entitled *Borrowed Finery* (1999), which was a finalist for the National Book Critics Circle Award in 2000.

Fox's characters often deal with rather intense situations in their lives, and many of Fox's novels have been called "somber," "dark," and "emotional." They've also been called "honest," because in her books, as in real life, there are no easy answers, and there isn't always a hero or heroine who saves the day. Fox's protagonists rely on their own resources— their intelligence and determination—to find their way in the world. Ultimately, at the heart of each of her books is a difficult journey of one kind or another—a journey made not only by Fox's characters, but also by her readers.

For example, take Paul Coleman, the adolescent protagonist of *Radiance Descending* (1997), whose younger brother, Jacob, has Down's syndrome. Jacob requires a lot of their parents' attention, and Paul often feels neglected. When the Colemans move from Long Island to New York City, Paul decides to start avoiding his younger brother, who has irritating habits like laughing all the time and messing up Paul's room. As it turns out, ignoring Jacob takes as much energy as paying attention to him, so Paul tries to find some middle ground. He begins to escort Jacob to his Saturday allergy shots, and through this routine, Paul is introduced to a whole new world—his brother's world. Paul grows to appreciate the slower pace of Jacob's life, and he eventually learns to be more compassionate.

Many of the characters in Fox's books learn the important skill of seeing the world through other people's eyes without being judgmental. After they endure hardships, they have a better understanding of what it is like to be in other people's shoes. Readers, too, gain a sense of compassion after reading about situations that might have previously been unfamiliar to them.

For example, in *Monkey Island* (1991), an eleven-year-old boy named Clay Garrity is abandoned by his father, who has just lost his job. Clay's mother is eight months pregnant and jobless, and she, too, ends up abandoning him in a welfare hotel where they have moved. Clay fears that he will be taken into custody by a social welfare agency, so he runs away to live on the streets. Eventually, he makes friends with two men who have also become homeless due to bad luck, and then he catches a terrible case of pneumonia. By the end of the novel, Clay is reunited with his mother. His experiences on the streets have shown him how difficult life can be, and through this realization, he is able to forgive his mother for abandoning him.

In this novel, like *Radiance Descending* and many others, Fox explores the themes of alienation and abandonment, resilience and resourcefulness, and compassion. Readers of *Monkey Island* who are not familiar with homelessness can learn through Clay's experiences how lonely and scary living on the streets can be. Readers will also come to realize that what happened to Clay's family could possibly happen to anyone.

In order to get across such somber and emotional stories, Fox chooses to write in a simple, clear, and direct writing style, with lots of suspense driving the story. Fox uses some advanced vocabulary words and writes about confusing emotional situations because she doesn't believe in talking down to young people or sugarcoating misfortune in order to protect them. Readers looking for laugh-out-loud stories that will have them in stitches from the first page to the last won't find that in Paula Fox's novels. Instead, they will find true-to-life characters with imagination, intelligence, and resilience. They will also find an author who respects children and adolescents as much as adults and who knows that they have lessons to teach as well as to learn.

1 A Fragmented Childhood

Paula Fox was born in New York City on April 22, 1923. Her childhood was not an easy one. Her mother, Elsie, was a hardhearted woman and a reluctant mother, and her father, Paul, was an on-again, off-again screenwriter and novelist. When Paula was only a few days old, Elsie and Paul left her in an orphanage; her grandmother, Candeleria, who traveled too much to care full-time for a child, placed Paula in the care of a kind couple who already had several children.

The family had too much on their hands, however, and soon after, Paula was given to a local minister named Reverend Elwood Amos

Corning. The reverend lived in Balmville, New York. For most of the first eight years of her life, Paula lived with Reverend Corning—whom she knew as Uncle Elwood—in an old Victorian house. They lived with the reverend's mother, who was kind but rarely spoke. Meanwhile, Paula's father kept irregular contact with Reverend Corning, sent money from time to time, and appeared one afternoon when Paula was five years old, only to leave again the next day.

Brief visits with her parents would become normal in Paula's life; when her parents returned, it was never for long. Shortly after Paul's visit, when she was five, Paula's parents sent for her to join them in Hollywood, California. Paula was there for only a few days before her mother, Elsie, decided she'd had enough—she wasn't cut out for motherhood, she said—and Paula was sent away again, this time to live with a friend named Mrs. Cummings, in Redlands, California.

From Redlands, Paula visited her parents four or five times. The attention she received from them was unpredictable and sometimes frightening. Her father, who was an alcoholic, frequently referred to her as "Pal" and her mother was distant, cold, and sometimes cruel.

After a year with Mrs. Cummings, Uncle Elwood showed up in California to take Paula back to the East Coast. Paula was grateful and relieved, but the blessing was short-lived. Paula had lived only a few short weeks with Uncle Elwood before her mother's mother, Candeleria, arrived to take Paula into her custody. Having to move in with her grandmother at age eight was a terrible disappointment for Paula. In her memoir, she wrote, "My parting from the minister was an amputation."[1]

An Early Love of Reading

Despite the turbulence of her early years, it was during this time that Paula began to realize that books were dependable friends. She remembers Uncle Elwood reading aloud to her from classic children's stories such as *Robin Hood*, *King Arthur and the Knights of the Round Table*, *Treasure Island*, and *Aesop's Fables*, among others. When she was only five years old, Paula learned her first lesson in how ideas translate into stories or words. She was sitting with Uncle Elwood as he prepared his sermon for the following Sunday. Uncle Elwood was stumped and asked the little girl for suggestions. She had been thinking about a recent picnic, where they had sat so close to the spray of a cascade that the water dampened their sandwiches. She told him he should write about waterfalls.

That Sunday, as she sat in the congregation at Sunday services, she was startled to realize that Uncle Elwood had taken her advice—the sermon was, indeed, about a waterfall. Even at her young age, Paula began to understand that words were meaningful and could inspire emotion, thought, and imagination. This was her first inspiration to become a writer.

These events, and the support of Uncle Elwood, encouraged young Paula to become an avid reader. In an essay Fox later wrote about the importance of books in her childhood, she said:

> I was taught to read when I was five. The old house where I lived in those days [with Uncle Elwood] was filled with books and not much else. The roof leaked, the well was always going dry, the wallpaper peeled, the furniture was patched and mended, the driveway up the long hill to the house was impassable in heavy rain or snow, and there was never enough money for repairs.
>
> But the books! They lined the walls of the rooms; they stood in columns on the floor; they were piled up in the attic on top of a river of

National Geographic [magazines] that cascaded down the crowded attic stairs.

In bad weather, when I couldn't go outside, I used to sit on those stairs and extract a *Geographic* as carefully as if I were playing pick-up sticks, so I wouldn't bring the whole attic down on myself. Among the glossy pages of the magazines, I met up with pygmies and Balinese dancers, cities built on water, mountain peaks yet unscaled, desert people and people who lived amid eternal snow, dragonflies and anacondas. On those attic stairs in an old house that seemed always on the verge of collapse, I began to sense huge possibilities.[2]

A Roller-coaster Adolescence

Paula lived for a while in a small brick house on Long Island with her grandmother and two uncles. She attended Public School 99, a one-room schoolhouse that stood next to a large cemetery. Paula, who was curious and adventuresome even at that young age, visited the cemetery every chance she could. She spent a lot of time by herself, exploring and using her imagination to make up wild fantasies. Paula's classmates on Long Island didn't know what to make of her—she was fair-haired and might have been mistaken for Swedish or Finnish if not for the dark skin and hair of her grandmother. She was teased off and on by her peers. In her memoir, *Borrowed Finery*, Fox explained how living with her grandmother made it difficult for her to fit in:

> One morning my grandmother made me a different breakfast from the usual toast and cereal. She minced garlic and spread it on a slice of bread that had been soaked in olive oil My arrival at school was greeted by my classmates with cries of mock disgust, hands outstretched to keep me at a distance.
>
> I was the foreigner in a school population made up largely of children from working-class Irish Catholic families. The final . . . evidence of my foreignness was my grandmother herself, when she appeared in school on those days set aside for parents to visit classes.
>
> She did not resemble any other mother. She was older, of course. And she had a thick Spanish accent . . . But I loved the bread soaked in oil and covered with garlic, and I didn't give it up once I'd tasted it.[3]

When two other foreigners arrived at the school—a French Canadian boy and an Armenian boy—Fox formed an alliance with them, accepting and even celebrating the ways she was different from most of her classmates. She wrote in her memoir that garlic was her saving grace, confirming her position as an outsider at her school. If not for the garlic, she might have continued trying to fit in and to be like everyone else, though it was clear even this early in her life, with her turbulent background and her love for reading and being alone, that she was different.

Off to Cuba

Soon, Paula left Public School 99 because she and her grandmother moved to Cuba to spend more than a year on a sugar plantation owned by a cousin. She didn't know where Cuba was, exactly, but she found it in an atlas at school. To Paula's eyes, the country looked like a green lizard lying across a blue sea.

On the plantation in Cuba, Paula had plenty of space to roam and play, including acres of manicured gardens on the estate where she and her grandmother lived, but she had few friends or companions. Her grandmother was busy most of the day tending to the cousin who owned the plantation. It was a while before Paula started school and made friends among her classmates and with her teacher, Señora García, who was in charge of one classroom full of children of all ages. In her memoir, Fox recounts vivid memories from this time:

> During my many months in Cuba, my grandmother had taken me to visit Tía Laura, my real great-aunt. She was retired, by then, and living in the country. We had supper with her and afterward went into the wild moonlit garden. A fire burned beneath a large black cauldron. I recall that she wore a black dress, silvered by the moonlight, and stirred *dulce de leche*, a Cuban sweet, with a huge ladle.[4]

While in Cuba, Paula wrote letters to Uncle Elwood. The only time she didn't receive a reply right away was when his mother, the silent but kind woman who had lived with Paula for the first eight years of her life, passed away. Though the woman wasn't Paula's own grandmother, she was sad for Uncle Elwood and remembered the woman fondly.

The Birth of a Storyteller

Though Paula and her grandmother were never very close, the person Paula would become as an adult was greatly determined by her grandmother's passion for storytelling. Candeleria told Paula stories from her life in Spain. These were sometimes funny, sometimes dreadful. As Fox would later recall, "What I [remember] most about her stories, told to me in fragments over the years I lived with her, was an underlying sorrowful tone, a puzzled mourning for the past."[5] Though she'd learned to love reading stories while in Uncle Elwood's care, it was perhaps Paula's grandmother who helped her make the leap from merely reading stories to telling them herself.

In September 1933, a revolution was led by Communist Fulgencio Batista Zalvidar (called Batista) against the liberal government of Gerardo Machado, then the president of Cuba. For several years, Cuba's economy had been deteriorating, and the price for sugar had dropped to all-time lows, despite the United States's support for the Machado government. In the midst of the chaos, facing a new Communist government, Paula and her grandmother fled to Long Island. In comparison to the sugar plantation, the one-room apartment they returned to was very small and crowded. By this time, Paula was ten years old and had already lived in more homes than many people do in a lifetime. She returned to P.S. 99, and immediately it seemed as if she'd never left at all. She began visiting regularly with her uncles and cousins in Spanish Harlem and she and her cousin Natalie often went to the movies.

During this time in New York, Paula continued to cultivate her love of reading. She and a few other schoolgirls found an abandoned shed near her apartment and decided to use it as a library. They collected and shared all of their books and dug up a few pieces of old furniture from the neighborhood. Eventually, winter came, and the shed grew too cold for the girls to continue meeting there. By the time they had to abandon it, however, Paula had acquired a real library card.

Family Reunion

When Paula was eleven, her parents returned to New York from Europe, where they had been living for several years. Paula went to meet their ship where it docked on the Hudson River and watched as Paul and Elsie walked down the gangplank to the pier. As they descended from the ship, in their sunglasses and fine clothes, Paula thought they looked as handsome as movie stars.

However glamorous they seemed, Paula soon learned that her parents had fallen on hard times. During the next month, while she continued to live with her grandmother and visit her parents occasionally, her father gave her a typewriter as a present, then took it back from her to sell it for cash. He also borrowed fifty dollars that Paula had been given by her aunt in Cuba. When, shortly thereafter, he sold a movie script for a large sum, he neither offered to return the typewriter—which naturally Paula had cherished, even for the short time she had it—nor repay the debt. Paula, thinking both debts too small to mention and fearing her parents' anger, kept quiet.

During this period, Paula spent one memorable afternoon shopping for shoes with Elsie, the mother she barely knew, at a department store on Fifth Avenue. The event was arranged by Paul, who every so often encouraged Elsie to spend more time with Paula. As Fox would later recount:

> She bought me two pairs of handsome shoes, one black kidskin, the other green suede. During the time that we were together, it felt as if we were continually being introduced to each other. I was conscious of an immense

strain, as though a large limp animal hung from my neck, its fur impeding my speech.

Each time, each sentence, I had to start anew. I could hear effort in her voice, too. The whole transaction, selecting, fitting, paying, wrapping, took less than twenty-five minutes. She smiled brilliantly at me in the elevator descending; the smile lasted a few seconds too long.

"Can you get home by yourself?" she asked me, as though I had suddenly strayed into the path of her vision. I nodded wordlessly. The shopping spree was over.[6]

Paula and her grandmother moved into a larger apartment along with Paula's uncle, Vincent, who woke everyone from sleep at night with loud nightmares. Once, they spent a long holiday weekend with Paula's parents on Martha's Vineyard. Months later, Paula left the Long Island apartment she shared with her grandmother and traveled with her parents by car to Florida, where they had planned to live together in a house that belonged to a friend of Elsie's. But a few days after they arrived at the house in Florida, Elsie and Paul changed their minds once again and drove back to New York, leaving Paula behind with only the housekeeper to look after her.

Paula felt they had not abandoned her so much as they had simply forgotten she existed altogether. She felt trapped by her age—twelve—because she was far too young to leave Florida and start a life on her own.

Life in Florida

Paula went to public school in East Jacksonville, Florida. She made a few friends, including a boy named Matt, who taught her how to scare away water moccasins (a type of poisonous snake) from the nearby wharf by jumping on the wharf before walking on it, and Mattie, an African American girl who worked in the house where Paula lived and with whom Paula played in the fenced-in yard behind the house. Perhaps her best friend at the time was Lee, a boy a few years older than she, who could already drive. Once, Lee was driving Paula to his house and they came to a stop in front of a huge snake lying across the road, its stomach swollen with a big meal. Fox recalls that Lee got out of the car, lifted the snake with both hands, and carried it to the side of the road. This showed not only courage but also a touching sensitivity toward animals that left quite an impression on Paula.

It was during Paula's time living in Florida that her father announced that he and Elsie were getting a divorce. He arrived in the spring to deliver the news and told Paula while they sat together on a bluff, overlooking a wharf and river. "I had not thought of them as married,"[7] Fox wrote. She didn't even understand how Elsie was enough of a real human being, made of flesh and blood, to have carried Paula in her belly for nine months. To Paula, her mother seemed alien.

After discussing the divorce for a bit, Paula's father abruptly changed the subject to, of all things, smoking cigarettes. At this point in time, Paula was twelve years old. Her father held out a crumpled pack of cigarettes and insisted Paula take one, even after she shook her head. Paula didn't take to smoking right away, but a few weeks later she and her friend Marjorie tried again, and this time the habit stuck. She would continue to smoke into adulthood.

The owner of Paula's house in Florida was a young woman named Mary. She arrived shortly after Paula's father and stayed for a few weeks, treating Paula like a friend and equal. Fox recalls that Mary encouraged her love of reading and books by giving her a copy of the classic novel *The Brothers Karamazov* (1879), by Fyodor Dostoevsky. Paul, who was by this time romantically involved with Mary, drove both Paula and Mary back to New York, and once again, Paula had to say good-bye to the friends she'd made and start her life again—elsewhere.

2 From Chaos into Adulthood

Paula went back to Long Island to her grandmother's apartment and saw her parents only occasionally over the next year or so. By this time, they were both dating other people, and her father's drinking problem was getting worse.

When she was fourteen years old, Paula spent some time with Mary's relatives in West Pittston, Pennsylvania, then drove with Mary to live in a rented house in Peterborough, New Hampshire.

Peterborough was a pretty town and the location of a popular artists' retreat, which lent the place a touch of glamour, as far as Paula was concerned. She was becoming more and more engaged in the world of books, and she was happy to learn that the town where she now lived was once home to Thornton Wilder, the American playwright and novelist, whose work she'd recently read. The estate where he had lived and worked was located deep in the woods, so Paula had to wear snowshoes to reach it. "When I came upon the fieldstone buildings," she wrote, "I forgot my purpose and felt only apprehension. I breathed in the [icy] air. It was still except for the soft slide of snow now and then from tree branches to the ground. I peered through a window into a room already dark in the early fading of daylight."[1]

The time spent in Peterborough was relatively happy for Paula. She was given her own room in Mary's rented home, which overlooked a wide stream. This period was the first time in Paula's life when she spent more than a few days at a time with her father, who was living at the house under the pretense that he was Mary's cousin. (Back then, it would have been considered scandalous for an unmarried woman and man to live in the same house.)

Another highlight of this period in her life was Paula's English class at school. It was here that Paula's teacher introduced her to poetry and Shakespeare. She made several good friends and had a few suitors at the Peterborough school, including a pharmacist's son, who left sodas in her locker as gifts, and a senior who took her to the movies. Mary, who at twenty-five years old was only a decade older than Paula, became her close friend and confidant. It was Mary she would go to with questions about boys and growing up.

But no chapter in Paula's childhood ever lasted very long. Before a year was up in Peterborough, Paula and her father were forced to leave because of his excessive drinking and the rumors about his relationship with Mary. The spring she turned fifteen, Paula lived in a small apartment rented by her father on Manhattan's Upper West Side. Sometimes her father was there, sometimes he wasn't—she never knew exactly where he went or when he would return.

Choosing a Path

When she was about sixteen years old, Paula's father started pressuring her to figure out what she wanted to do with her life. This motivated her to spend several years trying out her various talents and skills. She attended art school, modeled for sculptors, and practiced the piano. She spent several months working and living on Nantucket, an island off the coast of Massachusetts, with a friend and then was notified by her father that she would be attending boarding school in Canada the following year. She returned to Long Island and stayed with her grandmother until it was time to go to school. During this time, she spent one awkward afternoon visiting Elsie, her mother, in the New York apartment Elsie shared with a male companion.

Sainte-Geneviève, the small boarding school Paula attended for a year in Montréal, was housed in a rambling four-story structure. The boarders—the girls who lived on campus—played bridge every night and went to dances and balls with boys from nearby colleges. Paula had little money, so though she was frequently invited to balls or to go on dates, she usually had to borrow nice clothes to wear. She spent the Christmas holiday on Prince Edward Island with her father and Mary—who was, by this time, her stepmother—then later visited with her father in New York City over spring vacation. She had long since realized that in order to see her parents, she had to live apart from them. When they lived together, her parents inevitably fled.

Paula was waiting for her father to pick her up from school when France signed the armistice with Germany in June 1940. She was seventeen at the time. She and her father spent three weeks in a rented house in Halifax, Nova Scotia, then returned to New York City. There, Paul checked Paula into a women-only boarding house and, much to Paula's surprise, enrolled her in the Julliard School. At Julliard, she played piano and took singing lessons, paid for by Mary.

"My life was incoherent to me," Fox wrote about this period in her life. "I felt it quivering, spitting out broken teeth. When I thought of the purposes I had tried to find for myself the last year, to show my father that I 'wanted' something—piano, voice lessons, sculpture, none of the least use to me—when I thought of the madness of my parents where I was concerned, I felt the bleakest misery."[2]

All the time she was searching to find her passion, it was right there under her nose. From the time Uncle Elwood read to her as a little girl through her teen years, Fox had treasured books. It would be many years, however, before she would turn her love for reading into a passion for writing.

Working Life

When she was seventeen, Paula drove to California with a middle-aged woman named

Kay, a friend of Mary's. The trip was arranged by Paula's father. In Los Angeles, Paula's roller-coaster life only got bumpier.

She was briefly married to an actor who was twice her age; she was underage at the time of the wedding, so her father had to give his consent by telegram. The actor left on a merchant ship shortly after Paula found a job as a waitress in a Greek café; he was gone for months, and they broke up after he returned.

Paula stayed in California for eight years after that, working a string of odd jobs. She worked for a magician, then as a painter at a ceramics factory, then as an instructor at Arthur Murray's, a popular dance studio. She made friends with a Hungarian refugee who made designer clothes, and volunteered her services as a model in her friend's fashion shows. For Warner Brothers, a film studio, she read South American novels (using the Spanish skills she learned long ago in Cuba) and wrote reports about their potential as film scripts. It was during this time, when she was twenty years old, that she became pregnant and gave up the baby for adoption because she did not have the means to care for a child. She regretted the decision immediately but could do nothing to reverse it.

The Author Emerges

Fox returned once again to New York in 1948, when she was twenty-five years old. Soon after, she married a man named Richard Sigerson and had two sons, Adam and Gabriel. She divorced Sigerson in 1954 and attended Columbia University from 1955 to 1958, stopping just short of her degree. She taught in various schools in and around New York for the next several years, until 1962, when she married Martin Greenberg, who was a professor of English at C. W. Post College in Greenvale, New York. Martin was also an editor at a literary journal that had rejected Fox's fiction for publication. They are still married today, more than forty years later.

Almost immediately after the wedding, Fox, her sons, and her new husband moved together to Greece to live for six months. Greenberg had won a respected award called a Guggenheim Fellowship, which allowed him to study and work and gave Fox the time and space she needed to begin her career as a novelist. Of this period, Fox recalled:

I remember when I was finally able to quit my teaching job and devote myself full-time to writing. People asked me, "But what will you DO?" People have this idea that a life spent writing is essentially a life of leisure. Writing is tremendously hard work. There is nothing more satisfying, but it is work all the same.[3]

In Greece, with the time and support she needed, Fox wrote her first adult novel, *Poor George* (1967), followed shortly by her first children's novel, *Maurice's Room. A Likely Place* and *How Many Miles to Babylon?* (1967) were published soon thereafter. Once she'd committed to writing books, publication followed relatively easily. Though she is more widely known as a writer for young people, her adult novels have gained much critical praise.

Fox has said that she never consciously decided to write for either kids or adults. She believes that first and foremost she tells a story for herself, and the audience comes second. She has been fortunate in that her books for children and young adults have provided her the time and resources to write her less widely known books for adults. She said that she is especially interested in writing about children because they are experiencing many things for the first time, including life's small daily surprises as well as periods of loneliness and challenging events. She also has said that writing for children is not very different from writing for adults, because children also know about the difficult themes she explores in her adult work—for example, pain, betrayal, fear, and unhappiness—and they don't need to be protected from these harsh realities.

3 The Pleasure of Telling Stories

Fox's love for reading and storytelling was awakened and nurtured by her earliest father figure, Uncle Elwood, who read to her from a young age, and was encouraged by her grandmother, Candeleria, who told Fox zany stories about her life in Spain. Because of her experiences, Fox believes in teaching children to appreciate books from early in life, as soon as they can read. "Imagination can be . . . stifled," she says, "[b]ut it can be awakened. When you read to a child, when you put a book in a child's hands, you are bringing that child news of the . . . nature of life. You are an awakener."[1]

Fox believes that having a fertile imagination is the key to good storytelling. For her, storytelling depends more on imagination than on capturing real-life experiences. Sometimes, however, she uses her memories as a starting point for her novels, and like a tadpole turning into a bullfrog, the stories grow in an entirely new direction and take on lives of their own.

For example, one part of the book *One-Eyed Cat* (1984) was influenced by an experience Fox had when she was a child. In *One-Eyed Cat*, the main character, Ned, accidentally wounds a stray cat with an air rifle (a gun that shoots pellets or BBs using compressed air) and is tormented by guilt as a result—even to the point of becoming physically ill. He has kept his shameful secret to himself, and he believes that his shame will get bigger and bigger, haunting him for the rest of his life.

Although this story never happened to Fox as it is told, it was inspired by a memory from Fox's childhood, which she recalls in her memoir:

> Once the [neighbor] children brought along a sickly puppy and showed it to me. We passed its limp body among us, caressed it, and at last killed it with love. We stared,

stricken, at the tiny dog lying dead in the older boy's hands, saliva foaming and dripping from its muzzle.

Later that day, after the farmer and his family had departed, I told the minister I had had a hand in the death of the little animal. Although he tried to comfort me, to give me some sort of absolution, I couldn't accept it for many years.

Even now, I am haunted from time to time by the image of a small group of children, myself among them, standing silently at the back door of the house, looking down at the corpse.[2]

Notice how Fox has taken this sad, true-life memory and used her imagination and writing skills to transform it into *One-Eyed Cat*. It is because of her own familiarity with the shame and guilt of wounding a defenseless animal that she is able to write with authority and compassion about Ned's predicament.

Understanding Human Behavior

As previously mentioned, an active imagination can help both the author and the reader understand the circumstances of other people's lives and have more compassion. One important tool in novel writing is psychology, which is the science of the way people behave, especially in challenging situations. Successful authors must be very smart psychologists and always have their characters behave realistically, or else their readers won't believe a word they write. A big difference between psychologists who see patients and writers who develop characters is that the patients are real and the characters are fictional (though they might be loosely based on real memories). A writer can't make up realistic fictional characters, though, without using his or her imagination.

Paula Fox has a thorough understanding of human psychology. She understands human behavior as well as any children's author working today, and her complicated stories and character development prove it.

Take nineteen-year-old Ben, the main character in Fox's novel *Blowfish Live in the Sea* (1970). Ben hasn't spoken to his father in twelve years, and he has the odd habit of constantly writing the sentence "Blowfish live in the sea" on anything and everything in sight. Ben is a strange kid, and you might not understand him if you met him on the street.

Ben developed his quirky habit when he was a child, after his father came back from a trip to the Amazon with a souvenir gift: a painted blowfish. Ben was too smart for his dad, because he knew that blowfish didn't live in rivers—they live in the sea, which meant that his father had lied about where he'd gone. This one lie causes Ben so much pain that he doesn't speak to his father for twelve years.

During the course of the novel, Ben and his sister, Carrie, travel from New York to Boston to visit their father, and along the way begin to understand more about their past and each other. Because she understands human behavior and writes so well, Fox is able to communicate Ben's sad and strange life to the reader, inspiring compassion and tenderness.

Challenges Bring Opportunities

Like her characters, Fox had to undertake a long journey to finally find a place she could call home—she'd lived in New York, Florida, California, Pennsylvania, New Hampshire, Cuba, Canada, and Greece by the time her career as a writer was under way. After that, things started to settle down for her, and years later, in 1971, one of her adult novels, *Desperate Characters* (1970), was made into a film starring legendary actress Shirley MacLaine. With the money from the movie, she and Greenberg bought a century-old townhouse in Brooklyn, New York. Fox said in an interview with the newspaper, the *Hartford Courant*, that she was forty-seven years old when she bought the house in Brooklyn, but this was the first time in her life that she felt she'd found a true home. She and her husband have lived in the townhouse for more than thirty years now. Her two sons from her second marriage are grown men.

Life has not ceased to throw challenges into her path, however, and Fox continues to turn hardship into opportunity. About a decade ago, Fox was contacted by a woman who turned out to be the daughter she had given up for adoption when she was only twenty years old. In her memoir, Fox recalled the Saturday morning when she was sitting in her kitchen and a thick Federal Express envelope arrived. There was a hand-written note on top of a letter, and it said, "Go slow."[3]

Fox knew right away whom the envelope was from and what it contained. She called upstairs to her husband, "She's found me!"[4]

Fox's daughter's name is Linda. The two women exchanged letters for three months, sometimes twice a day. Then they arranged to meet each other in San Francisco, where, they agreed, if they got bored of each other, they would have other things to entertain them. But they didn't get bored of each other. As soon as they met in the airport, they sat down and talked animatedly for two hours. "She was the first woman related to me I could speak to freely,"[5] wrote Fox.

Paula and Linda have remained close, and Paula is also involved in the lives of Linda's children, her grandchildren. In fact, one of her grandchildren is a musician named Courtney Love, the leader of the grunge band Hole and widow of the popular Nirvana lead singer, Kurt Cobain. Fox said in an interview that Courtney reminds her of her own mother, Elsie. "[Linda] also told me that the reason [Courtney's] last name is Love," said Fox in the same interview, "is that Linda used to say, 'Courtney, love, come here.'"[6]

In 1997, Fox had another life-changing experience. While traveling in Israel with her husband, Fox was mugged by a man who struck her, took her purse, and left her bleeding from her head. She spent three weeks in a Jerusalem hospital and one week in Columbia Presbyterian Hospital, in New York City. All in all, it took nearly a year for her to get better. "It took me three months to write the first ten pages of [my memoir, *Borrowed Finery*],"[7] she told a reporter. In another interview, she explained how her discipline got her through her recovery.

> I wrote every morning, because my energy was highest then. I would get up at eight or eight-thirty, and start and play solitaire, and go to the typewriter, and play solitaire, and go to the typewriter. There were days when I couldn't move beyond a sentence, and then other days when I could write a whole page. There were days when I knew what I was about to do, and then I would go with relative speed—it would take me three hours to write two or three paragraphs. So those days encouraged me, for all the bleak times in between.[8]

One positive thing came from the nightmarish ordeal, however: after she recovered from her injury, she found that she no longer cared for cigarettes. This was no small change in her life, since she'd been a regular smoker since that first taste of cigarettes in Florida when she was twelve years old.

4 Realistic Characters and Themes

Overall, Fox's books are less concerned with plot than with character, meaning that what happens is less important than how the characters cope with the events of their lives. Many characters in Fox's novels find themselves in strange situations with no one to rely on but themselves. Many of her characters, too, are coping with the illness or death of a family member and the loneliness and grief that results.

For example, *The Village by the Sea* (1988)—a book for middle school readers—is about a ten-year-old girl named Emma who is sent to live with her unkind, alcoholic aunt for two weeks while her father recovers from surgery in the hospital. Emma copes with her anxiety about her father's health and her cruel aunt by building a miniature "village" on the beach with her new friend, Bertie. But because it is made of sand, the village is destined for destruction. Emma enjoys building the village so much that she isn't bothered much when it is destroyed. Afterward, she cherishes the memory of her creation. She returns home with a new sense of courage and compassion for her aunt. In *The Village by the Sea*, as in life, nothing lasts forever, and one's memories are ultimately as important as one's present-day reality.

Another of Fox's recurring themes appears in *A Likely Place* (1967), the story of a nine-year-old named Lewis who is so exasperated by the intrusion of the adults in his life that he thinks about running away. Adults are constantly taking Lewis places without asking him where he wants to go, telling him what he is feeling, and assigning him activities he doesn't enjoy and isn't good at. This leaves him feeling lonely, alienated, and misunderstood.

When Lewis's parents go away on a business trip and leave him with a fascinating, oddball babysitter named Miss Fitchlow, he gets a taste of what it's like to live without pushy adults around. Miss Fitchlow engages him in intelligent conversations, introduces him to yoga exercise and health foods, and allows him to go to the park alone. During the course of his time with Miss Fitchlow, Lewis carves out a place of his own in the park near his home. It becomes his private place where he can be alone with his thoughts and keep personal items like a candle and a pamphlet he found. He also befriends a man named Mr. Madruga, who doesn't speak English perfectly and needs Lewis to help him translate an important letter to his son.

In the end, Lewis's overprotective but well-meaning parents return, and Lewis greets them with a stronger sense of who he is and where he wants to go in the world. They haven't especially changed, but he has, which is the most important thing. Like many of Fox's books, *A Likely Place* has as much wisdom to teach to parents as it does to children.

Another one of Fox's novels for younger readers, *Dear Prosper* (1968), is narrated by an old dog who is writing a letter to one of his former owners, telling about the events that have occurred in his life. The story begins with the dog's birth behind a general store in New

Mexico, then continues through his escape to another town, where he is adopted and renamed by a sheriff. Prosper goes on to work as a ranch dog, and then to live in the lap of luxury with a rich new owner. He continues on many adventures and ends up living with a kind caretaker; in the end, he has led a contented life. Ultimately, the book is about overcoming hardships and long journeys.

Fox is able to capture a dog's view of his own life and at the same time, she relates the dog's long journey to that of most human beings. Like a human, Prosper forms loyal relationships as well as painful ones, overcomes hardships and adversaries, and at long last arrives at his true home, where he can feel both loved and needed.

Understanding Kids

Time and again, even in her early novels, Fox has proved that she has a great understanding of young people—even peculiar young people, like the main character of her first novel for young adults, *Maurice's Room* (1966). Maurice is an eight-year-old boy who is obsessed with collecting things. Maurice's collections aren't especially valuable or prizewinning; among his rare finds is a bottle full of dead beetles, a raccoon tail, rocks, and anything else that captures his imagination.

Only Maurice and his friend Jacob, who shares his love of collecting, are able to walk around in his junk-filled room without knocking items off their shelves. Maurice's parents are at their wit's end—they consider their son's collections "junk" and encourage him to pursue what they call more "constructive" and less peculiar interests. They force him to take trumpet lessons, which he hates. One day, though, they give Maurice a toy sailboat, which he loves, until he accidentally destroys it midsail when he and Jacob become distracted by some rusty bedsprings they spot in the pond.

When Maurice's parents decide to move to the country, Maurice gives the bedsprings to Jacob but packs up the rest of his collections, all of which are lost when the moving van goes over a bump and the back door opens accidentally. However, Maurice is consoled when he discovers that the barn at his new home is filled with unknown treasures, and he starts to build his collections all over again. During the course of the book, it is Maurice's parents who have to learn the difficult lesson of compassion; by the end, they have come to accept their son's passion for collecting. Many of Fox's young characters end up teaching their parents or other adults important lessons, instead of the other way around.

The Critics Weigh In

Critics have consistently praised Fox's sympathy with and portrayal of children, parents, and their often troubled relationships with each other and with the world at large. Notable children's literature critic Zena Sutherland wrote, "The special gift of Paula Fox is that of seeing from the child's viewpoint and maintaining that viewpoint while feeling the sympathy of an adult and the detachment of an artist. Her children move our hearts because they are so true, yet there is neither sentimentality nor pity in her writing."[1]

Critics also have praised Fox's clear writing style, her honesty, and her willingness to confront complicated and emotional issues. They are especially complimentary of Fox's characterization of adult characters, who are as likely to be as flawed and mixed-up as their kids—if not more so. Another critic wrote in the *New York Times Book Review*, "In an era when youthful distrust of adults is rampant, Miss Fox remains true to the concept that children need adults if they are to grow, though they must be fulfilled themselves and accept young people as individuals."[2]

It hasn't escaped the attention of the reviewers (all of whom are adults, by the way) that Paula Fox's writing style and choice of themes pay respect to her young readers. She does this by challenging readers to confront difficult writing and complicated topics, which is a sign of respect and admiration. Neither has it gone unnoticed that Fox's preference is for dark, emotional, complicated stories. One reviewer wrote in *Literature Resource Center*, "In her best children's books, Fox manages to discover what it is to be a vulnerable child struggling for a sure sense of self in a bewildering and often alien world."[3]

Critic John Rowe Townsend had this to say: "Of the new writers for children who emerged in the United States in the later 1960s, Paula Fox was quickly seen to be one of the most able. Her books were unusually varied; each had a distinct individual character, but at the same time each was stamped with her own imprint."[4]

A Darker Side

Many of Fox's books, especially those for adolescent readers, are darker in theme and tone than *The Village by the Sea* and *A Likely Place*. In these novels, Fox's writing is mysterious, somber, and thoughtful. Her most well-known novel, *The*

Slave Dancer (1973), is a good example of Fox's willingness to challenge young readers with difficult stories full of hardship and issues like slavery and racism. The novel takes place in the 1840s, and it is the story of a thirteen-year-old boy named Jessie, who is kidnapped from his hometown of New Orleans and put on a slave ship bound for West Africa. (Slave ships were sent during the slave trade to capture Africans and bring them back to the United States to work against their will.) Jessie is kidnapped because he plays the fife—a musical instrument that resembles a small flute without keys—and, after the ship reaches America and starts the voyage home again, he is forced to play music to the captured slaves so they will dance and exercise their limbs, which become cramped from living in too small a space during the journey across the Atlantic Ocean.

During the course of his journey back from Africa, Jessie befriends a slave boy named Ras, who is about his age. Eventually, Jessie and Ras escape the ship when the crew and many of the slaves drown in a storm. After a terrible struggle, they reach shore safely and are forced to go their separate ways although they have grown as close as brothers. Ras flees to the north, where he can be free, and Jessie makes his way back down south to New Orleans. Changed forever, Jessie finds that not only is he alienated from the home he once knew, but he also cannot stand the sound of music.

In addition to being a good example of Fox's more serious themes, *The Slave Dancer* is also written in Fox's straightforward and gripping style. The opening paragraphs indicate the somber tone of the book:

> In a hinged wooden box upon the top of which was carved a winged fish, my mother kept the tools of her trade. Sometimes I touched a sewing needle with my finger and reflected how such a small object, so nearly weightless, could keep our little family from the poor house and provide us with enough food to sustain life—although there were times when we were barely sustained.
>
> Our one room was on the first floor of a brick and timber house which must have seen better times. Even on sunny days I could press my hand against the wall and force the moisture which had coated it to run to the floor in streams. The damp sometimes set my sister, Betty, to coughing which filled the room with barking noises like those made by quarrelling animals. Then my mother would mention how fortunate we were to live in

A Note of Controversy

In 1974, *The Slave Dancer* won the Newbery Medal, and one critic called the book Fox's "most substantial work . . . a historical novel of weight and intensity which stands on its own, at a distance from her other books."[5] Another critic wrote that the novel "is historical fiction at its finest, for Fox has meticulously researched every facet of the slave trade and of the period."[6] Many critics agree that the novel is so sophisticated that it verges on being a book for adults rather than adolescents.

Some critics, however, had concerns about how the slaves were depicted in the book, as depressed or passive, and accused Jessie of never taking a stand against slavery despite his friendship with Ras, the slave boy.

Most reviewers, though, saw *The Slave Dancer* as a compassionate and fair portrayal of a horrible event. One critic called the novel a "story that movingly and realistically presents one of the most gruesome chapters of history, with all its violence, inhuman conditions, and bestial aspects of human nature—exposed but never exploited."[7]

New Orleans where we did not suffer the cruel extremes of temperature that prevailed in the north.[8]

Even when she is not writing about historical events like the slave trade, Fox's language is never overly dramatic or gimmicky. She always writes with a strong, authoritative style that hooks the reader and maintains interest.

For example, the opening to the previously mentioned *One-Eyed Cat* (the story of the boy who accidentally wounds a cat with an air rifle) is written simply and directly, with no flashy language to confuse the reader. This novel is similar to *The Slave Dancer* in tone and deals with the difficult themes of loneliness and compassion.

Notice how Fox starts from the first paragraph to tell the character's story and reveal his personality to the reader.

Ned Wallis was the minister's only child. The Congregational Church where the Reverend James Wallis preached stood on a low hill above a country lane a mile beyond the village of Tyler, New York. Close by the parsonage, a hundred or so yards from the church, was a small cemetery of weathered tombstones. Some had fallen over and moss and ivy covered them. When Ned first learned to walk, the cemetery was his favorite place to practice. There, his father would come to get him after the members of the congregation had gone home to their Sunday dinners. There, too, his mother often sat on a tumbled stone and watched over him while his father stood at the great church door speaking to each and every person who had attended service that day. That was long ago, before his mother had become ill.[9]

Building Suspense

In the excerpt above, Fox ended the paragraph with a sentence that leaves the reader wanting to know more about Ned's mother and about what will happen to Ned. This narrative tension fuels the reader's desire to continue reading, to know what happens next, and is present in all of Fox's novels. Tension is part of what makes Fox's novels so enjoyable to read.

In *Monkey Island*, the story of the boy who ends up homeless after both his parents abandon him, Fox once again explores themes of alienation, betrayal, and resourcefulness.

The opening of the novel provides a good example of how Fox grips the reader's attention from the first sentence without being overly dramatic with her language.

> Clay Garrity's mother, Angela, had been gone five days from the room in the hotel where they had been living since the middle of October.
>
> On the first evening of her disappearance, he'd waited until long past dark before going to a small table that held a hot plate, a few pieces of china, two glasses and some cutlery as well as their food supply: a jar of peanut butter, half a loaf of bread in a plastic sack, some bananas, a can of vegetable soup, and a box of doughnuts. His mother usually heated soup for their supper and made hot cereal for his breakfast in the pot that sat on the hot plate. Clay lifted the lid. There was nothing inside. During their first week in the hotel, she had made a stew that lasted them for three days. That was the only time she had really cooked.
>
> He ate a banana, then picked up the box of doughnuts. Beneath it, he found twenty-eight dollars and three quarters.
>
> He wasn't especially worried yet about her not coming home. She'd been gone entire days before, not returning until nightfall. But the sight of the money made him uneasy.[10]

Again, Fox uses narrative tension to build suspense and hook the reader from the first page. Why does the money make Clay uneasy? Where has his mother gone? You can be certain that Clay will be faced with difficult challenges throughout the book and likely learn important lessons from his journey— but to know more, you'll have to read it for yourself.

Sophisticated Themes for Sophisticated Readers

Fox's novels for adolescents are not always happy stories. Some of them, in addition to having dark themes, truthfully depict sadness, fear, anger, and desperation, none of which are easy to read about. But readers can always count on Fox to tell an engaging, honest story with a satisfying and realistic conclusion.

A good example of Fox's use of clear language to describe complicated, intense dramatic situations is *How Many Miles to Babylon?* (1967). It is the story of a young black child named James Douglas, who lives with his three aunts in the inner city. James has the habit of telling himself fantastical stories to cope with the harsh realities of his life, including abandonment by his father. Unfortunately, James falls in with a trio of kids who steal dogs and then claim the reward money when it is offered. They are all—including James—forced to go into hiding on Coney Island (in New York) when the police catch on to their scheme.

While in Coney Island, James sees the Atlantic Ocean for the first time and thinks about his roots across the ocean in Africa and about his mother, who is depressed and doesn't live with him. When James leaves the gang and makes it back to the small apartment where he lives, he must decide whether or not to tell the truth about where he's been and what he's been doing. He must also learn to accept the circumstances of his life, including his ill mother and stifling apartment, rather than continue to make up tall tales to escape his troubles.

Critics have said that *How Many Miles to Babylon?* is descriptive, beautifully written, complex, and poetic. "Even though the story is incredibly dark," wrote one reviewer in *Literature Resource Center*, "Fox nevertheless holds out hope for those who, like James . . . can through their own resourcefulness and courage endure in the [hardest] circumstances."[11]

"Resourcefulness" is a word that comes up a lot when referring to Fox's young characters. Like Fox herself when she was a child, her characters are often left alone in difficult or unfamiliar situations, and it is up to them to either find their way back home or create new homes for themselves. The lessons Fox's characters learn in their journeys through childhood are the same ones she learned in hers—to use your imagination to overcome life's difficulties.

In Fox's world—real and fictional—adults aren't always going to be the strong and dependable ones. Sometimes, it is up to the kids—like Emma on the beach in *A Village by the Sea*, Lewis in the park in *A Likely Place*, and Jessie on the slave ship in *The Slave Dancer*—to find their ways without interference or assistance from adults.

Grief and Resilience

In *Monkey Island*, Ned learned how to survive without a home or parents, and he eventually copes with his situation using his own determination and intelligence. Similarly, the thirteen-year-old narrator of *A Place Apart* (1980), Victoria, has to cope with a turbulent home situation when her father unexpectedly passes away. She and her mother are forced to move to a shabby house in another town, and one of Victoria's only new friends is an arrogant boy named Hugh, who tries to manipulate, or bully, her. Within a few months, another obstacle is thrown in her path when her mother announces her plans to remarry.

Eventually, Victoria learns how to manage her grief over her father's death, accept her new home, and form friendships with people who are positive influences. She even comes to accept her mother's new husband.

A reviewer wrote the following about *A Place Apart*:

> Victoria's biggest problem, and one that most adolescents will understand, [is] locating her territory, naming it, making sense of what's happening around her. She used to believe, she tells us, that "If I could describe one entire day of my life to someone, that person would be able to tell me what on earth life was all about." But that was before her father died, and the year that's covered by *A Place Apart* is the period of time it takes her to regain, however shakily, some sense of order and security

. . . *A Place Apart* is a book apart—quiet-voiced, believable, and often very moving.[12]

In many of Fox's books, including *A Place Apart*, characters are thrust into unexpected and challenging situations. Like Paul in *Radiance Descending* (1997) and Ned in *Monkey Island*, Liam, the main character of *Eagle Kite* (1996), must cope with a sudden and dramatic change in his home life when he learns that his father has contracted AIDS and is close to death. This news triggers a memory in Liam from two years earlier, when he saw his father embrace a young man on the beach. Though Liam's mother told him his father contracted the virus through a blood transfusion, Liam suspects otherwise. Meanwhile, his father, who is living apart from Liam and his mother, is wasting away and Liam must come to terms with all his conflicting emotions—anger, denial, shame, forgiveness, and grief. He suspects that his father is gay but cannot come to terms with it, especially since his mother denies it.

Liam's task is not simple, and neither is Fox's portrayal of it. As one critic wrote, "This will be a hard novel for teens to absorb, but well worth the effort."[13]

Times Are Changing

Until the mid-1980s, only a handful of young adult novels about homosexuality existed, and teens looking to read about being gay or having a gay relative were hard-pressed to find quality literature on the subject. The first young adult novel with homosexual content dates back to 1969, when an author named John Donovan wrote a book called *I'll Get There, It Better Be Worth the Trip* about a thirteen-year-old boy named Davy whose new friendship with another boy turns romantic.

For the next fifteen years, books with gay themes were few and far between; in fact, only four young adult novels were published with gay or lesbian themes between the years 1970 and 1976. (They were Isabelle Holland's *The Man Without a Face* [1970], Sandra Scoppetone's *Trying Hard to Hear You* [1974], Rosa Guy's *Ruby* [1976], and Mary W. Sullivan's *What's This About, Pete?* [1976].)

All told, as many as 100 books with gay or lesbian themes have been published for young adults since 1969, Fox's *Eagle Kite* included. Some of these have become instant classics, including Nancy Garden's *Annie on My Mind* (1982), the story of two high school seniors, both girls, who fall in love, and are then torn apart by prejudice. Other popular novels involve main characters who are not gay themselves but who must adjust to having close family members who are gay. *The Arizona Kid* (1986), by Ron Koertge, is the story of a sixteen-year-old boy named Billy who spends the summer in Tucson, Arizona, with his uncle, Wes, an openly gay man with many friends who are HIV-positive. *Jack* (1989), by A. M. Homes, is the story of a boy whose life is disrupted when his father comes "out of the closet."

At one time or another, almost all young adult novels that involve gay or lesbian characters have been challenged by groups who believe the books "promote" homosexuality. A challenge is when a group of parents, community members, or church officials attempts to remove or restrict a book from a school curriculum or library; a ban is the removal of the challenged book. Most challenged books are never removed because concerned parents, teachers, librarians, and other citizens fight to keep the books on library shelves. According to the American Library Association (ALA), which maintains an Office for Intellectual Freedom to keep records of all challenged books, 6,364 books were challenged between 1990 and

2000; of those, 515 were challenged because of material with a homosexual theme. (Other reasons cited for challenging books include sexually explicit material, occult or satanic themes, violence, and offensive language.) *Annie on My Mind*, *The Arizona Kid*, and *Jack* are all listed on the ALA's list of the 100 Most Frequently Banned or Challenged Books.

Despite the fact that challenges to books continue, society has come a long way since 1969—there are now dozens of young adult novels involving gay or lesbian characters on library and bookstore shelves, including Fox's well-loved novel *Eagle Kite*. Many of these contemporary books offer positive and affirming images of gays and lesbians and confront a range of relevant issues, including homophobia, coming out, and acceptance from friends, teachers, parents, and the community.

For Advanced Readers

Fox will never underestimate her readers' ability to understand complicated human dilemmas, and she won't ever write dishonestly about what growing up is like. She doesn't often write funny stories, though a sense of humor can be found throughout her work, especially in *The Little Swineherd and Other Tales*, a collection of short stories modeled after Hans Christian Andersen's folktales in which animal characters are used to satirize, or poke fun at, the way people behave in real life. In most of her novels, Fox uses humor to strengthen her characters' personalities and to enrich, or deepen, their experiences, but the stories themselves are not particularly comic. It might be difficult for some young people to read novels about homelessness, poverty, AIDS, death, and grief, but Fox always delivers a great story and portrays these hardships with honesty and kindness.

5 Recipe for Success

Some people think that writers rely on inspiration to get their work done, but this usually isn't the case. Most writers spend much more time thinking and trying to write than they do actually writing, and Fox is no exception. In an autobiographical essay for Random House, she wrote about the role of discipline in a writer's work.

> As I sit at my typewriter, working, there are moments when I feel I cannot write another word, when the sheer difficulty of discovering what I mean to say and how to say it is so [scary] that I want to stop forever. I haven't yet stopped. I stay in my chair, pen in hand, yellow-lined pad on the desk next

to the machine, doodling or writing down fragments of sentences, hoping some unifying
principle will, like a net, draw them together.
On the whole, most writing is the questions one
asks oneself. What has happened to me? Does it
have meaning? It's a peculiar process.[1]

Discovering the meaning of one's experiences
is only one part of the puzzle of writing a novel.
There's also imagination, psychology, and
memory. Each writer's stories depend on his or
her observations of human behavior and the
world at large, and each writer's perspective, or
outlook, is unique. Fox says that everyone's story
matters and that each story is one piece of a
larger puzzle. The more stories we read, the
more we learn about who we are, why we exist,
and what kind of world we live in.

Writing a novel also requires the discipline to
sit oneself down at a desk or computer even if no
words come. It takes discipline to figure out what
you want to say and how to say it.

Where Ideas Come From

There's no hard and fast way to make sure you
have plenty of things to write about. Some
authors say that you should write about what

you cannot get off your mind; some say you should write about things that have happened to you or your family. It's not always necessary for a writer to know exactly what she wants to say before sitting down at the computer or typewriter. Sometimes, the story reveals itself after several pages have been written. At this point the author might think to herself, "Aha! So *that's* what I wanted to write about." She might realize that while she thought she wanted to write a story about a girl who lost her cat, she really wanted to write about how the cat had protected her from feeling lonely after the death of a parent. Many writers complete several drafts, or versions, of a story before it is published, which gives them time to discover all the hidden meanings behind their stories. Sometimes what an author intends to write is very different from the final draft. In this way, writing is a very mysterious process.

No matter what an author chooses to write about, the most important aspect of good storytelling is that it reveals something honest about the world and what it means to be human. As Fox wrote in an essay, "Literature is the [territory] of imagination, and stories, in whatever [form], are meditations on life.

[Imagination] is the guardian spirit that we sense in great stories; we feel its rustling."[2]

Metaphors for Life

Fox believes that, in a sense, all stories are metaphors—something that represents something else—for larger stories. For example, in *How Many Miles to Babylon?*, the fantasy stories James tells himself represent his ideal life, free of troubles. (In the novel, James finds a ruby ring on the street and imagines that he is an African prince and the ring is a sign from his mother, who is in Africa preparing a place for him.) And in *One-Eyed Cat*, Ned's refusal to tell his parents about his crime against the cat represents his lack of understanding of human nature and his fear of being judged. When he reveals his secret, his mother teaches him that adults make mistakes, too.

Stories help readers understand the world better without having to go through all the hardships the characters go through. It can be difficult to really understand other people—friends, parents, or strangers—unless we know a great deal about their lives, thoughts, and hopes. Even with all this information, we might think we would behave differently if we were in their shoes. But when an author writes a story about a character—especially if the author writes well and understands human behavior, like Paula Fox—the reader can reach so far inside the mind of the character that he or she can understand the character's behavior. For example, after reading all about the particular circumstance of James's life in *How Many Miles to Babylon?*, it's possible to understand why he joins a dog-napping gang, even if you think dog-napping is morally wrong.

Storytellers like Paula Fox take a given situation—be it sad, challenging, hopeless, or strange—and create a whole world around it, a complicated and realistic human life. It is this ability to inspire compassion that keeps readers coming back to Fox's books decade after decade.

Interview with Paula Fox

SUSANNA DANIEL: You've said that you were unable to write full-time until you and your husband moved to Greece to live. What prompted your desire to be an author, and how long had it been your goal?

PAULA FOX: The six months we rented a house on a Greek island was the first block of time I'd had since I was sixteen. I began a novel, *Poor George*, and completed my first children's book there, *Maurice's Room*. I had written in my early twenties, but my stories were rejected.

SUSANNA DANIEL: If you had to credit two or three people in your life with encouraging you to be a writer, who would they be and how did they influence you?

PAULA FOX: I don't think any familial people encouraged me, although my father, when I saw him, always had books or suggested titles to me. Also, he was a writer, and that may have been one of the elements that led me to writing. My husband, Martin Greenberg, has encouraged me for the last forty years, though, and that has made up for a great deal.

SUSANNA DANIEL: What role do personal experiences and memories play in your fiction? In other words, to what extent has your work been influenced by your life?

PAULA FOX: I wonder if even science fiction isn't, ultimately, about one's personal life or some aspect of one's wishes, also a part of personal life. My life is, after all, the only one I really know deeply; nearly all of my stories arise from it.

SUSANNA DANIEL: You have been writing children's books since the 1960s. How do you think children's literature has evolved since then? Specifically, how have your books, themes, and characters changed?

PAULA FOX: I do believe the significance of children's literature has changed; it's seen as more significant now in the USA. It has always been of significance in England and in Europe in general.

SUSANNA DANIEL: Is there any advice—about life, writing, or anything else—you would give your twelve-year-old self if you could talk to her today?

PAULA FOX: I can't think what advice I would give my twelve-year-old self! Except to wait and see what happens next!

SUSANNA DANIEL: What advice do you have for children who want to be writers when they grow up?

PAULA FOX: I would advise children who wish to be writers to write about their own real experiences and thoughts and feelings as best as they can in whatever form—fairy tale or wizardry or, as it's called, real life—they choose.

SUSANNA DANIEL: You've held an array of jobs in your lifetime. How do you think writing books compares to other careers in terms of happiness and stability?

PAULA FOX: I've had a good many jobs. I always wanted to be a writer but sometimes I wish I weren't! Especially when I'm stuck and must call upon patience with myself to wait out whatever is preventing me from going on with a story.

SUSANNA DANIEL: You've said that discipline helped you write your memoir when you were recovering from your attack in Israel. In your opinion, how important is discipline—as opposed to, say, inspiration or passion—to a writer?

PAULA FOX: From discipline arise passions and inspiration. I go to my study every morning and I start to work. The moments of inspiration are few and far between, but they're worth all the disciplined work that is a preparation for them to arrive.

SUSANNA DANIEL: You seem, from reading your memoir and interviews, to possess an exceptional memory. How important is memory in the writing of fiction?

PAULA FOX: Memory is everything for a writer, especially, in my own case, visual memory.

SUSANNA DANIEL: Writing is a solitary exercise, and many of your books revolve around themes of abandonment, isolation, and alienation. How important is human connection in a writer's life?

PAULA FOX: Human connection to husband, children, friends is everything to some writers, me among them.

SUSANNA DANIEL: Is it essential, in your opinion, for a writer of children's books to have a family? How did your experiences as a mother influence your writing?

PAULA FOX: My experience as a mother did affect my experience as a writer. I saw how a story can be no larger than a mustard seed and yet hold a child's interest. Of course, it must be a very interesting mustard seed!

SUSANNA DANIEL: Do your characters share any of your personal traits? Which ones?

PAULA FOX: My characters share my own traits, especially those I find in other people. If one writes truthfully about oneself, one is usually writing about all the people one has known and that the self contains.

Timeline

1923 Paula Fox is born in New York City on April 22.

1931 Paula is permanently removed from the home where she has been living with a kind minister, Uncle Elwood, and taken, after a few stops, to Cuba to live with her grandmother on a sugar plantation.

1933 Paula and her grandmother return to New York City after a revolution in Cuba. In the next ten years, she lives in New York City, Los Angeles, New Hampshire, and Canada, where she attends boarding school.

1943 Fox gives up a daughter for adoption, then immediately regrets it.

1948 Paula Fox marries Richard Sigerson and has two sons, Adam and Gabriel, shortly after.

1954 Paula and Richard divorce.

1955 Fox enrolls in Columbia University and is a student for three years.

1962 Paula Fox marries Martin Greenberg, an editor whose journal has recently rejected her writing for publication. They move to Greece to live for six months.

1966 Fox publishes her first novel for children, *Maurice's Room*, to positive reviews. Her next two novels, *A Likely Place* and *How Many Miles to Babylon?*, are published within the next year and a half.

1971 Fox's highly praised novel for adults, *Desperate Characters*, is made into a movie starring Shirley MacLaine.

1975 Fox's best-loved and most controversial novel, *The Slave Dancer*, wins the American Library Association's most distinguished prize, the Newbery Medal.

1978 Fox's body of work is awarded the Hans Christian Andersen Award.

1979 *The Little Swineherd and Other Tales* is nominated for the National Book Award.

1983 *A Place Apart* is given the American Book Award.

1990 Around this time, Fox is contacted by the daughter she gave up for adoption forty-seven years earlier. They write to each other, then meet and become friends. They have remained close.

1999 Fox's memoirs, entitled *Borrowed Finery*, are published to rave reviews; the book is a finalist for the National Book Critics Circle Award the following year.

Selected
Reviews from
School Library
Journal

Amzat and His Brothers: Three Italian Folktales
1993

Fox retells three Italian folktales that were told to her by a friend who heard them from his grandfather when he was a child growing up in a pre-World War II Italian village. The tales are variations of familiar stories: "Mezgalten," for example, contains elements of "The Brementown Musicians" and "The Wolf and the Kids." Acts of violence may disturb some adults, as in the title story when Amzat and his wife trick his brothers into murdering their wives and then cause the drowning of the brothers. The third story shows the prejudice of villagers toward a woman and her son because of their habit of never bathing and the dull wits of the son. While the woman and son end their days living in a palace (and eventually learning the art of bathing), and the worst of their tormentors end up poorly, the depiction of the heckling is harsh. The people in these stories seem to be more rooted in real life than the usual archetypal folktale characters. A good collection of the region's lore would be welcome, but this isn't the one. McCully's pen-and-ink sketches add little.

The Eagle Kite
1995

Grades 8–12—Liam, a high school freshman, learns that his father is dying of AIDS. Suddenly, his comfortable family is in pieces, and his father has gone to live in a seashore cottage two hours from the family's city apartment. Distanced from both parents by secrets each of them seems compelled to keep, Liam remembers having seen his father embrace a young man years before—a friend, his father had said. In the remainder of the book, Liam and his parents wrestle with truths that encompass not just disappointment and betrayal, but intense love. This is far more than a problem novel. AIDS is integral to the plot, the issue is handled well, and the character who has AIDS is portrayed sympathetically, but the book's scope is broader than that. It is a subtly textured exploration of the emotions of grief that will appeal to the same young people drawn to Mollie Hunter's *A Sound of Chariots* (HarperCollins, 1972) and Cynthia Rylant's *Missing May* (Orchard, 1992). Dramatic tension is palpable, sustained in part by a dazed, timeless quality in Liam's slow reckoning with loss. The characters are neither idealized nor demonized, and Fox's take on Liam as a confused, seethingly angry, tight-lipped, surreptitiously tender teenager has the ring of authenticity. Some in the target audience may find the action too slow or the mood too dark, but those who persevere will be rewarded by the novel's truthfulness

Lily and the Lost Boy
1987
Grades 5–7—Another thought-provoking gem from Fox. Eleven-year-old Lily Corey, her

parents, and her older brother are spending three months on the Greek island of Thasos while Mr. Corey finishes a book. Lily has been flowering—enjoying her friendships with the islanders, her personal study of Greek mythology and archaeology, and her recent closeness with Paul (in their New England home town setting they were "normal" antagonistic siblings). But Lily's summer idyll ends when Paul becomes friendly with another American boy, Jack Hemmings. Jack is mysterious, erratic, defensive, self-destructive, and unloved. Lily resents his influence over Paul and the way in which he disrupts the even, satisfying flow of her lazy summer days. And yet Lily comes closer to an understanding of Jack than anyone, by sharing a catharsis in the young boy's life. Due to Jack's irresponsibility, the Coreys' stay on the island ends with a tragedy that brings the family closer to their unsophisticated Greek friends even as it marks the beginning of a permanent separation. Lily and Paul leave their innocence on Thasos and take away a new awareness of human fragility and dignity. Fox has created a sensitive portrait of three young adolescents who achieve varying degrees of self-knowledge during their stay in an alien but hospitable culture. The story is very low keyed, with lengthy descriptions that capture the atmosphere of the Greek island but that also slow down the pace of the story. Simply written, with strong characterizations and overtones of Greek tragedy, *Lily and the Lost Boy* is an excellent choice for readers who share Lily's own budding characteristics: thoughtfulness, integrity, sensitivity, and courage. A beautifully written story for thoughtful readers.

Monkey Island
1991

Grades 5–7—Eleven-year-old Clay Garrity's family had been what most people would consider an average family—until the magazine his father worked for went out of business and he couldn't find another job over the next year. Clay then experienced the gradual decline from that normal existence to one of abandonment by his father, the move to a welfare hotel and, at the beginning of the story, the disappearance of his mother who, with the added burden of a difficult pregnancy, is unable to cope with the daily struggle for survival. Clay eventually comes to a small park scornfully called Monkey Island for the homeless who live there. Here he is taken in by two men who share the wooden crate that offers them some shelter from the cold November winds. These three become a sort of family, holding on to some sense of humanity in a brutal and brutalizing world. For all of its harshness, *Monkey Island* is also a romanticized view of the world. Although Clay is not spared the hunger, fear, illness, and squalor of the streets, there is still a distancing from the more immediate types of violence that exist there. He is always on the edge of such danger, but no incidents actually touch him. In the end, it is pneumonia that brings him back into the social services system. After ten days in the hospital, the boy is placed in a foster home and shortly thereafter is reunited with his mother and baby sister in a conclusion that readers desire but that may strain credibility. This is a carefully crafted, thoughtful book, and one in which the flow of language both sustains a mood of apprehension and encourages readers to consider carefully the plight of the homeless, recognizing unique human beings among the nameless, faceless masses most of us have learned not to see.

The Moonlight Man
1986

Grades 6–10—Fox has always been adept at writing apparently simple stories which on closer examination prove to explore the essential meaning of relationships through carefully chosen incident and to illuminate our understanding of the human condition through the vicissitudes of her characters. In this case, fifteen-year-old Catherine Ames vacations in a cottage in Nova Scotia with a father whom she barely knows—a failed writer with a poet's philosophical tongue who is an alcoholic. A competent child/woman, Catherine, in a few days of trying to understand and cope, lives through the classic kaleidoscope of responses of family members to alcoholics: denial, anger, fear, loneliness, exhaustion, disgust, pity, grief, sympathy. Harry Ames binges, blames, makes unreasonable demands, apologizes, reforms, relapses. Catherine succeeds in admiring her father for his talents while deploring his behavior, strengthened by knowing that their time together will end soon. And end it does, in apparent friendship, yet Harry Ames' last words to his daughter suggest that he will not see her again. There's enough detail and incident about alcoholism here for a case study, but the story rises above the clinical in poignantly dramatizing the separation that differing life patterns can inflict on those who love one another.

Western Wind
1993

Grades 5–8—Elizabeth Benedict, eleven, has always enjoyed the company of her eccentric artist grandmother, but when her parents insist that she spend a month with her at her rustic summer cottage off the coast of Maine, the girl feels as though she's being exiled so her parents can spend more time with her new baby brother. Anger and jealousy gnaw at her, until, almost in spite of herself, she begins to experience and appreciate the quiet beauty of Pring Island. The rather abrasive elder Benedict at times embarrasses her granddaughter, quoting poetry and posing probing questions, while at the same time, revealing stories about her youth, her husband, and herself. At once charmed and exasperated by the island's only other inhabitants' overzealous, impulsive young son, Elizabeth spends time with him and learns to accept the wisdom he innocently reveals. His disappearance exposes some other truths, including the real reason she's been sent to spend time with Gran. In this wonderfully realized, sensational novel, Fox's unadorned prose is anything but austere. In a forthright manner, she sets each scene and paints her thoroughly compelling, complex characters. Readers may not like them all, but they will definitely be interested in them.

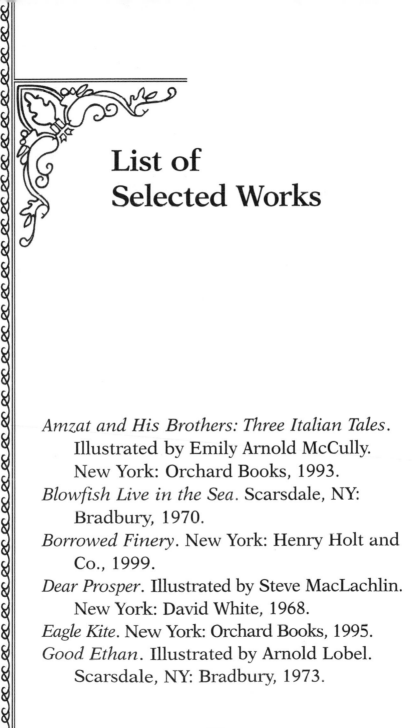

List of
Selected Works

Amzat and His Brothers: Three Italian Tales.
   Illustrated by Emily Arnold McCully.
   New York: Orchard Books, 1993.

Blowfish Live in the Sea. Scarsdale, NY:
   Bradbury, 1970.

Borrowed Finery. New York: Henry Holt and
   Co., 1999.

Dear Prosper. Illustrated by Steve MacLachlin.
   New York: David White, 1968.

Eagle Kite. New York: Orchard Books, 1995.

Good Ethan. Illustrated by Arnold Lobel.
   Scarsdale, NY: Bradbury, 1973.

How Many Miles to Babylon? Illustrated by
Paul Giovanopoulos. New York: David
White, 1967.

A Likely Place. Illustrated by Edward Ardizzone.
New York: Macmillan, 1967.

Lily and the Lost Boy. New York: Orchard
Books, 1987.

The Little Swineherd and Other Tales. Illustrated
by Robert Byrd. New York: Dutton
Children's Books, 1996.

Maurice's Room. Illustrated by Ingrid Fetz. New
York: Macmillan, 1966.

Monkey Island. New York: Orchard Books, 1991.

The Moonlight Man. Scarsdale, NY:
Bradbury, 1986.

One-Eyed Cat. Scarsdale, NY: Bradbury, 1984.

A Place Apart. New York: Farrar,
Strauss, 1980.

Portrait of Ivan. Illustrated by Saul Lambert.
Scarsdale, NY: Bradbury, 1969.

Radiance Descending. New York: DK, 1997.

The Slave Dancer. Illustrated by Eros
Keith. Santa Barbara, CA: ABC-CLIO,
1988.

The Stone-Faced Boy. Illustrated by
Donald A. Mackay. Scarsdale, NY:
Bradbury, 1968.

The Village by the Sea. New York: Orchard
    Books, 1988.
Western Wind. New York: Orchard Books, 1993.

List of Selected Awards

Guggenheim Fellowship (1972)
National Endowment for the Arts
    Grant (1974)
National Institute of Arts and Letters
    Award (1972)
Rockefeller Foundation Grant (1984)

***Blowfish Live in the Sea* (1970)**
National Books Award children's book
    category finalist (1971)

***The Little Swineherd and Other
Tales* (1978)**
National Book Award nomination (1979)

The Moonlight Man (1986)
New York Times Notable Book (1986)

A Place Apart (1980)
American Book Award (1983)
New York Times Outstanding Book (1980)

One-Eyed Cat (1984)
Newbery Honor Book (1985)
New York Times Notable Book (1984)

The Slave Dancer (1973)
Newbery Medal, American Library
Association (1974)

The Village by the Sea (1988)
Newbery Honor Book (1989)

Glossary

absolution Forgiveness.

alienation Emotional isolation, feeling alone or like an outsider.

amputation A removal by or as if by cutting, especially the surgical removal of a limb or digit.

anaconda A very large snake found in South America.

apprehension Anxiety, concern, or worry.

armistice A truce.

austere Severe or stern.

authenticity Believability or truth.

authority A forceful or convincing voice.

autobiography One's story of one's own life; memoir.

avid Enthusiastic.

bestial Resembling a beast in character or appearance.

captivity Any place where one cannot leave or move around freely.

captor One that has captured a person or animal.

cascade A waterfall or series of small waterfalls.

cauldron A large kettle or vat used for boiling.

chaos Confusion and disorder.

characterization The act of developing a character.

compassion Understanding other people's circumstances or putting oneself in their shoes.

confidant A person to whom one might tell secrets.

consent Permission.

custody The responsibility for another person, especially a child.

depicted Portrayed.

dictator An absolute and often oppressive ruler.

Dostoevsky, Fyodor Famous Russian novelist who lived from 1821 to 1881 and who wrote *Notes from the Underground* (1864), *Crime and Punishment* (1866), and *The Brothers Karamazov* (1879–80).

Down's syndrome A genetic condition that causes mild to severe retardation.

eccentric Strange and quirky.

eloquent Extremely well-spoken or vividly expressed.

embody To represent an idea in human form.

erratic Unpredictable and changeable.

estranged Separated emotionally for a long time.

exploited Used unfairly.

facet A feature or element of something.

fictional Imaginary or make-believe.

fife A small flute with six to eight finger holes and no keys.

gimmicky Using a new scheme or angle.

grunge Rock music incorporating elements of punk rock and heavy metal, popular in the late 1980s and early 1990s.

Guggenheim Fellowship Important award given annually to writers and artists.

Hans Christian Andersen Award Award presented every other year for lifetime achievement to children's authors and illustrators.

impeding Opposing or obstructing.

judgmental Critical or lacking understanding.

kidskin A soft leather made from the skin of a young goat.

manipulate To control someone's actions or feelings by unfair or dishonest means.

melancholy Sadness or depression.

memoir A story of one's life told from personal experience, or a biography.

metaphor In writing, when one thing is used to symbolize or represent something else.

mock To make fun of.

narrative The telling of an event through a story.

narrative tension The suspense that drives a story forward and keeps the reader engaged.

organic Natural, or made from living materials.

palpable Visible.

pick-up sticks An old-fashioned game for kids involving sticks one must gather within a certain amount of time.

pygmies Any of a small people of equatorial Africa ranging under five feet in height.

quivering Shaking.

rampant Widespread.

satirize To mock or ridicule.

scandalous Shocking or outrageous.

sentimentality Emotion for the sake of

emotion; based on feeling rather than thought.

social welfare agency Government organization that provides homes for kids who have been neglected by their parents.

suitor A man who is romantically interested in a woman.

tenacity Stubborn bravery or persistence.

themes The ideas in a novel or story that reappear in different forms.

tone In a story, the mood or feeling created by the words.

vicissitudes Sudden or unexpected changes that often occur in one's life.

vulnerable Capable of being hurt.

Wilder, Thornton American playwright and novelist whose works reflect human nature and universal truths.

For More Information

Due to the changing nature of Internet links, the Rosen Publishing Group, Inc., has developed an online list of Web sites related to the subject of this book. This site is updated regularly. Please use this link to access the list:

http://www.rosenlinks.com/lab/pfox

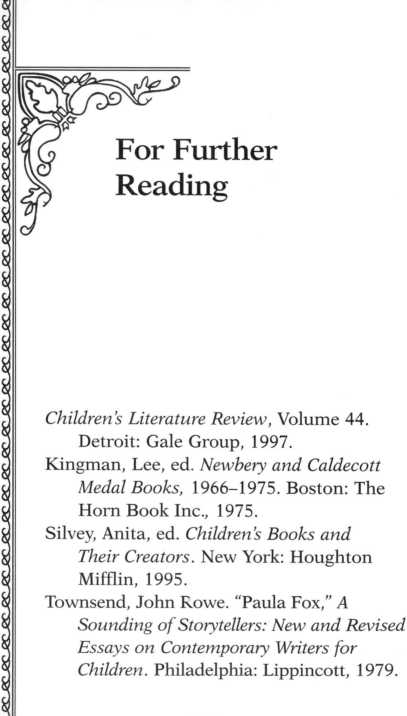

For Further Reading

Children's Literature Review, Volume 44. Detroit: Gale Group, 1997.

Kingman, Lee, ed. *Newbery and Caldecott Medal Books, 1966–1975*. Boston: The Horn Book Inc., 1975.

Silvey, Anita, ed. *Children's Books and Their Creators*. New York: Houghton Mifflin, 1995.

Townsend, John Rowe. "Paula Fox," *A Sounding of Storytellers: New and Revised Essays on Contemporary Writers for Children*. Philadelphia: Lippincott, 1979.

Bibliography

Broderick, Dorothy M. *New York Times Book Review*, November 9, 1969, (Part 2), p. 34.

Children's Literature Review, Vol. 16, 1989, Vol. 16, pp. 80, 255–269.

Fox, Paula. "About This Author." Random House. 2002. Retrieved January 2003 (http://www.randomhouse.com/teachers/authors/pfox.html).

Fox, Paula. *Borrowed Finery*. New York: Henry Holt and Co., 2001.

Fox, Paula. "Some Thoughts on Imagination in Children's Literature,"

Celebrating Children's Books: Essays on Children's Literature in Honor of Zena Sutherland. Betsy Hearne and Marilyn Kaye, eds. New York: Lothrop, Lee, and Shepard Books, 1981.

Fox, Paula. *Monkey Island.* New York: Orchard Books, 1991.

Fox, Paula. *The Slave Dancer.* Santa Barbara, CA: ABC-CLIO, 1988.

Hanscom, Leslie. "A Talk with Paula Fox: Consulting the Child Within," *Newsday,* December 13, 1987, p. 18.

Hawthorne, Mary. "Advancing Through Water," *New Yorker,* July 2, 2001.

Hedblad, Alan, ed. *Something About the Author,* Vol. 120. Detroit: Gale Group, 2000.

Literature Resource Center. Gale Group, 2002. Retrieved November, 2002 (http://www.galenet.com).

McGee, Celia. "Author Pages Through a Painful Past," *New York Daily News,* October 4, 2001, p. 55.

Sutherland, Zena. *Bulletin of the Center for Children's Books.* Chicago: University of Chicago, February 1970.

Townsend, John Rowe. *A Surrounding of Storytellers: New and Revised Essays on*

Contemporary Writers for Children.
Philadelphia: Lippincott, 1979.

Tyler, Anne. "Staking Out Her Territory," *New York Times Book Review,* November 9, 1980, p. 55.

Source Notes

Chapter 1

1. Paula Fox, *Borrowed Finery* (New York: Henry Holt and Co., 2001), p. 64.
2. Paula Fox, *Celebrating Children's Books: Essays on Children's Literature in Honor of Zena Sutherland*. Betsy Hearne and Marilyn Kaye, eds. (New York: Lothrop, Lee, and Shepard Books, 1981), pp. 24–34.
3. Fox, *Borrowed Finery*, p. 74.
4. Ibid., p. 132.
5. Paula Fox. "About This Author," Random House, 2002. Retrieved March 2003 (http://www.randomhouse.com/teachers/authors/pfox.html).
6. Fox, *Borrowed Finery*, p. 127.
7. Ibid., p. 129.

Chapter 2

1. Paula Fox, *Borrowed Finery* (New York: Henry Holt and Co., 2001), p. 139.
2. Ibid., p. 149.
3. Ibid., p. 183.

Chapter 3

1. *Literature Resource Center*, Gale Group, 2002. Retrieved March 2003 (http://www.galenet.com).
2. Paula Fox, *Borrowed Finery* (New York: Henry Holt and Co., 2001), p. 18.
3. Fox, *Borrowed Finery*, p. 209.
4. Ibid.
5. Ibid., p. 210.
6. Mary Hawthorne, "Advancing Through Water," *New Yorker*, July 2, 2001.
7. Celia McGee, "Author Pages Through a Painful Past," *New York Daily News*, October 4, 2001, p. 55.
8. Hawthorne.

Chapter 4

1. Zena Sutherland, *Bulletin of the Center for Children's Books* (Chicago: University of Chicago, February 1970), p. 96.
2. Dorothy M. Broderick, *New York Times Book Review*, November 9, 1969, Part 2, p. 34.
3. *Literature Resource Center*, Gale Group, 2002. Retrieved March 2003 (http://www.galenet.com).

4. John Rowe Townsend, *A Surrounding of Storytellers: New and Revised Essays on Contemporary Writers for Children* (New York: J. B. Lippincott, 1979), pp. 55–65.

5. Ibid.

6. Alan Hedblad, ed., *Something About the Author*, Vol. 120 (Detroit: Gale Group, 2000), pp. 106.

7. *Children's Literature Review*, Vol. 16 (Detroit: Gale Group), pp. 80, 255–269.

8. Paula Fox, *The Slave Dancer* (New York: Laurel Leaf, 1974), p. 1.

9. Paula Fox, *One-Eyed Cat* (Scarsdale, NY: Bradbury, 1984), pp. 1–2.

10. Paula Fox, *Monkey Island* (New York: Orchard Books, 1991), pp. 1–2.

11. *Literature Resource Center*, Gale Group, 2002. Retrieved March 2003 (http://www.galenet.com).

12. Anne Tyler, "Staking Out Her Territory," *New York Times Book Review*, November 9, 1980, p. 55.

13. *Children's Literature Review*, Vol. 16, 1982, Detroit: Gale Group, pp. 80, 255–269.

Chapter 5

1. Paula Fox, "About This Author." Random House, 2002. Retrieved February 2003 (http://www.randomhouse.com/teachers/authors/pfox.html).

2. Paula Fox, *Celebrating Children's Books: Essays on Children's Literature in Honor of Zena Sutherland*, Betsy Hearne and Marilyn Kaye, eds. (New York: Lothrop, Lee, and Shepard Books, 1981), pp. 24–34.

Index

About the Author:

Susanna Daniel is a fiction writer from South Florida who teaches creative writing at the University of Wisconsin at Madison. She has a BA from Columbia University and an MFA from the University of Iowa writers' workshop. Her fiction has been published in Harcourt's *Best New American Voices 2001*, *Epoch*, and *The Madison Review*, and she is currently at work on a novel.

Photo Credits

Cover and p. 2 © AP Photo/Gino Domenico

Designer: Tahara Hasan; Editor: Annie Sommers